The Gothic-Fantastic in
Nineteenth-Century Russian Literature

STUDIES IN
SLAVIC LITERATURE
AND POETICS

VOLUME XXXIII

edited by

J.J. van Baak
R. Grübel
A.G.F. van Holk
W.G. Weststeijn

The Gothic-Fantastic in Nineteenth-Century Russian Literature

Edited by

Neil Cornwell

AMSTERDAM - ATLANTA, GA 1999

∞ The paper on which this book is printed meets the requirements of "ISO 9706:1994, Information and documentation - Paper for documents - Requirements for permanence".

ISBN: 90-420-0615-3
©Editions Rodopi B.V., Amsterdam - Atlanta, GA 1999
Printed in The Netherlands

TABLE OF CONTENTS

Preface   1

Russian Gothic: An Introduction   3
NEIL CORNWELL

From Pantheon to Pandemonium   23
RICHARD PEACE

Karamzin's Gothic Tale: *The Island of Bornholm*   37
DEREK OFFORD

At the Origins of the Russian Gothic Novel: Nikolai Gnedich's   59
Don Corrado de Gerrera (1803)
ALESSANDRA TOSI

Does Russian Gothic Verse Exist? The Case of Vasilii Zhukovskii   83
MICHAEL PURSGLOVE

The Fantastic in Russian Romantic Prose: Pushkin's *The Queen of*   103
Spades
CLAIRE WHITEHEAD

Philosophical Tale or Gothic Horror Story? The Strange case of   127
V.F. Odoevskii's *The Cosmorama*
ROGER COCKRELL

Gothic Treatment of the Crisis of Engendering in Odoevskii's *The*   145
Salamander
CYNTHIA C. RAMSEY

Elena Gan and the Female Gothic in Russia   171
CAROLYN JURSA AYERS

Supernatural Doubles: *Vii* and *The Nose*   189
PRISCILLA MEYER

The Gothic in Gogol and Dostoevskii   211
IGNAT AVSEY

The Echoing Heart: Fantasias of the Female in Dostoevskii and   235
Turgenev
LEON BURNETT

Unknown Force: Gothic Realism in Chekhov's *The Black Monk*   257
ANN KOMAROMI

List of Contributors   277

Select Bibliography   281

Index   287

PREFACE

This collection is based on the proceedings (with extra contributions added) of a symposium on 'Nineteenth-Century Russian Gothic-Fantastic' held at the University of Bristol in July 1997 (under the auspices of the Nineteenth-Century Studies Group of the British Association of Slavonic and East European Studies).

The editor is grateful for the assistance of David Bethea in locating extra contributors (both potential and actual) and to the generous and invaluable efforts of Birgit Beumers in the final preparation of the volume.

The transliteration system used in this volume is that of the Library of Congress, minus diacritics. An exception to this is the omission of the soft sign at the end of names (e.g. 'Gogol', rather than 'Gogol'').

RUSSIAN GOTHIC: AN INTRODUCTION

NEIL CORNWELL

'Russian Gothic' as a term has not until recently enjoyed a great deal of currency in critical studies of Russian literature. The word 'Gothic' is commonly used in connection with, for instance, certain early works by Dostoevskii, or, to a lesser extent, of his later and more famous novels, which may be recognised as including Gothic elements or traces. Otherwise, what might have been termed 'the Gothic in Russian literature' has tended, with rare exceptions, to be submerged under the blanket heading of 'Russian romanticism' or 'the fantastic'. This situation, which has been noted by several of the contributors to this volume, may be partly explicable in terms of the vicissitudes of Soviet literary criticism, during the more depressing stretches of which even 'romanticism' and 'Dostoevskii' were dirty words and critical energies were certainly not to be expended on the Gothic or the supernatural. Furthermore, the burgeoning of interest in Gothic as a literary style, even in the West, is still comparatively recent.

Even the anthology entitled *Russian 19th-century Gothic Tales*, compiled by Valentin Korovin and published by Raduga in Moscow in 1984,[1] seems to have acquired that title for its English-language edition by chance (the Russian title being given as *Fantasticheskii mir russkoi povesti* ('The Fantastic World of the Russian Novella'). The range of stories included extends from Antonii Pogorel'skii and Orest Somov, in the 1820s, to Vladimir Odoevskii's *The Living Corpse* (*Zhivoi mertvets*: published 1844, but dated 1838) and A.K. Tolstoi's early story *Vampire* (*Upyr'*, 1841). Pushkin, Lermontov and Gogol are represented, as well as a number of the more minor figures of Russian prose (Mikhail Zagoskin, Osip Senkovskii and the poet Evgenii Baratynskii). The blurb to this collection, which has no general introduction, refers to 'enchanting flights of the imagination, vivid imagery borrowed from

---

[1] *Russian 19th-century Gothic Tales*, compiled by V. Korovin, Moscow, Raduga, 1984 (hereafter 'Korovin, 1984').

folk tale and legend, grotesque fantasy and utopian dreams of a distant, happy future'. While all this may have something in common with western definitions of the Gothic, we may prefer to stress alternative features – old castles, hapless maidens, wicked and grasping relatives, and mysterious revenants – as more characteristic of the genre. V.E. Vatsuro, the leading Russian commentator on the Gothic in recent decades, nominates '"gothic" heroes, conflict, and the basic motifs and technique of "mystery"' as the basic props of the Gothic narrative whole, with the castle and incest, for instance, as important subsidiary motifs.[2]

A certain input from folklore, and such further native medieval ingredients as chronicles and saints' lives apart, Russian Gothic can be said to derive from an amalgam of European infuences: the English Gothic novel, the tales of Hoffmann, the French *fantastique* and *frénétique* traditions, and the various schools of European idealist and esoteric thought.[3]

The English and European Background
'Gothic', as an ethnic and a cultural concept, of course originates in Europe, and the manuals of European history tell us that Gothic settlement developed from the east to the south and west. If anything, however, it remains more popularly associated with the north. Detailed considerations of the exact pre-medieval, medieval and architectural connotations of 'Gothic' aside, the cultural revival of the term, particularly in a literary sense, is generally viewed as developing in a

---

[2] V.E. Vatsuro, 'Iz istorii "Goticheskogo Romana" v Rossii (A.A. Bestuzhev-Marlinskii)', *Russian Literature*, 38, 1995, pp. 207-26 (208-09). Other articles by Vatsuro are cited below, or throughout this volume, and/or listed in the Select Bibliography. An invaluable general source on Anglo-Russian links over the period in question is M.P Alekseev's *Russko-angliiskie literaturnye sviazi (XVIII vek - pervaia polovina XIX veka)*, published as vol. 91 of *Literaturnoe nasledstvo*, Moscow, 1982.

[3] For an account of this topic and its impact on Russia (though concentrated on the Symbolist period and since), see Bernice Glatzer Rosenthal's, 'Introduction', to *The Occult in Russian and Soviet Culture*, edited by Bernice Glatzer Rosenthal, Ithaca and London, Cornell University Press, 1997, pp. 1-32. A full historical account of this area of thought is to be found in Antoine Faivre's study, *Access to Western Esotericism*, Albany, State University of New York Press, 1994.

reverse direction: from west to east.[4] Certainly, what is now regarded as the Gothic novel, together with the allied, or anticipatory, phenomenon of 'graveyard poetry', stems from eighteenth-century England. The eastward spread, however, soon mingled with kindred local currents and a process of cross-fertilisation ensued, embracing structure, style, setting, themes and common sources. A reverse wind quickly wafted the fashion back to England – and beyond, to Ireland and America – as well as returning it again to eastern Europe, from where some of its themes at least, such as that of the 'undead', appear to have originated.

The political, social, cultural and religious anxieties of the eighteenth century were felt Europe-wide (indeed, northern hemisphere-wide) and paraded themselves across the entire continent. Consequently, in the view of the Marquis de Sade:

> It was therefore necessary [for writers] to call upon hell for aid in the creation of titles that could arouse interest, and to situate in the land of fantasies what was common knowledge, from mere observation of the history of man in this iron age; ... [the Gothic genre was] the inevitable product of the revolutionary shocks with which the whole of Europe resounded.[5]

The craze for Gothic dates from Horace Walpole's classic formulation of the genre in *The Castle of Otranto* (1765), with its combination of economic and sexual intrigue, based on an accursed dynastic succession, to the accompaniment of supernatural manifestations in a southern European medieval Gothic-castle setting. Near-contemporaneous European works – and their successors (east and west) – may repeat, vary, extend or develope alternative emphases upon these – soon enough to be noted as stereotyped – ingredients. As some of the essays in this volume observe, Gothic fiction extended to, or shaded into, psychological analysis, the uncanny (in the senses outlined by Freud and reapplied by Todorov), horror (and/or 'terror' in

---

[4] For a discussion of the pre-history of Gothic, see Samuel Kliger, 'The "Goths" in England (1945)', reprinted in *The Gothick Novel*, edited by Victor Sage, Basingstoke and London, Macmillan, 1990, pp. 115-30.

[5] Count D.A. Sade, 'Idée sur le roman'; quoted from *A Handbook to Gothic Literature*, edited by Marie Mulvey-Roberts, Basingstoke and London: Macmillan, 1998, p. 204.

some differentiations), the fantastic (Todorov again), and the marvellous.[6]

A number of extra-literary cultural models were internationally shared, in addition to a primal Gothic or medievalist nostalgia. Pan-European literary images derived from the engravings of Piranesi (particularly the *Carceri d'Invenzione*); his impenetrable imaginary prisons and impossible blueprints, affecting Gothic writers from Walpole in England to Odoevskii in Russia, paralleled in their labyrinthine mental processes the most complex features of Gothic architecture. Images of tyranny or incarceration – within ruins, castle, prison, asylum or monastery – had their objective correlatives in the architectural monuments of real institutional power (which in turn took on a literary significance): Versailles, the Bastille, Charenton and Notre Dame within France; the Castel Sant'Angelo in Rome; the Piombi in Venice; Metternich's Spielberg; and the Peter and Paul Fortress in St Petersburg are prominent examples. Mental and structural landscape juxtaposed with the natural, as observed alpine scenery vied as a source of inspiration with the rugged vistas of Salvator Rosa and the symbolised depictions of Caspar David Friedrich. Various strands of idealist philosophy (including Jena Romanticism and Neoplatonism) joined with the Hermetic and esoteric traditions, plus an input from Jewish and eastern influences, to furnish Gothic writers with some sort of an ideological platform of the mystical, in addition to the Enlightenment-inspired social.

Just as feudalism, or the Ancien Régime, was threatened and finally confronted by revolution, so did constitutionalism subsequently do battle across Europe with reaction. Gothic fiction, as one facet of Romanticism, duly reflected this binary conflict. Traditional dynastic requirements opposed new value systems, as the past met the present and fate (or resignation) was challenged by rebellion. From this, within the Gothic idiom, followed a whole series of dualistic clashes. At a spiritual level the supernatural vied with the natural, as mysticism challenged, and was again challenged by, materialism; or religion by science (and cult by pseudo-science). On all planes death would

---

[6]See Tzvetan Todorov, *The Fantastic: A Structural Approach to a Literary Genre*, translated by Richard Howard, Cleveland and London, The Press of Case Western Reserve University, 1973; Sigmund Freud, 'The "Uncanny" (1919)', in Freud, *Art and Literature*, Harmondsworth: Penguin, 1990, pp. 335-76.

contend with life. On a socio-political, and an individual, level tyrant would rage against victim and victimisation would engender vengeance; incarceration would oppose freedom and hierarchy would strive to control individuality; heritage or inheritance would be threatened by subversion, actual or potential, and authoritarianism by permissiveness, while, on a sexual level in particular, repression would tilt against desire.

A historical period setting would often give way to the more recent past, or even contemporary surroundings, just as exotic locations would be replaceable by a more local topography, and the classic chronotope of the historic Gothic castle could be succeeded by a rural mansion or an atmospheric townhouse. Gothic in the novel, or tale, could extend to, or incorporate, poem or drama. Nevertheless – typically – Gothic writing would take the form of prose fiction; writers from northern (and mainly Protestant) Europe would set their main (or most Gothic) works in the (largely Catholic) south; east Europeans would frequently prefer a western (or at least partly western) setting; imposing edifice (whether menacingly metropolitan or forlornly remote) may well alternate with an awe-inspiring nature.

What we may now see as 'classical Gothic', then, will normally involve dynastic disorders, set at some temporal and spatial distance and in a castle or manorial locale; defence, or usurpation, of an inheritance will threaten (and not infrequently inflict) violence upon hapless (usually female) victims amid a supernatural ambiance. Often (but not always) the heroine will be saved, the villain unmasked and the supernatural phenomena dispersed (explained or confirmed, as the case may be). Variations on such a classic Gothic masterplot allow the genre to overlap with, or merge into, the fictional modes of psychological realism, the uncanny, the fantastic or the marvellous (in which, in Todorov's terms, the supernatural may be, respectively, resolved by realistic explanation, never resolved, or found, within the terms of the fiction, to exist). An emphasis on hesitation over the supernatural may result in what we might call 'fantastic Gothic'; the establishing of a philosophical, occult or religious system of dualism (involving perhaps the 'existence' of demonic emissaries, revenants, demon lovers, sylphs or salamanders, and confirmed contact or 'correspondences' between the two worlds) will push a work into the realm of what might be termed 'Romantic Gothic' (largely Germanic in origin, and termed *dvoemirie* in its Russian utilisation: to be revived and developed later in the nineteenth century as Symbolism). Further impetus in that direction would result in the Todorovian marvellous: a fictional world akin to that of Hoffmann's *The Golden Pot*, the 'distant lands' of the German Romantics, or pure fairy tale.

The 'occult' (a term often interchanged with 'esoteric'), according to Bernice Rosenthal, may be said to encompass: the 'occult sciences' (alchemy, astrology and magic); the Kabbala (Jewish and Christian); and 'the post-Renaissance doctrines of Rosicrucianism, Spiritualism, Theosophy and Anthroposophy' (incorporating, in their turn, elements from the more ancient teachings of Hermeticism, Gnosticism, Neoplatonism and early Christianity).[7] One offshoot of this was Freemasonry. Another important aspect was the concept of a 'living nature', which may be related to *Naturphilosophie* and the 'cosmic pantheism' of Schelling.[8] There was a considerable vogue for the occult in late nineteenth-century Russia, but the eighteenth-century influx of Freemasonry and esoteric elements within the Romantic movement were also important. In addition to the concept of *dvoemirie*, Russia had the phenomenon of *dvoeverie* (dual faiths), the coexistence, or blending, of paganism with Orthodox Christianity.[9] However, it is primarily what Rosenthal calls the 'practical side' of the occult – the 'attempt to enlist invisible or supernatural forces, divine or diabolic, to attain health, wealth, love, and other personal goals'[10] – that really brings it into convergence with the Gothic.

On the psychological side, the accentuation may fall on character analysis (most commonly of villainy) or on a crisis of identity, often introducing the *Doppelgänger* theme (which, in its turn, may resolve itself into a supernaturally or a psychically induced 'double'). Strong psychological elements of dream and fantasy are contained within the style of 'fantastic realism', a term particularly associated with the mature work of Dostoevskii.[11] Greater concentration on setting may

---

[7] Rosenthal, op. cit., p. 2.

[8] Ibid., pp. 3-4.

[9] Ibid., p. 10.

[10] Ibid., p. 5.

[11] See in particular: Leon Burnett, 'Dostoevsky, Poe and the Discovery of Fantastic Realism', in *F.M. Dostoevsky (1821-1881): A Centenary Collection*, edited by Leon Burnett, Colchester, University of Essex, 1981, pp. 58-86; Malcolm V. Jones,

define 'historical Gothic' or, if contemporaneous, 'society (or social) Gothic'; other emphases again may lead to 'horror' or 'criminal' Gothic; the idea of 'the carnival world of the gothic' prompts consideration of Gothic in terms of the theories of Mikhail Bakhtin.[12] A yet further sub-division is identifiable as 'artistic Gothic', in which Gothic elements are involved with, or subordinated to, themes from art or music, bringing into play artistic works or figures (painters or paintings, musical composers or works, the animation of images or statues). In all such cases, some elements at least of the basic, or classic, Gothic ingredients need to be present for the term 'Gothic' to remain justifiable. Beyond these widely attested categories of the European Gothic tale, vestigial Gothic traces are to be found throughout what is considered mainstream realist European fiction over the whole of the nineteenth century, leading towards a subsequent Neo-Gothic revival, in the main coincidental with Symbolism and *fin de siècle* Decadence.

European elements were, then, an important factor throughout the evolution of English Gothic. Not only were the settings of the most prominent examples of the English Gothic novel (by Walpole, Radcliffe, Lewis and others) European, but Beckford's *Vathek* (1786), like Wilde's Gothic-Decadent play *Salome*, a century later, was actually written in French. French, too, was the language of composition of *The Manuscript Found in Saragossa*, an extraordinary framed compilation of stories reflecting the darker side of a burgeoning European Romanticism, written between about 1797 and 1815 by the polymath Polish nobleman, Jan Potocki (who is alleged to have committed suicide in 1815 with a home-made silver bullet). European, as well as

---

Dostoyevsky After Bakhtin: Readings in Dostoyevsky's Fantastic Realism, Cambridge, Cambridge University Press, 1990; and id., 'The Evolution of Fantastic Realism in Russian Literature: Gogol', Dostoevskii and Bulgakov', in *Celebrating Creativity: Essays in Honour of Jostein Børtnes*, edited by Knut Andreas Grimstad and Ingunn Lunde, Bergen, University of Bergen, 1997, pp. 58-69.

[12] Jones, in *Dostoyevsky After Bakhtin*, suggests the term 'social gothic' (p. 120) and employs the phrase 'carnival world of the Gothic' (p. 125) in his discussion of *The Idiot*. For an attempt at elucidating the English Gothic novel in terms of Bakhtinian dialogism and heteroglossia, see Jacqueline Howard, *Reading Gothic Fiction: A Bakhtinian Approach*, Oxford, Clarendon Press, 1994.

English, influences and themes were also important in works by Charles Brockden Brown and Washington Irving, the first exponents of American Gothic; an Anglo-European element remained vital to this style of American fiction through successive works by Poe, Hawthorne and Melville, and on to Henry James.

In France, in the decade after Walpole had launched the Gothic novel in English, Jacques Cazotte published his short novel *The Devil in Love* (*Le Diable amoureux*, 1772). A work which was later to catch Todorov's attention, *The Devil in Love* was promoted in the late 1820s as the main instigator of the prose tradition of *le fantastique*, then approaching the height of its popularity in France. Cazotte's emphasis is on erotic temptation and demonology, but the psychological dimension and underlying dynastic concerns place *The Devil in Love* at the very least on the edge of the Gothic. Also on the French Gothic margins lurks the Marquis de Sade, who, perhaps not surprisingly included a baroque farrago of Gothic elements in his works, while 'sadism', in the modern sense of the word, is a phenomenon widely to be found in Gothic fiction (if seldom employed on quite the elaborate scale favoured by the 'divine Marquis'). Sade's overall impact on the wider development of Gothic, fantastic, Romantic and Decadent fiction, as on psychoanalysis, would be hard to underestimate (as elaborated in Mario Praz's seminal study, *The Romantic Agony*, first published in English in 1933). For instance, Charlotte Dacre's novel *Zofloya, or The Moor* (1806), which appeared chronologically mid-way between the Gothic romances of Radcliffe and Mary Shelley's *Frankenstein*, in addition to drawing on elements from both Radcliffe and Lewis, is at least equally close to Sade in its depiction of a heroine with a fully conscious commitment to vice and in its weighing, albeit at a less sophisticated level, of the attractions of criminality and the insidious progression of depravity.

Much of what might be called French Gothic fiction can be seen to stem from these prototypes, together with the impact of English Gothic and the German Romantics (in particular, from the cult status acquired by Hoffmann in the late 1820s). Such cultural cross-fertilisation is exemplified by the publication, in the *Revue de Paris* in 1829, of Scott's critical essay on Hoffmann. The revived vogue for *le fantastique* and *l'école frénétique* can be seen as Gothic offshoots. Crime, horror and incarceration loom large in the writings of Pétrus Borel. Crime and psychological intrigue underpin a number of works by Balzac, while earlier the psychological frontiers of nightmare had been tested by Charles Nodier. Gothic, or near-Gothic, works of one tendency or another emerged too in this period from such prominent writers as Victor Hugo, Jules Janin, Théophile Gautier, Alexandre Dumas *père*, Prosper Mérimée and Gérard de Nerval (the last named left the second part of his main contribution to the genre, *Aurélia, or Dream and Life*, in unrevised form when he hanged himself in 1855). Later additions to such a list would include Villiers de l'Isle-Adam and Guy de Maupassant.

From Germany, Gottfried Bürger's ballad *Lenore* (1773) provided his European and American successors with one of Gothic's archetypal figures: that of the revenant-bridegroom; the poem was translated into English by Walter Scott and into Russian by Zhukovskii (with versions and adaptations by others). Such an apparition manifests itself too at the climax of Schiller's influential and popular early story *The Ghost-Seer* (1784), itself influenced by Cazotte. This story, which – like *Lenore* – achieved multiple early translations into English, contains many of the ingredients of classic Gothic and the fantastic. Coleridge was a great admirer of Schiller, Byron was inspired by *The Ghost-Seer*, and it would be difficult to doubt that Maturin's *Melmoth the Wanderer* was influenced by it. Schiller's broader impact on Europe and Russia is, of course, well attested.

There also developed in Germany a genre of popular literature, known as the *Trivialromane*, analogous to and influential upon English Gothic fiction (see the famous listing in Jane Austen's *Northanger Abbey*). At the turn of the century, the remarkable stories of Heinrich von Kleist (1777-1811) and the extraordinary anonymously published *The Nightwatches of Bonaventura* (1804) are not without their Gothic qualities. Kleist's *The Beggarwoman of Locarno*, for instance, qualifies as a supreme example of a Gothic miniature (of just three pages). In his *The Foundling*, an historical Italian setting provides the backdrop for an uncanny doubling (of the foundling Nicolo and the dead Colino) in a series of confusions: of a portrait and its real life resemblances, and of the living and the dead, in sharp relief against polarities of good and evil. Not in entirely dissimilar vein, 'Bonaventura', in his sectionalised 'Night Watches', furnishes the reader with a unique admixture of apocalyptic vision along with the grotesque and the gruesome, underpinned with a substratum of cemetery nihilism.

Arguably, however, the most influential figure of German Romantic prose, in its Gothic-fantastic and *Märchen* modes at least, was E.T.A. Hoffmann (1776-1822). Several of his works can be identified as particularly Gothic in form, or as massively influential upon the later development of European Gothic-type fiction. *The Entail* (1817) is perhaps his most classically Gothic story, set in a sinsister Castle R., in which the narrator's sensitivities are heightened by reading Schiller's *The Ghost-Seer*, and by the presence in the castle of 'an evil family secret' and 'a dreadful ghost'; dynastic inheritance is the issue; buried treasure and murder unfold; the ghost of the murderer still wails from the ruins. More significantly, the by now already traditional figure of the manic monk is developed by Hoffmann in his own redoubtable contribution to the Gothic novel, *The Devil's Elixirs* (1816: a fundamental work of the European Gothic style, long overdue a reprint in its English translation!). Focusing on the dual concepts of the divided self and the vicissitudes (and the metaphysics) of coincidence, and presented through the time-honoured Gothic-romantic device of the 'manuscript', Hoffmann's novel deals with the expiation of the sins of a degenerate line, by means of conflict between forces of the divine and the demonic and redemption through love. Skilful exploitation of the multidudinous familiar trappings of Gothic horror build this work into a thrilling novel of suspense; and yet the darkness of Brother Medardus's life achieves its ultimate redemption, just as the manifold enigmas of interwoven plot and subplot are granted demystification. The main impact of this novel, however, arose from Hoffmann's treatment, in this most complex of his works, of crises of identity, bizarre and terrifying mental experiences arising under extreme duress, and the theme of doubles. Many subsequent works in the Gothic mode (by Nerval or Gogol; Poe or Dostoevskii; and indeed many others) would seem inconceivable without Hoffmann.

Russia

The involvement of a classical Pantheon of deities (demons, or diabolism) – even in Russian affairs – can be found in certain eighteenth-century texts, and is traced in the present volume (from a work of 1769 by Vasilii Maikov onward) in the essay by Richard

Peace. The first Russian Gothic story proper, however, appears to be *The Island of Bornholm* (*Ostrov Borngol'm*, 1794), by Nikolai Karamzin (see Derek Offord's essay). A Sentimentalist author of stories, poetry, essays and travelogues, Karamzin (1760-1826) subsequently turned himself into Russia's first major historian. Under the influence of English and European Preromanticism, Karamzin's stories emphasise Sentimentalist and historical themes, with a tinge of graveyard Gothic (as in his most famous tale, *Poor Liza*, of 1792). In just one instance, *The Island of Bornholm*, this formula is reversed, to result in a predominantly Gothic tale with the trappings of Sentimentalism.

Gothic works in Russia remained few and far between before the 1820s although a hitherto little known novel *Don Corrado de G[u]errera, or the Spirit of Vengeance and the Barbarity of the Spaniards* (1803), by Nikolai Gnedich (better known as the translator into Russian of *The Iliad*), is here exhumed for examination by Alesandra Tosi. The romantic poet Vasilii Zhukovskii (1783-1852) twice reworked Bürger's *Lenore* into Russian versions (*Svetlana*, 1808-12; and *Liudmila* (1808), and much later produced a translation (*Lenora*, 1831): see the essay in this volume by Michael Pursglove. Clara Reeve's *The Old English Baron* had been translated into Russian as early as 1792. French translations of English Gothic fiction were commonly known in Russia (where the educated élite were more accustomed to reading in French than in Russian), and translations of English fiction into Russian were frequently made from the French (as were many of the early translations into English of Russian works). Ann Radcliffe's novels appeared in Russian in the early 1800s, leading a wave of Gothic translations, along with certain works of others falsely attributed to her! These included Matthew Lewis's *The Monk* (no less), and *The Romance of the Pyrenees*, by a certain Catherine Cuthbertson. Obscure English authors of popular Gothic to achieve appearances in Russian in this period include Anna Maria McKenzie and George Walker.[13]

Vatsuro's work on the Gothic in Russia and Todorov's theory of the fantastic apart, the Soviet critic N.V. Izmailov had traced a tradition of

---

[13] See V.E. Vatsuro, 'A Radklif, ee pervye russkie chitateli i perevodchiki', *Novoe literaturnoe obozrenie*, 22 (1996), 202-25.

the fantastic in Russia.[14] This had been a somewhat negative category to Belinskii (involving the far-fetched, the supernatural and the otherworldly), but had been rather more frivolously approached by Osip Senkovskii (who had written tales of his own of this stamp under the name of 'Baron Brambeus'). Eastern influences (Senkovskii was himself an orientalist), folkloric motifs and the fairy tale all fed into the Russian fantastic, along with the idealist philosophy of Schelling and the impact of the Gothic and the ballad (identified by Izmailov as subgenres of Preromanticism); fate, revenge and the intervention of otherworldly powers (often resulting in gloom, tragedy, moralising and mysticism) lead this version of the fantastic to merge with Vatsuro's ideas of a Russian Gothic. Izmailov dates the beginning of this tradition proper to the stories of Pogorel'skii's cycle *The Double, or My Evenings in Little Russia* (*Dvoinik, ili moi vechera v Malorossii*, collected 1828);[15] he then traces it in some detail up to 1844, the year of publication of Odoevskii's in effect valedictory *Collected Works* (*Sochineniia*).

'Are there really such things?...[as Russian novels]', the aged Countess of *The Queen of Spades* (*Pikovaia dama*, 1834) asks her nephew; 'I want the sort where the hero doesn't strangle either his father or mother, and there are no drowned bodies'.[16] Russian prose fiction indeed matured slowly over the first quarter of the nineteenth century and, if there was a heyday of Russian Gothic fiction, it certainly fell in the second quarter. Aleksandr Bestuzhev (1797-1837), later known under the pen-name 'Marlinskii' after being imprisoned and exiled for his role in the Decembrist uprising of 1825 (and subsequently disappearing in action in the Caucasian colonial wars) published, under the impact of Radcliffe, Scott and Irving (plus touches of Shakespeare and Schiller), a number of Gothic tales in the 1820s and early 30s, mostly still untranslated into English.[17] These comprise, by general consensus, *The Traitor* (*Izmennik*) and *Castle Eisen* (*Zamok Eizen*, both

---

[14] N.V. Izmailov, 'Fantasticheskaia povest'', in *Russkaia povest' XIX veka: Istoriia i problematika zhanra*, edited by B.S. Meilakh, Leningrad, 1973 pp. 134-69 (135-7).

[15] See ibid., pp. 141-5.

[16] Alexander Pushkin, *The Queen of Spades and Other Stories*, translated by Alan Myers; edited by Andrew Kahn, Oxford, Oxford University Press, 1997, p. 76.

[17] See, however, 'The Terrible Fortune-Telling', translated by K.M. Cook, in Korovin, 1984, pp. 133-66.

of 1825); and a trio of 'mature' stories from the turn of the 1830s: *An Evening at a Caucasian Spa in 1824* (*Vecher na Kavkazskikh vodakh v 1824 godu*), *The Terrible Fortune-Telling* (*Strashnoe gadan'e*), and *The Cuirassier* (*Latnik*). Marlinskii combines strong Gothic elements with historical settings and folkloric motifs.[18] *The Cuirassier*, however, progresses to near-contemporaneity, a more sophisticated narrative technique, and the fullest range of Gothic motifs.

Another writer to pour Romantic-Gothic motifs into popular fiction in this period was the historian, dramatist and journalist Nikolai Polevoi (1796-1846). In particular, his tale *The Bliss of Madness* (*Blazhenstvo bezumiia*, 1833) is a potboiler of overt Hoffmannism (complete even with a framing device of a group of friends reading a Hoffmann tale). An obsession with a woman he believes to comprise half his soul leads the protagonist to his doom in a madhouse, in a narrative bestrewn with trappings of the occult, conjuring an Italian atmosphere in St Petersburg, and motivated on a realistic plane with card-sharping and fortune hunting. The main trio of characters in the embedded tale (sensitive artistic man, mysterious young woman, and demonic father-figure) are to be found too in Gogol's *Terrible Vengeance* (*Strashnaia mest'*) and recur later in Dostoevskii's *The Landlady* (*Khoziaika*). A not entirely dissimilar triangle occurs in Elena Gan's *Society's Judgement* (*Sud sveta*, of 1840); the proposition that Gan's works include at least an element of 'Female Gothic' (a concept all but unrecognised in commentaries on Russian literature of the period hitherto) is examined here by Carolyn Jursa Ayers.

Mikhail Lermontov (1814-41), by the end of a brief and stormy literary career, had left two unfinished works of Gothic fiction, *Vadim* and *Shtoss*. The latter is a tale of mystery and demonic card-playing, begun only months before Lermontov's fatal duel. *Vadim* (written 1832-34, published 1873), the principal product of Lermontov's prose juvenilia, comprises a little over a hundred pages of a historical novel of the Pugachev rebellion, apparently influenced by Scott and Hugo. The eponymous protagonist is a demonically depicted hunchback,

---

[18] See Vatsuro, 1995, who concentrates on *Castle Eisen* and *The Cuirassier*; on the former see also Lewis Bagby, *Alexander Bestuzhev-Marlinsky and Russian Byronism*, University Park, The Pennsylvania State University Press, 1995, pp. 128-33; and, on *The Traitor*, Lauren G. Leighton, *Alexander Bestuzhev-Marlinsky*, Boston, Twayne, 1975, pp. 78-82 and (on 'the tales of horror') pp. 98-106.

whose mission of righteous revenge in a family feud (against a tyrannical landowner, somewhat in the mode of Walpole's Manfred) turns, entangled in the mayhem of a Cossack uprising and fuelled by an unbridled jealousy inspired by designs of incest, into pure malevalence. A slightly grotesque concentration on beggars and mutilation gells with motifs of the monastery, confinement, torture and a labyrinthine cave, described in detail suggestive of both Gothic architecture and fiction.[19] This place, named Devil's Lair (*Chortova logovishcha*), where unclean spirits are thought to hold sway, is clearly destined to be the *locus* of a melodramatic climax – were the novel to have been completed.

The other major figure of Russian prose in this period, Nikolai Gogol (1809-52) incorporated Gothic settings or features into a number of his Ukrainian and Petersburg tales. An important example of the artistic Gothic is his Hoffmannian *The Portrait* (*Portret*, 1835; somewhat toned down Gothicwise in the revision of 1842), which projects a Gothic struggle of good and evil into the creative process, highlighting the eponymous evil-eyed and cursed painting. In the present volume, Priscilla Meyer treats the demonic Ukrainian story *Vii* with the Petersburg extravaganza *The Nose* (*Nos*) as a Gothic pair, or 'double', in themselves.

However, it might be argued, the most impressive body of fiction at least approximating to a genuine form of Russian Gothic writing belongs to Vladimir Odoevskii (1804-69). This would include several of the stories contained within his philosophical frame-tale *Russian Nights* (*Russkie nochi*: first integral publication 1844), along with a number of independent tales or novellas. Most notable of these are his 'dilogy' *The Salamander* (*Salamandra*, 1841) and *The Cosmorama*

---

[19] See Chapter 18 of *Vadim*: M.Iu. Lermontov, *Polnoe sobranie sochinenii v piati tomakh*, Moscow-Leningrad, 1937, vol. 5, pp. 65-71. The entrances to the cave system are through burial mounds, each of which 'serves as though as a vault for the dark underground gallery' (p. 67); also within is 'a wide round hall ... paved with stones [which] has four cavities in the shape of niches' and 'a four-cornered pillar [which] supports its clay vault, rather expertly formed' (p. 68) [translations mine: NC]. At one point (the end of Chapter 20 and the beginning of Chapter 21), the words 'fantastically' (*fantasticheski*) and 'Gothic hall' (*kak boi chasov v syroi goticheskoi zale*) appear within a dozen lines of each other (p. 84). For a published English translation (unavailable to me), see Mikhail Lermontov, *Vadim*, translated with an introduction by Helena Goscilo, Ann Arbor, Ardis, 1984.

(*Kosmorama*, 1839); Odoevskii is well represented in the current volume, with essays on these two works by Cynthia Ramsey and Roger Cockrell respectively. In addition, Odoevskii wrote shorter Gothic stories, such as *The Ghost* (*Prividenie*), which could almost be taken as a whimsical reworking of Hoffmann's *The Entail*. Two of his stories, 'The Improvisor' (*Improvizator*, from *Russian Nights* (word for word) and (to a lesser degree) *The Sylph* (*Sil'fida*, 1837), it has now come to light, were plagiarised – via a French translation of the 1850s – by the Irish-American fantastic-Gothic writer Fitz-James O'Brien (1828-62).[20] Frequently dubbed, though not of course entirely accurately, 'the Russian Hoffmann', Odoevskii includes a full gamut of occult and Gothic paraphernalia scattered through his collective tales: magical and alchemical effects, the suspension of time and place in an ultra-Gothic-Romantic extension – indeed the dissolution – of what is now seen as the Bakhtinian chronotope, supernatural arson and spontaneous human combustion, through to the walking dead. He also specialised in proto-science fiction and anti-Utopia, as well as artistic delirium, or a kind of manic *Künstlernovellen*, in tales based on Piranesi, Beethoven and J.S. Bach (in addition to his literary and governmental service careers, Odoevskii was, among yet other things, a musicologist and an amateur alchemist).[21]

Like Lermontov (but four years earlier), Aleksandr Pushkin (1799-1837) cut short his literary career through a fatal duel. No text can rival Pushkin's *The Queen of Spades* for the position of undisputed masterpiece of Russian Gothic. Neither has any comparable short Russian text (given its mere 30 pages in length) been accorded such massive critical attention. *The Queen of Spades* can be read as a Gothic tale *par excellence*, as Gothic parody, or – given that it is a prime example of the pure fantastic (and recognised as such by commentators stretching from Dostoevskii to Todorov: see Claire Whitehead's analysis in this volume) – in almost any number of yet further ways:

---

[20] See Neil Cornwell, *Vladimir Odoevsky and Romantic Poetics*, Oxford, Berghahn Books, 1998, pp. 157-67.
[21] For a full account of Odoevskii's career, see Neil Cornwell, *The Life, Times and Milieu of V.F. Odoyevsky*, London, Athlone, and Athens, Ohio University Press, 1986; on Odoevskii and the philosophical tradition (esoteric and Romantic), see pp. 91-114.

from society tale, to psychological study, to numerological puzzle.[22] Among the many possible sources tapped by Pushkin can be numbered *The Devil's Elixirs* and another Hoffmann story, *Gambler's Luck* – both of which feature hallucinations or obsessions with cards. The epitome of the 'Petersburg tale' in Russian literature, *The Queen of Spades* extends from its near contemporary metropolitan Russian setting back in time to the 1770s and geographically west, to the Paris of the Ancien Régime and the pseudo-occultism of the Count Saint-Germain. Economic drive, sexual exploitation, *idée fixe*, the clash of two eras and the judgment of fate all engage in what is a virtuoso performance of condensed prose. A recent commentator, Andrew Kahn, concludes that: 'Like all works of the supernatural and of the Gothic, *The Queen of Spades* tantalizes by a potential naturalistic explanation of the fantastic, and winks now and then at the pseudo-scientific'.[23]

In the following decade of the 1840s, Dostoevskii, who claimed to have read Radcliffe's novels while still a child, opened his career with a strong Gothic flourish, offering such works as *The Double (Dvoinik*, 1846) and *The Landlady (Khoziaika*, 1847).[24] However, his near encounter with a Tsarist executioner and an ensuing decade of Siberian exile turned him more toward the directions of political conservatism and psychological realism; nevertheless, residual Gothic elements are apparent throughout his *oeuvre* and made something of a come-back in his later period, both in his short stories of the 1870s and, in the case put forward in the present volume by Ignat Avsey, in his final novel, *The Karamazov Brothers (Brat'ia Karamazovy)*.[25] Similarly, another acknowledged master of Russian realism, Ivan Turgenev, included a

---

[22] For a variety of readings, see Neil Cornwell, *Pushkin's 'The Queen of Spades'*, London, Bristol Classical press, 1993. For a numerological analysis, see Lauren G. Leighton, *The Esoteric Tradition in Russian Romantic Literature*, University Park, Pennsylvania: The Pennsylvania State University Press, 1994, pp. 131-52.

[23] Andrew Kahn, 'Introduction' to Pushkin, *The Queen of Spades and Other Stories*, p. xxvi.

[24] Critical literature on *The Double* is widespread. For a recent attempt to rehabilitate the much-denigrated *The Landlady*, see Randi Gaustad, 'Rebuilding Gothic on Russian Soil: The Roles of Religion and Intertwining of Minds in Dostoevskii's *The Landlady*', in *Celebrating Creativity*, cited above, pp. 205-15.

[25] On this theme, see also Robin Feuer Miller, 'Dostoevsky and the Tale of Terror', in *The Russian Novel from Pushkin to Pasternak*, edited by John Garrard, New Haven, Yale University Press, 1983, pp. 103-21.

sprinkling of Gothic-fantastic tales amidst his works, including *Phantoms* (*Prizraki*, 1864) and the late story *Clara Milich* (1883); here, Leon Burnett concentrates on the story *Faust* (1856). Still within the 1840s, A.K. (or Aleksei) Tolstoi had published vampire tales.[26] Madness, of one type or another, was a frequent ingredient of Russian fiction, from Pushkin through to Vsevolod Garshin's *The Red Flower* (*Krasnyi tsvetok*, 1883) and Anton Chekhov's *Ward No. 6* (*Palata No. 6*, 1892). Other writers to essay something resembling a Gothic style include Nikolai Leskov and Aleksei Apukhtin. In the main, however, a relatively straight realism seemed to be the dominant force in Russian literature until the Symbolist movement emerged towards the end of the century, when Romantic and Gothic dualities returned with something of a vengeance. In that *fin de siècle* ambiance, even the medical realist Chekhov turned his hand to Gothic phantasmagoria – in one tale at least: *The Black Monk* (1894: see Ann Komaromi's essay), thus closing the (exactly) one hundred years of Russian Gothic analysed here (from Karamzin to Chekhov).

The demonic (or forms of diabolism, or the Satanic), witchcraft and other Gothic appurtenances continued to resurface in Russian literature, even into the Soviet period (most notably in the writings of Mikhail Bulgakov), while the city of St Petersburg (renamed Petrograd, Leningrad, and finally St Petersburg again) has continued to exercise its own Gothic-type mystique. Indeed, the St Petersburg theme (or 'text') in Russian literature (from Pushkin, Gogol and Dostoevskii, on to Andrei Belyi and beyond) could even be said to qualify as a sub-category of its own: 'St Petersburg Gothic'.

We have already seen a number of instances of cross-fertilisation at play in the literary developments outlined above. In recent times, Carlos Fuentes, writing of the literary origins of his novella *Aura*, traced its basic plot (through *The Queen of Spades*, its reworking in *The Aspern Papers* by Henry James, and analogously with the figure of Miss Havisham in *Great Expectations*) back to a Chinese tale, deriving in its turn from 'the traditions of the oldest Chinese literature, that tide

---

[26] See Alexei Tolstoy, 'Vampire', translated by Olga Shartse, in Korovin, 1984, pp. 525-95; Alexis Tolstoy, 'The Family of the Vourdalak' [written in French], translated by Christopher Frayling, in his *Vampyres: Lord Byron to Count Dracula*, London, Faber, 1992, pp. 254-79.

of narrative centuries that hardly begins to murmur the vastness of its constant themes: the supernatural virgin, the fatal woman, the spectral bride, the couple reunited'.[27] Such is the process by which literature evolves.

Cazotte's pioneering *The Devil in Love* made its impact on Schiller, Matthew Lewis and subsequently Hoffmann. We have already commented, in this respect, also on Schiller's *The Ghost-Seer* and Bürger's ballad *Lenore*. Mary Shelley's *Frankenstein* had its Russian connections[28] (not least in the final chase over the northern ice); moreover, Odoevskii reviewed her later novel *The Last Man*, the theme of which he later sketched in a powerful short work called 'The Last Suicide' (forming a part of *Russian Nights*). Poe's celebrated 'double' tale *William Wilson* derived from a Spanish sketch by Washington Irving, in its turn based on an abandoned project of Byron's drawn from Spanish literature and suggested to him by Percy Shelley: and there is no saying where its influence stopped. As for the Germanic influences on Poe, which were common also to Odoevskii (and Poe was admired by both Odoevskii and Dostoevskii, as well as, subsequently, by the French and Russian Symbolists) ... ; again, we cannot begin here to take such things further.

Among the direct influences on Odoevskii were Saint-Martin and Schelling. Odoevskii apart, Cazotte and Balzac were fascinated by the occult tradition and the *Illuminati* (see Balzac's novella *Séraphita*). Hoffmann, Gautier and Odoevskii, to name but three, were exercised by divided-self mental states. Cazotte, Bürger and Gautier portrayed diabolical lovers; vampirism featured in works by Hoffmann, Nodier, Gautier and A.K. Tolstoi. Schiller, Hoffmann and Odoevskii exploited the theme of the ghostly curse. Hoffmann, Balzac, Odoevskii and Gogol combined Gothic trappings with art or music. Pushkin, Eichendorff and Mérimée employed animated statues. Balzac even composed a sequel to Maturin's *Melmoth the Wanderer* (entitled *Melmoth reconcilié*); *Melmoth* had its impact on both Gogol and Dostoevskii. A number of

---

[27] Carlos Fuentes, 'How I Wrote One of My Books', in his *Myself with Others: Selected Essays*, London: Andre Deutsch, 1988, pp. 28-45 (38).

[28] For an exploration of this theme, see Richard Freeborn, 'Frankenstein's Last Journey', *Oxford Slavonic Papers*, New Series, 18 (1985), 102-19. See also Alekseev's research on Claire Clairmont and Russia: 'Moskovskie dnevniki i pis'ma Kler Klermont', in *Literaturnoe nasledstvo*, 91, pp. 469-573.

writers of Gothic-type fiction (and Russians not least) lived – or died, or nearly died – somewhat Gothic lives (by duelling, suicide, or even execution). And so we could continue. And thus, moreover, were assembled throughout European Gothic literature of the first half of the nineteenth century more than sufficient ingredients to fuel and fuel again – across Europe and into Russia – subsequent Gothic revivals and Neo-Gothic movements.

FROM PANTHEON TO PANDEMONIUM

RICHARD PEACE

From its very origins European literature has been closely associated with the dominant religion of its contemporary culture. The deeds of men and women in *The Iliad* and *The Odyssey* occur within the wider framework of the actions and desires of the Greek gods and goddesses who, for good or ill, interfere in the lives of mere mortals. The freedom of action claimed by the heroes of such works is depicted as dependent on the whims of supernatural beings and the petty quarrels that arise within a whole pantheon of deities. In Greek drama human behaviour seems even more predetermined by the supernatural and the iron laws of fate. Thus the Greek view of the human condition is one in which free will is largely illusory, and although human beings may be brought to account for their actions, their subjection to a supernatural superstructure ultimately frees them from responsibility. At the opening of *The Odyssey* Zeus himself views this human weakness with some scepticism: 'What a lamentable thing it is that men should blame the gods and regard *us* as the source of their troubles, when it is their own transgressions which bring them suffering that was not their destiny'.[1] Nevertheless, alienation of human responsibility is an important function of the supernatural framework, as it is presented in literature.

The advent of Christianity brought new values. In theory the old Pantheon was replaced by monotheism and the doctrine of free will. Yet the ancient world still exerted its influence. The monotheistic focus was perhaps not quite as clear as it was, for example, for the Jews. Polytheistic breaches occurred with the introduction of the doctrine of the Trinity, the promotion of the status of the Virgin Mary and the disciples as saints, followed by a host of minor, and often local, saints. Added to this was a distinct hierarchy of angels, and here a certain proliferation in respect to the ancient world may be observed, if, as the winged messengers of the divine presence, such creatures are to be

---

[1] Homer, *The Odyssey*, translated by E.V. Rieu, revised edition, Harmondsworth, Penguin, 1991, p. 4.

seen as the counterparts of Hermes. As with the Pantheon of the Greeks, intercession with the Father on behalf of earth-bound mortals, became a dominant role for those closest to God in Heaven – the Virgin and the saints. Yet the doctrine of free will added a notable difference: through prayer, mere mortals could themselves plead for intercession and seek divine backing for their own free actions.

There is yet one more figure that must be added to the Christian pantheon; one that for the purposes of my argument is the most significant – the devil. In Christian tradition, Satan was in fact an angel who had been thrown out of heaven and had set up his own kingdom in the nether world: 'Better to reign in hell than serve in heav'n', as Milton puts it.[2] We may see in this figure certain lineaments of the Greek god Pluto, but there is a distinct difference. Pluto, although god of the underworld, was not the embodiment of evil. The problem of evil was seen differently by the ancient Greeks. Although many areas of human activity had their own presiding deities: love, war, hunting, carousing – there was no supernatural incarnation of evil as such. The bad things that man experienced arose from dissensions among the gods themselves. Christian theology, however, polarised the problem of good and evil, and by offering man free will, forced him to choose between God and his ministers and Satan and his nefarious cohorts. The Christian pantheon, therefore, created its own dark mirror image.

In the Christian middle ages, the representation of God on stage in the mystery plays seemed to present no doctrinal problem. Yet, for the more sophisticated writer imbued with the spirit of classicism, the portrayal of the Christian equivalent of Zeus was a matter of the greatest delicacy. Thus only at the very end of his great poem *The Divine Comedy* does Dante even dare to suggest the ineffable, numinous presence of God Himself and, strangely, it is presented with echoes of that older Pantheon. The revelation, we are told, is as intangible as the 'Sybil's sentence' lost in the winds on flitting leaves; it is a mere moment, yet it is measured in time by another classical reference: Neptune's encounter with the Argonauts.[3] Despite such half-formed hints, Dante cannot possibly equate Heaven with Mount Olympus, and its hierarchy with the old Pantheon; but he, like Milton after him, seems less embarrassed by the description of hell.

---

[2] John Milton, *Paradise Lost*, Book I, line 263.
[3] Dante, *Paradiso*, Canto XXXIII, lines 66; 94-6.

Milton does boldly represent the Christian deity, yet he does so as the autocrat: his is the 'throne and monarchy of God'.[4] Satan, on the other hand, for all his arrogance, behaves more like a Greek democrat. Like Zeus, he calls a council to discuss proposed action:

> The great Seraphic Lords and Cherubim
> In close recess and secret conclave sat,
> A thousand demi-gods on golden seats,[5]

The venue, however, is not Mount Olympus: it is Pandemonium – the dark mirror image of the Christian pantheon. Here is a new hierarchy of the nether world, in which hell, as 'Pandemonium', has replaced Pantheon, and the old pagan world can be equated with the devil. Moreover, by calling Satan's solemn council a 'secret conclave',[6] Milton hints at other forces of evil – the Romish assembly of Cardinals – and even suggests the pagan Muslims in his references to the 'Soldan's chair', and 'Paynim chivalry'.[7]

For the Portuguese, the Muslims were certainly equated with the powers of evil, and, earlier in that same century in which Milton was writing, their national epic *The Lusiads* depicts Vasco da Gama sailing round the continent of Africa to find a sea route to India, not only as the emissary of trade, but also as the bearer of the Christian message. His enemies along the way are the old foes of Portugal, the Moors (that is to say the Arabs and their Muslim converts). Although Vasco da Gama prays to God, the text offers little evidence of His divine presence: the fortunes of Vasco's expedition are entirely in the hands of the Pantheon of Greek gods. Venus is on his side, and can intervene physically to pull his ships out of dangerous ports, but Bacchus is against them: they are attempting to conquer the East, which Bacchus regards as his own domain. In a particularly bizarre episode, Bacchus adopts human form and dresses up as a figure (perhaps even a priest) performing Christian rites amid clouds of incense at an altar decorated with images of the Virgin Mary and the Apostles. All this is to deceive the Portuguese into believing that the Muslim island of Mombasa has a

---

[4] Milton, *Paradise Lost*, Book I, line 42.

[5] Ibid., lines 794-6.

[6] Ibid., line 795.

[7] Ibid., lines 764-5.

Christian population and will offer them sanctuary.[8] The absurdity of
the scene is compounded, not only by the fact that the God of Wine is
taking the side of the teetotal Muslims against the bibulous Portuguese,
but also by the strange detail that the latter are the Lusitanians (as the
poem's very title itself suggests) and take their name from Luso, who
was a follower of Bacchus, and may even have been his son.[9]
Everything seems wrong in this strange episode, not least that Camõens
is treading on dangerous theological ground, and can only offer a single
line in mitigation of apparent blasphemy: 'O falso Deus adora o
verdadeiro' ('the false god was worshipping the true one').[10] The scene
may be tinged with comedy, but the role of the Pantheon in *The
Lusiads* is to be taken seriously.

At the other end of Europe, a century later, the Pantheon was portrayed
in entirely comic terms. In *Elisei, or Bacchus Annoyed* (*Elisei, ili
razdrazhennyi Vakh*). V.I. Maikov (1728-78), influenced by the French
satirist Scarron, presents his hero, the cabby Elisei, as a figure caught
up in a dispute between Ceres and Bacchus. Ceres complains to Zeus
that the drunkenness of the Russian peasant is ruining agriculture, all
the more so as they are turning her product, grain, into that of Bacchus
– wine. Bacchus defends drunkenness, which he believes is actually
being curtailed by the prices charged by the tax farmers, who have the
state's concession on the sale of alcohol. He sees a champion of his
cause in Elisei, the ruffian with a penchant for beating up such people.
The Pantheon has been summoned to resolve the quarrel, and, as
Bacchus hopes, also to get Elisei out of prison.

Maikov's gods have all the base features of human beings
themselves. He wishes to present them as rough barge haulers, *burlaki*:

> *I slovom, chtob moi bogini i bozhki*
> *Iznadorvali vsekh chitatelei kishki.*[11]
> ('And in a word, so that my goddesses and petty gods
> Should tear the guts of all my readers')

---

[8] *Lusiads*, Canto II, stanzas 10-12.

[9] Luís de Camõens, *Os Lusíadas*. Introduction by S.A. Benedito and Notes by A.
Leitão. Lisbon, Biblioteca Ulisseia de Autores Portugueses, [1987?], p. 245.

[10] *Lusiads*, Canto II, stanza 12, line 8.

[11] V.I. Maikov, *Elisei, ili razdrazhennyi Vakh, Pesn'* I, lines 24-5; in *Russkaia
literatura XVIII veka*, edited by G.P. Makogonenko, Leningrad, 1970, pp. 229-50.

Thus Zeus is discovered asleep after too much alcohol and is farting.[12] Neptune, instead of the sea, merely stirs a puddle with his trident and is abused by young peasant lads. Their parents beat the god, claiming that, now that they are baptised, they no longer pay him respect: '*Ne stanem boga chtit' v takom, kak ty, bolvane*' ('We are not going to respect a god in a blockhead like you').[13] Yet, for all their protestations, there is no sense of any true divine presence in the poem, even though the hero's mother prays to the saints for succour; and when the tax farmer prays all night to avert a thunder storm, his devotions merely present Elisei with the opportunity to slip into his wife's bed. Indeed, when Elisei wonders why (because of the machinations of Hermes) he is wearing women's clothes, he is interrupted by the woman who has sexual designs on him at the very moment that 'Christ' is on his lips: 'I know not by Christ...'. At this point his words were interrupted by the superintendress' ('"*Ne znaiu po Khriste...*" *Tut rech' preryvaet nachal'nitsa*').[14]

Maikov presents us not only with the complete degradation of the old Pantheon, but he also suggests, more clearly than Camõens, its identification with Satanic forces. Thus Elisei regards his transportation to the female prison by Hermes as the work of the devil,[15] and the tax farmer (who appears to be an old believer) seeks to attribute his own misadventures to Satan, devils and spirits. He summons a witch to be rid of them, and although later he calls a priest to absolve his sins, we are assured that this will not save him from hell.[16] Zeus, too, has power in the nether world: he can condemn people to hell.[17] Maikov's debased pantheon contains hints of Russian folklore (e.g. the house spirit – *domovoi*), and this is significant in as

---

[12] *Ibid.*, lines 263-5. Such details are reminiscent of Scarron:
     Juppiter le lance Tonerre
     Dormoit ayant bu trop d'un verre
     Et Junon qui n'avoit moins bu
     Dormoit sur un lit à cul nu.
(Paul Scarron, *Le Typhon*, Toussainet Quinet, 1664, Book I, p. 9)

[13] Maikov, *Pesn'* I, line 458.

[14] Ibid., *Pesn'* III, lines 49-50.

[15] Ibid., *Pesn'* II, lines 161-7.

[16] Ibid., *Pesn'* V, lines 94-106.

[17] Ibid., *Pesn'* V, lines 300-06.

much as folkloric elements, identified with the world of the devil, will in the next century constitute a new 'Romantic Pandemonium'.[18]

The hint is already there in the concept's originator; for we have seen that Milton likens the impious throng of spirits at Satan's council to 'fairy elves'.[19] Nevertheless, it was not so much Milton's proud Lucifer, as the more insinuating Mephistopheles of Goethe, that would condition the portrayal of evil in Russian nineteenth century literature. Thus the Russian romantic pandemonium would be a world inhabited, not by Milton's 'elves', but by spirits, witches and monsters heavily influenced by German romantic literature, even though a compromise between the classical paradigm and native folklore had already been attempted in the eighteenth century by such writers as M.D. Chulkov (1743-93), who devised a hierarchy of Slavonic gods (Perun, Veles, Lel', etc.) as 'Russian' counterparts of Greek deities.

The nineteenth century saw a resurgence of interest in the forces of the supernatural. It was, perhaps, in part, a reaction to the rationalism of the preceding century; in part, also, the reflection through art of those incomprehensible horrors let loose by the French Revolution. To that extent the new romantic pandemonium may be related to social upheaval, in the same way as Milton's own pandemonium is often linked to the earlier 'English Revolution'.

As we have seen, writers in previous centuries, often had ideological difficulties with the framework of the supernatural imposed on them by classical models. The spirit of freedom abroad after the French Revolution was inimical to hierarchies, and the new framework of the supernatural was perhaps less a framework than a dimly glimpsed scaffolding – a pandemonium of rebellious forces, nearer to a concept of 'pandemonium' in its modern sense. German romantic writers, particularly Tieck and Hoffmann, had a great impact on Russian literature at the beginning of the nineteenth century. Their influence may be traced particularly in the works of Odoevskii,

---

[18] Maikov's poem has other national elements. The central figure recalls that thuggish figure of the folk epics (*Byliny*), Vasilii Buslaev The Russian fairy tale also provides Elisei with his 'invisible hat' (*shapka nevidimka*), although there is an attempt to turn this into a classical element by likening it to the *aegis* (Maikov, *Pesn'* III, lines 284-8; *Pesn'* V, lines 352-4.

[19] See Milton, *Paradise Lost*, Book I, lines 777-88.

Vel'tman, Pogorel'skii and Gogol. At the same time, the French Revolution had unlocked the Pandora's box of nationalism, and this too shaped the course of Russian literature. The nascent nationalism of the Ukraine evoked an interest in the ethnography of the region, in particular, in Ukrainian folklore. The writings of Somov, Narezhnyi and the early Gogol rely heavily on such material, and this helped to initiate a literary preoccupation with the supernatural, reinforced by romantic models originating in Germany.

Somov's stories bear such titles as 'The Water Sprite. A Ukrainian Legend' (*Rusalka. Malorossiiskoe predanie*, 1829); 'The Werewolf. A Folk Fairy Tale' (*Oboroten'. Narodnaia skazka*, 1821); 'The Hobgoblin. The Tale of a Russian Peasant on the Highway' (*Kikimora. Rasskaz russkogo krest'ianina na bol'shoi doroge*, 1830); and 'The Witches of Kiev' (*Kievskie ved'my*, 1833). Similar features of Ukrainian demonology permeate the fabric of Gogol's early stories, *Evenings in a Village near Dikanka* (*Vechera na khutore bliz Dikan'ki*, 1831-32), and it is a significant feature of such writing that only the forces of evil are given manifest form: the force for good, Orthodox Christianity, is strangely non-manifest, and often reduced to the nominal and the semiotic – the sign of the cross.

For all the petty dissensions of the Pantheon, the classical world was ordered. Each deity had its allotted province, its determined role and specific character; all were relatives or dependants of Zeus. When, however, romantic pandemonium broke out, all such clarity was lost: evil manifested itself in bizarre and unpredictable forms. Satan, as an inverse Zeus, might be the father of these demons, spirits, witches and monsters, but their name was legion, and their forms and characters often non-specific.

Nevertheless, the crisis in the concept of a supernatural framework for literature predates Romanticism. It was, as we have seen, a direct consequence of the acceptance of Christianity. A multiplicity of deities was paganism; the supreme being was one, and could only be good; all that was not good must be the work of the devil. Decisions were now taken out of the hands of the gods: man himself must decide between good and evil, between God and Satan. Here was a polarisation, which writers – such as Camões, still influenced by classical models – could not fully assimilate to their aesthetic system. More overtly Christian writers, such as Dante and Milton, were still profoundly influenced by classical models, and although theirs was an ordered vision of the Christian polarity, with paradise at one end of the supernatural framework and hell at the other, their own artistic inclinations seemed to lie more with the pandemonic. They were both fascinated by hell and it is perhaps significant that Dante was led there by Virgil, no longer the classical poet of the Pantheon, but the pagan guide to *Inferno*.

The nineteenth century saw the development of another force which threatened to negate the very existence of the supernatural framework for literature – the growing preoccupation with realism. Yet, just as earlier the Pantheon and Christian values could exist, for a time, side by side without any real sense of integration, we see, particularly in the works of Gogol, that pandemonium could coexist with a nascent striving towards realism. The Naturalist school of the 1840s and early 1850s looked back to Gogol as their inspiration, yet their bleak depictions of everyday life in the cities were shorn of the supernatural codas which Gogol often appended to his bizarre accounts of St Petersburg life. His story *Nevskii Prospekt* ends with a warning to the reader that all is not what it seems on the capital's main thoroughfare, particularly with the approach of night, 'when the demon himself lights the lamps merely in order to show everything in an unreal light'.[20] If this is an instance of pandemonium subverting realism, his most famous story *The Overcoat* (*Shinel'*) effects justice for the wrongs inflicted on the little man, not through divine intervention, and certainly not by the efforts of human justice, but through the demonic pranks of a ghost.

In Maikov's eighteenth-century pseudo-epic, the intervention of the Pantheon in human affairs was inept and comic. The bungling of these clumsy gods is echoed in nineteenth-century depictions of pandemonium. In Vel'tman's novel *Heart and Thought* (*Serdtse i dumka*, 1838), the devil intends to marry off all the bachelors in the town, but miscalculates: they all fall in love with the same young girl, the novel's heroine. The incident reveals the way in which pandemonium has taken over from pantheon; for here, in effect, the devil has assumed the role of Cupid.

The ineptitude of diabolic forces provides much of the humour in Gogol's story *Christmas Eve* (*Noch' pered rozhdestvom*, 1832). Thus

---

[20] N.V. Gogol', *Polnoe sobranie sochinenii*, Leningrad, 1937-52, vol. 3, p. 46.

the devil burns his hands when trying to steal the moon. Yet this bizarre incident has its own 'realistic' commentary; for the only person to see the strange lunar dancing is a rural clerk leaving an inn on all fours. Behind the diabolical comedy, therefore, lies an ironic observation relating to the real world: the manifestations of drunkenness explained away as the work of the devil. In Maikov's world the Pantheon was responsible for the fortunes or misfortunes of the human protagonists, but they, unaware of these gods, blamed instead the forces of evil, even when they themselves were largely to blame. Indeed, Maikov with eighteenth-century directness had already made Gogol's point on drunkenness as the devil's work more explicitly:

> *Tak sp'iana Elisei o dele rassuzhdaet*
> *I, vinen byvshii sam, na d'iavola peniaet.*[21]
> ('So Elisei considers the matter in his drunkenness,
> And, being himself to blame, reproaches the devil'.)

In Gogol's early stories it is the forces of pandemonium which appear to shape men's ends and, although this is ostensibly a Christian world in which men have free will, Gogol's irony can suggest pandemonium as an excuse, enabling men to escape personal responsibility. To this extent the new romantic pandemonium performs a similar function to the old classical Pantheon. This may be seen in *The Lost Dispatch* (*Propavshaia gramota*), where it is clear that the irresponsible behaviour of the narrator's grandfather has brought about the loss of the all-important document, even though the grandfather seeks to ascribe his misfortunes to a series of diabolical interventions. Yet, if there is irony here, it returns to haunt the author himself. Thus Gogol would later claim that the second burning of the manuscript of *Dead Souls* (*Mertvye dushi*) was not of his doing – it was the work of the devil.

Behind the comic façade of Gogol's works, we often perceive a serious subtext, and, much as Freud could show the inner psychological relevance of the apparent outer workings of the Pantheon in *Oedipus Rex*, so one may also detect similar psychological features implicit in Gogol's use of pandemonium. Thus, although the author, in a would-be ethnographical footnote to his story *Vii*, is at pains to tell us that his incredible monster is 'the colossal creation of the imagination of the

---

[21] Maikov, *Pesn'* II, lines 166-7.

common folk', it is nothing of the sort. No such creature exists in Ukrainian folklore; the 'colossal imagination' is his own, which has dreamed up a new denizen of pandemonium to symbolise the warped conscience of the story's hero. Much the same could be said of that giant horseman who finally brings retribution at the end of *A Terrible Revenge* (*Strashnaia mest'*).

In Gogol's writing (and rewriting) in the 1840s, the forces of pandemonium are less overt. A similar movement away from the fantastic may also be seen in Vel'tman, in particular the unfinished novel *Adventures, Drawn from the Sea of Life* (*Prikliucheniia, pocherpnutie iz moria zhiteiskogo*, 1846-63). Nevertheless, in Gogol's later writing, the lurking presence of pandemonium can still be sensed behind his so-called 'naturalism'. In *The Overcoat* retribution is achieved not through satanic monsters, as in earlier stories, but through the intervention of what is taken to be the hero's own ghost (and, typically, Gogol suggests some ambiguity here). In his magnum opus *Dead Souls*, creatures of the nether world are merely invoked in his title. The move away from more bizarre aspects of the supernatural can be seen in Gogol's rewriting of *The Portrait* (*Portret*), which he undertook at this time, whereas in the rewriting of *Taras Bul'ba*, influenced as he was by *The Iliad*, Gogol hints, not at romantic pandemonium, but at a Christian pantheon, when he depicts the souls of dying warriors transported to heaven by angels, and presents Taras dying the death of a martyr with even a suggestion of crucifixion.

The accommodation of the supernatural to realism is even more evident in those who followed Gogol. In *The Double* (*Dvoinik*), Dostoevskii presents the fragmentation of the bizarre life of St Petersburg, not like Gogol in *Nevskii Prospekt* as a world hopelessly jumbled together and distorted by some demon, but as the perception of a mind under stress. Nevertheless, pandemonium exists in Dostoevskii's works, at least as a subliminal concept. When Raskolnikov is pushed to give an explanation for the murder of the old woman, he finally falls back on the 'Gogolian excuse' that it was not he who killed her but the devil.[22] Yet, in *The Devils* (*Besy*), unlike the Pushkin poem from which he takes his epigraph, Dostoevskii does not endow his novel with any hint of Satanic concretisation, but uses the

---

[22] F.M. Dostoevskii, *Polnoe sobranie sochinenii v tridtsati tomakh*, Leningrad, 1972-90, vol. 6, p. 322.

concept of pandemonium as a metaphor for the activities of the
nihilists. Indeed, his realistic interpretation of the fantastic elements in
Pushkin's story *The Queen of Spades* (*Pikovaia dama*) tells us more
about his own procedures than it does about those of Pushkin.[23]

Dostoevskii's last novel *The Brothers Karamazov* (*Brat'ia
Karamazovy*) suggests a Miltonic balance, with the figure of Christ at
one pole of a philosophical and moral argument and the devil at the
other. Yet these supernatural entities are accommodated to the realism
of his novel by the device of fiction within fiction. Christ merely
appears as a silent protagonist in an insert tale – Ivan's 'Legend of the
Grand Inquisitor', and Ivan's devil is but the hallucinatory figment of a
mind under stress. The serious, silent authority of Christ is in direct
contrast to the garrulous, comic presentation of the devil, but both are
psychological phenomena relating to an inner struggle within Ivan
himself. The devil is thus a projection of the negative aspects of Ivan's
own character, but in its comic presentation the figure looks back to
Gogol and forward to the Woland of Bulgakov's *The Master and
Margarita* (*Master i Margarita*). The presentation of the supernatural
as psychological phenomena of the real world is perhaps what
Dostoevskii had in mind when he spoke of himself as a 'realist in a
higher sense'.[24]

The realism of Tolstoi seems purer; it appears to lack all
supernatural elements. Yet even here the subliminal presence of
pandemonium can still be glimpsed. In *Anna Karenina* the figure of the
little peasant with the tousled beard may be a realistic detail from
Vronskii's earlier bear hunt, but he assumes a spectral dimension in
Vronskii's dream and, more suprisingly in that of Anna, as an
intimation of fate. At the end of his life, in the simple moralistic stories
he wrote for peasants, Tolstoi's clear-eyed realism can be breached. In
What Men Live By (*Chem liudi zhivut*, 1881), Tolstoi sets men's actions
in the framework of the Christian pantheon, when an angel, punished
by God, falls to earth and becomes the humble workman Michael.

---

[23] Ibid., vol. 30 (1), p. 192. See: M.A. Polivanova, 'Zapis' o poseshchenii
Dostoevskogo, 9 iiunia 1880 goda', in *F.M. Dostoevskii v vospominaniiakh
sovremennikov*, Moscow, 1964, vol. 2, pp. 361, 363. See also: Neil Cornwell, *Pushkin's
'The Queen of Spades'*, London, Bristol Classical Press, 1993, pp. 7, 64.
[24] Dostoevskii, ibid., vol. 27, p. 65.

Turgenev, that other pillar of the Russian realist novel, shows even clearer signs of plunging into the supernatural in old age with such stories as *The Song of Triumphant Love* (*Pesn' torzhestvuiushchei liubvi*) and *Klara Milich* (with its subtitle 'After Death'), though there had been a forerunner of his interest in the supernatural in the story *Phantoms* (*Prizraki*) of 1864. On the other hand, a story of 1871, 'Knock...Knock' (*Stuk... stuk   stuk!*), appears to poke fun at the idea of supernatural intervention. Even Dostoevskii, at the end of his career, succumbed to the overtly supernatural in that untypical story *Bobok* (1873).

Nevertheless, in Russian nineteenth-century realism, pandemonium underlying the surface of everyday reality is merely suggested through the literary devices of omen, symbol and metaphor. Such features communicate an ominous undertow to the banal everyday existence depicted in Chekhov's plays. This is not to say that more overt depictions of the supernatural had entirely died out. The ethnographically inspired works of Leskov and Mel'nikov-Pecherskii are prime examples. Indeed, in Mel'nikov-Pecherskii's major novel, *In the Forests* (*V lesakh*, 1871-74), which depicts the life of the 'old-believers', Christianity, both Orthodox and schismatic, is subverted by the remnants of a pagan pantheon represented by the old gods: Iarilo, Mat'-syra-zemlia and Grom-gremuchii.

The real dawn of the supernatural in Russian literature came with the millenial feeling that permeated the onset of the twentieth century. It is patent in the works of Merezhkovskii, Sologub and Blok. Nor, in the later Soviet period, was it completely eliminated by the prescribed doctrine of Socialist Realism. Older irrational beliefs could still be used to subvert the new rationalist orthodoxy, when writers such as Evgenii Shvarts, in his 'fairy story' plays, and Mikhail Bulgakov, in his novel *The Master and Margarita*, returned to nineteenth-century pandemonium in an updated form, in order to portray a new political dimension of evil and human impotence.

By way of conclusion, we may see that from its very beginnings European literature has depended heavily on a framework of the supernatural. In origin this was a religious dimension, but at the human level it implied an abrogation of individual responsibility. The aesthetic legacy of classicism was (and is) tenacious, but, with the advent of Christianity and a new pantheon, works of literature frequently exhibited a conflict between old aesthetic and new ethical criteria – most glaringly so in Camõens' epic poem *The Lusiads*. At the same time, such ideological equivocation provided ample scope for satire, and mock epics, such as (in Russian) Maikov's *Elisei, or Bacchus Annoyed*, not only parodied the classical form, but exploited it to make barbed social comment.

For more serious writers in the epic tradition, the tension between two supernatural hierarchies had to be resolved. With Milton, the pagan Pantheon in a real sense 'went underground' to be reinvented as Pandemonium and, significantly, this hierarchy of hell assumed greater artistic substantiality than the Parnassian heights of heaven. The identification of Pandemonium with forces alienated from heaven allowed the possibility of further association with folk beliefs and ancient pagan deities, also anathematised by the official church, and through this process 'pandemonium' became part of the romantic rejection of classical values themselves. Yet 'pantheon' went underground in yet another sense. The chaotic, often invisible, forces of pandemonium which, nevertheless, still shaped human behaviour, became metaphors in Gothic and romantic literature for the workings of the subconscious. Horrors that lay deep within the mind could be projected into the conscious world as the mysterious, and often terrifying, creatures of pandemonium and once again, as we see in the writings of Gogol, the existence of a supernatural world absolved human beings from ultimate responsibility.

Nevertheless, in the nineteenth century, this shadowy, reconstituted pantheon came into conflict with a new scale of literary values – realism. The dichotomy was as marked as that between the earlier rival pantheons of classical art and Christian doctrine. And yet, pandemonium was not easily suppressed, and even in the works of writers such as Tolstoi and Chekhov its dark, subliminal forces can be glimpsed beneath the realistic texture. As before, the tension between two incompatible systems provided rich material for humour and satire. The twentieth century has already yielded substantial proof that pandemonium lives on.

KARAMZIN'S GOTHIC TALE:
THE ISLAND OF BORNHOLM

DEREK OFFORD

The focus of N.M. Karamzin's early writings is not so much the characters, events or places described as the sensibility of the narrator. Given this fact, the narrator's moods assume great importance. These moods waver between, at one extreme, a Rousseauesque[1] optimism about the essential goodness of human nature and, at the other, a pessimism evoked by awareness of the vulnerability of individual happiness to evil, fate or human weakness and by reflection on the impermanence of human achievement. The two moods find expression in corresponding literary manners: on the one hand an idyllic or pastoral manner and on the other an elegiacism in which melancholy may shade into anxiety and even terror.

These moods and manners coexist throughout Karamzin's early writings. In his poem 'Recovery' ('Vyzdorovlenie'), published in 1791, an air of gloom, ennui and sorrow, compounded by fearful dreams, is dispersed by tender Nature and a sense of renewal brought about by the sun, dawn, stars and moon.[2] Again, in the poem 'The Graveyard' ('Kladbishche'), published in 1792, two voices offer opposing views of death: the first presents it as terrifying, associating it with howling winds, shaking coffins, rattling bones, toads nestling in skulls and snakes in nettles; the other presents it in terms of tranquillity and reconciliation through such images as a gentle breeze, birds singing on a grave, a dove on a bough, a rabbit in the grass and fragrant flowers.[3]

In the opening paragraphs of the most celebrated example of Karamzin's prose fiction, *Poor Liza* (*Bednaia Liza*, 1792), the two

---

[1] In general Karamzin reveres Rousseau as one of the creators of the new sensibility; see, for example, the description of the narrator's pilgrimage to Rousseau's former home at Vevey and to his grave at Ermenonville near Paris, and the reflections to which these visits give rise, in *Pis'ma russkogo puteshestvennika*: N. M. Karamzin, *Izbrannye sochineniia*, 2 vols., Moscow-Leningrad, 1964 (hereafter *Izb. soch.*), vol. 1, pp. 277-81, 490-96. However, see also note 36 below.

[2] 'Vyzdorovlenie', *Izb. soch.*, 2, pp. 15-16.

[3] 'Kladbishche', ibid., pp. 28-9.

moods are juxtaposed through contrasting views of the environs of Moscow. On the one hand the narrator paints an idyllic spring and summer picture of meadows and copses, a shining river rippling to the oars of fishermen's boats and plied by barges laden with grain from the provinces, grazing flocks, young shepherds singing simple songs under the shade of oak-trees and a distant view of Moscow's golden cupolas illuminated by the rays of the evening sun. On the other hand he offers a tableau of a deserted monastery with gloomy Gothic towers, where on autumn days the wind howls fearfully (*strashno*) among the walls and the graves overgrown with grass and in the dark passages between the empty cells. Here the narrator conjures up in his imagination the sad picture of an aged monk praying for release from his earthly fetters, now that he has lost all feeling, and describes scenes depicted on the gates of the monastery which make disturbing reference to troubled times in Russia's medieval past.[4]

In the voluminous *Letters of a Russian Traveller* (*Pis'ma russkogo puteshestvennika*) too both moods are present. The idyllic mood is much in evidence in Switzerland, a country of natural beauty, abundance, freedom and simplicity of morals which Nature has apparently made inaccessible to the vices.[5] The Alpine folk live a life that is pastoral – both literally and metaphorically. They graze their herds on the mountain slopes, sustaining themselves on the milk and cheese which they produce themselves, and live in that state of primeval innocence in which people, unburdened by the anxieties of modern life, are said to be capable of tender feeling and warm human relationships.[6] How well the Alpine shepherdesses, the narrator exclaims, understand the language of the heart![7] Karamzin pays apt homage to Gessner, the 'Swiss Theocritus', a writer dedicated to 'virtue and innocence'.[8] Karamzin's elegiac mood, on the other hand, finds expression in his travelogue in reference to old castles and ruins;[9] in a passage on a monk who had committed suicide;[10] in periodic

---

[4] *Bednaia Liza*, ibid., 1, pp. 605-06.
[5] See, for example, *Pis'ma russkogo puteshestvennika*, in *Izb. soch.*, 1, pp. 207, 225, 238-9.
[6] Ibid., pp. 262-3.
[7] Ibid., p. 266.
[8] Ibid., pp. 242, 245-6.
[9] Ibid., pp. 254-5, 274, 351, 401-02.
[10] Ibid., pp. 325-8.

reflections on the transience of human life and civilisations;[11] in his view of a tomb as a sanctuary;[12] and in his susceptibility to bouts of melancholy nourished by his reading of the eighteenth-century Scottish poet James Thomson[13] and the apocryphal Gaelic epos of Ossian.[14] This mood is particularly striking in a passage that seems to serve as a preliminary sketch for *Poor Liza*: wandering in the Bois de Boulogne on the outskirts of Paris, the traveller comes upon a gloomy, deserted sixteenth-century castle, one of whose chambers is inhabited by an old woman who has lost everything, including her beautiful daughter Luiza, whose sad story contains a number of details reproduced in Karamzin's sentimental tale.[15] Medieval buildings may even induce terror, as well as melancholy, as when the narrator visits a Benedictine monastery in Erfurt and in its lugubrious passages visualises a monster of medieval fanaticism.[16]

It will be seen that the elegiac passages in Karamzin's early writings contain quite numerous traces of elements which we now associate with Gothicism, such as frightening images and fearful dreams, a predilection for ruins and the graveyard, a sense of mortality, and the melancholy and even frissons of terror which such places may excite. However, these elements are difficult to disentangle from the general European Preromanticism which Karamzin imbibes and to which he himself contributes, and which in Russia goes under the name Sentimentalism.[17] Their existence in Karamzin's work predates the

---

[11] Ibid., pp. 274, 362-3.

[12] Ibid., p. 495.

[13] James Thomson (1700-48), author of 'Seasons', is mentioned or quoted in *Pis'ma russkogo puteshestvennika* on pp. 344-5, 572, 587.

[14] Ossian, or his poetry, is mentioned in ibid., pp. 172, 363, 598.

[15] Ibid., pp. 402-03. The old woman, whose story of course deeply affects and is carefully recorded by the sensitive traveller, had lived quietly and happily in a little hut with her daughter Luiza, in a time when the world was better and people had more goodness. Luiza loved to sing and would go to the woods to gather flowers. Creditors would bother them, but Luiza would talk to them and they would relent. However, Luiza died, leaving the old woman vulnerable. She had been driven from her home by creditors and was now stoically awaiting her death.

[16] Ibid., pp. 182-3.

[17] The terms 'Sentimentalism' and 'Preromanticism' are much confused in both Russian and Western writing on Russian literature of the second half of the eighteenth century: see G. S. Smith, 'Sentimentalism and Preromanticism as Terms and Concepts', in *Russian Literature in the Age of Catherine the Great*, edited by A. G. Cross, Oxford, Meeuws, 1976, pp. 173-84. In the present essay, the sceptical view towards which

appearance of the main landmarks of Gothic fiction at its highpoint in the 1790s, such as Ann Radcliffe's novels *The Mysteries of Udolpho* (1794) and *The Italian* (1797), Matthew Lewis's *The Monk* (1796), and other popular works such as Regina Maria Roche's *The Children of the Abbey* (1794) and *Clermont* (1798). Admittedly, some Gothic romances – William Beckford's *Vathek*,[18] Clara Reeve's *The Old English Baron*[19] and Sophia Lee's *The Recess*[20] – were translated into Russian in the years 1792-4[21] (the translation of Reeve's novel emanated from Moscow Masonic circles to which Karamzin was close[22]). But the early novels of Ann Radcliffe – *The Castles of Athlin and Dunbayne* (1789), *A Sicilian Romance* (1790) and *The Romance of the Forest* (1791) – became known in Russia, through French translations, somewhat later, in the late 1790s, and it was not until the early years of the nineteenth century that *A Sicilian Romance* and *The Romance of the Forest* were translated into Russian.[23]

It is therefore best to approach Karamzin's short tale *The Island of Bornholm* (*Ostrov Borngol'm*), published in the first number of Karamzin's almanac *Aglaia* in April 1794, not so much as an experiment in a distinctive new European manner – which was in any case not yet clearly defined or widely known in Russia[24] – but rather as

---

Smith tends is accepted: namely that Sentimentalism (which is 'a term found almost exclusively in Russian literary criticism and history') and Preromanticism are 'merely different names for the same literary movement' (pp. 173, 181). For an opposing point of view, according to which Sentimentalism and Preromanticism are different movements, see, for example, Rudolf Neuhäuser, 'Periodization and Classification of Sentimental and Preromantic Trends in Russian Literature between 1750 and 1815', in *Canadian Contributions to the Seventh International Congress of Slavists*, The Hague, Mouton, 1973, pp. 11-39 (especially pp. 31-3).

[18] Written in French in 1782 and published in English translation in 1786.

[19] The novel first appeared under the title *The Champion of Virtue: a Gothic Story* in 1777; the second edition, entitled *The Old English Baron*, came out in 1778.

[20] The novel was first published in 1783-5.

[21] See V.E. Vatsuro, 'Literaturno-filosofskaia problematika povesti Karamzina "Ostrov Borngol'm"', in *XVIII vek*, 8, Leningrad, 1969, pp. 190-209 (192): hereafter Vatsuro (1969).

[22] Ibid.

[23] V.E. Vatsuro, 'A. Radklif, ee pervye russkie chitateli i perevodchiki', *Novoe literaturnoe obozrenie*, 22, 1996, pp. 204-06, 223: hereafter Vatsuro (1996).

[24] The point is made explicitly by Vatsuro (1969), pp. 192, 194, who also mentions other writers who are known to Karamzin and who by degrees develop the literary technique of the Gothic novel: J.-P. Florian (1755-94), F. de Baculard d'Arnaud (1718-1805), abbé A. F. Prévost (1697-1763).

a development of a particular strand of Preromanticism represented by poets such as Thomson, Edward Young,[25] Thomas Gray and Ossian, as well as by novelists such as Clara Reeve and Ann Radcliffe.[26] What distinguishes the tale from Karamzin's other early work is not the use of Gothic motifs in it, but its saturation with them and the fact that these motifs are less obviously counterbalanced by an alternative idyllic vision. We need therefore both to identify the Gothic elements in the tale and to attempt to explain their unusual prevalence.[27]

1

The plot of the tale *The Island of Bornholm* revolves around a mystery which obsesses the narrator as he voyages from London back to his native Russia after lengthy travels abroad. No sooner has his boat left London than it has to dock at Gravesend to await favourable weather and the narrator goes ashore. Here he encounters a pale thin young man holding a guitar. Oblivious of the narrator, sighing and staring out to sea, the young man sings a sad prelude in Danish (which fortunately the narrator has learnt from a friend in Switzerland during his travels[28]) about Lila, the love he has left behind on the Baltic island of Bornholm,

---

[25] *Night Thoughts*, the most celebrated work by Edward Young (1683-1765), made a deep impression on Derzhavin as well as on Karamzin.

[26] Moscow Sentimentalists following in Karamzin's footsteps, such as P.I. Shalikov and F.V. Sibirskii, tended to see early Gothic works such as the novels of Ann Radcliffe in this light: see Vatsuro (1969), p. 192; and idem (1996), p. 204.

[27] The Gothic elements of *Ostrov Borngol'm* have been most fully explored by Vatsuro (1969). See also Gitta Hammarberg, *From the Idyll to the Novel: Karamzin's Sentimentalist Prose*, Cambridge, Cambridge University Press, 1991, pp. 182-202. For further discussion see Iu. Lotman, 'Evoliutsiia mirovozzreniia Karamzina (1789-1803)', in *Trudy istoriko-filologicheskogo fakul'teta* (*Uchenye zapiski Tartuskogo gosudarstvennogo universiteta*, 51), Tartu, 1957, pp. 122-62; Henry M. Nebel, *N. M. Karamzin: A Russian Sentimentalist*, The Hague, Mouton, 1967, pp. 145-8, 175; Anthony G. Cross, *N. M. Karamzin: A Study of His Literary Career 1783-1803*, Carbondale, Southern Illinois University Press, 1971, pp. 113-15; Rudolf Neuhäuser, *Towards the Romantic Age: Essays on Sentimental and Preromantic Literature in Russia*, The Hague, Martinus Nijhoff, 1974, pp. 180-82; idem, 'Karamzin's Spiritual Crisis of 1793-1794', in *Essays on Karamzin: Russian Man-of-Letters, Political Thinker, Historian, 1766-1826*, edited by J.L. Black, The Hague, Mouton, 1975, pp. 56-74; Natalya Kochetkova, *Nikolay Karamzin*, Boston, Twayne, 1975, pp. 86-9.

[28] The traveller in *Pis'ma russkogo puteshestvennika* befriends a young Danish chemist with whom he travels in Switzerland and France.

from which he has been banished for ever. At this point the narrator is led back to the boat by the captain, as the wind has changed. After a week-long voyage the boat puts in at Bornholm for the night. The narrator, his curiosity aroused by the reference to the island in the song he has heard at Gravesend, persuades the captain to allow him to go ashore with some sailors in a dinghy. Local fishermen agree to put the party up for the night and lead them to a grassy plain, at which point the narrator, accompanied by a thirteen-year-old guide, leaves the sailors in order to savour the sunset. He soon glimpses in the distance an old castle, which he makes for against the advice of his guide and reaches as night is falling. Ignoring his guide's advice to return to the fishermen's huts, the narrator requests hospitality and is led into the castle by a servant, who takes him to a little candle-lit room where he is greeted by a grey-haired old man weighed down by sorrow. The narrator is taken to a bed-chamber for the night but his sleep is troubled. Needing fresh air he goes to the window, notices a little door and goes out into the moonlit garden. A long avenue of oak trees leads him up to a sandy knoll in the side of which he sees a small opening. Following a passage and going down some steps he comes to an unlocked door and there, beyond an iron grille with a large lock, he finds a young woman asleep on a bed of straw. She awakes and it becomes apparent from what she says that she has been imprisoned for some terrible transgression and will remain in the cave until she dies. Emerging from the cave and overwhelmed by his impressions, the narrator falls asleep on the grass. He awakes as the sun is rising, to hear the servant telling the old owner of the castle that their visitor had entered the unlocked cave. The old man now recounts 'a most horrifying story' (*uzhasneishuiu istoriiu*) which explains what the narrator has seen, but which the narrator himself tantalisingly refuses to divulge. The narrator rejoins the sailors with whom he had come ashore and they return to the ship and set sail. The tale ends with the narrator standing on deck deep in sorrowful thought.[29]

Karamzin's tale contains many of the standard props of eighteenth-century Gothic fiction. At its centre stands what has been described as

---

[29] The tale is reprinted in *Izb. soch.*, 1, pp. 661-73; for an English translation, see *The Selected Prose of N.M. Karamzin*, translated by Henry M. Nebel, Evanston, Northwestern University Press, 1969, pp. 117-31. Since the work is very short, further page references will not be provided.

the 'major locus of Gothic plots, the castle',[30] perhaps inspired in this case by the ruined thirteenth-century castle of Hammershus at Bornholm's northern tip, once a stronghold of the Swedish bishops of Lund. Karamzin's narrative lovingly reconstructs the castle with copious architectural and decorative detail and abundant reference to its antiquity and current dilapidation. It is a large 'Gothic' building with pointed towers and is surrounded by a deep moat and a high wall with locked gates and raised drawbridges. The courtyard is overgrown with bushes, nettles and wormwood; a tall peristyle of ancient design leads to an iron porch. In the first hall, surrounded by a 'Gothic' colonnade, a lamp casts a pale light on rows of gilded pillars which have long since begun to crumble. Here and there lie pieces of cornice, chunks of pilaster and whole columns which have collapsed. There are long, narrow passages, down which the servant leads the narrator to a bed-chamber hung with ancient weaponry – swords, spears, armour and spiked helmets – and in which there stands a high bed decorated with carving and ancient bas-reliefs and covered by a golden canopy. Finally there is the secret underground cave, damp and cold, with a lamp hanging from the vault, in which a woman is cruelly imprisoned.[31]

Moreover, Karamzin's castle is pervaded by an atmosphere of superstition, gloom and threat that is typical of Gothic fiction. It is a place which people shun, the narrator's guide informs him, for 'God knows what goes on there!' At the castle gates the narrator is greeted by a disembodied voice asking him who he is. The old man in his first utterance forewarns his visitor that 'eternal grief dwells within the walls of this castle'. The master's servant is sinister and taciturn: he is a tall man in a long black coat who, as he leads the visitor through the castle several times, stares silently at him with his penetrating eyes. Sounds jar the nerves: doors slam shut, the drawbridge creaks when raised, footsteps ring out on the steps of the iron porch and the iron door of the bed-chamber closes with a frightening resonance. The narrator, left alone in the bed-chamber, begins to muse on the adventures which the castle may have witnessed in the past and even

---

[30] Fred Botting, *Gothic*, London, Routledge, 1996, p. 2.

[31] Karamzin's probable sources for the common Gothic motif of a woman's underground prison - passages in French works by Mme de Genlis (1746-1830) and Monvel (J. M. Boutet; 1745-1812) - are discussed in Vatsuro (1969), pp. 201-2. Other Gothic works in which the motif appears include *A Sicilian Romance* (Ann Radcliffe) and *The Children of the Abbey* (Regina Maria Roche).

takes on the persona of a graveyard poet, comparing himself to a man who amid the tombs looks upon the ashes of the dead and brings them back to life in his imagination. His sleep is disturbed by nightmares populated by characteristically Gothic images, both medieval and monstrous. He dreams that all the armour on the walls has turned into knights who come down and stand over him with bared swords, angrily demanding to know why he has intruded into 'terrible [*strashnoe*] sanctuary of the castle' and threatening to kill him for his impudent curiosity. Awakening from this nightmare, the narrator falls back into another in which a terrible thundering sound rumbles through the castle, the windows shake, the doors clang, the floor trembles and an ineffable winged monster flies towards the narrator's bed, roaring and hissing.[32]

However, neither lubugrious setting nor sinister atmosphere is an end in itself. Rather they provide a fitting backdrop to the revelation of some shocking secret. Like Ann Radcliffe's *A Sicilian Romance*, though less explicitly and with a dissimilar, irredeemable outcome, Karamzin's tale brings to light a terrible event that has ruined a family.

Karamzin leaves us in no doubt that the young man at Gravesend and the young woman in the cave are the lovers to which the young man's song alludes (although he does not explicitly tell us that they are). This inference seems to be confirmed by the narrator's admission that the old man's story does unravel the terrible secret of the unknown young man at Gravesend. Moreover, the young man and the young woman are paired in the narrative by many literary means. The same epithets are applied to them: 'pale' (*blednyi)*; 'languorous' (*tomnyi)*; 'unhappy' (*neschastnyi)*. They share many traits. Both stare with motionless eyes and utter their thoughts in a quiet voice. Both are near to death or associated with it. The young man is more an apparition than a human being; the narrator sees in his eyes the last ray of a life that is going out; his feelings are dead to external objects and he sees and hears nothing. The young woman, for her part, expects to die; her hand is white and withered; her heart, she says, has wasted away from grief, and a question dies on her pale lips. Both the young man and the young woman actually crave death: the young man ends his song with a vow to cast himself with his lover into the roaring waves; the young woman hopes her life will soon end. Furthermore, both elicit pity from

---

[32] For further discussion of the narrator's dreams, see Vatsuro (1969), pp. 200-01.

the sensitive narrator and in the descriptions of their encounters with him there is some syntactic symmetry.[33]

We are not told explicitly why the relationship of the young man and the young woman is illicit, or what their relationship is to the old man who is master of the castle. The young woman falls silent one word short of defining her relationship with the old man, when she instructs the narrator to tell the one who uttered the terrible curse on her that she bears her end without complaint and will die his 'affectionate, unhappy ...'. The missing word could be 'wife' and the transgression adultery. However, it is much more likely that the young woman is the daughter of the old man, that the young man is her brother and that the transgression is therefore incest, which so fascinates Gothic writers, beginning with Horace Walpole in his *Castle of Otranto* (1764). That her relationship with the young man *is* illicit is indicated by allusions to law and its infringement in the young man's song, by the thought of crime that immediately comes to the narrator's mind when he sees the young woman in the cave, and by the young woman's immediate avowal to the narrator that she kisses the hand that punishes her.

The dark secret which the Gothic tale in general unlocks is indicative of fears about the triumph of vice over virtue, and about consequent social disintegration, that were experienced by readers of the period (in the 1790s) when Gothic fiction was reaching the peak of its popularity.[34] In Karamzin's narrative, the transgression of which the narrator slowly becomes aware gives rise within him to a disturbing and seemingly irresolvable conflict between the demands of, on the one hand, mind and reason and, on the other, heart and feeling. This conflict finds expression in the tale in consideration of the competing claims to authority of convention and nature, human law and natural law. It is this tension that the young man's song bemoans:

> The laws condemn
> the object of my love;
> But who, oh heart, can
> resist thee?
> What law is more sacred

---

[33] When he sees the young man, the narrator observes: 'My gaze could not meet his' (*Vzor moi ne mog vstretit'sia s ego vzorom*); in the cave, on seeing the young woman, he remarks: 'my gaze again met hers' (*vzor moi eshche vstretilsia s ee vzorom*).

[34] Botting, p. 5.

than your innate feelings?
What power is stronger
than love and beauty?

For the young man Nature is the highest authority and he does not believe that he has sinned before her in yielding to his passion. Nature thundered, but did not strike the lovers in their embrace. Humans, on the other hand, are cruel and pitiless, as attested by the parental curse which the young man's love has brought down on him and as a result of which he has been banished from Bornholm. The tension between different conceptions of law which runs through the young man's song arises again when the narrator comes upon the young woman asleep in her prison. He cannot believe that she has committed some grave crime, for both her sweet countenance and his own heart assure him that she is innocent. It is significant in this regard that it seems to the narrator that the cave in which Lila is imprisoned is man-made rather than natural. The old man, on the other hand, cleaves to the established authority of convention: he is quite unable to understand why the heavens have unleashed their anger on a weak, grey-haired old man who has loved virtue and respected its holy laws. Thus for all his apparent benignity and civility, he conforms to a certain degree to the Gothic type of the tyrannical master of a feudal castle and the castle itself, seen in this light, takes on its characteristically Gothic role as the seat of medieval barbarism.

2

The tension between reason and feeling, mind and heart, convention and Nature which pervades *The Island of Bornholm* mirrors the conflict that was taking place in late eighteenth-century Russia between the broad cultural movements of Classicism and Sentimentalism, or Preromanticism. Karamzin's place in that conflict in the period before he wrote *The Island of Bornholm* is clear. His position is reflected in his preface of 1786 to his own translation of *Julius Caesar*, in which he expresses his admiration of Shakespeare for his ability to imitate Nature and to reveal 'all the most secret springs of a man, his innermost motives, the distinguishing characteristic of every passion' and rejects

Voltaire's criticism that Shakespeare disregarded rules and propriety.[35] Again, in his short essay 'What does an Author need?' ('Chto nuzhno avtoru?'), written in spring 1793, Karamzin upholds authorial sincerity and sensitivity as prerequisites for successful art. Rousseau, with his passionate love of mankind, is forgiven his failings and is set above other, more learned, writers who tell truths unwarmed by the love of a virtuous heart.[36] Karamzin's early stories *Poor Liza* and *Natal'ia, a Boyar's Daughter* (*Natal'ia, boiarskaia doch'*, 1792) themselves posed a challenge – psychological, social and moral – to the static, rationally ordered, gentry dominated, refined and symmetrical universe of Russian Classicism. Moreover the concept of virtue, so important to the eighteenth-century Russian mind, was redefined. The cultivation of virtue and nobility of character remained an admirable goal, but these qualities now found expression not so much in restraint of passion and adherence to a golden mean as in indulgence of the emotions and a sensitivity – which to the modern reader appears overblown – to an affecting impression. Thus, whereas for the post-Petrine satirist Kantemir, virtue is conceived in the Stoic sense as a means of protecting one from the vicissitudes of Fortune,[37] in *Natal'ia, a Boyar's Daughter* Karamzin's narrator is adamant that 'virtue itself cannot protect us from grief'.[38]

---

[35] See *Izb. soch.*, 2, p. 80. A similar defence of Shakespeare against Voltaire is mounted by Horace Walpole in the preface to the second edition of *The Castle of Otranto* (1765): see The World's Classics edition, edited by W.S. Lewis with a new introduction and notes by E.J. Clery, Oxford, Oxford University Press, 1996, pp. 10-14.
[36] *Izb. soch.*, 2, pp. 120-22. It should be noted though that in his essay 'Nechto o naukakh, iskusstvakh i prosveshchenii', written in the winter and spring of 1793 and published in the first number of *Aglaia* together with *Ostrov Borngol'm*, Karamzin expresses reservations about Rousseau's belief that enlightenment is a corrupting influence on man. If science and art are an evil, he argues here, then they are a necessary evil, for they are the fruits of man's innate curiosity and desire to improve his life both physically and morally. By showing us the beauties of sublime Nature, they elevate the soul and make it more sensitive and tender and stimulate in us a love of order, harmony and goodness and, conversely, an antipathy to disorder, dissonance and vice. The enlightenment which Rousseau reviles, then, is a 'palladium of good morals': *Izb. soch.*, 2, pp. 122-42 (esecially 124-9, 139-40). Even in this essay, though, Karamzin at the outset reiterates his reverence for Rousseau (pp. 122-3).
[37] See, for example, Kantemir's notes to line 423 of Satire V and line 121 of Satire VII, in Antiokh Kantemir, *Sobranie stikhotvorenii*, Leningrad, 1956, pp. 142, 167.
[38] *Izb. soch.*, 1, p. 652.

The tale *The Island of Bornholm*, for all its Gothicism, fits comfortably into the Sentimentalist framework,[39] for it is informed by the same sensibility as Karamzin's earlier writings. Like the narrator whose soul is famously mirrored in the letters of a Russian traveller, the narrator of *The Island of Bornholm* is brimming with emotion and dwells in the realms of heart, spirit and soul (*serdtse, dukh, dusha*) rather than reason (*razum*).[40] He is sensitive to the plight of the young man he sees at Gravesend, immediately recognising his unhappiness and sensing that he has been 'killed by Fate'. Having heard the young man's song, he is prompted 'by an involuntary inner impulse' to throw himself at the singer and press him to his heart, and is prevented from doing so only by the appearance of the captain of the ship, who comes to lead him away so that they may take advantage of the favourable wind that has begun to blow. When he lands on Bornholm, his sensitivity is almost immediately demonstrated by his desire 'to savour for a while yet the pleasures of the evening'.[41] Again, his first words to the young woman in the cave refer to his own sensitivity, which he hopes might help to ease her fate. And, when he leaves the cave, he again reveals his sensitive soul by reflecting on the grief of being

---

[39] Support for this assertion seems to be provided by Vatsuro's classification of *Ostrov Borngol'm* as close to an 'elegiac fragment', a term used by Karamzin himself to describe his work *Sierra-Morena* (1795): see Vatsuro (1969), p. 195. Vatsuro also notes here the static quality of the tale *Ostrov Borngol'm*, its lack of narrative in the normal sense, representing its main point of difference from the Gothic novel or tale.

[40] We might add that in retrospect, with the publication of the complete *Pis'ma russkogo puteshestvennika* in 1801, we also see a clear narratorial connection between *Ostrov Borngol'm* and the concluding pages of *Pis'ma russkogo puteshestvennika*. Like the narrator of *Ostrov Borngol'm*, the Russian traveller also sails down the Thames and on to the open sea in an English vessel, is racked for days on end by seasickness and marvels at the immensity of the sea, the howling of the storm and man's audacity in the face of Nature. This traveller also reads Ossian and translates Carthon on the voyage and, with his imagination filled with threatening Ossianic images, negotiates the perilous waters past the Norwegian cliffs on a dark and stormy night. Like the visitor to Bornholm, he makes a hackneyed reference to 'Neptune's kingdom' during his voyage (op. cit., pp. 596-600.) It should be noted though that the mood of the concluding pages of the travelogue is quite different from that of the Gothic tale: in the *Pis'ma*, Karamzin is full of wit and exultant as he approaches his native land after a long absence.

[41] The narrator has in fact spent the six days prior to his arrival on Bornholm prostrate and virtually unconscious as a result of seasickness. He would therefore appear to be altogether unprepared physically for the exertions of his stay on the island. However, verisimilitude, despite the claims of Karamzin's narrators, is not of great importance in Sentimentalist fiction!

excluded from the society of the free and joyful creatures with which Nature abounds, and on the presence of living signs of God's love, such as birdsong, gentle and fragrant breezes and velvety carpets of grass, even among the mossy cliffs of the north.[42]

3

And yet, if the narrator of *The Island of Bornholm* is identical in terms of his sensibility with the narrator of Karamzin's earlier sentimental tales and with his 'Russian traveller', nevertheless he does seem also to suffer a broader, more troubling spiritual disturbance than the exquisite melancholy induced by the individual plight of 'poor Liza' in 1792. The cause of this almost existential *Angst* may be sought partly in personal circumstances in Karamzin's life and in despondency at developments in Russia. Karamzin's contemporary and close friend A.A. Petrov had died in March 1793, an event which gave rise to the grief expressed in Karamzin's poem 'To a Nightingale' ('K solov'iu'), first published in the same almanac in which *The Island of Bornholm* appeared, in which the poet feels as if he has been orphaned and looks ahead to his own death.[43] Moreover, former Masonic friends of Karamzin's had received his *Moscow Journal* (*Moskovskii zhurnal*) coolly. Again, A.N. Radishchev had been arrested and exiled in 1790; the poet and dramatist Ia.B. Kniazhnin had died in prison in 1791; and the publisher, journalist, philanthropist and Mason N.I. Novikov had been arrested in 1792.[44] However, behind Karamzin's crisis of 1793-4, there also lie fears about the extinction of enlightenment and humanist values in the wake of the French Revolution.[45]

The early phase of the French Revolution – the storming of the Bastille, the measures taken against feudalism by the Constituent

---

[42] This passage is somewhat reminiscent of the reflections prompted in the narrator in *Pis'ma russkogo puteshestvennika* by the story of Luiza's mother in the deserted castle in the Bois de Boulogne (see note 15 above). How much magnificence there is in the physical world, the narrator muses here, and how much calamity there is in the moral world. How can the unfortunate person weighed down by the burden of his being, isolated among the multitude of the cold and the cruel, rejoice at the magnificence of the golden sun, the pure blue sky, the green meadows and woods (op. cit., p. 403.)?

[43] 'K solov'iu', *Izb. soch.*, 2, p. 32.

[44] See Neuhäuser, 'Karamzin's Spiritual Crisis ...' (cited note 27 above).

[45] As noted, for example, by Vatsuro (1969), p. 190; and Neuhäuser, 'Karamzin's Spiritual Crisis ...', pp. 67-8.

Assembly and the Declaration of the Rights of Man and Citizen in July
and August 1789 – do not seem to have troubled Karamzin unduly. It is
true that on first arriving in France, in August 1789, he finds that
villages in Alsace are in revolt, villagers are sewing cockades to their
hats, and a new uprising is beginning in Strasbourg, where soldiers
disobey their officers and are unruly in the streets.[46] Occasional
disturbing reports of events in France reach him in Switzerland in the
autumn of 1789 and the winter of 1789-90: he hears the fear expressed
that Swiss who have invested money in France will be bankrupted;[47]
and in Basle he witnesses the emotional reunion of a French noble
family, separated when the mother and father were forced to flee their
burning castle by villagers threatening to kill them.[48] He reports the
view that society in Paris, which he reaches in late March 1790, is not
what it was before the Revolution, because the wealthiest and most
noble families have fled into emigration.[49] He is made indignant during
a visit to Versailles at the thought of the Parisian mob attempting, on
the night of 5-6 October 1789, to arrest Marie-Antoinette and the king
at their palace, and he compares Versailles without the court to the
body without the soul.[50] (The degeneration is reflected in the fact that
in the best inn the narrator and his companions have to wait two hours
to be served a meal![51]) He is moved by the sight of the king and queen
in church and evinces sympathy and admiration for them.[52] Reflecting
at length on the Revolution in a letter dated April 1790, he presents
revolution as an act of folly and warns of the dangers of giving free rein
to popular sentiment, showing himself already to be a conservative
advocate of a stable political order in general, and an admirer of the
French monarchic regime and of the civilisation which flourished under
its protection in particular.[53] And yet the disorder which Karamzin
witnesses in Strasbourg seems quite good-natured and does not distract

---

[46] *Pis'ma russkogo puteshestvennika*: in *Izb. soch.*, 1, p. 202.
[47] Ibid., p. 291.
[48] Ibid., pp. 210-11.
[49] On the other hand, another Parisian tells the traveller that Paris had already declined
before the outbreak of the Revolution from the heights it had reached under Louis XIV
(ibid., pp. 378-80).
[50] Ibid., pp. 472-3.
[51] Ibid., p. 473.
[52] Ibid., pp. 380-1.
[53] Ibid., pp. 381-3.

him from his touristic pursuits, such as a visit to the majestic Gothic cathedral, from the top of whose tower, 725 steps high, it was frightening to look down on the town and the people, like insects, below.[54] And at the end of his description of his stay in Paris he reflects that he has lived peacefully and gaily there, a citizen of the world who has looked on the city's agitation with a tranquil soul. Neither the Jacobins nor the aristocrats have done him any harm.[55]

However, a revolution which at the time of Karamzin's sojourn in Paris in the spring of 1790 had had the character of an experiment in constitutional monarchy had, by the time he wrote *The Island of Bornholm* in 1793, taken on an altogether different complexion. The tension aroused in Europe by the attempted flight of Louis XVI and the royal family from France, and his arrest at Varennes in June 1791; France's declaration of war on Austria in April 1792 and the subsequent embroilment of the country in war with England, the United Provinces of the Netherlands, Spain and Prussia; the insurrection of August 1792, the involvement of the populace, the *sans-culottes*, in the Revolution and the ensuing ascendancy of the Montagnards and Jacobins over the more moderate Girondins; the trial of Louis XVI and his execution in January 1793; the establishment of the revolutionary government and the institution of the Terror in September 1793 and the execution of Marie-Antoinette in October of that year: all these factors and excesses had filled Karamzin with fear and revulsion by the time he came to prepare the first number of his new almanac in the winter of 1793-4. In these circumstances, it was difficult to sustain the optimistic mood represented by the pastoral manner. Instead, a mood of uncertainty, doubt, foreboding and moral confusion comes to the fore in a fictitious exchange of letters, which Karamzin wrote in late 1793 and early 1794, between characters to whom he gave the names Melodor and Filalet, or more particularly in the letter of Melodor with which the exchange opens.

Melodor (literally 'giver of music', who may be felt to represent Karamzin's poetic persona) gives voice to the crisis experienced by the optimistic lover of humanity who has imbibed the ideas of the eighteenth-century Enlightenment. Like a traveller sighing over what remains of Troy, he contemplates the ruins of all his hopes and plans

---

[54] Ibid., pp. 202-03.
[55] Ibid., p. 507.

(Melodor uses the word *razvaliny*, explicitly relating the favourite Gothic setting to the collapse of his spiritual world). He regards with horror the disintegration of the 'comforting system' devised in an age which, Melodor believes, had witnessed a softening of morals, a refinement of reason and feelings, an increase in the number of life's pleasures, the dissemination of a spirit of sociality and the establishment of milder governments and more amicable relations between peoples. Together with Filalet, Melodor had reflected on the moral world, the nobility of the human soul and man's greatness of spirit. They had joyfully embraced all mortals as God's creatures and regarded all of Nature as a heavenly garden in which the divinity of mankind was ripening. In short, they had convinced themselves that the human race was climbing towards universal spiritual perfection. And yet the century was ending in blood and flames: Europe, the repository of the arts and sciences, was being devastated by a ferocious war. Surveying the fate of various civilisations, Melodor confronts the possibility that there exists some unknown law according to which humanity suffers a Sisyphean destiny, aspiring to pinnacles of enlightenment only to be cast down, each time a summit is reached, into renewed barbarism. The replacement of a notion of continuous progress by the notion of an eternal alternation of day and night, truth and error, virtue and vice leads Melodor to question the purpose of existence.[56]

The mood expressed by Karamzin through Melodor to a certain extent mirrors that of Gothic fiction at this period, or, to put it another way, Gothic fiction is an apt medium for the expression of a mood such as Melodor's. For Gothic fiction, like Melodor's letter, gropes for a

---

[56] *Melodor k Filaletu*: in *Izb. soch.*, 2, pp. 245-51. In his reply, Filalet (literally 'lover of truth', who may be felt to represent Karamzin's philosophical persona) writes with resignation and tries to salvage hope amid the prevailing despair. He accepts that the moral order is not so clear to us as the physical order but, seeing God in the natural world, in the movement of the planets and the cycle of the seasons, refuses to believe that God has no function in the moral world and clings to a faith that there is a seed of goodness in the human heart which will again bear fruit when conditions are propitious (ibid., pp. 251-8). This air of resignation and fresh hope is expressed too in an epistle in verse to the poet Dmitriev, which Karamzin wrote in late 1793 in response to a lament by Dmitriev about the rapid passing of the period of happy youth ('Poslanie k Dmitrievu', ibid., pp. 34-8 - published in 1794, but not in the almanac *Aglaia*). The renewed faith that individual virtue and goodness may prevail is also reflected in the novella *Iuliia*, published in 1794 (see Neuhäuser, 'Karamzin's Spiritual Crisis ...', pp. 72-3).

formulation of the anxieties to which the French Revolution – among other factors, such as industrial revolution, urbanisation and attendant economic and social change – had given rise.[57]

The narrator of *The Island of Bornholm* shares the uncertainty of the age. He seems to have been confused by what he has witnessed even before he arrives on Bornholm. When the old man, who has long been cut off from the world, asks him whether love reigns on Earth, whether people worship virtue, whether peoples prosper in the countries the narrator has seen, the narrator's answer is ambiguous. The light of the sciences spreads more and more, he says, and yet blood still flows, the unfortunate still shed tears and people, while praising virtue, argue about its substance. On Bornholm the sight of Lila imprisoned in the cave prompts him to reflect on human cruelty and to ask why the Creator has given people the power to make each other and themselves unhappy. He seems though to have no clear answers to the questions that trouble him and the meaning of the tale is therefore perhaps less straightforward than some critics assume. His sympathies may seem to lie with Nature and sensibility.[58] And yet he is not confident enough of the legitimacy of the rights of Rousseau's natural man to protest at the treatment of the young woman according to the laws of convention, or to rail at the old man who has imprisoned her and who is in any case seen to share in the grief at the ruin of the family.[59] On the contrary, the narrator seems to accept what he has seen as *force majeure* and leaves the island without demurral.[60]

---

[57] It does not seem coincidental that the Gothic novel, if viewed as an appropriate vehicle through which to articulate a sense of moral crisis and social uncertainty, was at its most popular in the decade after the French Revolution (see Botting, p. 5).

[58] As argued by Hammarberg (op. cit., p. 199), who believes that the old man's practice of following the divine commandments 'more to the letter than to the spirit' is 'unacceptable to the Sentimental narrator'.

[59] That the old man too is crushed by this incestuous or adulterous affair is suggested by the fact that he shares traits with the young man and the young woman. He too speaks in a quiet voice and refers to his dying heart. The narrator likens him to a cold autumn day, one more reminiscent of a sorrowful winter than a joyful summer; the signs of sorrow in his heart do not disappear from his face for a moment, despite his best efforts to be hospitable.

[60] This fact does not seem altogether to warrant the conclusion of P.N. Berkov and G.P. Makogonenko, in their introductory article to the collection of Karamzin's works to which reference is made in this essay, that the emotional final paragraph of *Ostrov Borngol'm* shows that Karamzin sets the 'laws of heaven' and 'virtue' higher than the 'law of innate feelings' (see *Izb. soch.*, 1, p. 39). A similar position (that, in the light of

4

However, the trauma which Karamzin and his narrator have experienced as a result of the events of the early 1790s, in the case of the author, and the visit to Bornholm, in the case of the narrator, is not an entirely negative phenomenon. For Gothic aesthetics allow such experience a beneficial value: terror, so it is claimed, has an uplifting effect. The most influential eighteenth-century text on the subject is Edmund Burke's treatise *A Philosophical Enquiry into the Origin of our Ideas of the Sublime and the Beautiful* (1757). Burke contrasts beautiful objects, which are characterised by their smallness, delicacy, comprehensibility and perceptibility within the human gaze, with sublime objects, which were vast, magnificent, obscure, awe-inspiring and beyond the grasp of the rational mind. Sublime objects confronted the individual subject with an intimation of its own extinction and excited both delight and horror.[61]

Arguably, the narrator of *The Island of Bornholm*, too, gains some profit from his disturbing experience, by means of the access it affords him to a world beyond the mundane. The vocabulary of Gothic aesthetics – *velichestvennyi* ('majestic', 'awful', indeed 'sublime'), *neobozrimyi* ('boundless', 'immense'), *strashnyi* ('fearful', 'frightening', 'terrible'), *uzhas* ('horror') – is ubiquitous in *The Island of Bornholm* and sublimity and terror, intensified by a sense of the proximity of death, are ever-present and interlocking forces in the tale. The Thames, down which the narrator's boat speeds at the beginning of his voyage, is 'sublime'. The sweet inertia of the soul into which the narrator slips as he lies on the shore at Gravesend is 'the most striking and the most poetic form of death'. When the ship passes beyond the northern shores of England (or perhaps Karamzin means Britain) the birds which had soared over the vessel return to shore, as if frightened by the 'immensity' of the sea. Now the narrator – who appears to be the

---

events in France, Karamzin felt 'a need to subordinate one's passions to reason in the name of preservation of virtue') is adopted by P.A. Orlov, in his introductory article in the anthology *Russkaia sentimental'naia povest'*, Moscow, 1979, p. 16. However, the narrator of the 'elegiac fragment' *Sierra-Morena*, published in the second number of *Aglaia* in 1795, still does not accept that the dictates of the heart can be overcome, though one may struggle long and hard against its impulses: see *Izb. soch.*, 1, p. 676.
[61] See Botting, p. 39 (and pp. 4, 23-4).

sole passenger on board – is confronted by nothing but the roaring sea and misty sky, which present themselves as 'a sublime and terrifying object' and whose infinity (*beskonechnost'*) captivates him. He cites Wieland – though the notion goes back to classical antiquity – to the effect that in the open sea only a slender piece of wood separates the sailor from a watery death. On Bornholm itself, the narrator is titillated by fear. His reception in the castle by the sinister servant creates in him 'an impression of terror, mixed partly with horror, partly with a secret, inexplicable pleasure or, to put it better, with the agreeable expectation of something extraordinary'. Even the gloomy avenue of rustling oak-trees, leading to the cave where Lila is imprisoned, produces a certain reverence (*blagogovenie*) in him. At the end of the tale infinity is again invoked implicitly, as Bornholm is lost to view and the narrator is once more alone between the heavens and the sea.

The sense of horror is provoked above all by mountains, the natural phenomena that most deeply affected Preromantic artists, for it was in mountains that the presence of the Creator was most keenly felt. The taste for mountainous scenery, prefigured in the reverential descriptions of the Bernese Oberland in *The Letters of a Russian Traveller*,[62] is reflected now in repeated references to Bornholm's massive cliffs and crags. It is the 'fearsome cliffs' (*groznye skaly*) of the island that first present themselves to the narrator as he approaches. Thus confronted with the hand of Nature, the horrified narrator, as a trembling mortal, is compelled to acknowledge cold, silent eternity and implacable death. The green plain to which the narrator and accompanying sailors and fishermen ascend from the rocky shore, during what seems in retrospect an idyllic evening interlude before the Gothic nightmare, reminds the narrator of Alpine valleys. Later, as he roams the castle grounds in the middle of the night, he sees in the distance the rocky crags that surround the island like a jagged wall. The mossy cliffs that are terrible to behold, the granite crags and foaming sea, feature again in his reflections upon emergence from the cave as he contemplates the boundless spaces of Nature.[63]

---

[62] *Izb. soch.*, 1, pp. 256-8.

[63] Mountains are explicitly associated with horror and sublimity in *Sierra-Morena*: they are among the 'horrors [*uzhasy*] of Nature' which 'exalted, enraptured. nourished [*vozvelichivali, voskhishchali, pitali*]' the soul of the heroine (*Izb. soch.*, 1, p. 675).

5

There is, finally, one other ray of light in *The Island of Bornholm*, besides the possible personal enrichment of the narrator by his terrifying experience.[64] Like Karamzin's fictitious epistoler Filalet, in his reply to Melodor,[65] the narrator seems to preserve intact some hope for the future. This hope he sustains by distancing himself in three ways from the events he has witnessed and by establishing, as a self-conscious Russian, the 'otherness' of Bornholm.[66]

Firstly, the paragraph with which the tale begins establishes emotional distance between the narrator and the events he is to describe, by telling us that the narrator and his listeners are now securely protected in his beloved home from the hostile elements. Winter is setting in: summer and autumn have passed, greenery has faded, the trees have lost their fruit and leaves and snow is beginning to fall. The storyteller and his audience must say goodbye to Nature for the time being. The season of death is, of course, a fitting backdrop to the story which the narrator has to tell, but at the same time the narrator and his listeners may look forward to a joyful tryst with spring and in the meantime they may take shelter before a flaming fire of oak and birch.

Secondly, Bornholm is removed from the narrator's audience by its extreme physical and indeed metaphysical inaccessibility. In order to reach it, one has to cross the huge, empty, fearsome sea. The voyage lasts a week and in the course of it the narrator travels to the edge of human consciousness, passing six days incapacitated by seasickness with his eyes closed and his heart barely beating, before, on the seventh day, he comes back to life (*ozhil* is the word Karamzin uses). It is out of this journey to the seeming brink of terrestrial life that the narrator arrives at Bornholm. (It is perhaps indicative of the metaphysical

---

[64] It should be noted that Gitta Hammarberg interprets the whole tale as an idyll in which the sombre and terrifying features serve to throw the positive features of the work into sharper relief (op. cit., p. 202).

[65] See note 56 above.

[66] In this respect, as in others, Karamzin behaves in *Ostrov Borngol'm* like a typical Gothic author, for distancing is a stock device of the northern-European Protestant writers of the late eighteenth century, who in their romances often supposedly observe the history and mores of Catholic southern-European peoples in the late Middle Ages or early modern times

dimension of the journey that Karamzin nowhere refers to the narrator in this tale by the matter-of-fact, even somewhat touristic term *puteshestvennik*, which he applies to the narrator of his grand travelogue, but uses instead the more poetic and even quasi-religious word *strannik*.) Even when the narrator reaches Bornholm, he is able to set foot on the island only with difficulty. It is a perilous place for boats, the captain tells him, for there are rocks and shoals concealed on the sea bed and the island has fearsome cliffs on all sides.[67] Once the boat is anchored, the captain at first resists the narrator's entreaty that he be allowed to go ashore in a dinghy. It is only because the narrator, his curiosity aroused by the apparition at Gravesend, is unyielding, that the captain finally agrees to the request, and even then only on condition that his passenger return to the ship early the next morning.

Thirdly, and perhaps most importantly, the narrator establishes ethnic, cultural and religious distance between himself, his listeners and readers, on the one hand, and Bornholm, its history, inhabitants and customs, on the other. We are repeatedly reminded in the tale of the foreignness of the narrator in Bornholm. The narrator strikingly introduces himself at the castle gates as 'foreigner' or more literally 'man from another land' (*chuzhezemets*). The old man and Lila (twice) address him in the same way and the servant, reporting to his master that the narrator has found the cave in which Lila is imprisoned, describes him similarly as '*chuzhestranets*'.[68] Moreover, Russian civilisation is presented by both sides in the story, Danish and Russian, as different from, and superior to, what is termed 'Gothic'. Interested by the news that his visitor is Russian, the old man asserts that the ancient inhabitants of Bornholm, and of the nearby Baltic island of Rügen, were also Slavs, but that the Russians were illuminated by Christianity at an earlier date. The Russians were already building magnificent temples devoted to the one God and glorifying the Creator in their hymns while the Baltic islanders, blinded by error, were still offering bloody pagan sacrifices to their idols. This association of Bornholm with paganism – and implicitly with human sacrifice – is

---

[67] Karamzin is granting himself some fictional licence here: whereas the northern part of the island is composed of granite and does indeed have a rocky cliff coast, the undulating southern part, composed of sandstone, limestone and shale, has a dune coast.
[68] The narrator is also addressed twice as '*molodoi chelovek*' ('young man') by the old man; and as '*neschastnoi*' ('wretch')and '*derzkoi*' ('audacious') by the knights in his dream.

pursued when the thought of druids springs to the narrator's mind, as he roams the castle grounds in the middle of the night and he imagines that he is drawing close 'to the sanctuary where all the secrets and horrors of their worship are preserved'.[69]

Perhaps, then, the Russians should not in the final analysis be too troubled by Karamzin's anxieties about Western Europe and by his narrator's Gothic experience. The relationship between Russia and other nations was not, in Karamzin's time, being structured exclusively in terms of the antithesis of East and West with which we are familiar from nineteenth-century (and twentieth-century) Russian thought. It was also being conceived in terms of an opposition, inherent in Preromantic literature in general and Gothic literature in particular, between North and South. (It is the 'North' that the traveller in *The Letters of a Russian Traveller* sees himself as representing, even in central European Switzerland.[70]) The Russians, a subtext of *The Island of Bornholm* seems to tell us, are one of the northern peoples whose historical moment is approaching and who, even among the northern peoples themselves, enjoy pride of place by virtue of their spiritual heritage, and perhaps by virtue of a native goodness and sensitivity represented in the tale by the narrator. These qualities may help to protect them, in their cosy family hearth, from the cataclysmic events sweeping Europe. Seen in this light, Karamzin's apparently exceptional experiment with the Gothic mode in *The Island of Bornholm* is not only an apt expression of his pessimistic mood in 1793-4 but it also chimes both with his early Sentimentalism and with the defence of conservative values with which he was to be concerned during the second half of his career, as political thinker and historian in the age of Alexander I.

---

[69] Germanic pagans and druids also come to the narrator's mind in *Pis'ma russkogo puteshestvennika* (*Izb. soch.*, 1, p. 106), as he travels away from Russia, in the vicinity of Königsberg.

[70] Ibid., pp. 266, 291. He also looks forward from the River Elbe, near the beginning of his journey, to his return to his 'distant northern homeland' (p. 151).

AT THE ORIGINS OF THE RUSSIAN GOTHIC NOVEL: NIKOLAI GNEDICH'S *DON CORRADO DE GERRERA* (1803)

ALESSANDRA TOSI

Nikolai Gnedich (1784-1833) has been widely acknowledged as one of the most significant authors in early nineteenth-century Russia and most of his translations and poetical works have been extensively investigated – by contemporaries as well as by modern scholars. During his lifetime, Gnedich was esteemed primarily for his translations, and in particular for his monumental version of *The Iliad* (which Pushkin admiringly described as 'one of the few works which proudly places Russian literature ahead of Europe'[1]). Subsequently, the writer's original lyric poetry attracted much critical attention. Irina Medvedeva, for example, the editor of Gnedich's complete poems in the Soviet 'Biblioteka poeta' series, regards his verse as 'the most significant and original part' of the writer's literary output.[2] As a rule, however, scholars have confined their researches to Gnedich's 'classical' works written after 1811, the year in which he embarked on the painstaking translation of *The Iliad* – the *magnum opus* which established his reputation as a literary figure.[3] Consequently, the body of work appearing during the first decade of the century, which included

---

[1] A. Pushkin, 'Opyt otrazheniia nekotorykh neliteraturnykh obvinenii'; quoted by I. Medvedeva, 'N.I. Gnedich', in N.I. Gnedich, *Stikhotvoreniia*, 2nd edition, Leningrad, 1956, p. 5. See also P. Tikhanov, *Nikolai Ivanovich Gnedich. Neskol'ko dannykh dlia ego biografii po neizdannym istochnikam*, St Petersburg, 1884.
[2] Medvedeva, p. 5.
[3] A rare exception is Rudolf Neuhäuser, who deals in some depth with Gnedich's early works: see R. Neuhäuser, *Towards the Romantic Age: Essays on Sentimental and Preromantic Literature in Russia*, The Hague, Martinus Nijhoff, 1974. Mostly, little mention is made of the author's early production; see C. Moser, *The Cambridge History of Russian Literature*, revised edition, Cambridge, Cambridge University Press, 1992, pp. 108, 112; M. Gasparov, 'Nikolai Gnedich', in *Histoire de la littérature russe. Le XIX siècle. L'époque de Pouchkine et de Gogol*, edited by E. Etkind *et al.*, Paris, Fayard, 1996, pp. 397-8; *Istoriia russkoi literatury*, edited by N. Prutskov, 2 vols, Leningrad, 1980-81, 1, p. 259; W.E. Brown, *A History of Russian Literature of the Romantic Period*, 4 vols, Ann Arbor, Ardis, 1986, 1, pp. 257-76.

Gnedich's only original narratives, has been systematically neglected and still needs to find its rightful place within the context of the author's *oeuvre* and of nineteenth-century literature as a whole.

In the present paper we shall examine one of the first original narrative works by Gnedich, *Don Corrado de Gerrera* [*Guerrera*], published in Moscow in 1803 (and, as yet, never reprinted). Textual analysis of the work will be preceded by a brief investigation of the literary sources of *Don Corrado* and of the reception accorded to this first Russian Gothic 'novel of horror'.[4]

* * *

For Gnedich, the decade from 1800 to 1810 marked the beginnings of what would prove to be a long-lasting interest in ancient languages and cultures, and was characterised by a 'romantic' fascination with Shakespeare,[5] English graveyard poetry,[6] Milton and the tragedies of Schiller.[7] Such a heterogeneous ensemble of authors was seen by the avant-garde of Russian *literati*, including Aleksei Merzliakov, Iakov Galinkovskii, Andrei Turgenev and Vasilii Zhukovskii,[8] as embodying

---

[4] On Gothic 'horror' and 'terror', see note 33 below.

[5] For a review of Shakespeare's impact on Russia, see M.P. Alekseev, *Shekspir i russkaia kul'tura*, Moscow-Leningrad, 1955.

[6] Excerpts from James Thomson's *The Seasons* (1727-30) were published in Russian journals, from 1781 (first complete translation, by D. Dmitrevskii: 1798). Edward Young's *Night Thoughts* (1742-45) began appearing in a prose version in Kheraskov's journal *Vechera* in 1772, followed by two indirect translations from German versions (1778; 1780) in Novikov's *Utrennii svet*, and one from French (1806). An incomplete translation of Thomas Gray's *Elegy Written in a Country Churchyard* (1750) came out in *Pokoiashchiisia trudoliubets* (1784); a complete prose translation was published in 1785.

[7] On the reception of Milton in Russia from the eighteenth century to Soviet times, see V. Boss, *Milton and the Rise of Russian Satanism*, Toronto, University of Toronto Press, 1991. For an accurate list of the first Russian translations of Schiller's tragedies, see C.E. Passage, *The Russian Hoffmannists*, The Hague, Mouton, 1963, p. 17, n. 1c). See also R.Iu. Danilevskii, 'Shiller i stanovlenie russkogo romantizma', in *Rannie romanticheskie veianiia. Iz istorii mezhdunarodnykh sviazei russkoi literatury*, edited by M.P. Alekseev, Leningrad, 1972, pp. 3-95 (hereafter: Danilevskii).

[8] Andrei Turgenev (1781-1803) was the oldest of four brothers (one of whom, Nikolai, was later a Decembrist); all played an active role in Russian cultural life during the reign of Alexander I. Andrei and his brother Aleksandr started a literary circle ('The Friendly Literary Society', 1801), in which younger Muscovite writers discussed contemporary German literature (works by Goethe, Schiller, Kotzebue and Wieland

the common archetype of the poet-genius whose work encapsulated the 'new' romantic ideals of creativity, originality and aesthetic freedom.

The young Gnedich shared their enthusiasm, publishing in 1803 the first Russian translation of Schiller's tragedy *Fiesko*,[9] re-workings of Ossian's songs,[10] excerpts from Milton's *Paradise Lost*[11] and, in 1808, a translation (into Russian, via the French version by Ducis) of Shakespeare's *King Lear*. Gnedich's predilection for recent West European literary trends is also reflected in two novellas (or *povesti*), *Moritz, or the Victim of Revenge* (*Morits, ili zhertva mshcheniia*, translated from German), the original story *Unhappy Love* (*Neschastnaia liubov'*),[12] and the novel *Don Corrado de Gerrera*.

were examined and partially translated). See A. Saburov, 'Aleksandr Turgenev', in *Pis'ma Aleksandra Turgeneva Bulgakovym*, edited by I. Luppol, Moscow, 1939, pp. 5-6; F. Vigel', *Zapiski*, 2 vols, Moscow, 1891-92, 2, pp. 217-19; A. Pypin, *Ocherki literatury i obshchestvennosti pri Aleksandre I*, Petrograd, 1917, pp. 189-221; Iu. Lotman, 'Pisatel', kritik, perevodchik Ia. A. Galinkovskii', *XVIII vek*, 4, 1959, pp. 248-9; Kh. Shmidt, 'Esteticheskie vzgliady Andreia Turgeneva', *Uchenye zapiski MGU*, 295, 1960, pp. 35-55. See also A. Veselovskii, *V.A. Zhukovskii, Poeziia chuvstva i serdechnogo voobrazheniia*, St Petersburg, 1904, pp. 59-60 and passim.

Merzliakov played an important role in promoting Schiller and in the new literary trends within the circle of young writers attending Moscow University in the early 1800s. Their perception of Shakespeare as a romantic author *ante litteram* was borrowed from the *Sturm und Drang* writers (particularly Schiller, a great admirer of Shakespearian tragedy). Thus Preromantic German authors acted as a vehicle for the then Russian avant-garde's romantic interpretation of Shakespeare. From 1804 both Merzliakov and Gnedich, together with Batiushkov, joined the 'Free Society for the Lovers of Philology, Science and Arts': see A. Egunov, '"Plody uedineniia" N. Gnedicha', *XVIII vek*, 7, Moscow-Leningrad, 1966, p. 313.

[9] See S. Kibal'nik, 'Nikolai Ivanovich Gnedich', in *Russkie pisateli, 1800-1917*, edited by P. Nikolaev *et al.*, 3 vols, Moscow, 1989-94, 1, p. 586. Whilst Kostka, reviewing the fortunes of Schiller in late 18th and early 19th-century Russia, omits Gnedich's translation (E. Kostka, *Schiller in Russian Literature*, Philadelphia, University of Pennsylvania Press, 1965, pp. 13-17), Egunov (op. cit., p. 317) and Danilevskii (op. cit. pp. 50-3) stress the importance of Gnedich's early works for the reception of Schiller in Russia.

[10] See Gnedich's *Posledniaia pesn' Ossiana* (Moscow, 1804) and *Krasoty Ossiana* (Moscow, 1806).

[11] In 1805 Gnedich translated part of Book III of Milton's masterpiece (see Boss, p. 116).

[12] The translation of *Moritz* came out in a separate edition (Moscow, 1802), signed with Gnedich's pseudonym, 'N. G-ch'. Both works were published in Gnedich's early collection (poems, stories and plays), *Plody uedineniia* (1802: authorship initially attributed to the little-known M. Dmitrevskii). More recently, however, Egunov (pp. 312-19) has provided convincing textual evidence that *Plody uedineniia* was one of the

* * *

At the time of its publication *Don Corrado* met with mixed, often negative, responses from readers and exceptionally caustic reviews from critics. To understand the strong reactions aroused by Gnedich's novel, we need to consider this question within the context of the general reception of the Gothic novel – a narrative form which at the turn of the century was rapidly rising to literary prominence among Russian readers, although fiercely opposed by the great majority of critics.

The first Gothic novel to appear in Russian was Clara Reeve's *The Old English Baron* (1777), translated into Russian in 1792,[13] although, it may be assumed that, even earlier, a number of readers were reading English Gothic novels – either in the original or in French translation. The genre gained great popularity in the last decade of the eighteenth-century, amid numerous translations, imitations and original re-workings of the 'tales of terror' (*romany uzhasov)*, most notably Karamzin's *The Island of Bornholm* (*Ostrov Borngol'm*, 1794). However, the Gothic novel reached the peak of its fame with the Russian reading public in the decade 1800-1810, a cultural and literary phenomenon dubbed by Vatsuro the 'Gothic wave' (*goticheskaia volna*) of Russian literature.[14] During this period *romany uzhasov* flooded the book-market in their various forms, meeting the demand from enthusiastic readers and beginning to influence contemporary

---

first books by Gnedich, an argument seemingly confirmed by the existence of Gnedich's signed translation of *Moritz*.

[13] See V.E. Vatsuro, 'Roman Klary Riv v russkom perevode', in *Rossiia i Zapad*, edited by M.P. Alekseev, Leningrad, 1973, pp. 164-5 (hereafter: Vatsuro, 1973).

[14] See V.E. Vatsuro, 'Iz istorii "goticheskogo romana" v Rossii (A.A. Bestuzhev-Marlinskii)', *Russian Literature*, 38, 1995, 209 and passim (hereafter: Vatsuro, 1995). The numerous titles of Gothic works listed in Sopikov's bibliography provide clear indications of the extent of the phenomenon and of its popularity amongst early 19th-century Russian readers: V.S. Sopikov, *Opyt rossiiskoi bibliografii*, 4 vols, St Petersburg, 1813 (reprinted by A. Suvorin, St Petersburg, 1904-08), 2, pp. 174-5 and passim; and 1, p. 52. See also G. Gennadi, *Spravochnyi slovar' o russkikh pisateliakh i uchenykh umershikh v XVIII i XIX stoletiiakh i spisok russkikh knig s 1725 po 1825*, 3 vols, Berlin-Moscow, 1876-1908, vol. 3, pp. 228-9 and passim.

writing.[15] As has been noted, English Gothic literature, and Ann Radcliffe's novels in particular,[16] enjoyed constant success in Russia throughout the nineteenth and early twentieth centuries, inspiring a long line of writers, stretching from Karamzin[17] and Zhukovskii, to Bestuzhev-Marlinskii[18] and Somov, to Dostoevskii and Bunin.[19]

Notwithstanding its popularity with writers and the public at large, the genre met at this time with widespread resistance from literary critics who were all but unanimous in their rejection of this Gothic wave flooding Russian letters.[20] The literary exploitation of horror, violence and supernatural forces, and the creation of Satanic types along with the dark tones typical of the genre, not only clashed with the 'moralising' principles underlying both the Sentimentalist and Classical conceptions of literature dominating at the time, but also challenged the aesthetic ideals endorsed by a number of *literati* for a rational and balanced prose, engaged in civic issues.[21] In terms of subject matter,

---

[15] See V. Sipovskii, *Ocherki iz istorii russkogo romana*, 1, St Petersburg, 1909, pp. 17, 19 and passim (hereafter: Sipovskii, *Ocherki*).

[16] Radcliffe was the most popular author of Gothic novels in Russia. Her works were intensively translated at the beginning of the nineteenth century. In 1802 alone, for example, seven translations of her novels appeared, either from the English originals or from French editions: see Sopikov, 2, loc. cit.

[17] See V.E. Vatsuro, 'Literaturno-filosofskaia problematika povesti Karamzina "Ostrov Borngol'm"', *XVIII vek*, 8, 1969, pp. 190-209 (hereafter: Vatsuro, 1969).

[18] See Vatsuro (1995).

[19] See N. Kozmin, *O perevodnoi i original'noi literature kontsa XVIII i nachala XIX veka v sviazi s poeziei V.A. Zhukovskogo*, St Petersburg, 1904. On this theme see also: V. Troitskii, *Khudozhestvennye otkrytiia russkoi romanticheskoi prozy 20-30-kh godov XIX veka*, Moscow, 1985; V. Vinogradov, 'The School of Sentimental Naturalism', in *Dostoevskii and Gogol': Text and Criticism*, edited by P. Meyer and S. Rudy, Ann Arbor, Ardis, 1979, pp. 165-6; Vatsuro, 1973, p. 164; J. Mersereau, *Russian Romantic Fiction*, Ann Arbor, Ardis, 1983, pp. 54-5; L. Grossman, *Poetika Dostoevskogo*, Moscow, 1925, pp. 20-1; D. Peterson, 'Russian Gothic: The Deathless Paradoxes of Bunin's "Dry Valley"', *Slavic and East-European Journal*, 31, 1987, pp. 36-49; and M. S. Simpson, *The Russian Gothic Novel and its British Antecedents*, Columbus, Ohio, Slavica, 1986.

[20] See Vatsuro (1969), pp. 191-2. A similar phenomenon had occurred in 18th-century England, where the Gothic novel was a popular genre among readers, but not one uniformly well received by critics: see J. Howard, *Reading Gothic Fiction: A Bakhtinian Approach*, Oxford, Clarendon Press, 1994, p. 149.

[21] Theodore Ziolkowski lists, among various reasons for the success of the Gothic novel in Western Europe, two aspects which help in understanding the decidedly negative reaction the genre met from Russian critics: 'Psychologically it signalled a turn from the portrayal of manners in an integrated society to the analysis of lonely, guilt-

narrative texture and artistic treatment, the Gothic novel was considered from the literary point of view an incoherent and defective genre, an aesthetic judgement often driven by – and interwoven with – the rejection of its content on ethical grounds. The pages of journals through the 1810s and early 1820s reveal critics' preoccupation with the alleged immorality, sensationalism and stylistic coarseness of this new genre, which was increasingly competing with Sentimentalist narratives of the edifying type for the preference of the reading public. A number of articles simply dismissed the Gothic novel with a touch of irony, directed at its characteristically dreamy – or rather, nightmarish – features. This was the case, for example, with an article published in 1806 in *The Lover of Literature* (*Liubitel' slovesnosti*): 'Thus at first sight it would seem that if somebody was to be granted the gift to write in his sleep, then he could, without any difficulty, write such a novel;'[22] and with the better-known 'Plan for a Novel *à la* Radcliffe', targeting the blend of the marvellous, the romance tradition and the threatening atmosphere – a topical mixture in the genre:[23]

> Robbers and dungeons,
> Half a dozen owls on a tower;
> The moon just gleaming through the gorges
> In the distance – the roaring of the wind, the howling of the wolves;
> My heroes dream of
> A Dragon in fire, a Griffin in flight;
> Dread, horror streams behind them
> There you have a novel à la Radcliffe![24]

---

ridden outsiders. In literature it exemplified a longing for adventure in explicit departure from the moralizing and essentially conservative tone of sentimental-domestic novels. In short, the Gothic romance stands out as one of the earliest and most conspicuous symptoms of the incipient reaction against Enlightenment'. T. Ziolkowski, *Disenchanted Image: A Literary Iconology*, Princeton, Princeton University Press, 1977, p. 84.

[22] 'O nekotorykh noveishikh angliiskikh romanakh', *Liubitel' slovesnosti*, 2, 1806; cited in V. Sipovskii, *Iz istorii russkogo romana i povesti*, St Petersburg, 1903, p. 247.

[23] On the influence of the romance tradition on Gothic, see G. Beer, *The Romance*, London, Methuen, 1970, pp. 55-7.

[24] 'Razboiniki i podzemel'ia, / S poldiuzhiny na bashne sov; / Luna chut' svetit skvoz' ushchel'ia, / Vdali - shum vetrov, voi volkov; / vo sne moim geroiam snitsia / Drakon v ogne, letiashchii Grif; / Strakh, uzhas v sled za nimi mchitsia... / Vot vam roman à la Radklif': O.S. [Orest Somov], 'Plan romana à la Radklif', *Khar'kovskii demokrit*, 5, 1816, p. 61.

Other critics were more earnest in the expression of their concerns over the popularity enjoyed by the *roman uzhasov*. Reflecting the widespread rejection by eighteenth and early nineteenth-century Russian and Western European critics based on arguments of an ethical nature,[25] a number of reviews attacked the alleged immorality of Gothic narratives, which were accused of carrying to an extreme the immoral seeds embedded in much of the novel genre as a whole.[26] Petr Makarov, for example, blamed Lewis's *The Monk* (which had been attributed to Radcliffe) for its 'absence of any moral purpose'.[27] The critics' concern over the powerful influence of Gothic novels on the reader's imagination, and the belief that the Gothic novel represented a potential source of danger for public morality, remained a *topos* in early nineteenth-century criticism of the genre. By probing the most remote provinces of human fears, Gothic novels were believed to deflect the reader from the path of virtue, especially in the case of the 'impressionable' and 'weak' minds of the young and of women [!]. The widespread popularity of Gothic novels (that is to say a 'masculine' genre *ante litteram*, at least as far as contemporary opinion was concerned[28]) among women, particularly those of noble birth, was

---

[25] See D. Budgen, 'The Concept of Fiction in Eighteenth-Century Russian Letters', in *Great Britain and Russia in the Eighteenth Century: Contacts and Comparisons*, edited by A.G. Cross, Newtonville, Oriental Research Partners, 1979, pp. 65-83; Sipovskii, *Ocherki*, 1, pp. 21-31.

[26] Reviewing the critical reception of the Gothic novel in England, Fred Botting remarks that 'between 1790 and 1810 critics were almost univocal in their condemnation of what was seen as an unending torrent of popular trashy novels. Intensified by fears of radicalism and revolution, the challenge to aesthetic values was framed in terms of social transgression: virtue, property and domestic order were considered to be under threat': F. Botting, *Gothic*, London, Routledge, 1996, pp. 21-2.

[27] P. Makarov, 'Retsenziia na Monakha', *Moskovskii Merkurii*, 3, 1803, p. 139. It was not infrequent in early 19th-century Russia that books written by lesser known authors were published under the name of more popular writers, as in the case of Matthew Lewis's *The Monk*. Makarov's remarks may be compared with the similar arguments expressed, for example, in an English review of Lewis's work (*The English Critic*, 7 June 1796, p. 677; noted by Botting, p. 20).

[28] O.O.O.,'Vzgliad na povesti, ili skazki', *Patriot*, May-September 1804; reprinted in V. Sipovskii, *Iz istorii russkogo romana i povesti*, 1, 1903, pp. 242-4 (p. 243): hereafter 'Vzgliad na povesti ...'. In fact, at the opposite extreme, the Gothic novel has often been claimed by feminist scholars as a 'female' genre: either directly, on grounds of its authorship and audience, or in terms of its thematization of female anxieties. In this regard, Claire Kahane provides an interesting psychoanalytical explanation of why

considered exceedingly disgraceful.[29] In the periodicals Russian critics
expressed surprise and concern at the fact that the 'gentle sex' not only
read, but actually wrote, novels in this most unfeminine and gory of
genres. Ann Radcliffe was often cited as a notorious example:

> The English woman Radcliffe devoted her pen to the most terrifying fantasies,
> such as could be contrived not by the heart of a woman but by the imagination
> of the most inflamed fanatic. We can only hope that the English Muses, having
> frightened us for a moment with the wild horrors of Radcliffe's imagination,
> will soon charm us with pleasant descriptions in the taste of Marmontel.[30]

* * *

The negative response of contemporary critics to the Gothic genre is
also apparent in the reviews of *Don Corrado*.[31] However, in this case,
the novel's disturbing subject-matter and its terrifying atmosphere in
equal measure disconcerted critics and readers. The crude display and
tight succession of murders, tortures and rapes, all described in
accordance with the narrative techniques of the novel of horror,
appeared especially shocking to a reading public accustomed to the less
crude content of mere narratives of terror: the Gothic themes tempered
by Sentimentalist overtones that characterised the popular work of

---

Gothic literature has always been perceived as especially congenial to the female
imagination and has attracted so many women readers in different times and countries;
she points to the 'deep motivation' of the genre, the spectral presence of a dead mother
signifying the problematics of femininity which the heroine must confront: C. Kahane,
'The Gothic Mirror', in S.N. Garner *et al.*, editors, *The (M)other Tongue: Essays in
Feminist Psychoanalytic Interpretation*, Ithaca, Cornell University Press, 1985, pp.
334-51.
[29] Cf. P. Makarov, p. 218.
[30] 'Vzgliad na povesti ...', p. 243.
[31] As Devendra P. Varma has pointed out, in England the Gothic movement towards
fantasy and romance was connected with the development of a larger reading public.
Thus the profession of letters depended on the taste of readers, rather than on that of a
patron: D. Varma, *The Gothic Flame*, Metuchen, New York and London, Scarecrow
1987 (first published London, A. Barker, 1957), p. 220. In Russia the
professionalisation of literary activities was in its initial stage. The 'Gothic flood' of
English novels at the turn of the century, and especially the original endeavours in the
genre by such Russian writers as Karamzin, and later Zhukovskii and Gnedich, provide
further evidence of a similar development of the book market toward more popular
tastes.

Radcliffe, Karamzin's *The Island of Bornholm*,[32] and the imaginative supernatural of Zhukovskii's ballads and *povesti*. No Russian writer had yet gone to Gnedich's extreme in adopting the excesses of the European Gothic novel of horror.[33]

S. Zhikharev, an acquaintance of the author, condemned, for example, the uninterrupted chain of frightening episodes described in *Don Corrado*, a rejection only partially mitigated by the acknowledgement of their powerful effect on the reader's imagination ('Thus a cold shiver makes one's flesh creep'[34]); and of the moral calibre of the author ('This novel is the work of a most kind and wise man'[35]). P. Makarov's review of *Don Corrado* published in *The Moscow Mercury* (*Moskovskii Merkurii*) is decidedly more averse. The critic stigmatised the exaggerated display of 'Gothic horrors', the supposedly inconsistent behaviour of the violent hero, together with the 'indifferent' tone (*khladnokrovie*) of the narrator who would not superimpose his moral judgement on the villain's wrongdoing: 'Don Corrado stabs, stifles, strangles all – himself not knowing why – without distinction of age or sex, relatives and strangers, enemies and friends – anybody his hand can reach. From the first to the last page this novel provides only descriptions of murders, poisoning and crimes narrated with astonishing cold-bloodedness.' [36]

The rejection of *Don Corrado*, as a capricious succession of horrors by contemporary critics, has been followed by general neglect from modern scholars.[37] On close analysis however, Gnedich's novel reveals

---

[32] See Vatsuro (1969); and Derek Offord's essay in the present volume.

[33] The majority of scholars agree on the distinction between two branches of the Gothic novel: the 'novel of terror' and the 'novel of horror', or *Schauer-Romantik*. The first, the main examples of which are works by Walpole and Radcliffe, is based on the build-up of expectations of dreadful events, through a refined suspense technique; the second, which includes the narratives of Lewis, Beckford and Maturin, by contrast, aims at shocking the reader with a succession of fully described horrors: see D. Seed, 'Gothic Definition', *Novel*, 14, 3, 1981, pp. 270-74. Varma (pp. 129-31 and 206) adds a third group: the Gothic-historical novel, identifying Walpole's *The Castle of Otranto* as its major example.

[34] S. Zhikharev, *Zapiski sovremennika*, 2 vols, Moscow-Leningrad, 1934, 1, p. 259.

[35] Ibid.

[36] See P. Makarov, *Moskovskii Merkurii*, 4, 1803, pp. 54-5 (hereafter *Moskovskii Merkurii*).

[37] *Don Corrado* has not been re-printed since its 1803 publication, a circumstance which largely explains the scant scholarly attention paid to Gnedich's novel. The most striking case is that of Simpson (see note 19 above), who, in his book on the Russian

itself to be a rich work, skilfully wrought to conform to a precise aesthetic design, and meriting a reconsideration of its place in Russian literary history. As we shall demonstrate, the first original 'novel of horror' to appear in Russia was grafted on to a rich literary tradition, extending from Milton and Shakespeare, to the 'Graveyard School', to Schiller and Lewis. A number of Preromantic aesthetic and philosophic issues form its complex ideal framework, which is expressed through the literary conventions, narrative techniques and plot devices of the English Gothic novel.

* * *

According to most scholars, the Gothic novel absorbs and reworks multiple literary sources into a highly codified genre, sharing common aims and narrative devices.[38] These range from the characteristic atmosphere of mystery and apprehension aimed at stimulating the reader's imagination, to analogies in settings, character types and plot devices.[39] Gnedich's work forms part of this tradition, incorporating elements derived from the rich store of the author's Romantic literary interests into the generic mould of the Gothic novel of horror.

Don Corrado de Gerrera, or the Spirit of Vengeance and the Barbarity of Spaniards (*Don-Korrado de Gerrera, ili Dukh mshcheniia i varvarstva Gishpantsev*) is a weighty volume of nearly four hundred pages, structured in two parts and nineteen chapters. Set in Spain at the time of Philip II, the plot revolves around the eponymous villain-hero.

Gothic novel from Karamzin to Turgenev, although briefly treating Gnedich's translation *Morits* as if it were an original work (pp. 35-6), gives *Don Corrado* only a passing mention (p. 18). Brown (op cit., 1, p. 259) superficially dismisses the work on the grounds that 'it is said to have no great merit as a novel, which is not unlikely'. N. Petrunina, although providing an interesting hint regarding a possible literary source for the novel in Schiller ('*Don Corrado* in terms of style and themes is close to the rebellious tragedies of the young Schiller and to German literature of the *Sturm und Drang*'), does not investigate the issue, nor provide further information on the work as a whole: see her 'Proza 1800-1810', in *Istoriia russkoi literatury*, op. cit. (note 3 above), 1, p. 66. Similarly, see N. Belozerskaia, *V.T. Narezhnyi*, St Petersburg, 1896, p. 36, who maintains that Gnedich borrowed his content 'from a foreign novel or *povest*'' whose 'original, unfortunately, we have not been able to find'[!]. Neuhäuser (op. cit., pp. 226-33) and Egunov (pp. 313-19) represent exceptions to the rule.

[38] See Vatsuro (1995), p. 209 and passim.

[39] See R. Hume, 'Gothic Versus Romantic: A Reevaluation of the Gothic Novel', *PMLA*, 84, March 1969, pp. 282-90 (284).

Under cover of his position as an officer in the royal army, Don Corrado perpetrates an impressive number of crimes, including manslaughter, the malicious seduction and rape of innocent maidens, the confinement and starvation of his own father, and responsibility for the murder of his brother. The escalation of his misdemeanours is eventually put to an end by the young and brave Don Ribero, who reveals the cruel Corrado's crimes and consigns him to the Inquisition. The unrepentant villain ends his life in agony.

As with most Gothic novels, the historical setting in *Don Corrado* is only vaguely depicted. Conforming with the clichés typical of Enlightenment literature, which Gothic writers often exploited, medieval Spain is represented as the epitome of religious fanaticism and political reaction. It is possible that the choice of the historical setting had been inspired by Schiller's tragedy *Don Carlos* (1787), a work certainly familiar to the young Gnedich, who, as we have seen, was a keen admirer of the German author.[40] In that tragedy, Philip II's Spain is represented, as in *Don Corrado*, as a kingdom dominated by violence and superstition. Schiller, however, driven by a powerful revolutionary impulse foreign to Gnedich, does not linger on the description of horrifying events. In Schiller's play, description of the frightful is secondary to criticism of the political and religious oppression, an aim revealed throughout the tragedy: '[The] Spanish army is burning farms and countryside, Spanish soldiers are building gallows in every town. Spanish officers behead people for their love of freedom. Spanish priests burn them for their religion.'[41] As was typical of many Gothic writers, Gnedich borrowed the theme of medieval irrationality and religious fanaticism enhanced by the Mediterranean setting – seen as an alien and potentially threatening environment – to tinge the plot with a gloomy pseudo-historical atmosphere.[42]

---

[40] *Don Carlos* was staged for the first time in Russia in 1787 at the Petersburg Court Theatre and in Riga a few months later: see Kostka (op. cit., note 9 above), p. 13.

[41] F. Schiller, *Don Carlos*, Birmingham, Oberon, 1987, p. 12. As Kostka points out (pp. 14-17), notwithstanding the political ideals conveyed in Schiller, this aspect was generally ignored in Russia, at least until the reign of Nicholas I. The German writer was mainly perceived as one of the major representatives of romantic aesthetics. Karamzin, for example, after having attended a performance of *Don Carlos* in Berlin in 1789, expressed enthusiasm for the 'Romantic' qualities of the play: 'What a force in his emotions! What picturesque language!' (Neuhäuser, pp. 107 and 112).

[42] Lewis's *The Monk*, for example, fully exploits this narrative device. Cf. also the narrative function of the Italian setting in several of Radcliffe's works.

Geographical space (mainly Spain, and to a minor extent England and Germany) and temporal co-ordinates (the sixteenth century, or the 'Dark Ages' of European history) thus provide an appropriate canvas for the succession of Corrado's devilish deeds. This intent is anticipated early on in the piece, both in the subtitle (*Dukh mshcheniia i varvarstva Gishpantsev*[43]) and in the Introduction.

The grim tones of the subtitle are further stressed in the introductory pseudo-historical information provided:

> Who does not know the Spaniards – the *epitome of superstition and violence*? the Spaniards [sic] – where not only the mob, blinded by false convictions, wanders in *the darkness of superstition*, [...] but even the Nobles, even the Sovereigns serve us as examples, the best of which is King Philip II, whose whole life has been driven by the high goal of committing crimes [...]. 50,000 innocents became the victims of the *superstition and violence* of Philip; 8,000 have fallen by the hand of his favourite, the grandee de Alba, and *who after all that can be astonished at the deeds of de Gerrera?* [44]

The setting described in the Introduction creates a suitable atmosphere for the terrifying events narrated in the opening pages, where a sequence of crimes committed by Don Corrado unfolds in nightmarish succession. The forceful effect of the opening episode is enhanced by the insertion into the narrative thread of the characters' dramatic dialogues and theatrical gestures – a stylistic device, widely employed throughout the novel, to which we shall return. The atmospheric suggestion of the passage, as elsewhere in *Don Corrado*, is intensified by the exploitation of striking visual oppositions (arising from stark colour contrasts and by the sudden shift of a light/visible scene into a dark/hideous one) and poignant acoustic effects (built on the tension between a silence loaded with suspense, vis-à-vis the sudden breaking of sound). A dead calm precedes the horror of the 'frightful scene' gradually discernible from the obscurity of the night: '*Imagine* a deep and extensive valley, completely covered by *ash* and *piles of dead*

---

[43] Makarov observed that 'the Spaniards would be upset by such a title. The author determines the features of a country after the features of a character who is not historically grounded, being himself imaginary': *Moskovskii Merkurii*, p. 53.

[44] N. Gnedich, *Don-Korrado de Gerrera, ili Dukh mshcheniia i varvarstva Gishpantsev*, Moscow, 1803, [5]-[6]. Here and hereafter the italics are mine, unless otherwise stated; hereafter reference is by page number in the text.

bodies, and the stream which waters it mingled with the *blood* and stopped in its flow, choked by corpses; *wails and moans rend the air.*' (I, 9-10)

Whilst the horrendous bloodshed of innocent victims ('mothers, elderly, youngsters') is described at length, the disclosure of its perpetrator, according to the suspense technique typical of the genre, is delayed for a few pages. Eventually a rhetorical question uttered by the indignant narrator ('Can this possibly be the deed of man?') heralds the appearance of the murderer who:

> ... splattered with blood [...], smiles with joy, with a contented gaze on his face contemplates the plundering. This is Don Corrado de Gerrera, admiring the deed he has accomplished *with his own hands!*[45] This is a *monster*, produced by *aberrant nature*, this is a *horror of existence*. These are brutalities to make mankind shudder; his heart is dead to the *voice of nature*. (I, 12-13)

Thus the reader, according to a narrative pattern frequently exploited by Gothic writers, is frontally attacked with detailed scenes aimed at shocking and disturbing him or her, and only then introduced to the villain responsible for the horrendous crimes.

The strong tones and gruesome events described in the first pages are not fully supported at this stage by a convincing plot, or by psychological insights in explanation of the hero's behaviour. Progressively, however, the intersection of different narrative layers on the one hand, and the introduction of a more complex and nuanced characterisation of Corrado's personality on the other, bring the work to a level of artistic accomplishment.

The first step in this direction is taken with interpolated flashbacks to the hero's formative years, a device often encountered in Gothic novels to provide the villain with psychological background and individual characterisation. Through the framed story, inserted toward the middle of the first part, the narrator describes the first two decades of Corrado's life: his childhood in Spain, followed by wanderings through Europe in his youth. The account of Corrado's upbringing and past experiences marks a breakthrough in the narrative structure of the novel. Firstly, through this device, wider spatial and temporal co-ordinates are introduced into the picaresque-like adventures of the

---

[45] Italics in the original.

young Corrado. Secondly, and most importantly, these episodes provide the reader with insights into the villain's earlier life and psychology, which partly explain the vicious character and the extreme evil of his subsequent deeds. Furthermore, the narrative structure as a whole gains momentum from the depiction of Corrado's personality and past; the fragmentary material of the first chapter is now organised around an intriguing protagonist giving unity and meaning to the long chain of gruesome events.

Born in a barbaric country and brought up amongst 'pirates who owned vessels on which they sailed, robbing and killing, without consideration for either the sex or station of their victims,' Corrado, 'who was still a child, was nourished by the same air breathed by the villains' (I, 105-06). The encouragement of his immoral father plays an important role in the formation of a child endowed with an extraordinary personality which circumstance turns to evil purposes. Thus, the 'gifted' son, once embarked on the path of crime, easily surpasses the example set by his father (and indeed any other imaginable example!): 'Right from his infancy Corrado was sly and cunning and his father loved him. He turned sixteen, and he surpassed his father, which is not surprising, given the fact that he was born with a manly character: he was born for high deeds'(I, 107-09).

Henceforth, Corrado's inexhaustible thirst for power and glory dominates his existence, leading to the series of crimes described through the novel: 'Nothing attracted him as glory did; he looked at it with greedy eyes. Thus every victory aroused in him an ardent flame. He wanted to gain renown, and falling on innocent victims, plundering and killing them, he thought he would win the laurels [of glory]' (II, 112-13). Thus the sequence of horrors related in the first chapters of the novel becomes – at least in retrospect – plausible.

The psychological insights into Corrado's exasperated craving for universal fame and power are further explored in the course of the work. The Gothic villain gradually acquires the traits of a Faustian character, a Prometheus, attempting to demonstrate his superiority over any human or natural law. This solitary struggle undertaken by the fierce Corrado to prove his supremacy becomes the ideational frame for the second part of the narrative, underpinning the escalation of the villain's crimes and eventually engendering his tragic death. Although fully developed only later in the narrative, important hints in this respect are again detectable in the initial pages. Particularly revealing is the choice of a passage from Schiller's *The Robbers* (*Die Räuber*) to serve as the *incipit* to the novel:[46] 'Look, look! all the *laws of the world* are broken, the *bonds of nature* are severed; an ancient hostility has risen from *hell!*' These lines, which serve as an epigraph on the title page immediately under the characteristic Gothic title, anticipate and prelude the frightful atmosphere of the work. Furthermore, they interject the ideational conflict underlying the whole novel, between the body of rules governing human and natural life ('laws of the world', 'bonds of nature') on the one side, and the chaotic principle embodied by Don Corrado ('ancient hostility'), on the other. Such opposition rests on antithetical pairs (humanity/inhumanity, light/darkness, God/Satan) whose dense religious and literary references convey the symbolic meaning of the text.

Similar basic dualities underlie the opening scene, centred on the nightmarish aftermath of a slaughter perpetrated by the villain-hero. In the episode which introduces Corrado into the narrative (I, 12-13), the derogatory qualifiers associated with the villain ('monster', 'dread of nature') opposed to his innocent victims, and the stress placed on his behaviour against nature ('his heart is deaf to the voice of nature'), vis-à-vis that of devout men, provide hints as to Corrado's Titanic personality and aspirations, setting the stage for the development of the main motifs and themes of the novel.

Throughout the narrative, the portrayal of the main character is constructed on the accumulation of epithets similar to those quoted above, highlighting the 'inhuman' and 'unnatural' traits of Corrado's personality. The villain is depicted alternatively as a beast or a devilish creature, a 'tiger' and a 'monster', who, characteristically, stares at his victims with a devilish grin: 'with a smile of joy, with a contented gaze he contemplates the plundering' (II, 12). Such features are further enhanced by means of contrasting the passionate Corrado with characters of heavenly perfection described in Sentimentalist style. Such features are particularly evident in the case of the heroines who, without exception, fall prey to the beastly desires of Corrado. Their

---

[46] *Die Räuber* marked the beginning of Schiller's fame in Russia. A re-worked German version of the play by K.M. Plümlicke was translated for the first time in 1793 by N. Sandunov and, according to Zhikharev's *Zapiski*, was first performed in Moscow in 1805; see also Danilevskii (op. cit., note 7 above), pp. 37-41.

virtues, beauty and innocence make them particularly vulnerable to
Corrado's seduction, for, as has been noted in regard to the English
Gothic novel, modesty and delicacy encourage sexual aggressiveness in
the Gothic villain.[47] The young Sharlotta, for example, is described as
the 'flower of her sex' (*tsvetok svoego pola*), whose naive affection for
Corrado eventually decides her tragic destiny: 'She returned his
caresses with *the innocence of an Angel*. Poor Sharlotta, what a
rapacious *beast* has broken into your heart' (II, 127). Similar is the
representation of Corrado's main victim, his wife-to-be Olimpia, whose
idealised portrayal is clearly reminiscent of Sentimentalist narrative
devices ('my rough brush is not able to portray her beauty; I will only
say that she was one of the three Graces...': II, 138). Interestingly, to
her seduction, as to Sharlotta's, are attached the metaphorically
opposing images of predator and prey: 'Oh you, young, good hearted,
candid; – a *wolf* can easily catch an innocent little *sheep*' (I, 64).

Corrado aspires to make himself immune to the feelings of love and
compassion and thus to become 'inhuman', an attribute which he
perceives and cherishes as a mark of superior moral and physical
strength. 'Inhumanity' becomes a necessary attribute *and* a
distinguishing mark of the villain's dream of omnipotence. At the height
of his power, Corrado expresses this belief in the form of a
melodramatic monologue: 'The bloodsucker stares with a devilish
smile at the quivering limbs of the murdered. "So – he utters, here's the
amiable offspring of nature – Ah! How it trembles, how it curses me.
Curse, curse! Offspring of hated nature! Yet this is still only a trifle, a
beginning on the way to hell"' (II, 145-146).

Don Corrado's violent and nihilistic behaviour, increasingly
motivated by his dreams of omnipotence, challenges any obstacle,
including his own human limits, as expressed in a second dramatic
monologue:

> Oh! *I possess so much strength, so much courage, so much hatred* to torment
> all your [nature's] favourites – and I will utterly annihilate even you. Away from

---

[47] See R. Mise, *The Gothic Heroine and the Nature of the Gothic Novel*, New York,
Arno Press, 1980, pp. 111, 118 and 223. Mario Praz recognises in the idea of pleasure
obtained through sadistic or masochistic cruelty a theme characteristic not only of the
Gothic novel, but of romantic literature as a whole: see M. Praz, *La carne: la morte e il
diavolo nella letteratura romantica*, Florence, Sansoni, 1984. See also C.A. Howells,
Love, Mystery and Misery: Feeling in Gothic Fiction, London, Athlone, 1978, p. 12.

the sight of humanity! Stifle rage, silence the smallest voice of regret! *Make my heart one of stone*! Then, once broken free from a throng of Furies, I will hunt all the favourites of nature until the seas will be stained with their blood, until the stench of their corpses will rise to the height of the skies. I long for blood. (II, 145-147)

Thus, as in Lewis's *The Monk,* Corrado increasingly behaves like a fiend in human shape, an overpowering, Miltonic 'superman' in front of whom men and nature alike shrink.[48] The villain thus acquires the traits of a tragic romantic hero and the reader, although repelled by Corrado's sadism, is at the same time attracted by the exceptional stature of a character whose Titanic struggle is doomed to failure. Once the ephemeral nature of his dreams of supremacy is revealed, the hero is spiralled into the abyss of torture, death and eternal damnation.

Whilst the first part of the novel is dedicated to the depiction of Corrado's success, which is obtained at the price of extreme violence, the second part reveals the descending phase in the hero's life. The height of Corrado's power is marked when he is given a Gothic castle as a reward for a crime he has committed. Corrado's mansion, which is placed in a remote and deserted location beside an old cemetery,[49] is characteristically adorned with gloomy crypts and mouldy vaults:

> Amid the mountains of the Sierra Morena was situated a Gothic castle. On the southern side a river ran close by; on the northern and eastern sides it was surrounded by thick forests. The castle was encircled by a wall made of stone which had at each corner a high Gothic tower; beneath one of them there was a fairly large underground cave. There reigned a perpetual night; there was only dampness and coldness, there lived frogs and mice. (II, 5-7)

---

[48] Corrado's victims and associates are terrified by his ruthlessness. The natural environment also seems to retract before the villain's 'unnatural' behaviour. After one of the many bloody deeds perpetrated by Corrado, for example, 'Nature reacted with horror: the sun hid itself behind black clouds, the clouds spread out' (I, 82).

[49] On the characteristics of Gothic buildings, see M. Praz 'Introductory Essay', in *Three Gothic Novels,* edited by P. Fairclough, Harmondsworth, Penguin, 1968, pp. 7-34. See also Botting, op. cit., pp. 32-8. The influence of motifs and atmosphere from Macpherson's songs may be also detected. This observation is further supported by the fact that, shortly after publication of *Don Corrado,* Gnedich translated and reworked a number of Ossianic poems which he probably already knew in 1803.

As is apparent from the passage above, Corrado's castle is represented according to the typical literary conventions of the West European Gothic novel. However a number of other Preromantic genres contribute to the depiction of particular areas in the proximity of the medieval mansion. The decaying cemetery adjacent to the castle, for example, contains the whole gamut of images of death characteristic of graveyard poetry, a genre interacting with the Gothic novel,[50] whilst the most probable source for the depiction of the cemetery (and of the near-by dungeon) appears again to be Schiller's *Fiesko,* a play which Gnedich had translated only a few months before the publication of *Don Corrado.*[51]

The castle, representing the focal point in Gothic novels, has been recognised by Bakhtin as the fundamental chronotope of the genre; the decaying mansion of the villain is the place where the vestiges of past centuries, old legends and spells meet with present times, an encounter producing fantastic and fearsome events.[52] Furthermore, a strong narrative significance is attached to the castle, for its gloomy setting incites an upsurge of the supernatural forces latent in the narrative. The Gothic mansion is thus a place full of mysterious implications, a *lieu*

---

[50] The literary model provided by English Gothic literature clearly played a major role in the depiction of Corrado's castle. It might, however, be inferred that, as was often the case in the West, an additional source of inspiration was probably provided by actual examples of Neo-Gothic buildings. The Gothic revival in literature and architecture represent two inter-related cultural phenomena in late-18th, early-19th-century Western Europe. This linkage between the two easthetic spheres is also observable in Gnedich's Russia, where the Gothic 'revival' experienced by contemporary architecture coexisted with a fashion for the 'medieval' novel of terror. See D. Shvidkovsky, *The Empress and the Architect: British Architecture and Gardens at the Court of Catherine the Great,* New Haven and London, Yale University Press, 1996, pp. 195-210.

[51] Compare Gnedich's depiction of the cemetery (II, 157) and the dungeon (II, 6) with these excerpts from Schiller's tragedy. For instance, Verrina thus menaces his daughter Bertha: 'Down into the lowest vault beneath my house! There whyne and cry aloud! Be the life painful as the tortures of the writhing worm. May you drag thy hoad of misery throughout the endless circle of eternity!' (Act I, scene 4). Further on, an old cemetery is thus described: 'the church-yard where corruption preys on the moulding carcasses, and Death holds his abhorred feast - where shrieks of tormented souls delight the listening devils, and sorrow sheds her fruitless tears into the never-filling urn' (Act III, scene 1). See F. Schiller, *Fiesco, or the Genoese Conspiracy: a Tragedy,* translated by G.H. Nöhden and J. Stoddart, Dublin, Printed for J. Archer, 1799.

[52] See M. Bakhtin, *Literaturno-kriticheskie stat'i,* Moscow, 1986, p. 278. See also Praz, 'Introductory Essay' to *Three Gothic Novels.*

symbolique in which the supernatural events, carried to their extreme, often lead the narrative to a tragic closure.

Don Corrado conforms to the features of the genre, not only by the description of the castle and its chronotopical connotations, but also by the narrative and symbolic function assumed by the Gothic building. The atmosphere breathed within the mouldy walls of his ancient mansion induces a dramatic and tragic turn in Corrado's life. Initially the villain-hero finds his perfect dimension in his newly acquired castle, the dark and gloomy space he had yearned for since his childhood when: 'his soul was thrilled by frightening events. When the storm chased a black cloud, when the thunderclap left everybody stunned; then – oh! then he felt happy' (II, 109-110). In the castle Corrado builds a miniaturised hell, within whose perimeter he feels able to govern the world by imposing his rule of violence and terror. Thus the villain's father, potentially able to reveal his son's criminal past, is confined in the cave underneath one of the towers, his brother is killed,[53] while his angelic wife is constantly watched by Corrado's frightful attendant Vooz and forced not to pass beyond the confines of the thick forest surrounding the castle, which mark the spatial boundaries of her husband's absolute power.

While Corrado is at first comfortable within the enclosed and threatening space of his Gothic mansion, this environment will soon contribute to precipitating the dramatic reversal in his fortunes. Stirred by the gloomy castle atmosphere, the remorse lying in Corrado's subconscious rises to the surface, taking the shape of dreams and apparitions which haunt the hero's mind. Starting from sleep, the terrified villain imagines being confronted with the phantoms of those he has wronged. Thus, although he is of outstanding physical and mental strength, the hero's psychological balance begins to be undermined by the memory of horrors perpetrated. Corrado is unable to avoid, or to control, the shattering effect of gloomy recollections which seize him in the form of hallucinations and nightmares. Visions,

---

[53] Fratricide often marks the apex of the tragedy in both Gothic novels and *Sturm und Drang* dramas, including Schiller's *The Robbers* (see V. Shklovskii, *O teorii prozy*, Moscow, 1928, p. 50). *Morits, ili zhertva mshcheniia* (the German work translated by Gnedich in 1802), probably structured after Schiller's play, fully develops the theme of the inimical brothers, typical of early romantic literature (cf. R. Neuhäuser, *The Romantic Age in Russian Literature: Poetic and Aesthetic Norms. An anthology of Original Texts (1800-1850)*, Munich, Verlag Otto Sagner, 1975, p. 73).

apparitions and other supernatural phenomena contribute to blur the
boundaries between dreams, visions and reality, eventually leading
Corrado into a mental breakdown: 'he became thoughtful; anxiety was
portrayed on his forehead. Thus, the voice of conscience thundered, but
he closed his ears and did not listen to it. His face expressed fear and a
tortured conscience' (II, 50-51).

Thus, in keeping with a narrative device often employed by Gothic
writers, supernatural events, magnified by a haunted environment,
provide insights into the most remote regions of the human mind. The
character's subconscience proves able to terrify and cause the most
unbearable sufferings to the otherwise unconquerable villain:

> 'Ah, my peace – oh, I would sacrifice thousands of pistoles to stifle this damned
> thunder, to free my head from this dream – a dream which is the main cause for
> my anxiety!' – Thus the thunder of conscience struck the villain, he felt it and
> trembled. An overpowering fear and suspicion grew in his soul, he dreaded that
> somebody would reveal his deeds. (II, 55)

Despite deep psychological suffering, however, Corrado will not
repent, unlike his assistant Richard, and vigorously fights to suppress
signs of any psychological weakness which could reveal in him the
much despised quality of 'human frailty'. Corrado remains until the end
faithful to his role as a demonic, supernatural figure whose principles –
if not spirits – remain unbroken, even under threat of the Inquisition's
tortures. Whilst, in the first chapters of the novel, Corrado is depicted
as a melodramatic character whose extravagant emotions are designed
to excite the last possible twinge of sensation, he gradually emerges as
a powerful romantic hero – an alien soul depicted in his lonely and
extreme struggle to rise above the crowd. It is precisely in this dream of
unrelenting super-humanity pursued by Corrado that the reader finds
the plausible cause of the villain's unscrupulous conduct, eventually
leading to his fall and to his death at the hands of the Spanish
Inquisition.[54]

Given the powerful image of the villain, conveyed with stylistic
intensity throughout the work, the scene which brings the novel to a
close after Corrado's death appears rather blunt and feeble. In depicting
the happiness finally achieved by Olimpia and her rescuer Don Ribero,

---

[54] See Varma, pp. 189-90.

Gnedich employs modes of the Sentimental idyll which contrast sharply with the Gothic tones used in the rest of the work. Tongue-in-cheek innuendo is detectable in the bucolic finale: 'Their life was comparable to that of a quiet May – obscured from time to time by light clouds: their life flowed by like a clear brook which was occasionally troubled by raindrops' (II, 209).

* * *

Devendra P. Varma has suggested that villains in the Gothic novel of horror share the same lineage with, and similar characteristics to, the romantic (or, in Mark Simpson's view, the 'Byronic'[55]) hero. Both the Gothic novel of horror and the romantic novel would reflect an attraction for, if not a glorification of, the exceptional individual who knows no laws and no limits, opposed to the ordinary mortals who surround him or her. Quite clearly, the creation of Corrado – a character altogether unique in Russian literature of the period – is much indebted to Gnedich's early literary interests: Milton and Shakespeare, the English Gothic writers, Schiller and Goethe: all authors who had variously interpreted and romanticised the Miltonic image of the Devil often associated in their works with the myth of Prometheus.[56] Within this literary framework, Gnedich gives birth to the first modern 'demon' to appear in Russian fiction, a precedent followed by a vast progeny of Russian heroes – of Raskolnikovs and Stavrogins – whose dream of super-humanity lead them to a tragic fight against all human conventions and moral rules.

As we have now seen, the young Gnedich, attracted by '[all] that exceeded the usual state of things',[57] as one contemporary put it, introduced into Russian prose the 'exaggerated' style and literary themes of the novel of horror and of Western-European early Romanticism as a whole. In *Don Corrado* the author sharply breaks with both the Classicist and the Sentimentalist traditions, deliberately opposing the aesthetics of rationality, harmony and elegance with one of freedom and unbridled imagination in the choice and treatment of the most extreme subject-matter.

---

[55] Simpson, p. 11.
[56] See Boss (op. cit., note 7 above), pp. 157-8 and passim.
[57] See Zhikharev, pp. 259-60.

To emphasise the historical perspective, Gnedich, with his *Don Corrado*, broadened the themes hitherto treated in Russian prose, depicting the violent passions and extreme aspirations of the hero, introducing the topics of the mysterious and the uncanny and, more generally, drawing attention to aspects of reality new in the development of the Russian novel. These thematic choices required the exploration of new literary techniques which the author derived and re-elaborated from the recent works of English and German authors. Like the first Gothic writer, Horace Walpole,[58] Gnedich strove to renovate a contemporary prose language and style inadequate for the depiction of themes of horror and the supernatural. His narrative experimentation provides the novel with a complex stylistic structure which includes interpolated poetry, framed stories and, most notably, 'theatrical' speeches and gestures.[59] Furthermore, dramatic dialogues are frequently employed to enhance the poignancy of the narrative and to convey the romantic image of Don Corrado.

Again like Walpole, who professed to have been inspired by Shakespearean tragedy in the conception of *The Castle of Otranto*, Gnedich turned to the theatre, in particular to the plays of Schiller, a writer who had already influenced authors such as Radcliffe and Lewis.[60] In *Don Corrado* the stylistic role played by both Schiller's work and the Gothic novel is noticeable, mainly in the emphasis on dramatic devices, which Gnedich had already employed in *The Fruits of Solitude* (*Plody uedineniia*, 1802). A. Egunov has argued that Gnedich's early collection of narratives, pieces and poems, the characters' discourse in the prose works closely resembles the speeches of personages in the plays.[61] In *Don Corrado* the author further expands the stylistic potentialities of theatrical devices (particularly of

---

[58] See Horace Walpole's 'Preface to the Second Edition' of *The Castle of Otranto*, Oxford, Oxford University Press, 1996, pp. 9-14.

[59] The utilisation of theatrical devices in prose genres was to become a key element in later 19th-century prose. As Willem Weststeijn points out, the alternation of prose and drama is a characteristic feature of romantic fiction in Russia: see his 'Narrative Devices in Russian Romantic Prose', in A. van Holk, editor, *Dutch Contributions to the Tenth International Congress of Slavists, Sofia, 14-22 September, 1988*, Amsterdam, Rodopi, 1988, p. 329.

[60] See Simpson, pp. 15-18 and 35. For an account of the influence of Matthew Lewis's work in early 19th-century Russia, see V.E. Vatsuro, 'G. P. Kamenev i goticheskaia literatura', *XVIII vek*, 10, 1975, pp. 271-7.

[61] See Egunov, pp. 313-14.

dialogue and monologue), to high dramatic effect: a technique well-established in Gothic fiction as a whole.[62] Entire sections of the novel are given over to long melodramatic discourses and monologues (which sometimes fill half the overall length of a chapter) from the main characters. Furthermore, throughout the work, the third-person form (the utterance of the omniscient narrator) alternates with theatrical speech by the characters (the first-person speech graphically evidenced in the text). This establishes a balance between the two voices, empowering the characters – and particularly the villain-hero – to intervene directly in the narrator's presentation of events by interjecting into the narrative their own viewpoint, subjective perceptions and emotional discourse.

As we have seen, Nikolai Gnedich's *Don Corrado*, the first novel of horror to appear in Russia, relied upon German and English prototypes that had recently been brought to the attention of his contemporary Russian writers and readers. Additionally, on a basic canvas of the themes, setting and plot of the Gothic novel, the author experimented with the narrative modes and techniques indicated above; these innovative devices enabled Gnedich to convey the extreme emotions of his characters and to give a convincing narrative shape to the 'new' themes of the grotesque, the sublime and the supernatural. In that respect, Gnedich's early novel draws Russian prose closer to the avant-garde of West European literature, shedding seeds which were eventually to germinate fully in the generations of Russian writers to follow. On the fertile literary background of early Russian romantic prose and folklore, the 'second wave' of European Romanticism (the French *École frénétique*[63] and the German *Kunstmärchen* of Tieck and Hoffmann[64]) laid deep roots, influencing authors such as Bestuzhev-Marlinskii,[65] Pushkin, Odoevskii, Vel'tman, Gogol[66] and Dostoevskii.[67]

---

[62] See Howells, p. 16.

[63] See R. Busch, 'Russian Freneticism', *Canadian-American Slavonic Studies*, 14, 2 1980, pp. 269-83.

[64] See A.B. Botnikova, *E.T.A. Gofman i russkaia literatura (pervaia polovina XIX veka). K probleme russko-nemetskikh literaturnikh sviazei*, Voronezh, 1977, pp. 12-13 and passim.

[65] See N. Kovarsky, 'The Early Bestuzhev-Marlinsky' in *Russian Prose*, edited by B.M. Eikhenbaum and Yury Tynyanov, Ann Arbor, 1985, pp. 109-26 (121-2).

The discovery of the dark side of human existence (the sinister, the nocturnal, the demonic, the torn subconscious of extreme heroes), which Gnedich's novel, Karamzin's tales and Zhukovskii's ballads first introduced into the realm of Russian high literature, would become an integral and pivotal theme in Russian prose from the 1820s. As Vatsuro remarks:

> The history of the penetration into Russia of the 'Gothic novel' and its reception by Russian readers and authors represents a whole chapter in the evolution of Russian literature. It would not be overly bold to assert that, disregarding this influence, our notion of the stylistic changes and of the shaping of Romanticism would inevitably be incomplete and even distorted.[68]

---

[66] See. A. Swensen, 'Vampirism in Gogol''s Short Fiction', *Slavic and East European Journal*, 37, 4 1994, pp. 490-509; R. Busch, 'Gogol' and the Russian Freneticist Cycle of the Early 1830s', *Canadian Slavonic Papers*, 22, 1, 1980, pp. 28-42.

[67] See G. Fridlender, *Dostoevskii i mirovaia literatura*, Moscow, 1979 p. 217. Interestingly, the young Dostoevskii was captivated by readings - Shakespeare's plays, Schiller's tragedies - which were very similar to those engaging Gnedich at the onset of his career as a writer. The influence of such authors wass clearly reflected in Dostoevskii's early works, in particular the now forgotten dramas *Boris Godunov* and *Maria Stuarda* (Fridlender, p. 67.

[68] Vatsuro (1973) p. 146.

DOES RUSSIAN GOTHIC VERSE EXIST?
THE CASE OF VASILII ZHUKOVSKII

MICHAEL PURSGLOVE

Although the adjective 'Gothic' is readily applied to a particular kind of Russian prose fiction by modern Western critics, its Russian equivalent ('*goticheskii*') has been rarely used by Russian critics. Its usage appears to be almost entirely restricted to describing English novels and is felt to be so unfamiliar a term that it is frequently put in quotation marks.[1] Nineteenth-century critics avoided the word completely, preferring terms such as 'horror novel' (*roman uzhasov), '*roman noir' (*chernyi roman*), 'novel of mystery and horror' (*roman tain i uzhasov*), or even the splendidly, though no doubt unintentionally, ambiguous, term *uzhasnyi roman*, used by the aptly named journal *The Well-Intentioned* (*Blagonamerennyi*) in 1818 to describe the novels of Ann Radcliffe and François Ducray-Dusmenil.[2]

Whatever the literature under discussion, modern critics assume that prose is the appropriate Gothic medium and, in general, show a marked reluctance to countenance the possibility of Gothic poetry. A few compilers of reference books admit the possibility of Gothic elements in poetry. Thus, speaking of the Gothic novel, Sir Paul Harvey finds that some 'elements of atmosphere and characterization' in them derive from eighteenth-century 'graveyard' poetry.[3] Ian Ousby claims that the influence of the Gothic novel can be felt in 'some Romantic' poetry, citing Coleridge's *Christabel* (1816) as an example,[4] while the

---

[1] For a discussion of this, see N. Cornwell, 'Vladimir Odoyevsky and Russian Gothic', *Rusistika*, 3, June 1991, p.26 (revised in his *Vladimir Odoevsky and Romantic Poetics*, Providence and Oxford, Berghahn Books, 1998, pp. 145-56).
[2] Quoted in V.E. Vatsuro, 'A. Radklif, ee pervye russkie chitateli i perevodchiki', *Novoe literaturnoe obozrenie*, 22, 1996, pp. 202-25 (210).
[3] P. Harvey, editor, *The Oxford Companion to English Literature*, Oxford, Clarendon Press, 4th edition, 1963, p. 345.
[4] I. Ousby, editor, *The Cambridge Guide to Literature in English*, Cambridge: Cambridge University Press, 1988, p. 405. More recent studies which do analyse 'the poetic tale of terror', in addition to examples in prose, include: Robert Miles, *Gothic*

anonymous author of the entry 'Gothic' in the *Modern Encyclopaedia of Russian and Soviet Literature* (*MERSL*) directs the reader towards Zhukovskii's ballads and Lermontov's *Demon*.[5] Some theoreticians of the fantastic in literature also cautiously admit the possibility of Gothic poetry. Neil Cornwell, for instance, takes as his point of departure Todorov's celebrated 'notion of hesitation on the part of the reader between a natural and a supernatural [...] explanation of the events presented in the narrative' and warns us that:

> Poetry, in all its forms seems to me to require, and normally to achieve, an attitude of mind and a degree of suspension of belief on the part of the reader, or listener, quite distinct from those pertaining to prose fiction.

He then adds:

> Furthermore, in cases where reader hesitation of the type here envisaged might arise – perhaps in certain narrative rather than lyric poetry – the effect is likely to derive at least as much from the incantatory quality of poetic form and language as from narrative content.[6]

* * *

The mention of narrative poetry, together with the hint in *MERSL* – not to mention his dates (1783-1852) – all suggest that the hunt for Gothic poetry in Russian may lead to Vasilii Andreevich Zhukovskii. Indeed, it must also be remembered that Zhukovskii made his name as a poet/translator with *Sel'skoe kladbishche* (1802), his version of Thomas Gray's *Elegy in a Country Churchyard* (1750), the most celebrated of the graveyard poems which Harvey saw as an influence on Gothic literature. The poem thus falls in the decade which Vatsuro has dubbed the time of the 'Gothic wave' (*goticheskaia volna*) in Russian literature.[7] There is a further connection between Zhukovskii's

---

Writing 1750-1820: A Genealogy, London, Routledge, 1993; and Anne Williams, *Art of Darkness: A Poetics of Gothic*, Chicago and London, University of Chicago Press, 1995.

[5] H. Weber, editor, *The Modern Encyclopaedia of Russian and Soviet Literature*, Gulf Breeze, Florida, Academic International Press, vol. 8, 1986.

[6] N. Cornwell, *The Literary Fantastic From Gothic to Postmodernism*, New York and London, Harvester Wheatsheaf, 1990, pp. 4, 48.

[7] V.E. Vatsuro, 'Iz istorii "goticheskogo romana" v Rossii (A.A. Bestuzhev-Marlinskii)', *Russian Literature*, 38, 1995, pp. 207-26 (209).

translation and the Gothic novel, in that its phraseology appears to have been influenced by Russian versions of the poem *Night*, one of the poems appended by Ann Radcliffe to her novel *The Romance of the Forest* (1791), which, like *The Mysteries of Udolpho* (1794), bears the subtitle 'interspersed with some pieces of poetry'.[8]

Zhukovskii's narrative poems are mainly cast in the form of literary ballads, a *genre* which is almost synonymous with his name. Between 1808 and 1839 Zhukovskii wrote forty of them, almost all of them based on foreign models. Interestingly, the author of the standard work on the *genre*, Michael Katz, is almost unique in not flinching from applying the adjective 'Gothic' to verse. Specifically, he attaches it to the collection of verse put out by Sir Walter Scott and Matthew 'Monk' Lewis in 1801, *Tales of Wonder*, and to some of Robert Southey's ballads (six of which were translated by Zhukovskii).[9] It should be noted, too, that Lewis's popular ballad, *Alonzo the Brave and the Fair Imogine* (1798), has a storyline involving marriage to a corpse, closely resembling that of Bürger's *Lenore*, which Zhukovskii translated three times.[10] Katz sheds light on his understanding of the term 'Gothic' when he writes of the ballad *Lila* (1815), by the little-known writer Aleksandr Meshchevskii: 'The setting of the poem consists of the most common Gothic motifs: *mgla, ten', grob, petukh*'.[11]

It is the presence of such motifs in Zhukovskii's work which seems to have attracted the attention of his contemporaries and, indeed, given rise to satire. In 1810 Konstantin Batiushkov wrote in his poem *Apparition (Prividenie)*:

...но из могилы,
Если можно воскресать,

---

[8] Vatsuro, 1996, pp. 217-22.

[9] M. R. Katz, *The Literary Ballad in Early Nineteenth-Century Literature*, Oxford, Oxford University Press, 1976, p.11. The six Southey ballads translated by Zhukovskii are: *Rudiger (Adel'stan); Lord William (Varvik); The Old Woman of Berkeley. A Ballad Showing how an old Woman rode Double and who rode before her (Ballada, v kotoroi opisyvaetsia, kak odna starushka ekhala na chernom kone vdvoem i kto sidel vperedi); Donica (Donika); God's Judgment on a Wicked Bishop (Sud bozhii nad episkopom);* and *Queen Oracca and the Five Martyrs of Morocco (Koroleva Uraka i piat' muchenikov).*

[10] Although Zhukovskii did not translate Lewis's ballad, he may have had it in mind when translating Schiller's ballad *Durand* as *Alonzo.*

[11] Katz, p.133.

Я не стану, друг мой милый,
Как мертвец тебя пугать.
В час полуночных явлений
Я не стану в виде тени,
То внезапу, то тишком
С воплем в твой являться дом.[12]

A few years later, A.F. Voeikov, in his *Madhouse* (*Dom sumasshedshikh*), wrote:

Вот Жуковский, в саван длинный
Скутан, лапочки крестом,
Ноги вытянув умильно
Черта дразнит языком.
Видеть ведьму вображает:
И глазком ей подмигает,
И кадит и отпевает,
И трезвонит, и ревет.[13]

The diarist Aleksandr Turgenev, in his *Letter from Florence to Simbirsk* (*Pis'mo iz Florentsii v Simbirsk*, 1835), reviewing Galdini's opera *Maria di Brabante* comments: 'There are more witches on stage than there are in Zhukovskii's ballads';[14] and in his memoirs, published in 1864, Filip Vigel points to the same Gothic motifs in Zhukovskii's work:

> Nourished on the classics and on French literature, and on submissive imitations
> of the same ... we saw something monstrous in his [Zhukovskii's] choices.
> Corpses, visions, demons, murders by moonlight; all this belongs to the *skazki*
> and even to English novels; instead of Hero awaiting [her] drowning Leander,

---

[12] '... but if it is possible to rise from the grave, I will not frighten you, my dear friend, as a corpse. At the midnight hour of apparitions neither surreptitiously nor suddenly will I appear wailing in your house.' [The prose translations here supplied are my own: MP].

[13] 'Here is Zhukovskii, wrapped in a long shroud, his paws crossed, his feet protruding delicately, teasing the devil with his tongue. He imagines he can see a witch: he winks at her, sprinkles incense, intones the funeral service, roars, makes a great noise.' Quoted from ibid., pp. 102-3.

[14] A.I. Turgenev, *Khronika russkogo. Dnevniki (1825-1826gg.)*, Moscow-Leningrad, 1964, p.49.

he presented us with a madly passionate Lenore with her galloping corpse of a lover.[15]

Here Vigel points to the most obvious candidate for 'Gothic poem' in Zhukovskii's work, or rather to the three most obvious candidates, since Zhukovskii produced three works based on *Lenore*.

Two of them – *Svetlana* (1808-12) and *Liudmila* (1808) – are reworkings of the original, while the third, *Lenora* (1831) is a translation. *Liudmila* gave rise to a celebrated polemic in the Russian literary press when, in 1816, Petr Katenin produced yet another version of *Lenore*, this one entitled *Ol'ga*. The contestants in this debate were, on behalf of Zhukovskii, another celebrated translator, Nikolai Gnedich, and, on behalf of Katenin, the playwright Aleksandr Griboedov. Gnedich finds solecisms and vulgarisms (famously, *svoloch'*) in Katenin's Russian, whereas Griboedov, in a wonderfully witty riposte, finds that Katenin's roughhewn style is much nearer to Bürger's original and that Zhukovskii's version reduces the original to gentle sentimentality. Griboedov's preference for Katenin's poem found support from Pushkin who, reviewing Katenin's work in 1833, wrote:

> The first noteworthy work of Mr Katenin was a translation of Bürger's famous *Lenore*. This was already well known here from the inaccurate and charming imitation done by Zhukovskii, who made of it the same thing Byron made of *Faust* in his *Manfred*: he weakened the spirit and form of his model. Katenin perceived this and got the idea of showing us *Lenore* in the energetic beauty of its original creation. He wrote *Ol'ga*. But this simplicity and crudity of expression, this *scum* which replaced the *ethereal chain of shadows*, this gallows in place of rural scenes illumined by the summer moon, struck unaccustomed readers unpleasantly, and Gnedich undertook to state their opinions in an essay, the unjustness of which was exposed by Griboedov.[16]

To say, as Griboedov does, albeit in inimitable fashion, that Zhukovskii tones down Bürger's original, is to voice what has become a cliché of

---

[15] F.F. Vigel', *Zapiski*, Moscow, 1928, p.342 (reprinted by Oriental Research Partners, Cambridge, 1974). The passage can also be found in Katz, op. cit., pp. 41-2.

[16] The articles by Gnedich ('About the Free translation of Bürger's Ballad *Lenore*'), Griboedov ('Concerning the Analysis of the Translation of Bürger's Ballad, *Lenore*') and Pushkin ('The Poetic Works and Translations of Pavel Katenin') can be found in C. Rydel, editor, *The Ardis Anthology of Russian Romanticism*, Ann Arbor, Ardis, 1984, pp.386-94; 395-403; 432-3.

Zhukovskii criticism. When for example, an entirely Zhukovskian 'wilderness owl' appears in Stanza 11:

Чу! совы пустынной крики[17]

Griboedov affects surprise that the lovers should take this as a signal to depart on a nocturnal ride, commenting: 'It seems to me that the cry of owls is not alluring at all, but would have kept Liudmila from this nocturnal trip. And this *hark* is repeated too much'.

As well as adding Sentimental features to the original, in *Liudmila* Zhukovskii also eschews the Todorovian hesitation which Bürger evokes when describing his heroine's fate: she is 'zwischen Tod und Leben' – *polmertvaia* in Zhukovskii's 1831 translation – whereas in *Liudmila* she is stone dead – *mertvaia*. There is a moral to *Liudmila*: she is exhorted to 'be obedient to heaven' (stanza 6) since the complaints of mortals are pointless (stanza 21), whereas there is no explicit moralising in the German original. As for *Svetlana*, Zhukovskii prefaces the whole story with a description of fortune-telling on the Eve of Epiphany, while at the end of the poem his heroine is neither *polmertvaia* nor *mertvaia*, since the whole episode is revealed to have been a dream. The Soviet critic Ts.S. Vol'pe, writing in 1936, maintains that, by setting this frightening tale within the framework of a dream, Zhukovskii, so far from creating a Gothic ballad, was parodying the genre in general and his own *Liudmila* in particular.[18]

* * *

It is therefore more profitable to consider Zhukovskii's 1831 translation, rather than the sentimentalised *Liudmila,* in the search for a Russian Gothic poem.[19] From the very first two lines of the poem it is clear that Zhukovskii intends fear to be a major theme in the work, so much so that he uses 'terrifying' (*strashnyi*) and 'fright' (*ispug*) in places where their German equivalents are missing from the original.

---

[17] 'Hark! The cries of the wilderness owl'

[18] Quoted in Katz, p.57.

[19] Bürger's *Lenore* and Zhukovskii's *Lenora* can be found in parallel in *Zarubezhnaia poeziia v perevodakh V.A. Zhukovskogo v 2 tomakh*, edited by A.A. Gugmin, Moscow, 1985, vol. 2, pp. 26-41. All the other Zhukovskii poems referred to here can be found in V.A. Zhukovskii, *Sobranie sochinenii v chetyrekh tomakh*, Moscow-Leningrad, 1959, vol. 2.

Леноре снился страшный сон,
Проснулася в испуге.[20]

There are other examples of Zhukovskii's out-Gothicking Bürger. In stanza 2, for instance, there is blood galore in the Russian, but none in the German:

И кровь лилась, лилась... доколь
Они не помирились.[21]

In stanza 4 the cursing of God's world is confined to the Russian version:

Она свет божий прокляла.[22]

Similarly, in stanza 10, only Zhukovskii warns of the torments of hell:

Страшись мучений ада.[23]

In stanza 21, the howl of the sorrowful owl, an import from *Liudmila*, is heard only in Zhukovskii's poem: an additional Gothic feature to add to the ravens, the grave, the coffin, the tolling of the bell, and the song for the dead which occur in both the German and the Russian.

Fear and horror are undoubtedly major themes in Zhukovskii's translation of *Lenore* and, indeed, in many of Zhukovskii's forty ballads, where the words 'terror' (*strakh*), 'terrifying/terrible' (*strashnyi*), 'horror' *(uzhas)*, and 'horrifying/horrible' (*uzhasnyi*) recur frequently, as do such words as 'funereal' (*grobovoi*) and 'gloomy' (*mrachnyi*).[24] Curiously, however, while frequently describing or

---

[20] 'Lenora dreamed a terrible dream and woke up in fear.' and 'Lenore fuhr ums Mogenrot / Empor aus schweren Träumen:' (Lenore started up at dawn out of heavy dreams:); literal English translations of *Lenore* are taken from *The Penguin book of German Verse*, edited by Leonard Forster, Harmondsworth, Penguin, 1957 (revised 1959), pp. 178-90.

[21] 'And the blood flowed and flowed ... until peace was made between them.'

[22] 'She cursed God's world.'

[23] 'Beware the torments of hell.'

[24] Precise figures for *mrachnyi, strashnyi, uzhasnyi* and *grobovoi* can be found in Katz, pp. 202, 210, 216 and 228.

mentioning fear and horror, Zhukovskii does not actually induce these emotions in his readers. Bürger's German in *Lenore* is direct, earthy, and dramatic, while Zhukovskii's Russian in *Lenora* tends to the anodyne. This is particularly noticeable in the most Gothic part of the poem, Lenore's nocturnal ride with her spectral lover. Take, for instance, the line which first recurs in stanza 20 and is subsequently repeated several times:

> Hurra! die Toten reiten schnell![25]

Here Bürger uses an exclamation and an active verb. On the other hand, Zhukovskii's version

> Гладка дорога мертвецам[26]

omits the exclamation and, by resorting to the non-existent verb 'to be', considerably softens the impact of the line.

In the following stanza (21), Bürger exploits the possibilities of German word formation to produce *Totensang, Totenbahre,* and *Leichenzug* ('funeral chant', 'bier' and 'funeral procession'), thus reinforcing the grisly image of the living dead. Zhukovskii's translation, while attempting to mimic the internal rhymes of the original, is much less forceful, less dynamic, and more mellifluous:

> «Но кто там стонет? Что за звон?
>   Что ворона взбудило?
> По мертвом звон; надгробный стон;
>   Голосят над могилой».
> И виден ход: идут, поют,
> На дрогах тяжкий гроб везут,
>   И голос погребальный,
>   Как вой совы печальный.[27]

---

[25] 'Hurrah! the dead ride quickly!'
[26] 'Smooth is the road for corpses'
[27] 'But who is it groans there? What is that ringing? What has roused the raven? They are tolling the bell for a dead man. They are intoning a funeral lament over the grave. A procession comes into sight. They walk, and sing, and drag a heavy coffin on a hearse. And the voices of the burial party are like the mournful shriek of the owl.'

A comparison of Zhukovskii's translation of stanza 30 with the German original invites a similar conclusion:

> Ha sieh! Ha sieh! im Augenblick,
> Huhu! ein gräßlich Wunder!
> Des Reiters Koller, Stück für Stück,
> Fiel ab, wie mürber Zunder.
> Zum Schädel, ohne Zopf und Scopf,
> Zum nackten Schädel ward sein Kopf;
> Sein Körper zum Gerippe,
> Mit Stundenglas und Hippe.[28]

> И что ж, Ленора, что потом?
>   О страх!.. в одно мгновенье
> Кусок одежды за куском
>   Слетел с него, как тленье;
> И нет уж кожи на костьях;
> Безглазый череп на плечах;
>   Нет каски, нет колета;
>   Она в руках скелета.[29]

If further evidence is required, the reader need look no further than the final couplets of stanzas 22 and 25, where Zhukovskii's version is demure compared to the robust original, in which a bed is called a bed:

> Komm, Pfaff, und sprich den Segen,
> Eh wir zu Bett uns legen. (stanza 22)

> Tanz uns den Hochzeitreigen,
> Wann wir zu Bette steigen! (stanza 25)[30]

---

[28] 'Ah look, ah look! In that moment ugh! a gruesome miracle! The horseman's uniform, piece by piece, dropped off like rotten tinder. His head turned into a skull, a naked skull without scalp or queue; his body became a skeleton with hour-glass and scythe.'

[29] 'What, Lenora, what happened next? O dreadful sight! In an instant scraps of clothing, one after another, came off him like rotting flesh. Already there is no skin on his bones; the skull on his shoulders is eyeless; there is no helmet, no cuirass. She is in the arms of a skeleton.'

[30] 'Come, parson, and pronounce the blessing before we go to bed!'
'Dance the bridal dance for us when we get into bed!'

Bürger's bed is clearly too strong for Zhukovskii's sensibilities, and in both stanzas he omits mention of it completely:

Нам дай на обрученье,
Пастур, благословленье. (22)[31]

Скачу, лечу жениться...
Ко мне! Повеселиться! (25)[32]

Bürger's *Lenore* has enough in it of the macabre, the gruesome, the dramatic, and the shocking to be termed 'Gothic', though I have found no critic who actually uses this adjective to describe it. The anonymous author of the entry on Bürger in the fifteenth edition of the *Encyclopaedia Britannica* calls *Lenore* 'spectral', while Neil Cornwell observes that the poem 'provided European and American Gothic with the archetypal figure of the bridegroom-revenant'.[33] Because it is a translation, rather than a version, of this poem, Zhukovskii's *Lenora* is probably among the *more* abrasive of his works. Abrasiveness is not, however, a quality readily associated with Zhukovskii. In different degrees *Svetlana*, *Liudmila* and *Lenora* all tone down Bürger's original. Though Zhukovskii frequently mentions fear, he does not inspire fear in his readers, or even the *frisson* of fear, the 'sweet horror' (*sladkii uzhas*) aimed at by the followers of Karamzin, who introduced the Gothic novel into Russia. In modern terms, Zhukovskii's ghosts, corpses, demons and the like belong more to a fairground Ghost Train than to *The Texas Chainsaw Massacre*.

* * *

Among the five English versions of *Lenore* which appeared in the 1790s, the best is Walter Scott's *William and Helen* (1796). This, incidentally, transposes the action into a medieval setting, more usual for Gothic literature, whereas both *Lenore* and *Lenora* allude to the aftermath of the Battle of Prague (1744). Zhukovskii was to turn directly to Scott in his narrative poem *Underground Judgment* (*Sud v podzemel'e*), but his main inspiration in the English-speaking world was

---

[31]'Pastor, give your blessing on our betrothal.'
[32] 'I gallop, I fly to be wed... Come to me! Let us make merry!'
[33] Cornwell, *The Literary Fantastic*, p. 59.

Robert Southey. An examination of his six versions of ballads by Southey shows that, in five of them, the pattern we have seen with *Lenore* is repeated: the original poem is toned down to produce what is basically a sentimental ballad, with perhaps only one or two stanzas in each poem exhibiting familiar Gothic features.[34] A good example is his version of *The Old Woman of Berkeley. A Ballad Showing how an Old Woman Rode Double and who Rode Before her*, which bears the equally cumbersome title *Ballada, v kotoroi opisyvaetsia, kak odna starushka ekhala na chernom kone vdvoem i kto sidel vperedi.* (1814). This work has some claims to inclusion in the Gothic cannon in that it appears to have influenced the most Gothic of Gogol's stories, *Vii.* Furthermore Zhukovskii boosted the role of Satan in his version, a fact which caused difficulties with the censorship. On closer inspection, however, the same pattern emerges. Despite a liberal sprinkling of *uzhas* and *strakh* throughout the poem, only a handful of the forty-seven quatrains have the macabre Gothic quality of stanza eight:

> Здесь вместо дня была мне ночи мгла;
> Я кровь младенцев проливала,
> Власы невест в огне волшебном жгла
> И кости мертвых похищала.[35]

Zhukovskii himself seems, to judge by a comment in a letter to A.I. Turgenev, to have seen this poem as marking the end of his flirtation with the Gothic: 'Yet more devils, yet more tombs! But that's the last poem of this type. Don't get the idea that I wanted to go down in history on the basis of nothing but devils.'[36] However, he was not yet done with Gothic paraphernalia. What is more, the last of six translations from Southey exhibits enough sustained use of Gothic motifs to justify calling it a 'Gothic poem'. This is his version of the ballad *Donica* (Russian: *Donika*).[37] The original poem was published in 1797, the same year, incidentally as the culminating Gothic novel by Ann Radcliffe, *The Italian*. Zhukovskii's version appeared in 1831, the same

---

[34] See K.H. Ober and W.U. Ober, 'Zukovskij's Early Translations of the Ballads of Robert Southey', *Slavic and East European Journal*, 9, 1965, pp. 181-90.

[35] 'For me the daylight was the fog of night; I spilled the blood of infants, I burned the hair of brides with magic fire, and stole the bones of corpses.'

[36] Zhukovskii, *Sobranie sochinenii*, vol. 2, p. 456.

[37] R. Southey, *Poems*, 1797, pp.175-82 (reprinted Oxford, Woodstock Books, 1989).

year as his translation of *Lenore*. *Donika* is not as close to *Donica* as *Lenora* is to *Lenore*. Southey's castle has a name – Arkinlow – and turns out to be located in Finland, while Zhukovskii gives no clue as to the location of his ballad. Southey's suitor of the eponymous heroine has the Germanic name Eberhard (Evrar in Zhukovskii), but her father is nameless. As if to compensate for this, Zhukovskii gives him the equally Germanic name of Romuald. Zhukovskii keeps Southey's metre – iambic – and stanza length – four lines. However, whereas the odd-numbered lines in Southey are unrhymed iambic tetrameters, in Zhukovskii they are iambic pentameters with feminine endings. Otherwise Zhukovskii's poem matches Southey's poem stanza for stanza, apart from two places where he reduces a two-stanza section to one, thus reducing the overall length from twenty-nine stanzas to twenty-seven.

Throughout its twenty-seven stanzas, *Donika* appears to have most of the prerequisites for being termed 'Gothic', as laid down, for example, in Vatsuro's study of the Gothic novel in Russia.[38] The first stanza has, for instance, what Vatsuro claims is the *sine qua non* of the Gothic novel: a gloomy, ancient, and forbidding-looking castle:

> Есть озеро перед скалой огромной;
>   На той скале давно стоял
> Высокий замок и громадой темной
>   Прибрежны воды омрачал.[39]

Zhukovskii's castle is located, as in the typical Gothic novel, in the midst of an equally sinister landscape. The lake at the foot of the massive cliff on which the castle stands is an object of fear, shunned by fishermen (stanza 2) and thirsty cattle (stanza 3). It has mysterious qualities, being calm when the weather is stormy and *vice versa*. From the lake, whenever death threatens the inhabitants of the castle, comes a 'horrible whisper' (*uzhasnyi shepot*), precisely the sort of sinister sound which Walter Scott noted as an omnipresent feature of the Gothic novel. In the castle dwells the eponymous heroine of the poem and her father Romuald – a remarkably benign figure for a Gothic castle-owner.

---

[38] See Vatsuro, 1995.

[39] 'There is a lake before a huge cliff; on this cliff a tall castle has long stood and, with its huge bulk, darkened the waters by the shore.'

Donika, like all Gothic heroines, is pursued by the powers of evil, which take over her body as she walks beside the lake with her betrothed Evrar. She swoons, appears to recover, but is now a living corpse. Her father's castle, which at first seems like a place of refuge set amid a sinister landscape, now reverts to its familiar Gothic role as a place which, for all its apparent impregnability, cannot resist the forces of evil and becomes a prison for the hapless heroine-victim. During the marriage ceremony, performed in the cathedral within the castle walls, she is transformed into a 'gloomy demon' (*mrachnyi bes*) who 'gives a horrible howl, and flees' (*Uzhasno vzvyl i uletel*). '*Uzhasno*' is, of course, one of the standard clichés in the Gothic lexicon.

The appearance of this word in the last line of *Donika* is reinforced by *uzhasnyi* (stanza 4) and *uzhas* (stanza 25), as well as *strashit'sia* (stanza 2), *strakh* (stanza 12) and *strashnoe* (stanza 20), together with *pugala* (stanza 11) and *pugali* (stanza 19). The poem also contains such familiar Gothic words as *taina* (stanzas 13 and 22), *omrachal* (stanza 1), *mrachnyi* and *trup* (both stanza 27). In almost every case these are Zhukovskian embellishments on Southey's text, which contains very little of the standard Gothic lexicon. A comparison of the last quatrains of each poem serves to illustrate this:

> That instant from her earthly frame
> Howling the Daemon fled, ·
> And at the side of Eberhard
> The livid form fell dead.

> Сама ж она с ним не стояла рядом:
> Он бледный труп один узрел...
> А мрачный бес, в нее вселенный адом,
> Ужасно взвыл и улетел.[40]

Here, for example, the concept embodied by the adverb *uzhasno* is entirely absent from Southey's poem. The same is true of the other two uses of the same root *uzhasnyi* (stanza 4) and *uzhas* (stanza 25).

* * *

---

[40] 'She herself was not standing beside him: he gazed upon nothing but a pale corpse...
And a gloomy devil, placed by hell within her, howled horribly, and flew away.'

Writing in 1843,[41] Belinskii implies that Zhukovskii had gone beyond the Gothic ballad. He claims that, *before* Zhukovskii, the ballad was 'a short story about love, usually unhappy, graves, crosses, ghosts, night-time, moonlight, and sometimes *domovye* and witches'. He does, however, characterise Zhukovskii's poetry as belonging to the 'Romanticism of the Middle Ages' (*romantizm srednikh vekov*), a romanticism of gloom (*mrak*), which Europe has long since left behind. As an example of this Romanticism of the Middle Ages, Belinskii points to the ballad *Donika*, which is, indeed, a much better candidate for the title of 'Gothic' than *Lenora*. Belinskii, however, found both poems equally unsatisfactory and, at the end of his second article on Pushkin, put them in the 'weak' category – together with, among others, *Ballada, v kotoroi opisyvaetsia...* (Zhukovskii's version of *The Old Woman of Berkeley*).

Not everyone shared Belinskii's low opinion of *Donika*. When the Acmeist poet Nikolai Gumilev edited a collection of Southey's ballads (published in 1922), the poem was given pride of place, being placed second only to Gumilev's own translation of *The Surgeon's Warning* (*Predosterezhenie khirurga*).[42] Despite his low opinion of both *Donika* and *Lenora*, Belinskii was far more complimentary about *Liudmila*, which he included among numerous pieces by Zhukovskii which he described as 'completely outmoded and yet of historical interest, without which no edition of Zhukovskii's works would be complete'. In the same category he places the ballad *Gromoboi* (1810). This ballad, together with *Vadim* (1814-17), forms *The Twelve Sleeping Maidens* (*Dvenadtsat' spiashchikh dev*), described as 'an ancient tale in two ballads' (*starinnaia povest' v dvukh balladakh*). Uniquely among Zhukovskii's poems, it is based on a prose work, the novel *Die zwölf schlafenden Jungfrauen, eine Geistergeschichte* (1794-6) by Christian Heinrich Spieß. The ghost story is, of course, related to the Gothic novel, and, once again, there are Gothic elements in Zhukovskii's version of this tale of a pact with the devil. Interestingly, the section which Belinskii chooses to quote at length is the most Gothic section of

---

[41] V.G. Belinskii, *Polnoe sobranie sochinenii*, 13 vols., Moscow, 1953-59, vol. 7, pp. 132-222.

[42] Sauti [Southey], Robert, *Ballady*, St Peterburg, 1922. The collection contains three further translations by Zhukovskii: *Adel'stan*, *Sud bozhii nad episkopom*, and *Ballada, v kotoroi opisyvaetsia...* (I am indebted to Michael Basker for this information).

the poem and includes the following stanza which is replete with Gothic imagery:

И всё в ужасной тишине;
    Окрестность как могила;
Вот...каркнул ворон на стене;
    Вот... стая псов завыла;
И вдруг... протяжно полночь бьет;
    Нашли на небо тучи;
Река надулась; бор ревет;
    И мчится прах летучий.
Увы!.. последний страшный бой
    Отгрянул за горами...
Гул тише... смолк... и Громобой
    Зрит беса пред очами.[43]

* * *

Although the ballad, with its emphasis on narrative, is the obvious poetic vehicle for the Gothic, the narrative poem (*poema)* can also serve this purpose. Zhukovskii wrote relatively few of these – sixteen in all – of which one, *Sud v podzemel'e*, shows some Gothic features. Written in 1831-2 (and published in 1834), it is an abbreviated version of, rather than a translation of, the second canto of Walter Scott's *Marmion* (1808).[44] For the most part, it is a historical narrative, telling of the gathering of nuns from Whitby on the holy island of Lindisfarne. The nuns' sea journey is described and their escape from the 'stifling captivity' (*dushnyi plen*) of their monastery is echoed by hints of an escape from their vows of chastity:

У той был резвым ветерком
Покров развеян головной,
Густой шелковой струей
Лились на плечи волоса,

---

[43] 'And everything is horribly silent; the surroundings are like the grave; here a raven croaked on a wall; there a pack of dogs began to howl; and suddenly, and slowly, the clock struck midnight; clouds filled the sky; the river swelled, the forest roared, clouds of ashes rushed by. Alas! The last terrible battle has broken out beyond the mountains... The rumble is quieter, dies down, and Gromoboi sees a devil before his eyes.'

[44] See J. Reed, editor, *Sir Walter Scott: Selected Poems*, Manchester, Carcanet Press, 1992, pp. 96-115.

И груди тайная краса
Мелькала ярко меж власов,
И девственный поймать покров
Ее заботилась рука,
А взор стерег исподтишка,
Не любовался ль кто за ней
Заветной прелестью грудей.[45]

The playful eroticism of this passage is largely absent in Scott's poem, where the equivalent passage reads:

Rear'd o'er the foaming spray;
And one would still adjust her veil,
Disorder'd by the summer gale,
Perchance lest some more worldly eye
Her dedicated charms might spy;
Perchance, because such action grac'd
Her fair-turn'd arm and slender waist.
Light was each simple bosom there,
Save two, who ill might pleasure share,
The Abbess and the Novice Clare.

Indeed, the eroticism of the last three lines in Zhukovskii seems to stem from a mistranslation of the original, particularly the word 'bosom'. The poem continues in leisurely fashion, with descriptions of the abbeys of St Hilda and St Cuthbert, and a friendly debate among the two groups of nuns about the relative merits of the two saints. Then, in the eleventh section of the poem, there is a dramatic change of tone:

Так весело перед огнем
Шел о житейском, о святом
Между монахинь разговор.
А близко был иной собор,
А суд иной происходил.[46]

---

[45] 'The headwear of one was ruffled by a frisky breeze. Her thick, silky hair streamed on to her shoulders, and the secret beauty of her breast could be clearly glimpsed through her hair. Her hand was concerned to catch her maiden's veil, but her eyes watched secretly to see whether anyone was admiring the intimate charms of her breasts.'

The equivalent section – the seventeenth – in Scott reads:

> While round the fire such legends go,
> Far different was the scene of woe,
> Where, in a secret aisle beneath,
> Council was held of life and death.

The trial in question is that of a young nun who has attempted to escape from Lindisfarne to meet her lover. Her punishment, described in lingering detail fit to grace any Gothic novel, is to be immured alive in a secret underground cell in the abbey. The last six sections of the poem are replete with all the familiar Gothic vocabulary, none more so than the section twelve, in which the underground cell is described:

> Там зрелся тесный тяжкий свод;
> Глубоко, ниже внешних вод,
> Был выдоблен в утесе он;
> Весь гробовыми замощен
> Плитами пол неровный был;
> И ряд покинутых могил
> С полуистертой резьбой,
> Полузатоптанных землей,
> Являлся там; от мокроты
> Скопляясь, капли с высоты
> На камни падали; их звук
> Однообразно тих, как стук
> Ночного маятника был;
> И бледно, трепетно светил,
> Пуская дым, борясь со мглой,
> Огонь в лампаде гробовой,
> Висевшей тяжко на цепях;
> И тускло на сырых стенах,
> Покрытых плеснью, как корой,
> Свет, поглощенный темнотой,
> Туманным отблеском лежал.
> Он в подземелье озарял

---

46 'Thus the conversation of the nuns ranged merrily before the fire over the everyday and the sacred. But nearby was another cathedral and another trial was going on.'

Явленье страшное тогда.[47]

Here Zhukovskii takes twenty-three lines, against Scott's thirteen, to describe this most Gothic of locations. For all its archetypically Gothic theme – the brutal incarceration of a virgin – *Sud v podzemel'e,* like all Zhukovskii's ballads except *Donika,* cannot be regarded overall as a Gothic work. It does, however, have the distinction of containing the recorded use of the adjective *goticheskii* in Zhukovskii's work.[48] It comes in the ninth section of the poem, which records the various resting-places for St Cuthbert's mortal remains after the sack of Lindisfarne. Finally they came to rest in Durham, referred to as

Святой готический Дургам.[49]

Here Zhukovskii follows Scott, who writes of 'Durham's Gothic shade'. That Durham Cathedral, the greatest romanesque building in Britain, contains not a single Gothic arch is an irony that the only Russian poet to whom the word 'Gothic' can be meaningfully applied would surely have appreciated.

* * *

There are other isolated works by other authors which would bear investigation as Gothic poems: Meshchevskii's *Lila,* Katenin's *Ol'ga,* Pletnev's *The Gravedigger* (*Mogil'shchik,* 1820), Pushkin's *The Bridegroom* (*Zhenikh,* 1825), and Lermontov's *The Demon* (*Demon,* 1829-41). Only Zhukovskii, however, consistently introduced Gothic

---

[47] 'There could be seen a cramped, heavy vault; it had been excavated deep into the cliff, below the level of spring floods; the uneven floor was all paved with gravestones, and a line of abandoned graves appeared, half trampled into the earth, with carving half worn away; because of the dampness, drops gathered and fell on to the stones from above. Their sound was uniformly quiet, like the tick-tock of a nocturnal pendulum; the candle in the funerary icon, which hung from heavy chains, shimmered palely, and struggled with the mist; the light, swallowed by the darkness, glinted dimly, foggily, on the damp walls, which were covered with mould, as if with scabs. In the dungeon the light illuminated a terrible spectacle.'

[48] Belinskii also uses the adjective *goticheskii* in the section of his article on Pushkin which deals with Zhukovskii. Although the context is Zhukovskii's 'Romanticism of the Middle Ages', the adjective is used to describe cathedrals rather than a literary genre (Belinskii, op. cit. p.175).

[49] 'Holy Gothic Durham'

motifs into his work and, in *Donika*, produced a rare, possibly even a
unique, example of the Russian Gothic poem.

THE FANTASTIC IN RUSSIAN ROMANTIC PROSE: PUSHKIN'S *THE QUEEN OF SPADES*

CLAIRE WHITEHEAD

Introduction

In a letter dated 1880, Dostoevskii offered advice to Iu. F. Abaza on how a fantastic story ought to be written by praising the example set by Pushkin in *The Queen of Spades* (*Pikovaia dama*):

> ...the fantastic in art has its limits and its rules. The fantastic must be so close to the real that you *almost* have to believe in it [Dostoevskii's emphasis]. Pushkin, who gave us almost all artistic forms, wrote 'The Queen of Spades'- the epitome of the art of the fantastic. You believe that Hermann really had a vision, exactly in accordance with his view of the world, and yet, at the end of the tale, that is when you have read it through, you cannot make up your mind: did this vision emanate from Hermann's nature or was he really one of those who are in contact with another world, one of those evil spirits hostile to man. ... That's art for you![1]

Almost one hundred years later, Dostoevskii's insistence upon uncertainty as the key to writing fantastic stories found its echo in the work of Tzvetan Todorov. In his *Introduction à la littérature fantastique*, Todorov offers the following definition of the fantastic as it operates within literary narratives:

> In a world which is indeed our world, the world we know, without devils, sylphs or vampires, there occurs an event which cannot be explained by the laws of this same familiar world. The person who experiences this event must opt for one of two possible solutions: either it is a case of an illusion of the senses, of a product of the imagination and the laws of the world thus remain intact; or the event did actually take place, it is an integral part of reality, but this reality is governed by laws which are unknown to us. ... The fantastic occupies the duration of this uncertainty. Once we choose one or other answer,

---

[1] F.M. Dostoevskii, *Polnoe sobranie sochinenii v tridtsati tomakh*, Leningrad, 1972-90, vol. 30, kn. 1, p.192; quoted in translation from Neil Cornwell, *Pushkin's 'The Queen of Spades'*, London, Bristol Classical Press, 1993, p. 7.

we leave the fantastic for a neighbouring genre, the uncanny or the marvellous. The fantastic is the hesitation experienced by someone knowing only the rules of the natural world when they are confronted by an event which is supernatural in appearance.[2]

For Todorov, the hesitation experienced by a reader between two mutually exclusive interpretations for events described is the fundamental element in all fantastic narratives. Dostoevskii's letter reveals that the description of the dead Countess's visit to Hermann in *The Queen of Spades* causes him to hesitate between a natural explanation (the vision is a product of the protagonist's imagination) and a supernatural one (the visit did actually occur and the protagonist enjoys links with 'another world'). Transposing Todorov's definitions onto Dostoevskii's comments would lead to a classification of Pushkin's story as belonging to the category of the 'pure fantastic'. Such a classification is applied to those narratives in which no single explanation is given for apparently supernatural events and where, therefore, the hesitation of the reader remains unresolved at the end.

The appearance of Todorov's study in 1970 marked a watershed in the field of criticism of fantastic literature. It moved decisively away from the type of thematic discussions which had characterised its predecessors. Informed by a structuralist ideology, Todorov's work gives priority to the literary text and to the rules and constructs functioning within this text; it sets out, to a certain extent, the 'limits and rules' which Dostoevskii considered to be operating in the genre. By means of a quasi-scientific and systematic approach, Todorov proposes a set of three rules governing the existence of the fantastic, a set of three properties which achieve the unity of a fantastic text and, finally, a set of three functions of a fantastic text.[3] These triads of rules,

---

[2] Tzvetan Todorov, *Introduction à la littérature fantastique*, Paris, Editions du Seuil, 1970, p. 29 (for English editions, see Select Bibliography).

[3] Todorov's proposed rules governing the existence of the fantastic are: i) the text must oblige the reader to consider the characters' world as a world of living people and to hesitate between a natural and a supernatural explanation of the events described therein; ii) this hesitation can be felt equally by a character and the reader; if by a character then this hesitation becomes a theme of the work; iii) the reader must adopt a certain position as regards the text: s/he must refuse equally an allegorical and a poetic reading of the text. His three essential properties of a fantastic text are: i) a certain use of figurative or metaphorical language; the fantastic is born from taking metaphorical

properties and functions represent a valuable contribution to the critical field, as they can, and have, been used as a basic guide to the reading of fantastic narratives. However, despite the undoubted progress achieved by Todorov's work, they should be accepted neither as wholly reliable nor as exhaustive. Indeed, the purpose of the present paper is to endeavour to redress one particular shortcoming in Todorov's work through a reading of Pushkin's *The Queen of Spades*. This shortcoming appears in Todorov's first rule governing the existence of the fantastic, which states that 'the text must oblige the reader to consider the characters' world as a world of living people and to hesitate between a natural and a supernatural explanation of the events described therein'.[4]

Although Todorov clearly identifies the role of the 'implied reader'[5] in the literary contract, the statement 'the text must oblige the reader to ...' illustrates his failure to recognise the presence of a creative persona behind the fictional text. To apply Roman Jakobson's terminology, he fails to posit an addresser opposite the addressee of the message. Whilst it may be accounted for by Todorov's structuralist ideology, this failure means that insufficient attention is paid to the fundamental question of *how* hesitation is provoked. Todorov is content simply to state that 'the reader hesitates over the interpretation to be given to events', whilst ignoring the fact that, within literary discourse, each event must, necessarily, be perceived through poetic and narrative constructs selected by the implied author. It is insufficient simply to state that an event inspires hesitation; one must be aware of the techniques and stratagems at the level of discourse which contribute to the uncertainty experienced by the reader. The present paper will investigate the techniques employed by Pushkin in *The Queen of Spades* in order to

---

language literally; ii) the habitual, though not exclusive, use of a first-person narrator; iii) the presence of an ascending line of plot development where the appearance of the fantastic is the climactic point. Todorov sets out the three functions of a fantastic text as follows: i) the fantastic produces an effect on the reader that other genres are incapable of doing; ii) the fantastic serves the narrative by maintaining suspense; iii) the fantastic also serves a tautological function and thus permits the description of a fantastic universe which has no existence outside of language.

[4] Todorov, op. cit., p.37.

[5] Todorov is careful to point out that, when he talks about 'the reader', he does not mean to refer to a 'real' reader, but rather to a reader who is implicit in the text, whose role and function is encoded in the text. For Todorov's term '*le lecteur implicite*', I use the accepted formulation 'implied reader'.

plant hesitation in the mind of the reader.[6] This investigation will
borrow from the theories of discourse analysts such as Gérard Genette
and Susan Lanser. The work of these two specialists has greatly helped
to clarify the impact that the choice of narrative structures can have on
reader response. An additional but complementary aim of this paper
will be to use Pushkin's story as a testing ground for other claims made
by Todorov as to the properties and functions of the genre of the
fantastic.

1

The Queen of Spades unsettles the reader from the outset by its *in
media res* opening:

> There was a card party in the rooms of Narumov, an officer of the Horse
> Guards. The long winter night had passed unnoticed and it was after four in the
> morning when the company sat down to supper. Those who had won enjoyed
> their food; the others sat absent-mindedly in front of empty plates. But when
> the champagne appeared conversation became more lively and general.[7]

This unsettling effect can be traced to the fact that these opening lines
provide the reader with incomplete information: the reader is simply
informed that one (unspecified) day a group of (unidentified) people
were playing cards at Narumov's. Adapting ideas initially formulated by
William Labov, Mary-Louise Pratt identifies six elements which make
up every literary narrative, of which the second is what she labels the
'orientation'. According to Pratt, the orientation of a literary narrative
'serves to identify in some way the time, place, persons, and their
activity or situation, and occurs immediately before the first narrative
clause as a rule'.[8]

---

[6] For an earlier reading of *The Queen of Spades* in terms of the Todorovian fantastic,
see Cornwell, op. cit., pp. 64-5; and, more fully, in idem, *The Literary Fantastic: from
Gothic to Postmodernism*, New York and London, Harvester Wheatsheaf, 1990, pp.
113-21.
[7] Alexander Pushkin, *The Queen of Spades*, translated by Rosemary Edmonds,
Harmondsworth, Penguin, 1958, p. 153 (henceforth page numbers in the text refer to
this version). For an annotated Russian text, see A.S. Pushkin, *Pikovaya dama*, edited
by J. Forsyth, London, Bristol Classical Press, 1992.
[8] Mary-Louise Pratt, *Toward a Speech Act Theory of Literature*, Bloomington, Indiana
University Press, 1977, p. 45. In his *Language in the Inner City* (Philadelphia,

In the case of *The Queen of Spades*, the reader is provided with only limited information as regards the time, place and persons in this narrative. Alongside this insufficient orientation, a further factor unsettles the reader. The verbs in the opening two sentences (*igrali* and *seli*) appear in the plural past tense form, but each lacks an accompanying subject; the missing subject could be either 'we' (*my*) or 'they' (*oni*). The absence of this determining subject means that the reader is unable to establish clearly the nature of the relationship between the narrating voice and the speech act. Is the narrator part of the group playing cards (and thus a participating character in the story he is telling), or is he simply an outside recorder of events (a narrator who observes the other characters without interacting with them in the fictional world)? To borrow terms proposed by Susan Lanser,[9] in these opening lines the narrator could possess heterodiegetic authorisation (that is, a narrator who is not a character in the story), homodiegetic authorisation (a narrator who is also a character in the story), or autodiegetic authorisation (a narrator who is also the central protagonist of the story he tells). The opening lines of any narrative are crucial in terms of the initial impact made upon the reader and the unsettling nature of this introduction, due to incomplete information and an unidentified narrator, will have consequences which will be felt throughout the story.

The third sentence of the opening paragraph reassures the reader by resolving the ambiguity surrounding the identity of the narrating voice. The demonstrative pronouns 'those' and 'others' indicate that the narrator does not number amongst the characters he is describing. This narrator is an uninvolved recorder of the action, rather than a

---

University of Pennsylvania Press, 1972), William Labov states that a fully developed oral narrative is made up of six elements: abstract, orientation, complicating action, evaluation, resolution and coda. In her work, Pratt adapts these six elements and their definitions in order to apply them to literary, rather than oral, narratives.

[9] Susan Lanser, *The Narrative Act*, Princeton, Princeton University Press, 1981. Using the basic methodology proposed by Gérard Genette in his *Discours du récit* (in *Figures III*, Paris, Seuil, 1972), Lanser's work constructs a poetics of point of view which she describes as being: '...a structurally coherent inventory of potential properties or a set of questions to "ask" of each text' (p.112). She identifies three aspects essential to an understanding of the question of point of view: *Status* - the relation of a textual speaker to the literary act; *Contact* - the interactions between speakers and listeners; and *Stance* - the attitudes of textual personae to the represented world. The identification of the authorisation of the narrative voice is an aspect of Lanser's category of *status*.

participant in it. The identification of the narrator as possessing heterodiegetic authorisation will encourage certain expectations from the reader as to how this discourse should be related. The traditional third-person (heterodiegetic) narrator conventionally has the authority of omniscient privilege and, as an uninvolved observer of actions, is also expected to occupy a stance of objectivity as regards the message he is relating. The presence of a heterodiegetic narrator contradicts Todorov's claims for the properties of a fantastic text which he outlines in the following way:

> In fantastic stories, the narrator usually says 'I'. ... The exceptions are almost always texts which, from a variety of points of view, distance themselves from the fantastic. ... The represented narrator suits the fantastic perfectly. He is preferable to a simple character who could lie. But he is equally preferable to the non-represented narrator for two reasons. Firstly, if the supernatural event was reported to us by such a narrator, we would soon be in the genre of the marvellous. ... The second reason, which is linked directly to the definition of the fantastic, is that the first-person who 'tells' is he who most easily allows identification between the reader and the character because, as we know, the pronoun 'I' belongs to everybody.[10]

Todorov prefers the use of an autodiegetic narrator to that of a heterodiegetic narrator because the presence of this latter would lead to a story falling into the category of the marvellous, rather than the pure fantastic. This shift of categories is due to the fact that, conventionally, a reader cannot doubt the information provided by a heterodiegetic narrator and the presence of doubt is essential for the existence of the fantastic. As we shall see, however, there do exist techniques which can be used to introduce hesitation into the narrative of a heterodiegetic voice. Equally, the decision to employ a heterodiegetic voice in a narrative does not rule out the possibility of encouraging sympathy between the reader and the character.

In the opening chapters of *The Queen of Spades*, the heterodiegetic narrator does not wholly conform to the expectations concerning his authority and privilege. Following the opening descriptive lines of the story, the reader is presented with an extended period of dialogue between the card players. During this dialogue, the public narrator

---

[10] Todorov, pp.88-9.

intervenes seven times to utter a total of only twenty words. On six of these seven occasions, the narrator interrupts, simply to attribute speech to identified characters, and on only one of these does he provide any additional information: '...exclaimed one of the party, pointing to a young officer of the Engineers' (p. 153).

However, other parts of direct speech remain unattributed by the narrator. The result of such non-attribution is two-fold: on the one hand it renders the speech more 'free', and so gives the reader a greater sense of mimesis, but it also demands a greater degree of active participation on the part of the implied reader in order to reconstruct the correct flow of the dialogue. The effort required of the reader is further increased due to the fact that he knows almost nothing of the characters involved in this dialogue. Coupled with the minimal information conveyed in the orienting paragraph, the presence of unattributed dialogue forces the reader into a position of much greater participation than might be conventionally expected. The minimal presence of the voice of the heterodiegetic narrator persists as Tomskii recounts the anecdote concerning his grandmother and her gambling.

According to the model proposed by Susan Lanser, Tomskii must be considered a 'private narrator'[11] for the duration of his telling of the anecdote. A private narrator occupies a narrative level immediately below that of the public narrator and is capable of addressing only those characters within the confines of the fictional world. Whilst private narrators may be taken as displaying a greater degree of mimetic power than the public narrator, they are considered to enjoy a lesser degree of authority. Tomskii is a character (and narrator) bound to the story world as an actor, and this means that his narrative act is subject to limitation and bias.[12]

---

[11] In her discussion of narrative levels, Lanser distinguishes three levels of persona in addition to the extrafictional voice, whose consciousness may participate in the organisation of the narrative: public narrator, private narrator and focalisor. Lanser clarifies the second of these personae in the following terms: 'The private narrator is usually a character in the text, bound to the fictional world, and dependent upon the existence of that world for his or her authorisation to speak. The private narrator is frequently delineated for us by a public narrator or by other characters [...]; because it forms part of the fictional situation, the immediate communicating context of the private narrator is more easily represented in the text than is the context of the public voice.'

[12] In her *Narratology: Introduction to the Theory of Narrative* (translated by Christine van Boheemen, Toronto, Toronto University Press, 1985), Mieke Bal classifies the type of narrators, using terms distinct from those employed by Genette and Lanser. Bal

What is ironic during the telling of the anecdote, however, is that Tomskii is revealed as a seemingly more reliable and accomplished narrator than the story's public narrator. Tomskii clearly announces the beginning of his tale with the request: 'Well, listen then' (p. 154), after which his voice dominates the narrative for the following three pages. In his telling of the tale, Tomskii identifies for his listeners the historical and geographical location of the action, provides identities and names for the participating characters and, through reference to actual historical figures (the Duc d'Orléans, Richelieu, and the Count Saint-Germain), he makes explicit claims for the truth of his story. All of these represent criteria not fulfilled by the public narrator at the beginning of *The Queen of Spades*. The provision of this informative orientation means that the reader does not need to work as hard to make sense of Tomskii's tale as he has had to in the opening paragraphs of the story. The opening of the story has been unsettling for the reader, but there is a distinct change in tone and nature when the voice of the public narrator is replaced with that of a private one. Whilst we are still at a very early stage of the narrative, the implied reader is being made wary of the reliability of the public narrator; doubts are being instilled that may have important consequences at a later stage.

The reader's expectations concerning the conventional authority of the public narrator begin to be fulfilled during the second chapter. This chapter opens with a scene in the dressing room of Tomskii's grandmother, the Countess ***, and the public narrator describes her personality thus:

> The countess had not the slightest pretensions to beauty – it had faded long ago – but she still preserved all the habits of her youth, followed strictly the fashion of the seventies, and gave as much time and care to her toilette as she had sixty years before. (p. 157)

Such commentary clearly shows that the knowledge possessed by the public narrator extends far beyond what is simply observable from an external perspective. The provision of such additional information and

---

prefers to distinguish between external narrators (EN) and those which are character-bound (CN): that is they not only narrate, but also act within the story world. Unlike external narrators, character-bound narrators are subject to bias and limitation, particularly affecting their focalisation but which must also extend to their narrative acts.

commentary is a capability of this narrator that has been missing during the opening chapter. As well as displaying a more extensive knowledge, the public narrator also provides the reader with clear proof of his omniscient privilege.

During the course of attributing the dialogue between Tomskii and his grandmother, the narrator comments: 'The girl at the window raised her head and made a sign to the young man. He remembered that they concealed the deaths of her contemporaries from the old countess, and bit his lip' (p. 158). He thus clearly displays his ability to gain direct access into the minds of the characters inhabiting the fictional world. The combination of this display of omniscience and the additional commentary upon the Countess means that the narrator now conforms more closely to the expectations for his role held by the implied reader. The reader's confidence in the competence of the public narrator is further encouraged by a subtle change in the phraseology employed. For example, following an exchange between the Countess and Lizaveta as they are preparing to go out in the carriage, the narrator intercedes in order to offer his own explicit judgement of the ward's situation: 'Indeed, Lizaveta Ivanovna was a most unfortunate creature' (p. 160). The qualifying phrase 'indeed' (*v samom dele*) displays an authority and conviction which has not previously been a trait of this narrator. The impression given of the narrator's superior knowledge is reinforced by the presence of 'certainly' in the statement: 'The countess was certainly not bad-hearted ...' (ibid.), as well as the use of generalisations such as: 'like all old people...' (ibid.).

The section of dialogue which precedes these comments has illustrated the situation between the Countess and Lizaveta, but the narrator now interjects to help guide the reader's reactions by providing his own judgement. This type of authoritative statement, which gives a relatively objective judgement of the situation, is far more in line with the expectations placed upon a narrator recording actions from an external perspective.

However, the narrator's display of knowledge and omniscience, along with his increasing use of authoritative terminology, does not mean that all questions concerning his reliability are resolved. For instance, during the exchanges between Tomskii and Lizaveta, the reader is intrigued by the latter's questions concerning the identity of Tomskii's friend. During this discussion, the voice of the public narrator is completely withdrawn (the parts of speech are left unattributed) and, when it does reappear, it provides only minimal information of the type found in the opening chapter: 'The girl laughed and made no answer' (p. 158). If the omniscient privilege previously displayed by the narrator is to be believed, he must be in possession of knowledge concerning both the identity of the friend and the reason for Lizaveta's particular interest. The failure on the part of the narrator to provide this information has two particular consequences: firstly, the interest of the reader is further provoked; and secondly, the reader is reminded that this narrator does not uniformly fulfil his contract of providing full and reliable information.

The inconsistent omniscience of the public narrator in the opening chapters of *The Queen of Spades*, coupled with the use of a private narrator who appears more reliable, illustrates how, contrary to Todorov's claims, hesitation can indeed be introduced into a story guided by a heterodiegetic voice. We will now see how Pushkin manages to overcome the second problem that Todorov considers as arising in stories narrated by a heterodiegetic narrator: namely, the difficulty in encouraging sympathy between the fictional characters and the implied reader. Following the exchanges between the Countess and Lizaveta in chapter two, the heterodiegetic narrator's voice returns to the fore to comment upon the ward's situation and to lead the narrative back to a point one week before the previous scene:

> ... one morning Lizaveta Ivanovna, sitting at her embroidery-frame by the window, happened to glance out into the street and see a young Engineers officer standing stock-still gazing at her window. She lowered her head and went on with her work. Five minutes afterwards she looked out again – the young officer was still on the same spot. [...] She got up to put away her embroidery-frame and, glancing casually into the street, saw the officer again. This seemed to her somewhat strange. (pp. 161-2)

The above passage reveals the telling technique of shifting the narrating focalisation between the public narrator and the fictional character, in this case Lizaveta. During the opening pages of the story, despite illustrations of the narrator's omniscient privilege, descriptions have generally been restricted to that which can be externally observed. In this passage there is a switch between what the narrator presents as observable and what is visualised by Lizaveta as she sits at the window. These switches in focalisation are signalled by the repetition (on three occasions) of the verb *vzglianut'* ('to look') in the original, after which the reader is presented with a scene as observed by the character. The switches in focalisation mean that the reader is informed only of what is known and seen by the character; the more knowledgeable perspective of the narrator is withdrawn. Therefore, the reader is told that a young officer stands below the window, but because his identity is not presently known to Lizaveta (it may or may not be known to the narrator), it is not revealed to the reader.

In the closing lines of the second chapter, a further switch in focalisation to the perspective of Hermann is signalled by the verbs of observation (*smotret'* and *uvidel*), as he arrives outside the Countess's house. All observations which follow this introductory verb clearly come from the perspective of the character, rather than that of the narrator: 'In one of them he saw a dark head probably bent over a book or some needlework. The head was raised. Hermann caught sight of a rosy face and a pair of black eyes. That moment decided his fate' (p. 164). This same scene has already been narrated from the perspective of the public narrator and of Lizaveta. Therefore, the reader knows whose head Hermann is observing and that Lizaveta is not bending over a book, but over her embroidery. The presence of the modalising phrase 'probably' is a clear signal that the perspective belongs to the character observing from the street with a limited perspective.

The result of these switches in the narrative point of view is to give the implied reader the impression of being in closer contact with the characters in the fictional world. During such shifts, the public narrator can be said to be inhabiting the medium of the focalising character in order to give the reader the impression of being, as Susan Lanser would say, 'on the scene' or 'in the mind' of the character. By placing the implied reader in closer contact with the characters in the fictional world, the strategy of shifts in focalisation encourages sympathy between the two.

These shifts in point of view also create a potential problem for the implied reader. In both of the above examples, despite the fact that the narrating perspective shifts, the narrating voice remains that of the public narrator. While the fictional character focalises, s/he does not report these perceptions directly in his or her own voice. On both occasions, the sustained presence of the voice of the public narrator leads to what can be referred to as instances of dual voice. In *The Queen of Spades*, the intermittent presence of dual voice causes particular difficulties when the implied reader is confronted with modalisation phrases such as 'it seemed', or 'as though' (*kazalos'*). In the description of Lizaveta first spotting the engineer gazing up at her window, the phrase '[t]his seemed to her somewhat strange' (p. 162) does not cause any difficulty, because it can clearly be identified as a statement from the narrator illustrating his ability to gain direct access to the thoughts of this character. However, a little later, the reader encounters the statement: 'The young man seemed to be grateful to her for looking out ...' (ibid.). In this case, it is difficult to state definitively whether the statement should be attributed to the perspective of the narrator or to that of the character. What can be said is that this modalisation phrase should not come from the public narrator: having established his omniscient privilege, nothing should 'seem' to this narrator. The presence of such a modalisation phrase contravenes the expectations concerning this narrator's ability to give full and reliable information.

This same problem arises a little further on in the story, in the description of Hermann's second arrival outside the Countess's house. The reader encounters the statement: 'It was as though some supernatural force drew him there' (p. 164). Again, because of the confusion of dual voice, it is difficult confidently to attribute this 'as though' either to the fictional character or to the public narrator. The lack of an attributing 'to him' (*emu*) in both of these cases is crucial. The use of this type of modalisation phrase clashes with the assured phraseology, such as 'certainly' and 'in fact', which has been encountered earlier. The difficulty in assigning such modalisation phrases to one definitive source, and the subsequent inability to believe (or not) in the existence of the 'supernatural force', leads to uncertainty and hesitation for the reader.

2

The preceding discussion – of the initial difficulty in identifying the narrative voice, the inconsistent omniscience of this narrating voice, and the switches in narrative focalisation leading to instances of dual voice – clearly illustrates that Todorov's dismissal of heterodiegetic narration as unsuitable for fantastic stories is hasty. Such strategies succeed in introducing an uncertainty which might not normally be expected to be found in a heterodiegetic narrative. Equally, the shifts in point of view facilitate the identification between the implied reader and the characters, which Todorov considers much easier to achieve in a text narrated by a first-person narrator. However, although uncertainty and hesitation are introduced in the opening chapters of *The Queen of Spades*, we have not yet encountered any direct intervention of the supernatural which will illustrate more clearly the type of techniques employed in fantastic stories. The fifth chapter of Pushkin's story is the most important in terms of the investigation into narrative techniques provoking hesitation. This chapter, like all the others in this story, is preceded by an epigraph, this time attributed to Swedenborg, which states:

> *That night the dead Baroness von W. appeared before me. She was all in white and said: 'How do you do, Mr. Councillor?'* (p. 176)

The story's third chapter has described the unexpected death of the Countess, when Hermann confronts her and demands to be told the secret gambling formula. The fact that this epigraph refers to the ghostly visitation of a dead woman dressed 'all in white' arouses an expectation in the reader that some event linked to ghostly visits will be described. By its mention of supernatural events, this epigraph recalls the one preceding the entire story: '*The queen of spades betokens the evil eye – Modern Guide to Fortune-Telling.*' Therefore, this fifth chapter opens with a clear encouragement to the reader to expect the incursion of the irrational into the world of the rational.

The chapter begins with the public narrator providing a clear and precise temporal location for the action taking place. He declares: 'Three days after that fatal night, at nine o'clock in the morning, Hermann repaired to the Convent of ***, where the last respects were to be paid to the mortal remains of the dead countess' (ibid.). Such concrete information has been missing from the previous chapters, even when switches in temporal location have been effected. This explicit reference to concrete time contrasts strongly with the suggestion in the epigraph of the appearance of the supernatural. Such references to time serve to anchor events firmly in the rational world by employing a scheme recognisable to, and shared by, all readers. In addition to this temporal reference, the opening lines of the chapter provide a simple and straightforward summary of plot details, which clearly locate the reader in the time-line of the *fabula*. The voice of the heterodiegetic narrator is once again to the fore, providing an impersonal narration of concrete facts and information. The reader's confidence in the narrator is further encouraged when the latter exercises his omniscient privilege, in order to provide an insight into Hermann's psychological state at this moment: 'Though he felt no remorse he could not altogether stifle the voice of conscience which kept repeating to him: "You are the old woman's murderer!"' (ibid.).

There is a clear discrepancy between the impression created by the chapter's epigraph and that of the opening lines. Unsurprisingly, however, for this narrator, the situation is not as straightforward as it may initially seem. Whilst the opening lines reassure the reader as to the narrator's competence, and provide a description of a recognisable reality, they also prepare the ground for the appearance of the supernatural. The narrator gives an explicit commentary on the character of Hermann and on the type of beliefs that he holds: 'Having very little religious faith, he was exceedingly superstitious. Believing that the dead countess might exercise a malignant influence on his life, he decided to go to her funeral to beg and obtain her forgiveness' (ibid.).

Taken with the chapter's epigraph, this commentary provokes an even greater level of expectation of the appearance of the fantastic. The voice of highest authority within this discourse characterises the protagonist as a man possessing many superstitious beliefs, including one which states that a dead woman is able to exert an influence upon his life from beyond the grave. Despite the fact that the narrator does not offer any judgement on the beliefs of the protagonist, the fact of their being stated further encourages the reader's belief that the supernatural will make an appearance.

Indeed, the reader does not have to wait long to see this expectation fulfilled. The narrator describes how Hermann approaches the Countess's coffin:

> He knelt down on the cold stone strewed with branches of spruce fir, and
> remained in that position for some minutes; at last he rose to his feet and, pale
> as the deceased herself, walked up the steps of the catafalque and bent over the

corpse ... At that moment it seemed to him that the dead woman darted a
mocking look at him and winked her eye. (p. 177)

These lines illustrate how this first long-awaited direct appearance of
the fantastic is communicated in the space of a single statement.
Throughout its length, Pushkin's story is characterised by a brevity of
expression which is maintained even when the fantastic is introduced.
The impact of this event is increased precisely because its description is
so short-lived, lasting no longer than the wink of the Countess's eye.
The description of the Countess winking at Hermann causes the implied
reader to hesitate. The reader hesitates because, clearly, the fact of a
dead woman winking cannot be explained by the rules operating in the
rational world. Such things do not take place in our familiar world. The
reader is confronted with a dilemma: does this dead woman actually
wink at Hermann, or is there some other explanation for what happens?
For Todorov, the recognition of this event as apparently contradicting
the rules of the rational world, and as presenting an ambiguity of
interpretation, would be sufficient for the story to broach his category
of the pure fantastic. It is possible, however, to identify other
techniques over and above the simple description of events which
contribute to the uncertainty experienced by the reader.

It is the inclusion of three particular narrative techniques which
means that the reader hesitates, not simply because a supernatural event
is described but because the description itself may be untrustworthy.
The first of these techniques has already been touched upon: shifts in
the narrative point of view. During the description of Hermann kneeling
on the floor and then approaching the coffin, the point of focalisation is
alongside him but, importantly, still external to the character. This
perspective is clearly illustrated by the fact that the reader is only
supplied with a description of the coffin once Hermann has succeeded
in breaking through the crowd which surrounds it: 'The church was
full. Hermann had difficulty in making his way through the crowd. The
coffin rested on a rich catafalque beneath a canopy of velvet' (p. 176).
Crucially, however, the suspension points which separate 'bent over the
corpse' and 'at that moment' in the lines quoted earlier signal a further
shift in focalisation. This shift moves the experiencing perspective from
a position alongside but external to the protagonist to one which is
more internal. This switch to a perspective closely associated with the
protagonist will necessarily have an effect on the type of information

being supplied to the reader. The reader must now recognise that information is being supplied by a character directly involved in the action, whose observations are constrained by human limitations, and who possesses less authority in the text than the public narrator. The reader undoubtedly hesitates when told that the dead countess in the coffin winks at Hermann; however, the fact that this event is described from a perspective internal to an experiencing character means that the reader cannot be sure of the complete reliability of the information.

The fact of the introduction of an apparently supernatural event, however, is not the sole reason for reader hesitation. The reliability of information is further called into question by the presence of the modalisation phrase 'it seemed to him'. The presence of this modalisation phrase clearly tells the reader that it only *seemed* to Hermann that the dead Countess winked at him, not that the Countess *did* wink at him. Because of the additional 'to him' in this modalisation phrase, there can be no confusion as to whether it 'seemed' to the protagonist or to the narrator that the dead Countess winks at Hermann. However, the ease in identifying the source of this modalisation phrase still raises an interesting question as to the degree of hesitation provoked: does the fact that this phrase comes from the consciousness of the protagonist create more or less hesitation than if it came from the narrator? The reader hesitates when this event is described, not simply because it contravenes the rules governing the rational world, but also because its description is clearly indefinite and incomplete. In order to resolve the uncertainty surrounding this event, the reader is in need of further information from the highest authority within the text: from the public narrator.

The third reason contributing to the hesitation provoked during this passage is precisely the lack of any such additional information. Following the single-sentence description of the Countess's wink, the internal perspective of the protagonist is replaced by a more external viewpoint (typical of the public narrator) which provides a 'bird's eye' view of the scene in the church:

> Hermann drew back, missed his footing and crashed headlong to the floor. They picked him up. At the same time Lizaveta Ivanovna was carried out of the church in a swoon. This incident momentarily upset the solemnity of the mournful rite. (p. 177)

The external perspective is clearly illustrated by the fact that, at this point, the narrating voice is able to describe two events occurring simultaneously in different parts of the church. This type of observation would not be possible from the point of view of a character directly involved in the action, and shows that a perspective enjoying omniscient privilege is now guiding the reader. The return of the less limited perspective of the public narrator encourages the reader to expect the additional information necessary to decide between a natural or supernatural interpretation for the Countess's wink. However, as the above lines illustrate, the public narrator seems to ignore this event, fails to provide any of the desired information, and chooses instead to report an absurd conversation concerned with the possibility that Hermann is the Countess's illegitimate son. By failing to provide the reader with helpful additional information, the narrator guarantees that the hesitation provoked by this event is not only not resolved, but sustained.

The second direct appearance of the fantastic follows closely on the heels of the first, separated by only one paragraph. This paragraph, however, is of importance for the interpretation of the fantastic events which follow it:

> The whole of that day Hermann was strangely troubled. Repairing to a quiet little tavern to dine, he drank a great deal of wine, contrary to his habit, in the hope of stifling his inner agitation. But the wine only served to excite his imagination. Returning home, he threw himself on his bed without undressing, and fell heavily asleep. (ibid.)

These lines represent a pre-emptive potential explanation for the apparently supernatural events described in the remainder of this fifth chapter. By describing the heavy drinking bout upon which Hermann embarks, the narrator is providing what could be viewed as a rational explanation for the visit of the dead Countess: Hermann is not actually visited by the dead woman, but simply experiences a drunken hallucination. This description in no way resolves the hesitation experienced previously, nor does it preclude the reader hesitating during the second appearance of the fantastic. This limited impact is due to the fact that the description is pre-emptive and is never explicitly signalled as being the reason for Hermann's vision. During the description of Hermann's drinking, his return home and falling asleep, the voice of the public narrator is at the forefront of the discourse. What is perhaps most crucial is that the narrator also describes the fact that Hermann does wake up:

> It was night when he woke and the moon was shining into his room. He glanced at the time: it was a quarter to three. Sleep had left him; he sat on the bed and began thinking of the old countess' funeral. (ibid.)

The fact that this information is provided by the narrator means that the reader will believe it to be truthful and reliable. The reader should not doubt that the events which follow occur when the protagonist is awake; they are not part of a dream. Any reader who attributes what happens to the protagonist's dreamworld is contradicting the explicit indications provided by the narrator. We have noted earlier the impact of references to concrete time and this is a technique employed once again as the narrator notes the exact time at which Hermann wakes up. The impression of a rational atmosphere pervading this scene is reinforced by the measured construction of the sentences in the above lines. In the original Russian, this paragraph contains three sentences, each of which is divided in half by a colon. In her translation, Rosemary Edmonds replaces the first of these with the conjunction 'and', maintains the second, and replaces the third with a semi-colon. As Heidi Faletti remarks during a discussion of the technique of parataxis, '[t]he use of a colon is especially forceful and points to the immediate consequence of an incident or the effect of an event or perception on a character.'[13] The causal link between the two halves of the sentences (highlighted by this strong punctuation) must be considered to be a narrative technique intended to represent the predominance of the rational world at this point in the scene. The actions or facts described in the second half of each of the sentences are natural and logical consequences of those described in the first half. It is precisely the lack of causal links between events that characterises the world of the irrational. Despite the hesitation provoked by the description of events at the funeral, the narrator is persuading the reader to believe in the reality of this scene.

---

[13] Heidi Faletti, 'Remarks on Style as Manifestation of Narrative Technique in *The Queen of Spades*', *Canadian-American Slavic Studies*, 11, 1, 1977, pp. 114-33 (115).

The description of the second appearance of the fantastic employs certain of the same techniques noted as being used in the funeral scene. In particular, this similarity holds for the technique of shifting the point from which the events of the narrative are focalised. The Russian critic N.K. Gei contends that, in the paragraph following the description of Hermann waking up, there is a two-fold shift in focalisation.[14] The first shift is in the visual perspective guiding the narrative and is effected in the following sentence: 'Just then someone in the street looked in at him through the window, and immediately walked on' (pp. 177-8). This sentence clearly shifts the point of focalisation away from that of the public narrator to a point located inside the room and alongside Hermann. As was the case for the description of the Countess's wink, the reader is now experiencing the scene from a visual perspective identical to that of the protagonist. Accompanying the shift in visual focalisation, there is also a shift in audible perspective signalled in the following sentence: 'A moment later he heard the door of his ante-room open' (p. 178). The implied reader is now in the position of experiencing events at the same time and from a similar location as the protagonist. According to Gei, these shifts in the perspective of the narrative last throughout the reporting of the fantastic event until the reversing of the actions signalling the shift are described. That is, the visual and audible perspectives move back to the narrator following this sentence: 'Hermann heard the street-door click and again saw someone peeping in at him through the window' (ibid.).

Despite these shifts in perspective, the language employed during these lines still belongs to the public narrator. As in the description of the Countess's wink, the reader is confronted with a narrative in which both narrator and protagonist are present as informing personae. Gei notes this fact and comments that: 'The confusion of the narrator's and the character's narrating perspective, allowing the ambivalence of the obvious and the improbable, gives rise to deepened and graphically expressive narrative levels'.[15]

Following the paragraph containing the three sentences of measured construction, the narrative moves onto a much less secure footing. The paragraph describing the entry into Hermann's bedroom of a figure

---

[14] N.K. Gei, *Proza Pushkina: Poetika povestvovaniia*, Moscow, 1983.
[15] Gei, p. 189.

eventually identified as the dead Countess succeeds in making the reader experience a strong sense of hesitation. As in the first appearance of the fantastic, this hesitation can be traced to three major narrative reasons above and beyond the simple description of an irrational event. The first of these is the repeated use of indefinite pronouns. During the four paragraphs which complete this fifth chapter, the reader is confronted by the use of the indefinite pronoun 'somebody' on three occasions. The first occasion has been noted above in the sentence which shifts the visual perspective ('someone in the street'). The second occurs six lines later in the sentence: 'But he heard an unfamiliar footstep: someone was softly shuffling along the floor in slippers' (ibid.). The third appears in the sentence quoted above, which shifts the narrative perspective back to the public narrator. The repeated use of this indefinite pronoun forms a strong contrast with the straightforward information provided in the paragraph beginning 'he woke up' and undoubtedly introduces a feeling of hesitation. This use is justified by the fact that the narrating perspective belongs to Hermann, who is placed in the room, and because of his limited perspective he cannot be aware of the identity of the persons performing the actions. The use of the indefinite pronoun proves to be an effective tool for the introduction of hesitation precisely because it thwarts the reader's desire and need to possess full knowledge of scenes and events. The indefinite pronoun is typical of fantastic discourse which, as Rosemary Jackson suggests, often presents its readers with 'objects or characters which are either nameless or unnameable'.[16]

The lack of identity given to the person performing the actions during this scene is further reinforced by the use of two verbs with passive force. The first appears in the third sentence of the paragraph beginning '[a]t that moment' and states: 'A moment later he heard the door of his ante-room open' (ibid.: *chto otpirali dver'*); and the second occurs only four lines later as the unidentified figure enters Hermann's bedroom: 'The door opened and a woman in white came in' (ibid.: *dver' otvorilas'*). Verbs in their passive form represent a telling narrative construct in the provocation of hesitation, because they describe actions without revealing the identity of the performer. In the second example, the use of the reflexive form gives the impression that

---

[16] Rosemary Jackson, *Fantasy: The Literature of Subversion*, London, Methuen, 1981, p. 40.

the door opens of its own accord, that the action is performed by the object itself. This technique complements the use of the indefinite pronoun by describing actions whilst leaving their performers unidentified. The combined effect of the presence of indefinite pronouns and verbs in the passive form is that of providing the reader with an uncertain and imprecise description, in clear contrast to the assured information previously supplied. The use of these two techniques leads to what could be referred to as a gap in cognition, where the reader is prevented from being able to make a definite connection between the actions described and the identity of their performers. This lack of identity is unsettling because it flouts the norms which operate in 'realist' discourse and which inspire a reader with confidence. According to Philippe Hamon, '[i]n the realist programme the world is describable, open to denomination', and realist discourse is 'characterised by a marked redundancy and foreseeability of its content'.[17]

At this stage, *The Queen of Spades* is presenting the reader with a world in which objects and characters are not open to denomination and it is this which makes him/her hesitate. Along with the use of indefinite pronouns, this decision to employ verbs with passive force is explained by the switch in narrative perspective. The reader is being informed of events from a point of focalisation alongside the protagonist inside the room: the fact that Hermann cannot see who opens the door means that the reader cannot be informed of it.

A third and final reason contributing to the hesitation experienced by the reader during this description is one already noted in our discussion of the first appearance of the fantastic. Because of the limited perspective during the description of the Countess's appearance, the reader is left in need of further information from an authoritative source – if he/she is to resolve the ambiguity and choose one interpretation over another. Following the departure of the Countess, the perspective of the public narrator returns to the fore. However, as earlier, the narrator fails to provide any of the necessary additional information and simply contents himself with a description of Hermann's actions following the visitation:

---

[17] Philippe Hamon, 'Un discours contraint', *Poétique*, 16, 1973, pp. 411-45 (422).

> It was a long time before he could pull himself together and go into the next room. His orderly was asleep on the floor: Hermann had difficulty in waking him. The man was drunk as usual: there was no getting any sense out of him. The street-door was locked. Hermann returned to his room and, lighting a candle, wrote down all the details of his vision. (ibid.)

The narrator is, presumably, in a position to give the reader more information which could help decide if Hermann was actually visited by a ghost, or whether the vision was simply a product of his imagination. However, the narrator does not do so, either here or at any other point in the remainder of the story. What these lines do contain is a reference to what has just happened as a 'vision' and, by mentioning the fact that the door is locked, the narrator does implicitly state that the figure Hermann has seen cannot be his batman. Nevertheless, this inference is not sufficiently explicit to indicate definitively the presence of either the natural or the supernatural. The narrator fails to help the reader solve the ambiguity between the (at least) two possible interpretations and so, as this fifth chapter closes, the hesitation remains.

Conclusion

The final chapter of the story describes how Hermann puts the gambling formula revealed to him by the Countess into action. On three consecutive evenings Hermann visits the gambling tables of Chekalinskii: on the first evening he plays the three and it wins; on the second evening he plays the seven which also wins; on the third evening Hermann believes he has played the winning ace, only to discover that he has, in fact, laid the queen of spades and lost all his money. *The Queen of Spades* ends with a brief epilogue providing the reader with information concerning the fates of Hermann, Lizaveta, and Tomskii, but with none which could help to dispel hesitation. As the story closes, the hesitation provoked by the description of events which contradict the rules operating in the rational world has not been resolved. The continued presence of hesitation in the mind of the reader means that Pushkin's story, as suggested by Dostoevskii in his letter, must belong to what we now understand as Todorov's category of the pure fantastic. The reader of the story is unable to opt confidently either for a rational explanation for events, which would place it in the category of the 'uncanny', or to give a definitive supernatural interpretation, which would place it in the category of the 'marvellous'.

It is hoped that this paper has succeeded in illustrating that it is indeed possible to investigate, on a narrative level, how hesitation is planted in the mind of the reader of Pushkin's *The Queen of Spades*. Whilst Todorov's study of the fantastic represented an invaluable leap forward in this particular field of criticism, its failure to address the question of *how* left further work to be done. This can be undertaken by a close reading of any fantastic short story, paying close attention to the types of narrative technique employed. Todorov's desire to provide readers with neat patterns and easily digestible rules also meant that certain aspects and characteristics of the genre were oversimplified. Our reading of Pushkin's story has clearly illustrated how the introduction of hesitation into a narrative guided by a heterodiegetic voice is far from impossible. Indeed, the techniques used to overcome the restraints imposed by the conventions of a heterodiegetic voice may well make such stories richer in their artistry. The identification of the types of technique employed to introduce ambiguity and uncertainty clearly shows the insufficiency of merely stating that 'a narrative event inspires hesitation'. Experiencing an event in a fictional text is very different from doing so in the real world. How a reader reacts to and interprets an event in a story is wholly determined by the poetic structures employed by the storytelling voice. In *The Queen of Spades* Pushkin demonstrates that the techniques of switches in point of view, the exploitation of indefinite pronouns, and the absence of customary additional commentary can be used as devices to unsettle and to remove the reader's ability to provide definitive explanations. As Dostoevskii had declared, 'you cannot make up your mind'.

PHILOSOPHICAL TALE OR GOTHIC HORROR STORY? THE STRANGE CASE OF V.F. ODOEVSKII'S *THE COSMORAMA*

ROGER COCKRELL

For anyone investigating V.F. Odoevskii's *The Cosmorama* (*Kosmorama*), one of the most immediately striking points about the story is its relative 'invisibility'. When it was first published in 1840[1] it seems to have attracted little response, apart from that of an anecdotal nature.[2] Even the prolific Belinskii – who from 1840 to 1846 was the chief literary critic of *The Notes of the Fatherland* (*Otechestvennye zapiski*), the journal of which Odoevskii himself was one of the editors and in which *The Cosmorama* had first appeared – refers to the story only in passing, amongst a list of other works which had come to his attention.[3] As if to reinforce the notion that this was not really a literary work worth discussing, *The Cosmorama* was never republished until the very end of the Soviet period.[4] In these circumstances it is hardly surprising that, during this gap of one and a half centuries, the story has

---

[1] 'Kosmorama', *Otechestvennye zapiski*, 1, VIII, 3 (1840), pp. 34-81.
[2] See, for example, Neil Cornwell, *The Life, Times and Milieu of V.F. Odoyevsky*, London, Athlone, 1986, p. 269 (all subsequent references will be to Cornwell, *Odoyevsky*).
[3] V.G. Belinskii ('Russkaia literatura v 1840 godu'), *Polnoe sobranie sochinenii*, 13 vols, Moscow, 1953-59, vol. 4, p. 441.
[4] 'Kosmorama', which had been omitted even by Odoevskii himself from his 3-volumed *Sochineniia* (St Petersburg, 1844), was finally reprinted in V.F. Odoevskii, *Povesti i rasskazy*, Moscow, 1988. It also appeared in the anthology *Russkaia i sovetskaia fantastika*, Moscow, 1989, pp. 175-224, from which edition page references here are supplied in the text. It now enjoys greater availability than ever before, with the publication of a student edition: V.F. Odoevskii, *Kosmorama / The Cosmorama*, edited by Roger Cockrell, London, Bristol Classical Press, 1998. For an English translation, see Vladimir Odoevsky, *The Salamander and Other Gothic Tales*, translated by Neil Cornwell, London, Bristol Classical Press, 1992, pp. 89-132.

featured relatively rarely in either Russian or Western literary criticism.[5]

A number of critical works dealing with themes which are directly relevant to Odoevskii's story either ignore it or cursorily dismiss it. Although, for example, *The Cosmorama* contains a specific, if somewhat cryptic, reference to Goethe's *Faust*, it is not even mentioned by André von Gronicka in his two-volumed study of Goethe's place in Russian literature and thought.[6] Again, in his chapter on the Russian short story from 1830 to 1850, Victor Terras, as might be expected, writes at some length on Odoevskii's collection of stories *Russian Nights* (*Russkie nochi*), which he describes as 'the chef d'oeuvre of Russian philosophic romanticism',[7] but the closest he apparently comes to *The Cosmorama* is his remark that 'Odoevsky wrote a number of stories not included in *Russian Nights*. Most of these are totally Hoffmannesque and not very good'.[8] As if in direct contradiction of this assertion Charles E. Passage had stated categorically that Odoevskii 'never wrote a Hoffmannian story', and that 'the revelations of the Cosmorama, in so far as we learn of them, are figments of a philosophy' to which 'Hoffmann contributed nothing at all'.[9] In such examples *The Cosmorama* is, somewhat frustratingly, an absent

---

[5] It has not of course been ignored entirely. See: Cornwell, *Odoyevsky,* pp. 60-1; idem, *Vladimir Odoevsky and Romantic Poetics*, Providence and Oxford, Berghahn Books, 1998, pp. 151-2 (and passim); idem, 'Perspectives on the Romanticism of V.F. Odoyevsky', in *Problems of Russian Romanticism*, edited by Robert Reid, Aldershot, Gower, 1986, pp. 169-208; P.N. Sakulin's monumental *Iz istorii russkogo idealizma. Kniaz' V.F. Odoevskii: myslitel'-pisatel'*, vol. 1, Part 2, Moscow, 1913, pp. 82-90; and Jo Ann Hopkins Linburn, 'A Would-be Faust, Vladimir Fyodorovich Odoyevsky and his Prose Fiction', unpublished PhD dissertation, Columbia University, 1970.
[6] André von Gronicka, *The Russian Image of Goethe*, Philadelphia, University of Pennsylvania Press, 1968. The significance of the *Faust* reference will be discussed later in the present essay.
[7] Victor Terras, 'The Russian Short Story 1830-1850', in Charles A. Moser, *The Russian Short Story: A Critical History*, Boston, Twayne, 1986, p. 16.
[8] Ibid., p. 18.
[9] Charles E. Passage, *The Russian Hoffmannists*, The Hague, Mouton, 1963, pp. 113-14. This is not the place to analyse this vexed question in detail. We may note, however, that Odoevskii himself played down the influence of the German writer on his fiction, acknowledging his mastery and genius as the creator of a special type of fiction, but rejecting the idea of any substantive link: 'Primechanie k "Russkim nocham"', V.F. Odoevskii, *Russkie nochi*, Leningrad, 1975, pp. 189-90.

presence somewhere in the wings, almost, but not quite, knocking on the door.

There may be good reason for such reticence. *The Cosmorama* is tantalisingly incomplete, and possesses an unsympathetic narrator (whose name changes mysteriously from Vladimir Petrovich to Vladimir Andreevich in the course of the story). Although, furthermore, there are a number of colourful and exciting supernatural scenes which embrace 'as full a gamut of occult and Gothic paraphernalia as may be encountered in any work of Russian romanticism',[10] these, at least at first reading, do not appear to be well integrated into the story as a whole. It is not only, however, the story's overall structural coherence which is in doubt; the overblown prose and exaggerated language of such passages give rise to questions concerning the tonality of the story and the author's aim in writing it. To what extent are such scenes to be viewed as a parody? How far, indeed, is the author to be taken seriously at all? The reactions of some of Odoevskii's contemporaries to the supernatural aspect of his work were far from flattering: just before *The Cosmorama* was published, the critic I. I. Panaev remarked that 'the prince [Odoevskii – RC] is going completely off his head and is writing such muck [*gadost'*] that it makes you ill to read it'.[11] And even some of those who do not share Belinskii's aversion to the fantastic in literature[12] may agree with his judgement, apropos of Odoevskii's occult tales in general, that:

> so long as the author maintains his grip on reality, his talent, with its poetic insights and unusual intelligence, remains as attractive as ever; but as soon as he lapses into the fantastic, the astonished reader is forced to ask himself whether the author is joking or speaking seriously.[13]

---

[10] Cornwell, 'Introduction' to *The Salamander and Other Gothic Tales*, p. 5.

[11] *Literaturnoe nasledstvo*, vol. 56, Moscow, 1950, p. 135. Although it is not made explicitly clear, Panaev's reference is almost certainly to *Kosmorama*.

[12] Commenting on Dostoevskii's story *The Double* (*Dvoinik*), in 'Vzgliad na russkuiu literaturu 1846 goda', Belinskii wrote: 'These days the place for the fantastic is not literature, but the lunatic asylum; it should be the responsibility of doctors, not poets': Belinskii, *Polnoe sobranie sochinenii*, vol. 10, pp. 40-1.

[13] Belinskii, 'Sochineniia kniazia V.F. Odoevskogo', *Polnoe sobranie sochinenii*, vol. 8, pp. 297-323 (313). Other occult tales by Odoevskii include *The Sylph* (*Sil'fida*, 1837), *The Live Corpse* (*Zhivoi mertvets*, 1838) and *The Salamander* (*Salamandra*, 1844).

* * *

Without in any way questioning or underestimating the importance of parody, experiment, and the use of various forms of romantic irony in Odoevskii's work,[14] this article argues that his primary intention in writing *The Cosmorama* is in fact unequivocally serious, having as its central theme the fallibility of man's perception of reality and his innate inability to understand the forces that govern the world. To be human, Odoevskii seems to be saying, is to fail really to know or to comprehend the universe. This notion is revealed and explored through the use of the contrasting dualisms of appearance and essence, reason and unreason, reality and dream, sophistication and naivety, and language and silence. In P.N. Sakulin's words, Odoevskii wanted, when writing *The Cosmorama* and other such tales, 'to exploit poetical moments in the world of the marvellous, the mysterious, and to instil into his readers a deeper understanding of life, as a great riddle, largely still unknown to people'.[15] Such a view implicitly counters Belinskii's objection that the fantastic in Odoevskii should be seen as a separate and unwelcome element meriting only ridicule. Despite certain reservations concerning the fantastic passages and their place in the story, it seems most probable that Odoevskii introduced them into *The Cosmorama* to support and emphasise his philosophical idea, rather than to question or subvert it. In the course of the story, furthermore, the author uses such passages to relate this central epistemological theme to psychological and moral questions. If people apparently experience abnormal events, does that mean merely that they are mentally deranged? And if they are unable to distinguish what is 'real', to what extent can they be held responsible for their actions?

Odoevskii structures the opening of *The Cosmorama* so that his main philosophical idea is reflected in the way that the story is told. The reader finds a succession of different perspectives on reality, each nesting within the one before. The first section, entitled 'A Warning from the Publisher', is followed by an introductory passage from an adult narrator, Vladimir, who then proceeds to relate an event from early childhood, in which there features a magic box, the 'cosmorama'

---

[14] See Cornwell, *Odoyevsky*, p. 38.
[15] Quoted in ibid., p. 61.

of the title.[16] The cosmorama in turn provides, for the young Volodia at least, a gateway into another world which is distinct from the child's own experience, but which at the same time is connected with it in some unfathomable way.

It is possible of course to treat the story as passive entertainment, as an inconsequential item of curiosity – much in the same way as Volodia's aunt views the cosmorama as simply an artefact or a toy, from which, in the cold light of morning, she can pull out a string of paper pictures. But the mirroring of form and content in the opening pages, together with the deliberate interweaving of the familiar with the strange, may give us pause for thought. We may have been struck, furthermore, by the story's Neoplatonist epigraph: '*Quidquid est in externo est etiam in interno*'.[17] If the existence of an epigraph acts in general as a promissory note from the author that he will help his readers with an interpretation of the story that is to follow, then the actual statement here – that there is a link between what is outside and what is inside – may provoke us into a more active and self-aware consideration of the text. When, in other words, we read the opening pages of Odoevskii's work, we are conscious that we are simultaneously looking *at* a story called *The Cosmorama* as well as looking *into* a cosmorama, an enchanted and enchanting box, which offers both Volodia and the reader endlessly intriguing possibilities – Tennyson's 'gleaming untravelled world, whose margin fades for ever and ever as we move'.[18]

The importance of the reader's role is clearly highlighted in the publisher's warning, contained in the story's opening lines. We are told that he has acquired a strange manuscript at an auction. The condition of the manuscript is of such high quality that he has been able to send it

---

[16] Odoevskii himself, apparently, owned a 'cosmorama', or some such toy: see Cornwell, *Odoyevsky*, pp. 309-10, note 96.

[17] The quotation may be taken from the English mystic and philosopher John Pordage (1607-81): see *Russkaia i sovetskaia fantastika*, p. 617.

[18] *Ulysses*, 1833. There is an interesting parallel between *The Cosmorama* and Novalis's *Heinrich von Ofterdingen* (1802), in which the hero Heinrich comes across a volume written in an unfamiliar script. It becomes clear that the figures represent himself, his family and his acquaintances - all dressed in costumes from another era - and that we are dealing with a series of haunted portraits, anticipating the lives of existing people in a mysterious and miraculous way. For further discussion of Novalis's novel, see T. Ziolkowski, *Disenchanted Images*, Princeton, Princeton University Press, 1977, pp. 104-5.

for printing without any alteration on his part. Nevertheless, he anticipates that there will be complaints from his readers that he has not provided them with an explanation of its apparently incomprehensible passages. The publisher hastens to assure everybody that he is preparing a commentary in which everything will be explained as clearly as '2 x 2 = 4' (p. 175). The comfortable premise – that we are here dealing with a world which is based on notions of mathematical certainty – is, however, immediately undermined by the opening section of the manuscript itself. In the introduction to the narrative section, we hear of the existence of a 'chain of incomprehensible marvellous adventures and circumstances', of which the first-person narrator has been not merely witness and participant, but also, using his own word, 'victim'. Like Dostoevskii's Underground Man, speaking two decades later (and incidentally using the same mathematical formula – 2 x 2 = 4 – to devastatingly ironic effect), the narrator seems anxious to go out of his way to establish his own unreliability: 'I must confess that, affected by everything that I have seen and being in no condition to distinguish reality from the mere play of imagination, I am unable to this day to account for my feelings' (p. 176). A few lines later, and we find the narrator stating categorically that anything in his story that the reader finds impossible to understand will also be incomprehensible to him.

The narrator starts his story with scenes from his childhood. He recounts how, as a five-year-old boy, he (Volodia) has been sent a toy by a certain Doctor Bin, the family physician of his aunt and uncle, with whom he is living, having been orphaned. This toy – the cosmorama – takes the form of a box covered with coloured paper on which are etched flowers, faces and various figures in gold. Although Volodia is told that he will only be able to gain access to the toy when he is 'clever enough' to use it, he is so fascinated by it that he creeps down at night to examine the box. In its side there is a glass window through which he can clearly make out a series of beautiful, richly decorated rooms, around which are walking a number of completely unknown and wealthily dressed people. Suddenly, in one of the more distant rooms, he sees his aunt embracing a strange man who is obviously not his uncle. His 'real-life' aunt suddenly appears before him, but when he tells her what he has just seen in the cosmorama she angrily takes him back to his room. The two realities overlap, however, for he very soon finds out that the unknown man, a young Hussar officer, not only exists but also obviously enjoys the company of his aunt. Odoevskii here adds yet another level of irony, for the adult games, including betrayal, deceit and almost certainly adultery, that now transpire are presented to the reader solely through the innocent eyes of a five-year-old:

> I had come to like Paul very much ... particularly his Hussar's uniform; he lived in our house and I was always running to see him in his room, behind the orangery; he also seemed to like toys very much, because when he was sitting with auntie in his room he would keep on sending me off to the nursery for some toy or other. (p. 179)

Thus, for Volodia, a magic door has been opened which gives him a privileged insight into a dual, or parallel, universe. Returning as a young man to Moscow, after an absence of some years, he chances again on the cosmorama and once more breaks through the veil into this alternative universe. This time he sees himself standing beside a beautiful woman whispering pleasantries which resound tonelessly in his ears, causing him, in the real world, to leap away in horror. A little later, while talking to Doctor Bin, he finds himself listening to the doctor's double, warning him of the calamitous effect of his gift. The one, the 'real' Doctor Bin, acts and speaks in a direct and uncomplicated manner; the other, his cosmoramic double, is full of sorrow and foreboding. Although he is totally unaware of the existence of this dual universe, Doctor Bin nevertheless notices the disturbing influence of the cosmorama on Vladimir. He therefore orders that the object be destroyed, but it is already too late: as the cosmoramic Doctor Bin has warned, the magic gateway, once opened, can never be closed; access to the other world, moreover, will be random, lying completely outside Vladimir's control.

From this point on, Vladimir increasingly turns from a rational being, a 'condescending person of the nineteenth century', as he describes himself (p. 194),[19] into somebody who is unable to relate to reality in any meaningful way. By the end of the story, he has become an incoherent and gibbering wreck, describing himself as the denizen of two worlds, living in one but belonging to the other, in which he acts as

---

[19] Vladimir himself is unaware of the irony.

involuntary participant and 'instrument of torture' (p. 224). This pathway to doom has been marked for Vladimir by a series of seemingly fortuitous, but mysteriously interlinked, events of an ever more violent and grotesque nature. A distant relation with whom he becomes acquainted, Sonia (or Sophia), in real life an ingenuous and pure-hearted girl, is in her cosmoramic persona transformed into a Satanic creature; lustful, insolent and cunning, she enjoins Vladimir not to believe in her innocence and naivety, which are in reality a trap to seduce him to give up everything and follow her. Vladimir, however, having already arrogantly decided that (the real) Sonia lacks the maturity to be able to capture the imagination of 'a young man at the height of his powers' (p. 195), rejects her and becomes intimately involved with a married woman, a Countess Eliza. This turns out to be a particularly rash move, as it provokes the wrath of a jealous husband who returns from beyond the grave to exact his revenge;[20] if we are to accept Vladimir's account at face value, he is witness and sole survivor of a spectacular conflagration which destroys the Countess, her children, her house and all its possessions. He himself manages to escape only by being led out of the fire by an ethereal Sophia; he learns later that she has died from burns that have mysteriously appeared over all her body. He himself lives on, buried alive, in a wasteland of tormented despair.

* * *

The Cosmorama is an unsettling and challenging text. Each page, each paragraph even, poses new problems. Any confidence that we may have in thinking that we have understood the course of events, or the essential traits of a particular character, is quickly undermined. The questions relate as much to genre as to interpretation. If we turn to Todorov for assistance with regard to the former, it would seem that Odoevskii's story might conform to his well-known definition of the fantastic as 'that hesitation experienced by a person who knows only the laws of nature, confronting an apparently supernatural event'.[21] Just

---

[20] The Russian critic V.N. Grekov claims that the fact that the Count, who is aided by demonic forces, succeeds in exacting his revenge is 'proof of the unfairness of the social structure': *Russkaia i sovetskaia fantastika*, p. 8.

[21] Tzvetan Todorov, *The Fantastic*, Ithaca, New York, Cornell University Press, 1975, p. 25.

as with everything else connected with this story, however, this is not an entirely satisfactory answer. If we focus for the moment on the perception of the fictional hero, as opposed to the reader, then certainly Vladimir is just as Todorov describes: a rational being who has to face apparently fantastic events. By the end of the story, he finds himself standing precariously balanced on the threshold between two realities: 'this world' and 'the other'.[22]

Nevertheless, 'hesitation' is not really the appropriate term in his case, for it implies that the person concerned is in full control of his faculties, able to weigh up the alternatives in a reasonably objective way. He must, as Todorov states, 'opt for one of two possible solutions',[23] by deciding whether what he has just experienced actually happened, or whether there is some other rational explanation. But Vladimir becomes so traumatically involved in events that he is incapable of choosing between the alternatives in this fashion. Once he has become trapped within the enchanted orbit of the cosmorama, the emphasis shifts increasingly from rationality and periods of relative lucidity to derangement and a sense of terror.

What of the reader's perception of events in *The Cosmorama*? To what extent is the question of hesitation relevant here? Clearly influenced by Todorov, David Punter arrives at a definition of a possible sub-genre of the fantastic which he terms 'paranoiac fiction'; by this, he means:

> ... fiction in which the reader is placed in a situation of ambiguity with regard to fears within the text, and in which the attribution of persecution remains uncertain and the reader is invited to share in the doubts and uncertainties which pervade the apparent story.[24]

In this connection it might be useful to summarise the reader's position after the opening introductory paragraphs, and before the start of the

---

[22] Christine Brooke-Rose defines the 'pure fantastic' as a sub-genre 'represented by the central line - a frontier between two adjacent realms'; this is precisely where Vladimir is situated: see her *A Rhetoric of the Unreal: Studies in narrative and structure, especially of the fantastic*, Cambridge, Cambridge University Press, 1981, p. 64. For a full discussion of the fantastic as a genre, see Neil Cornwell, *The Literary Fantastic: From Gothic to Postmodernism*, New York and London, Harvester Wheatsheaf, 1990, pp. 3-41.

[23] Todorov, p. 25.

[24] Quoted in Cornwell, *The Literary Fantastic*, p. 53.

story itself. He or she has to assess the credibility of a narrator who, betraying many of the classic signs of paranoia, openly acknowledges his doubts and fears, and states that he has no explanation for what he is about to describe. Add to this, firstly, the fact that the reader has already been assured by another, 'more objective' figure, the publisher, that the reader has no cause for concern and that everything will be explained; and, secondly, that the reader is not sure of the position adopted by the author, who has announced, as it were, his presence by introducing an unusual and somewhat cryptic epigraph. In these respects we can see that Punter's criteria have been fulfilled almost to the letter. The possibility, even perhaps probability, that the narrator's mind has become unhinged, will of course occur to the reader, but the door at this early stage is being left open; a pattern has been established in which the reader's ambiguous feelings towards the hero parallel those of the character towards his own narrative. And, even, although for many the scales will tip perceptibly, as the story develops, towards rational explanation as a resolution of the ambiguity, the doubts are not entirely erased.

On the one hand, we note that, with very few exceptions, the opening of the door into the fantastic is associated in one way or another with sleep and its associated activity, dreaming.[25] Thus, on the evening after the five-year-old Volodia has first been introduced to the cosmorama ('the enchanting box'), he drifts in and out of sleep, picturing to himself the box with its golden flowers and flags, imagining that it would melt away and that from it would emerge 'beautiful children in gold dresses, beckoning him to come to them'. He succeeds in persuading his nanny[26] to leave the room so that he can go down to see the box by 'pretending to be asleep'. Later, the first appearance of the vengeful husband is preceded by the narrator going to

---

[25] In this respect, Odoevskii's story echoes Goya's aphorism 'El sueño de la razón produce monstruos' (1799), the title he gave to No. 43 of his series of sketches, *Los Caprichos*. Although this is usually translated as 'The sleep of reason engenders monsters', J.B. Monleón has argued that 'sueño' should be translated here as 'dream'; that it is *dreaming*, rather than sleep, that gives rise to the supernatural, thus implying a blurring of the boundaries between reason and unreason: José B. Monleón, *A Specter is Haunting Europe: A Sociohistorical Approach to the Fantastic*, Princeton, Princeton University Press, 1990, pp. 40-2.

[26] Volodia's nanny is only one of a whole network of practically invisible servants who feature in this story.

sleep, dreaming an idyllic dream which becomes transformed into nightmare, waking up, racing over to his beloved Eliza in the middle of a thunderstorm whose raging has already formed part of his nightmare, and finding that Eliza has herself just woken from her own nightmare. Again, the description of the husband's second visitation on New Year's Eve, including the fateful and fatal conflagration, is set within the framework of Vladimir 'temporarily' falling into a deep sleep while waiting for his assignation with Eliza – and then, after it is all over, waking up in his own room. We note that at this point he 'sees himself', as if, in the intervening period, he has been in an astral out-of-body state and returns to look down momentarily on his own sleeping self. The only physical trace of the fire is a black stain on his hand which had been grabbed by the dead man's hand.

The story is punctuated, moreover, by regular appearances of the person who is its most tangible symbol of 'normal' reality: the solid, not to say stolid, figure of Doctor Bin. Whereas his cosmoramic counterpart is, as in Sonia's case, a totally different personality – a gloomy and Cassandra-like figure who turns up on the odd occasion to shout dire warnings of catastrophe at the uncomprehending Vladimir – our 'normal' Doctor Bin belongs to the 'there, there; take this – you'll feel better in the morning' school of medicine. The line of communication between this Doctor Bin and Vladimir operates more effectively, since the latter is generally willing to swallow any mixture that he is prescribed. Finally, even at the very end of the story, when Vladimir has become totally deranged, the ever-faithful Doctor Bin is still present, attempting, now alas in vain, to assure him that all his terrible experiences have been the result of a heightened imagination.

Nonetheless, despite the temptation to agree with the doctor's summary of Vladimir's position and state of mind, not all the question marks have been eliminated. There is, for example, the black stain on Vladimir's hand, mentioned above. Secondly, there is the undoubted fact of Sophia's death from unexplained burns received on the night of the fire; under normal circumstances, there would have been no reason for her to have been at the Count's house. Thirdly, there is no evidence to suggest that the occasion of Vladimir's second privileged insight into the cosmorama can be explained away by the possibility that he might have been asleep. Lastly, and most substantially, there is independent 'real-world' confirmation of the fact that the Count, having died to everybody's satisfaction, returns from the grave. There *may* of course be rational explanations, even in these instances, but they are not immediately obvious within the story; we must deduce that Odoevskii is keeping open the possibility of an alternative, non-rational, explanation.

* * *

Although, however, questions of genre and interpretation are linked, the suspicion persists that, even if it were possible to resolve beyond any doubt the problem of textual ambiguity in *The Cosmorama*, our understanding of the story would not necessarily be enhanced. The argument needs to be refocused away from questions of the fantastic, and whether or not the events as described by the narrator have been real or imagined, and on to textual and other issues. We are, to be sure, dealing with an incomplete story, but can we nonetheless discern in *The Cosmorama* any unifying principle or principles, other than the general one advanced by Sakulin, that the story presents the reader with a universe that is mysterious and almost certainly beyond rational understanding?

Embedded within *The Cosmorama*, in the early conversations between Vladimir and Sonia, we find a cluster of references to other texts. Within the space of a few pages there are discussions and comments on a quotation from *Hamlet*, a scene from Goethe's *Faust*, one of La Fontaine's fables ('The Dragon-Fly and the Ant'), and a short moralising allegory which Vladimir attributes to the German writer and academic Krummacher.[27] The discussions in these scenes reveal a striking contrast in attitude between Vladimir and Sonia: the former is characterised by Onegin-like condescension and general affectation of intellectual superiority; the latter by ingenuousness and innocence. Vladimir learns to his astonishment, for example, that Sonia has never heard of the French Revolution. Nonetheless, there is an ironic reversal at work here, for the reader soon realises that it is actually Sonia who is playing the dominant role in their relationship; it is she who is most affected by the La Fontaine fable, and it is she who indicates her interest in the allegory. Vladimir, certainly, has lent her *Hamlet* (together with many other literary works) to read, but again it is she

---

[27] Friedrich Adolph Krummacher (1767-1845), German poet and professor of theology.

who draws his attention to the line, 'There are more things in heaven and earth, Horatio, than are dreamt of in your philosophy' (p. 190).[28] From each of these references the reader may be able to infer certain ideas and themes which relate to an understanding of the story as a whole. The famous quotation from *Hamlet* could, of course, have stood as the story's epigraph. The La Fontaine fable[29] lacks an explicit moral, but Sonia's tearful attack on the hard-hearted attitude of the ant suggests the significance of ethical considerations within the story, and also points to the compassionate and self-sacrificial (i.e. non 'ant-like') role which she herself is to play. The Krummacher apologue, deriving in part from Plato's allegory of the cave, contains the implied moral injunction that privation and adverse circumstances must be overcome by faith; only by acting according to one's innermost beliefs, and by following one's heart rather than one's reason, will it be possible to emerge out of the darkness (of ignorance and falsehood) and into the full light of day.

Most challenging and cryptic of all, however, in terms of an interpretation both of the passage itself, as well as of its wider implications, is the Goethe reference. The scene which particularly interests Sonia is the brief and enigmatic episode which appears towards the end of *Faust 1*, entitled *'Nacht. Offen Feld'*. Faust and Mephistopheles are racing on horseback to the prison where Gretchen is held captive, when they pass by the Rabenstein, the place where, the reader may with hindsight infer, her execution is being prepared. Strange figures are gesturing mysteriously in a way which Mephistopheles claims is witchcraft, but which Faust interprets as an act of consecration. Mephistopheles is concerned to urge them both on and they gallop away. When Sonia singles this scene out for comment, Vladimir admits that he has never understood it. Sonia, however, who a little later is to confess that ideas come into her mind without her being aware of their origin, is astonished that he should be so lacking in perception:

---

[28] The Russian original has *'nashim mudretsam'* ('our philosophers').

[29] Sonia would presumably be referring to the Russian translation by the fabulist I.A. Krylov, 'Strekoza i muravei' (1808). La Fontaine's 'La Cigale et la fourmi' appeared as the first fable of Book 1 of his *Fables* (1668).

> How can that be possible? It's the most comprehensible, the most lucid scene!
> Do you really not understand that Mephistopheles is deceiving Faust? He's
> afraid – it's not witchcraft that's going on, but something quite different... Oh, if
> only Faust had stopped!... (p. 190)

What is it about this passage that is so important for Sonia? Is it that
she sees something here that touches upon Vladimir's fate and maybe
her own as well? As she points out, Mephistopheles is deceiving Faust;
why, we are not absolutely certain, but the assumption must be that
Faust is at the time unaware that Gretchen is to be executed and that the
place of execution which is being prepared is indeed the Rabenstein.
Whatever the interpretation of this extraordinary passage within
Faust,[30] in *The Cosmorama* its role can be seen, firstly, as emphasising
the gulf between perception and reality in Vladimir; and, secondly, as
acting as a premonition of Sonia's own violent death. But it is, I think,
possible to go further than this.

Late in his career, ten years after the publication of *The Cosmorama*,
the Russian poet V.A. Zhukovskii wrote an article which discussed this
very same scene. According to Zhukovskii, Mephistopheles is urging
Faust onwards, precisely because what he sees at the Rabenstein are not
the forces of black magic and witchcraft – there would, after all, be no
reason why Mephistopheles should be afraid of these – but heavenly
angels who are preparing and consecrating the place where Gretchen is
to die, symbolising the triumph of faith, weakness and essential purity
of heart over reason, cynicism and pride.[31] Here Zhukovskii is
unwittingly offering us an interesting perspective on *The Cosmorama*,
which helps to focus our attention not merely on abstract questions of
knowledge and perception, but also on the significance of the
relationship between Sonia and Vladimir. Echoes of
Margareta/Gretchen in Goethe's *Faust* can be observed both in Sonia's
self-sacrifice to save Vladimir, and her final message to him that he
should seek purity of heart, for that is 'the highest good' (p. 221). We
can also surmise that, had Odoevskii provided us with a continuation to

---

[30] Analysis of this particular scene in the critical works and commentaries on *Faust.
Part 1* to which I have had access is unfortunately not very illuminating. Brief but
interesting comments can be found in Michael Beddow, *Goethe: Faust 1*, London,
Grant and Cutler, 1986, p. 84 and W.H. Bruford, *Goethe's 'Faust 1': Scene by Scene*,
London, Macmillan, 1968, p. 82.
[31] 'Dve stseny iz Fausta', in V.A. Zhukovskii, *Estetika: Kritika*, Moscow, 1985, p. 355.

The Cosmorama, Sonia's role as mediator to save Vladimir spiritually as well as physically may well have become more explicit.[32]

Vladimir himself possesses the Faustian qualities of intellectual arrogance and, above all, pride. And it is pride which, in his case at least, is linked with suffering, for at the very end of the story he states that he can only find relief from his torment (and even then not always) when, having cast aside all pride, he weeps the tears of pure repentance. If we ask ourselves why he suffers so much, the primary cause would seem to be the diabolical forces which were first unleashed as a result of his privileged insight into the cosmorama. From this point of view, the debate as to whether or not such forces are real or part of his imagination is irrelevant; the suffering would be as real. But what then does he have to be penitent about? After all, unlike Faust, he did not enter knowingly into a bargain with the devil. It was not his fault that he was given the magic box as a toy when he was a five-year old: the this-world Doctor Bin did not know what he was doing, and his alter ego admits that he miscalculated in giving Volodia the toy. The question of moral responsibility, let alone the need to repent, therefore, surely does not arise in this instance. However, the cosmoramic Doctor Bin goes on clearly to imply that Vladimir has it within his own power to save himself and that what happens to him is not totally predetermined: 'Save yourself from the fatal law!' ('*Sokhrani sebia ot rokovogo zakona!*'), Vladimir is told (p. 184). His subsequent behaviour is a betrayal of this injunction.

The view of Vladimir as simply a victim of circumstance cannot therefore be sustained. The combination of pride with selfish egoism has fatal consequences, particularly in so far as his relationship with women is concerned. To Sonia, even though he acknowledges the uniquely soothing and calming effect which her innocence and pureness of heart have on him, he reacts with haughty indifference. Like so many superfluous characters in Russian literature, with whom he shares more than a passing resemblance, Vladimir's inability to respond emotionally

---

[32] For the significance of the figure of Sophia to the Gnostics, and the part that she plays as 'Mediatrix' between the spiritual and material kingdoms, see Samuel D. Cioran, *Vladimir Solov'ev and the Knighthood of the Divine Sophia*, Waterloo, Ontario, Wilfred Laurier University Press, 1977, pp. 18-21. See also Cornwell, *Odoyevsky*, pp. 104-5.

on a truly equal and mutually satisfying plane manifests itself when it is too late, only after she has already sacrificed herself for him.

His affair with the Countess is equally calamitous. They are drawn together, it seems, not by love at all, but by an implacable force which saps their will-power and destroys the norms of reason and convention. He is attracted towards her as powerfully as he was once attracted towards the cosmorama. Their feelings for each other are portrayed in terms largely of pride, and pride in turn is described as a 'cup into which all mankind's sins are poured', while their lips involuntarily touch the seductive beverage (p. 196). Reason and logic, with their veneer of cool sophistication, vanish – to be replaced by primitive, barbaric emotion:

> I stood motionless before her... My heart was torn by a feeling of grief which it had never before experienced; I felt my blood racing hotly through my veins, and my fast-beating pulse ringing deafeningly in my temples... I tried to summon to my aid all the powers of reason, all the experience acquired during a long lifetime of cold calculation... But all that dimly came to my mind were dark sophistries: crimes, thoughts of anger and blood, shutting off from me, like some crimson veil, all other emotions, thoughts and hopes... At this moment, within an outwardly cultivated, refined and rational European, there raged a wild savage, spurred on by bestial impulse. (p. 198)

Although, a little later, Vladimir returns to the utopian dream of his youth, holding out the promise of 'solitude, warm climate, a beautiful and intelligent woman, and a long succession of happy days, full of life-giving love and peace ...' (pp. 200-01), such a vision can now never be realised.

During the Count's climactic return from the dead, such empty and egotistical dreams are replaced by the understanding, achieved through Vladimir's transcendent powers of perception, that there is no action, word, or thought, however insignificant, which can exist in isolation and which does not have, over the course of time, the most profound and often damaging consequences. Everything is mysteriously interconnected, as if by some magic ladder, and even impulses which may seem to be morally good at the time can be transformed into bestial and soulless emotion.[33] For Vladimir, however, even though he

---

[33] See 'Kosmorama', p. 206. Odoevskii's interest in the idea of a universe governed by the principle of hidden causes and effects is reflected in the epigraph to his story *The*

reacts to such visions with all the transcendent fervour of an Old Testament prophet, understanding comes too late to save him; the poison of 'a long lifetime of cold calculation' has done its work.

* * *

We see then *The Cosmorama* as imbued with the concept of a universe which has magic and mystery at its heart, and which defies rational explanation, reflecting Odoevskii's enthusiastic acceptance of the ideas of Schelling and German Romanticism, and his angry rejection of the mechanistic pseudo-scientism of Francis Bacon and the crass materialism of Jeremy Bentham, accusing them, along with other English philosophers, of 'being preoccupied with screws and wheels and behind the wheels – with gold!'.[34] Although, however, the universe that Odoevskii presents in *The Cosmorama* is apparently unfathomable, it is neither random nor chaotic, since it is bound together by an elaborate and invisible network of interconnecting causes and effects. It is precisely because of man's lack of awareness of such determinism, moreover, that the concept of moral responsibility is retained. Thus the story can be seen as a synthesis of the romantic and rational impulses within Odoevskii;[35] for those with little taste for the supernatural and the fantastic, for that matter, it could also be viewed as containing a vision of the universe sufficiently 'marvellous' to render the presence of such elements unnecessary.

Live Corpse (Zhivoi mertvets), which was written the year before *The Cosmorama*; here he writes of responsibility being 'connected with each word, with each apparently insignificant action, with each impulse of a man's soul': quoted in Cornwell, *Odoyevsky*, p. 62. This story is also translated in Odoevsky, *The Salamander*, op. cit., pp. 66-88.
[34] Von Gronicka, op. cit., p. 123.
[35] For a discussion of the intuitive and the rational in Odoevskii, and the importance of the idea of synthesis in his philosophy, see Cornwell, *Odoyevsky*, pp. 78-82.

GOTHIC TREATMENT OF THE CRISIS OF ENGENDERING IN ODOEVSKII'S *THE SALAMANDER*

CYNTHIA C. RAMSEY

I

The novella *The Salamander* (*Salamandra*), by Russian Romantic writer and philosopher Prince Vladimir Fedorovich Odoevskii (1804-1869), first appeared in print in 1841, though not in its current incarnation. The story existed as early as 1838, when A.A. Kraevskii, editor-in-chief of *Notes of the Fatherland* (*Otechestvennye zapiski*), wrote to Odoevskii, inquiring as to the 'health' of *The Salamander* and encouraging him to send the manuscript as quickly as possible into his 'matrimonial embraces' (*supruzheskie ob''iatiia*). What is now Part II of the novella, 'El'sa', was first published under the name 'The Salamander' in *Notes of the Fatherland* in the earlier part of 1841, while Part I was published later that same year as a separate story under its current name 'The Southern Shore of Finland at the Beginning of the Eighteenth Century' (*Iuzhnii bereg Finliandii v nachale XVIII stoletiia*). A third part, entitled 'Undine' (*Undina*) remained unfinished, perhaps inspiring Odoevskii's understanding of his resulting novella as a 'dilogy' (*dilogiia*)[1], instead of the previously conceived 'trilogy'. Only in 1844 did Odoevskii publish the two stories as one in his *Collected Works* (*Sochineniia*).[2]

I would like to thank my colleagues and friends Samuel Kimball and David Vernikov for their insightful close readings of earlier drafts of this essay. My graditude also goes to Dan Ramsey for his broad knowledge of mythology, Scandanavian and other.

[1] *The Dictionary of Foreign Words* (*Slovar' inostrannykh slov*, 6th edition, Moscow, 1964) defines *dilogiia* as 'two novels or dramatic words linked by a unity of theme' (cited by Neil Cornwell in *V.F. Odoyevsky: His Life, Times and Milieu, 1804-1869*, London, Athlone, 1986, p. 309, n. 90).

[2] *Sochineniia kniazia V.F. Odoevskogo*, 3 vols., St Petersburg, 1844. For further information on the literary evolution of *The Salamander*, see M.A. Tur'ian's *Strannaia moia sud'ba: O zhizni Vladimira Fedorovicha Odoevskogo*, Moscow, 1991, pp. 308-9.

It seems no mistake that *The Salamander* existed as two independent works, since, as Simon Karlinsky notes, the novella is concerned with exploring a certain 'duality' or 'two-worldedness' (*dvoemirie*): the contrast 'between two views of reality, one based on the rational Western European traditions of Enlightenment and the other on old tribal customs and animistic beliefs'.[3] In Part I, the division is represented in terms of the difference between the 'primitivism' of rural Finnish life and the industrial urban spirit of the booming new Russian capital at the beginning of the eighteenth century. In Part II, however, the two sides have shifted: they occur within Russian society itself during the nineteenth century. Representing yet another generation of Russian 'fathers and sons', the German Romantic mystics of the 1820s and the 'materialist' rationalists of the 1840s, *The Salamander*'s two parts also diverge formally – in stylistic register, tone, point of view, and narrative frame. Indeed, Neil Cornwell suggests that Parts I and II belong to different genres: Part I contains characteristics of an historical novel, bearing a resemblance to Pushkin's unfinished *The Blackamoor of Peter the Great* (*Arap Petra Velikogo*), while Part II is a full-blown Gothic tale, complete with past tragedy, haunted house, and mystic alchemical experiments and apparitions.[4]

The challenge in reading *The Salamander*, then, lies in understanding how Parts I and II can be seen as two halves of a whole which complement each other, rather than as two separate stories which merely share a cast of characters. In this essay I present a possible avenue for that understanding: *The Salamander*'s unity dervies from its explication of the motif of sexual engendering, especially in relation to the genre of Gothic literature. The Gothic's preoccupation with sexuality is hardly a critical novelty. Laura Bayer-Berenbaum, for example, sees sexuality as the means by which characters transgress, often spectacularly, the 'normal', in order further to contaminate the enclosed space of the everyday. Within Gothic literature, she writes:

---

[3] Simon Karlinsky, 'A Hollow Shape: The Philosophical Tales of Prince Vladimir Odoevsky', *Studies in Romanticism*, 5:3, Spring 1966, pp. 169-82 (178).

[4] See Cornwell's 'Introduction' to Vladimir Odoevsky, *The Salamander and Other Gothic Tales*, translated by Neil Cornwell, Evanston, Northwestern University Press, 1992, p. 6; and the essay 'Vladimir Odoevsky and the Russian Gothic' in his *Vladimir Odoevsky and Romantic Poetics: Collected Essays*, Providence, Berghahn Books, 1998, pp. 152-3.

'Homosexuality, sodomy, incest, rape, or group copulations are inserted into ordinary experience in order to destroy the boundary line between the normal and the perverse, infecting the normal with the germ of the perverse so that all behaviour becomes susceptible to possible perversion'.[5]

The trope of the hero-transgresser is familiar in Russian Gothic literature, eventually overtaking even Dostoevskii's hyper-rationalist protagonists. In fact, V.E. Vatsuro sees Russian literature as fertile soil for the Gothic; the work of Gothic novelist Ann Radcliffe, he writes, 'was felt to have a kind of Russian spirit within it, as if the Gothic novel, with its excesses, its exotic settings, its flaunting of previous rules of literary logic, its questioning of moral values, struck an exceptionally receptive chord in Russia.'[6]

In supporting my reading of *The Salamander* as a Gothic work devoted to explicating the crises surrounding issues of engendering, I will first examine the main subtext of the first 'historical' part of Odoevskii's story, the Finnish epic collection *The Kalevala*. I will then briefly discuss two key English novels within the European Gothic tradition. Primarily concerned with problems of generating creativity and procreativity, they provide a context for the more 'Gothic' second part of the story. The main portion of the essay, however, will centre on how Part I of the *The Salamander* novella, rife with issues of sexuality, prepares for its fully Gothic realisation in Part II.

II

In 1835, Finnish folklorist and district health officer Elias Lönnrot published the first edition of *The Kalevala*.[7] *The Kalevala* was the result of years of work during which Lönnrot compiled tens of thousands of lines of Finnish oral heroic poetry and edited them to create 'a more or less continuous narrative'. One of Lönnrot's

---

[5] Linda Bayer-Berenbaum, *The Gothic Imagination: Expansion in Gothic Literature and Art*, East Brunswick, Associated University Presses, 1982, p. 40.

[6] Cited in Mark S. Simpson, *The Russian Gothic Novel and its British Antecedents*, Columbus, Ohio, Slavica, p. 19.

[7] All background information here on *The Kalevala* is provided in Keith Bosley's excellent 'Introduction' to his 'The World's Classics' translation of *The Kalevala*, Oxford, Oxford University Press, 1989, pp. xiii-xiv. Canto and line references from this edition of *The Kalevala* are hereafter inserted in the text of this essay.

motivations in taking on such a mammoth project was to shape his national heritage into one great historical epic work, on the order and magnitude of Homer's *The Iliad* and *The Odyssey*. Keith Bosley points out that *The Kalevala* is a 'double anachronism', since it is not only a nineteenth-century work which describes ancient myths and legends, but is also 'an epic produced at a time when epic was regarded as a thing of the past'. For access to *The Kalevala* in Russian, Odoevskii owed thanks to the research of his friend Iakov Grot, a Russian philologist specialising in Finnish studies, who had translated parts of *The Kalevala* into Russian and published them in *The Contemporary* (*Sovremennik*), 1839-40.

Odoevskii's opening authorial 'commentary' (*primechanie*) to *The Salamander* hints at the importance of *The Kalevala* as a subtext to his novella. At the end of the commentary he claims: 'In general the life, legends and belief of [the Finnish] people deserve attention in the highest degree and are an unvalued store of treasure for literary works'.[8] Earlier he praises Grot's research: 'We cannot judge the Finns without having penetrated their lands and acquainted ourselves with their family routine' (*s ikh semeinym bytom*) (133 / 141). Together, both statements suggest that to understand an entire culture, one must observe that culture on the miniature scale of the family. Within a single family, there can be no greater concerns than those of paternity and birth, the most basic question of our origins. This question constitutes the very meaning of 'family', and therefore that of a people and their collective identity.

Odoevskii addresses this concern with national origins when he explains that Lönnrot collected Finnish 'folk songs' which he later discovered 'are part of a whole harmonious poem' (*chasti tseloi stroinoi poemy*) and thus 'furnished new proof for adherents of Wolf's

---

[8] All textual quotes from *The Salamander* are taken from Neil Cornwell's collection of Odoevskii's works in translation, *The Salamander and Other Gothic Tales*, pp. 133-212. Unless otherwise noted, I have only altered Cornwell's translation in his transliteration, to match with the Library of Congress system used throughout this essay. Any supporting Russian textual quotes of *The Salamander* are taken from 'Salamandra', in V.F. Odoevskii, *Sochineniia v dvukh tomakh*, edited by V.I. Sakharov, Moscow, 1981, vol. 2, pp. 141-219. One set of page numbers alone indicates Cornwell's English translation; when both the English and the original Russian are given, the page numbers are both given (separated by a slash: the Cornwell translation given first and the *Sochineniia* original second).

views on the origins of *The Iliad* (*o proiskhozhdenii Iliady*) (133 / 142). *The Kalevala,* therefore, according to Odoevskii, illuminates familial as well as literary origins.[9] The importance of Odoevskii's statement lies in its representation of a desire for knowledge of origins. Lönnrot's Romantic vision of Finland, a Grand Duchy of the Russian Empire since 1809, being 'born' as an independent nation worthy of its own epic past, speaks to the desire of all nationalists for their countries to be creations of their own engendering, and not merely a part of some other empire's familial scheme. However, as *The Kalevala* itself suggests, sorting out issues of paternity and engendering is problematic, and in fact these lie at the heart of individual and national crises.

The Kalevala is framed by two significant birthing scenes. The first canto, appropriately enough entitled 'In the Beginning', describes the Finnish creation myth of the world. The 'air-girl', a daughter of nature, is impregnated by the wind and the sea, and endures a horrific pregnancy: in the midst of 'fiery birth-pangs' and 'hard belly-woes' (Canto 1: lines 137-8), 'She bore a hard womb / a difficult bellyful / seven hundred years / nine ages of man; / but no birth was born / no creature was created' (1: 127-32). Finally this 'air-lass', or 'water-mother', gives birth to seven eggs, out of which are created the world: 'an egg's lower half / became mother earth below / an egg's upper half / became heaven above; / the upper half that was yolk / became the sun for shining / the upper half that was white / became the moon for gleaming; / what in an egg was mottled / became the stars in the sky / what in an egg was blackish / became the clouds of the air' (1: 233-44). Another difficult engendering in the same canto sees the birth – again by the 'water-mother, air-lass' – of *The Kalevala's* main protagonist, Väinämöinen. However, this time the paternal source of the procreation is unknown: though the mother is clearly identified, *The Kalevala* remains ambiguous about the identity of Väinämöinen's father. As with the creation of the world, the gestation period is abnormally long – thirty years. In fact, tired of waiting, Väinämöinen finally enacts his own birth: 'When the moon did not loose him... / he shifted the stronghold gate / with his ring finger / slid the lock of bone / with his

---

[9] The fact that Odoevskii was mistaken in his belief that Lönnrot's poems formed a 'whole harmonious poem' is not in itself extraordinary: this was the same Romantic era which had embraced the false Gaelic epics of Ossian, and several scholars were misled by Lönnrot's seamless editing job into seeing an original whole.

left toe, came / with his nails from the threshold / with his knees from the doorway' (1: 315-24).

In the course of *The Kalevala*, the question of birthing arises repeatedly, thus repeatedly bringing the epic back to the issue of origins. For example, a young upstart named Joukahainen challenges Väinämöinen's authority during a contest of 'singing' the 'deep Origins / of eternal things' (3: 186-7). When Joukahainen loses, he saves his own life by promising his sister Aino to Väinämöinen in marriage. Aino, hearing of her brother's bargain, despairs, though she is consoled by her mother that she will be able to produce children of Väinämöinen's 'good stock' (3: 544). However, in the next canto, Aino succeeds in escaping the arranged marriage by drowning herself, thus thwarting Väinämöinen's plans of fathering a great line of descendants. Furthermore, the renegade hero, 'wanton' Lemminkäinen, is characterised as controlled by sexual desire: 'he kept going with women / staying out all night / making merry with lasses / capering with braided heads' (11: 17-20). In fact, his lust for women eventually costs him his life, and he is forced, as happens so often in *The Kalevala*, to call on his mother to resurrect him (Canto 15). And in the forty-fifth canto, in both a re-telling of the Pandora myth and a mirrored version of *The Kalevala's* own creation myth, the blind daughter of death, Tuoni, suffers a difficult pregnancy and eventually gives birth to all evils in the world: stitch, colic, gout, rickets, boil, scab, cancer, and plague (45: 163-70). The midwife of this birth is Louhi, evil witch of the Northland and main antagonist in *The Kalevala*, and the birth takes place in a swamp, a place associated with death in Finnish culture.

The final canto in *The Kalevala* finishes the cycle of procreative tales, vividly retelling both the fall of mankind and the virgin birth. The young maiden Marjatta over-assiduously sees to the preservation of her purity. She won't participate in any activity which signifies procreativity: milking cows, eating eggs, riding in a carriage pulled by stallions, and so on. One day she is tempted by a talking berry, eats it, and is thereby immaculately impregnated. Thrown out of the house by her unbelieving mother and father as a 'demon's bitch' and 'whore' (50: 163, 187), Marjatta responds with prophetic words reminiscent of the Virgin Mother's: 'I am not a whore at all / no kind of scarlet woman: / I am to have a great man / to bear one of noble birth / who will put down the mighty / vanquish Väinämöinen too' (50: 195-200). She is forced to give birth in a stable in the woods, and when her son arrives, she 'swath[s] him in swaddling cloths' (50: 338). Her infant vanishes from her, and after much searching Marjatta finds him in the swamp, which, according to Bosley, 'recall[s] the practice of leaving illegitimate babies to die if no one admitted paternity' (p. 676). Thus the lack of a generally acknowledged father for the infant endangers his life, and causes the 'old man' to refuse to christen and name him. Old Väinämöinen is called in to inquire into this case, and recommends the child be buried. An infanticide is avoided only when the two-week-old child speaks up to condemn Väinämöinen for his judgment and to defend himself. For this miracle the infant's life is spared; he is then quickly christened by the old man and named King of Karelia.

This infant of the last canto, of course, serves as a wonderful symbol for Finnish nationalism, a cause furthered by the publication of *The Kalevala*, and a goal only realised in 1917. However, as the brief look at some of its main plot points demonstrates, *The Kalevala's* position as a Finnish nationalist document, rallying the people towards the 'birth' of an independent Finland, is ambiguous at best. Though the story of the birth of Christ establishes a holy paternity for the son born to an unwed mother, the son born at the end of *The Kalevala* cannot name a particular paternal figure; as the stories preceding this last one should show, questionable origins lead to problems in the future.

III

The Salamander realises the underlying crises of engendering not only from its Finnish literary subtext but from its Gothic literary context. Two canonical works of English Gothic literature in particular, *The Castle of Otranto* and *Frankenstein*, exhibit the same concerns with procreation and paternity as Odoevskii's work, providing a heritage of anxiety surrounding origins, one of the central features of Gothic literature.

Horace Walpole's *The Castle of Otranto*, subtitled *A Gothic Story* and published in 1765, is generally accepted to be 'the first of the true Gothic novels'.[10] It is significant that a work regarded as having engendered an entire literary movement is so concerned itself with

---

[10] According to *The Oxford Companion to English Literature*, edited by Margaret Drabble, Oxford, Oxford University Press, 1995, p. 411.

engendering. Manfred, a tyrannical Italian prince in the thirteenth century, is obsessively concerned with siring an heir for his castle, estate, and title. When his son Conrad is crushed to death at his wedding by the helmet of an old statue, old Manfred decides impulsively to divorce his wife Hippolita and marry Conrad's fiancée Isabella. Isabella refuses and is aided in escape by a peasant boy, Theodore, whose origins are, appropriately, unknown. Searching for Isabella, Manfred is told that she is with her new lover in the courtyard, and rushes down to kill her, only to find that he has stabbed his own daughter Matilda. His attempt to block the cycle of engendering is thus rewarded with the death of his sole remaining descendant. The end of the novel reveals that such malfeasance is, in fact, inherited: Manfred's grandfather originally poisoned the good prince Alfonso, the castle's rightful owner, whose statue supplied the piece which originally killed Conrad and set the plot in motion. Theodore is proven the descendant of Alfonso and therefore the rightful inheritor of the castle and title; Isabella marries Theodore, to further protect the paternity of the castle's heirs; and Manfred and Hippolita are sent off to religious exile where, because they must take vows of celibacy, they will no longer have the opportunity to play further destructive engendering games.[11]

If *The Castle of Otranto* claims paternal rights to the Gothic Romantic literary canon, *Frankenstein* may claim to be its most famous son; it, too, is preoccupied with procreative crises.[12] Interestingly enough, Mary Shelley begins her 1831 introduction to the novel's slightly revised second publication with an 'account of the origin of the story' (p. v). Towards the end of the introduction, in which she tells the now-famous account of how she, her husband Percy Bysshe Shelley, and Lord Byron all agreed to write ghost stories to pass the time one a

---

[11] For discussion of *The Castle of Otranto*, see *The Oxford Companion to English Literature* (p. 178) and Chris Baldick's 'Introduction' to *The Oxford Book of Gothic Tales*, edited by Chris Baldick, Oxford, Oxford University Press, 1992 (p. xvi).

[12] *The Salamander* shares some narrative affinities with *Frankenstein*: *Frankenstein* begins in St Petersburg, where young adventurer Robert Walton writes to his sister; Victor Frankenstein, the young chemist who discovers 'the cause of generation and life' (Mary Shelley, *Frankenstein*, New York, Dover Publications, 1994, p. 31: pages numbers hereafter are given in the text), begins his scientific studies entranced with alchemy, which occupies Iakko and the old count throughout Part II; and Victor shares the same type of potentially crisis-ridden brother-sister relationship with Elizabeth Lavenza as Iakko shares with El'sa.

rainy summer in Switzerland, Mary Shelley writes: 'And now, once again, I bid my hideous progeny go forth and prosper. I have an affection for it, for it was the offspring of happy days' (p. ix).

Shelley's repeated references to endangered engenderings throughout the novel refract the novel's central crisis, the miscreation of the monster. Both Victor's mother Caroline and the adopted daughter Elizabeth are described as being left 'an orphan and a beggar' (pp. 15, 17) by the death of their respective fathers. (We also learn that Elizabeth's mother had died giving birth to her.) Inspired by a scientific account of electricity, Victor gives up his studies of alchemy 'and all its progeny as a deformed and abortive creation' (p. 22). Victor then begins working obsessively to create a 'new species' that would 'bless [him] as [their] creator and source',[13] insisting, 'No father could claim the gratitude of a child so completely as I should deserve theirs' (p. 32). Victor's desire to become the sole progenitor of a living creation removes the mother from the procreative equation. Such a hubristic appropriation and reduction of reproduction results in the novel's crisis, the accursed 'birth' of the monster. Victor's transgression informs his post-procreation nightmares: he dreams of Elizabeth, his fiancée, but when he kisses her he realises that he is instead embracing his dead, worm-eaten mother. This confusion of generations reflects the confusion of progeneration embodied in Victor's creature, and the violence of the birth continues to reproduce itself in the infanticide of his brother William, as well as the execution of Justine Moritz and the murders of Henry Clerval and Elizabeth.

The remainder of the novel traces Victor's effort to resolve this crisis. When he and his creation meet for the first time since the monster's birth, they argue about Victor's responsibility as 'miserable origin and author' of the monster (p. 69). In this textual moment Shelley makes a metaliterary connection between herself as creator of her novel and Victor Frankenstein as creator of his creature; later Victor will refer to his life story as a 'hideous narration' (p. 146), further mirroring Shelley's naming of her novel as 'hideous progeny' (p. ix). Though he could in theory stop the monster's violence by creating him a mate, Victor destroys his work at the last minute for fear of engendering greater violence: 'one of the first results of those sympathies for which the daemon thirsted would be children, and a race

---

[13] Victor designates himself as the monster's 'creator' repeatedly throughout the novel.

of devils would be propagated upon the earth, who might make the very existence of the species of man a condition precarious and full of terror' (p. 121).

Frankenstein anticipates *The Salamander* most pointedly in the relationship between Victor and Elizabeth. After Victor is cleared of Henry's murder, he receives a letter from Elizabeth in which she addresses the problematic nature of their dangerously ambiguous sibling/lover relationship. Elizabeth asks Victor if he loves another, since, she says, 'as brother and sister often entertain a lively affection towards each other, without desiring a more intimate union, may not such also be our case?' (p. 138).[14] In refusing to acknowledge the various engendering crises in his life, Victor fails to confront the incestuous implications in his relationship with Elizabeth. Instead, he insists on quickly marrying her upon his return to Switzerland. However, the horror of the crisis is made clear when the monster strangles Elizabeth on the wedding night. On the night when marriages are traditionally consummated sexually, Victor's two engendering crises – one creative, the other procreative – meet and are resolved in a single stroke: Elizabeth's murder and the monster's promised revenge.

IV

'The Southern Shore of Finland at the Beginning of the Eighteenth Century' establishes the family roots of the characters who will later become the two main protagonists of *The Salamander*. As the title of Part I suggests, the story of begins during the time of the Great Northern War between Sweden and Russia. On August 19, 1700, Peter I joined forces with Augustus II of Saxony and Poland and declared war on Charles XII of Sweden.[15] These forces of history raged over Finland, a part of the Kingdom of Sweden since the end of the Thirty Years' War. In accordance with his own edict, Odoevskii begins *The Salamander* with a single humble family in Finland. At the head of the

---

14 As Chris Baldick shows in his comparison of the 1818 and 1831 versions of *Frankenstein*, Elizabeth was originally portrayed as Caroline Beaufort's orphaned niece, and thus Victor's cousin, making any sexual relationship between the two of them even more problematic: see Baldick's *In Frankenstein's Shadow: Myth, Monstrosity, and Nineteenth-century Writing*, Oxford, Clarendon Press, 1987, p. 199.

15 See Nicholas V. Riasanovsky, *A History of Russia*, 4th edition, New York, Oxford University Press, 1984, pp. 221-6.

family are two elderly Finns, a poor fisherman Rusi and his wife Gina, who live in a modest hut on the banks of the Vuoksi. In the novella's first lines, Gina laments the fact that she must now bring in the wood, since her son Pavali has been drafted into military service for Sweden. With her father away fighting in the war, little El'sa is cared for by her grandparents Gina and Rusi, and thus her familial position is endangered. In an even more precarious straits is twelve-year-old Iakko, an orphan whose patrilineage is left unknown and therefore open-ended throughout the novella; he is cared for by the old couple but has actually been adopted by El'sa's father. Thus the two generations represented at first are separated by an intermediary generation whose absence already brings hardship to the family and portends no good.

In the tradition of the singers of *The Kalevala*, Rusi then contextualises the war within the spectrum of Finnish mythology.[16] First, he describes a time of 'earthly paradise' in Finland, when the Sampo performed all tasks for the maintenance of human life – carrying wood, building houses, baking bark-bread, singing songs – while the people 'just lay in front of the fire, turning over from one side to the other' (p. 137). Thus the existence of the Sampo in Rusi's version of the myth leads to a type of infantilisation of the Finnish people, in which they are helpless to care for themselves. This laziness in turn angers the father-figure Väinämöinen, who punishes the people by hiding away the Sampo in the ground. Rusi thus deduces that the *Ruotsi* (the Swedes) and the *Veineleisi* (the Russians) are engaged in a war with one another on Finnish territory in order to claim the national treasure of the Sampo.

Rusi then begins a description of the two warring powers. Significantly, his story hinges on the origins of the two leaders. About the great military leader Charles XII, Rusi says:

Hardly had the king come out of his maternal womb [*iz materinskogo chreva*] than he stamped his foot on the ground and said: what Iumala has given me, Pergola will not take from me. And he went around the earth with an iron

---

16 This 'Finnish Legend' within *The Salamander* is one of Odoevskii's most intriguing narrative performances. From his own time, in the late 1830s, he re-creates the telling of the Great Northern War, in the early 1700s, from a 'foreign' cultural perspective and genre. I agree with Karlinsky in his judgment that *The Salamander* merits examination from the standpoint of twentieth-century cultural anthropology (Karlinsky, op. cit., p. 179).

> sword; wherever he came to, he would wave his sword and people would die.
> (137 / 145)

The reference to the King's military prowess straight out of the womb is based on the fact that Charles XII ascended the throne at the age of fifteen in 1697 and amazed the surrounding invaders with his military genius.[17] Charles' connection with an 'iron sword' (*zheleznyi mech*) provides also an important mythical connection with *The Kalevala*, in which Väinämöinen searches for the origins of iron in order to heal his wounded leg (Canto 9).

However, as great as the Swedish king's origins are, 'The tsar is obviously stronger than the king', as Rusi explains, 'for he knows how he was born' (*ibo on znaet, kak on rodilsia*: 137 / 145). That birth is described as an inversion of Aphrodite's:

> They say he came straight out of the sea. There was a severe storm, the waves washed over the earth, ships sank, rocks tumbled from the shores into the sea. The [Swedish] king sat up on the shore, waved his iron sword and ordered the rocks to get up from the sea, but the rocks didn't obey. The king got angry, the sea raged even more, when suddenly it parted and from the water came the Tsar of the Russians. With one hand he raised the rocks and with the other he pointed all round and said: everything I see is mine. (p. 138)

This creation myth of Peter I identifies him with the Finnish epic hero Väinämöinen in two ways: he effectively enacts his own birth, and he can derive power from the ability to tell of his own origins – 'he knows how he was born'. Peter I also proves his might against Charles XII, whose iron sword is blunted by his more humble human origins, the 'maternal womb'. Rusi continues his 'Finnish legend' in a further mythification and glorification of Peter I: his forbidding of beards in Russia, the building of the Russian Navy, and even the creation of St Petersburg. Even when the sea sides with Charles XII, 'cramped within [its] shores' by the construction of Petersburg (p. 139), Peter is able to triumph over nature, commanding the sea to freeze, and thereby crosses over to invade Sweden. Later in the text, Peter I will be identified 'in the first place as a giant, and secondly in the guise of a miraculous mage who had subjected the elements' (p. 148).

---

[17] See Riasanovsky, op. cit., p. 221.

As a Russian, Odoevskii cements his patriotic viewpoint within a supposedly impartial outside narrator, but points to the actual bias of the narrator by embedding the old name for Russia (*Rus'*), into Rusi's name. The legend in fact ends with the telling of 'strange dreams' in which the Finnish people embrace the Russian invaders; Rusi tells of:

> ... huge rocks raising themselves up from the shores of Suomi [i.e., Finland], swimming across under the legs of the Russian Tsar, so that he went higher and higher; the Suomi people ran up the heap of rocks and the Tsar of the Russians was sheltering them with his huge hand. ... And above the city again is the Russian Tsar in a gold wreath; he is carried on heavenly clouds and from his wreath there fall on to Suomi golden sparks, which shine like a thousand suns. It's wonderful! Wonderful! (p. 140)

Thus while mythologising Peter I's height and strength, Rusi advocates him as the appropriate protector-cum-father to the Finnish children. The historical images are an appropriate reflection of a family 'orphaned' through the absence of El'sa's father in the war between the would-be fathers.

The war eventually comes to this family in the sound of approaching cannon, but before its full-scale arrival Rusi forces El'sa to use her magical visionary powers to see in the fire the murder of her father by Swedes. Gina is killed moments later in the hut by the same Swedish soldier, now wearing a Finnish coat, whom she accuses, 'You killed my son, and you want to kill my husband too!' (p. 143); Rusi then avenges her death in a dramatic act of self-sacrifice by drowning himself and the retreating soldier. These events place El'sa and Iakko in peril, as they are left without any parent-figures. As El'sa hides, Iakko is taken by the advancing Russian troops as a guide. Inflamed by thoughts of revenge, Iakko manages to save the life of Russian commander, Lieutenant Zverev, in battle by killing two Swedish soldiers. For this act of bravery, he is presented to Peter I on the battlefield as a hero: 'Lieutenant Zverev took Iakko by the hand and the tall black-haired man, before whom everyone removed their hats, patted him on the cheek and uttered something to those around in a language that was incomprehensible to the Finn' (p. 146).

Iakko's fate is then to continue participating in great moments of Russian history: he is taken to St Petersburg, and from there sent on to Europe for formal education as one of the tsar's emissaries. In the space of eleven years. Iakko has become 'an excellent physicist and mechanical engineer', and he has changed his name to 'Ivan Ivanovich Iakko' (p. 147). By displacing his former first name to his last, Iakko keeps a semblance of his Finnish heritage and claims his familyhood (through his last name, his *familiia*) for his own. However, by taking the most common Russian name and patronymic, Iakko announces his assimilation into the new Russian intellectual corps of Peter I, and in fact disguises the question of his patrilineage through Russification. It is interesting to note that in Holland Iakko is watched over by 'old Zverev', the father of the Lieutenant Zverev, whose life Iakko had saved on the Finnish battlefield. The narrator tells us that old Zverev loves Iakko 'like his own son' (*kak rodnogo*: 147 / 154).

The issue of patrilineage continues to haunt Iakko upon his return to St Petersburg to be presented to the tsar. In mythopoetic language mimicking that of the 'Finnish Legend', the narrator proclaims the 'miraculous times' of the Russian Empire and the great intellect of its emperor in dealing with 'internal improvements':

> The disorder of local affairs, the means of communication, the education of the people: all of this was entering Peter's mind and, from the heights of the throne, like powerful seed [*kak moguchee semia*], was falling on to fertile Russian ground [*na plodonosnuiu russkuiu zemliu*]. (148 / 155)

As the etymological roots of words like 'seed' (*semia*) and 'fertile' (*plodonosnyi*) suggest,[18] Peter I (through his 'seminal' thoughts) takes on the double role of the creative genius of his young empire and *pro*creative *progenitor* of a whole new people. The image of Peter I as great genius genitor reflects the earlier portrayal in the 'Finnish Legend' of Peter as a great father to the infantilised Finnish people. He

---

[18] *Semia* in Russia, as in English ('seed'), carries strong secondary connotations of physical procreation (*sperma* = 'sperm', 'semen') and metaphorical procreation (*potomstvo, rod* = 'posterity', 'lineage'): see *Slovar' russkogo iazyka*, vol. 4 (Akademiia nauk SSSR), Moscow, 1961, p. 106,; and *The Oxford Russian-English Dictionary*, second edition, Oxford, Clarendon Press, 1990, p. 727. It should also be noted that the word for 'seed' in Russian (*semia*), shares its root with the Russian word for 'family' (*sem'ia*), and thus is semantically linked to this word, as well as being very close orthographically in Russian.

The Russian word for 'fertile' here (or, more literally, 'fruitful': *plodonosnyi*), has as its root the word *plod*, meaning not only 'fruit', but 'fetus': *Slovar' russkogo iazyka*, vol. 3, p. 196 (*plod* = '*zarodysh u cheloveka i mlekopitaiushikh'*) and *Oxford*, p. 523.

will 'shelter them with his huge hand' (*prikryvaet ikh svoei ogromnoiu rukoiu*: 140 / 148) from St Petersburg, described at Iakko's return from Europe as 'the new capital of the reformer of Russia, which had only just risen from the Finnish marshes' (p. 147). Clearly, Peter I is not only fertilizing Russia, the 'fatherland' (*otechestvo*), with his 'powerful seed', but Finland as well.

Peter I's metaphorical fathering of Finland complicates the issue of Iakko's paternity, especially when given his prophetic meeting with Peter in Finland. Upon returning to Petersburg from Holland, Iakko is presented to Peter, assigned the honour of creating the nation's first typography and printing presses, and falls before the tsar in gratitude and love. 'And so,' the narrator concludes, 'the half wild Finn, under the mighty hand of Peter [*pod moguchei rukoiu Petra*], was to become one of the instruments of the Russian enlightenment' (149 / 156). The modifier '*moguchii*' ('mighty') is the same one used to describe Peter I's 'seed' (*moguchee semia*), and its repetition less than a page later indicates the same kind of procreative connectedness between Peter I and the Finnish orphan Iakko that it indicated between the Russian tsar and infantilised Finland.

The plot then turns to Finland in 1722, where Iakko has come to claim El'sa and bring her back to St Petersburg. By this point, Iakko's transfer of national paternity is nearly complete: he has almost entirely forgotten his native language and refuses to recognise the land of Rusi and Gina as his own. Two important characteristics of El'sa reinforce Iakko's transformed identity: firstly, as foretold by her ability to see the death of her father in the fire, she is known in her village as a sorceress with prophetic powers. Secondly, she expresses herself with an innocence that is child-like, embracing Iakko when convinced of his identity and naively assuming they will now marry. In fact, her lack of sophistication regarding urban societal conduct between men and women frightens the now-modernised Iakko; the idea of spending three days in a carriage with El'sa leads him to believe that 'the very innocence, the very straightforwardness of her feelings could be disastrous for them both' (p. 152). When El'sa reluctantly agrees to accompany Iakko back to Petersburg, Iakko arranges for her to ride in a separate carriage with the village pastor's wife. As final proof of his alienation from his native (*rodnoi*) land, he mentions in passing to the pastor that '*our* Russian carts are no good at all on *your* mountains' (p. 153; italics Odoevskii's).

Back in St Petersburg, Iakko places El'sa with his old father figure Zverev, to whom he explains his familial relationship with El'sa as that of sister and brother. Zverev agrees to take her in, and in fact looks after her with 'fatherly kindness' (*s ottsovskoiu dobrotoiu*: 158 / 165). This familial relationship between El'sa and the Zverevs continues the brother-sister link between Iakko and El'sa, since Zverev, who loves Iakko 'as a son', now becomes a father figure to them both. When El'sa takes (or is assigned) the Russian name 'Lizaveta Ivanovna' (with no last name given), the text for a third time presents El'sa and Iakko as sharing a father. This identification of Iakko and El'sa as brother and sister through a shared partonymic indicates a future conflict of sexual desire.

Complicating the issue, the narrator goes on to report that, since El'sa's arrival in Petersburg, Iakko is suffering a crisis of indecision: should he marry El'sa, who is beautiful and connected to his childhood, but half wild and uncultured, or Zverev's daughter Mar'ia Egorovna, less radiant than El'sa but attractive enough and – more importantly – successfully socialised as a member of Petersburg court society and future wife of a high-ranking government official? Later on, the jealous El'sa succeeds in winning a temporary lead over Mar'ia by threatening to go back to Finland with another Finn in Petersburg, since, 'At the thought of their homeland [*o rodine*], [Iakko's] heart automatically beat faster: the charms of El'sa, his childhood playmate, seemed to him all the greater and to part from her, to part for evermore, seemed to him unthinkable' (164 / 171). Once again, Iakko makes the logical semantic link between his 'homeland' (*rodina*) and his birth (*rozhdenie*), since they both come from the same etymological root (*rod-*).

In light of their brother-sister relationship, Iakko's discomfort with El'sa's open feelings of sexual desire for him (and his return of those feelings) signifies a greater worry than El'sa's unsophisticated behaviour in society: that is, the possible violation of the incest taboo. After all, though Iakko's connection to Mar'ia Egorovna could also be construed as familial, their relationship is not as clearly marked as sister-brother as that of El'sa and Iakko. Also, Iakko has more to fear from El'sa than from Mar'ia as a hero-transgressor: she is a sorceress, identified at several points in the novella as a 'witch' (*ved'ma*) with prophetic powers. Against the pleasant artificiality of the Zverevs' adopted Western European lifestyle – old Zverev is primarily concerned with what is and isn't 'seemly' (*tak sleduet*) – El'sa represents authenticity; and against the rising city of Petersburg, she represents nature and its powers. When choosing a dress for a ball, El'sa chooses 'bright red', Mar'ia a pink one (p. 158). Set up from this point onwards as the chief transgressor of societal man-created laws, El'sa, not unreasonably it would seem, appears to the worried Iakko as the riskier woman. She threatens to undermine the fatherland by bringing Iakko into a symbolically incestuous union, when seen in the light of their shared origins.

After El'sa's attempt to bewitch Mar'ia in the race for Iakko, and her subsequent discovery, El'sa is brought into a room with Iakko, Zverev, and his wife to confess her transgression. But because of the 'intermingling' of moonlight, firelight from the stove, and candlelight (p. 165), El'sa falls into a state of possession of the sort shown earlier in the text when she sees the murder of her father, and which has earned her the title of 'sorceress'. She speaks in a strange voice, saying that her attempt to put a spell on Mar'ia was a 'childish joke' (*rebiacheskaia shutka*), and calls the magical centre in the fire 'the scarlet halls of my little sister' (*alye palaty moei sestritsy*: 166 / 173). Talking of the 'magnificent halls' of her fiery vision, El'sa continues her descent into childhood:

> In the middle of those halls a child's face [*litso rebenka*] appeared to me, one exactly like mine; it would smile, beckon me in, disappear in streams of flame and appear again with the same smile. 'Little sister, little sister [*Sestritsa, sestritsa*], – it would say to me, – when shall you and I be united?' And my heart would long for this beautiful child [*k prekrasnomu rebenku*] ... Do you hear, Iakko, what little sister says; you are the only thing we lack; the mighty power of old Rusi vitalised you too, you silly [*nerazumnyi*]; you are ours, Iakko! (pp. 166-7; 174)

El'sa's vision of a return to her homeland is a return to her childhood, an idea which terrifies Iakko, and not only because of his reluctance to leave his new-found wealth and societal stature. Such a return would bring him back to his uncertain birth and paternity, to a time when he and El'sa were raised as brother and sister, which, given his desire for El'sa, he cannot contemplate.

Having witnessed this extraordinary scene of possession, Iakko and the Zverevs call a doctor, who prescribes opium and caffeine to keep El'sa drugged and submissive. El'sa can only protest her drug regimen in dreams and visions, in which she sings full verses of what will later become *The Kalevala*. Thus even while the Westernised rationalists try to erase El'sa's transgressive connections with primitive forces, El'sa manages to maintain contact with the ancient oral tradition of her birthplace. Visiting her, Iakko for the last time contemplates marrying her. However, by this stage of his Russian repaternilisation, Iakko can only see the idea in terms of a mechanised and Westernised viewpoint: 'To marry her? The very thought turned Iakko cold. He could not help comparing his situation with a fine machine, in which just one wheel had been wrongly installed, which had the effect of spoiling the motion of all the other wheels' (p. 172).[19] However, not having fully transferred his birth allegiance to Russia, Iakko is still able to feel despair when observing El'sa's beauty: 'his native sky [*rodnoe nebo*] shone at him in her eyes, the fabulous world of his childhood [*basnoslovnyi mir detstva*]' (172 / 179). The word 'fabulous' (*basnoslovnyi*) denotes that which is 'mythological', 'legendary', indicating that Iakko's childhood may be subconsciously connected with a myth which he wants concealed.[20]

El'sa escapes from Petersburg back to Finland during the Great Flood of November 1722 with Iusso, the young Finn with whom she had previously teased Iakko. Thinking she had perished in the flood, Iakko falls into a long fever which mimics El'sa's earlier possession. When Iakko is informed of the true whereabouts of his 'sister' on coming out of the fever, he resigns himself to a Russian paternity and asks Mar'ia Egorovna to marry him, which she accepts. In the last scene of Part I, Iakko makes a last visit to Finland to see El'sa once more before his marriage. As his sleigh races along, 'A sad feeling weighed on Iakko's soul; he was travelling over his native earth [*po zemle rodnoi*], which was at the same time foreign [*chuzhaia*] to him' (175 /

---

[19] The 'machine' reflects the conflict contained in Peter I's reign (and condensed into Iakko's crisis of identity) between that which is 'folk' or 'native' and that which is 'Western' or 'modern', and therefore 'foreign'.

[20] The reference to a 'mythological' or 'legendary' childhood refers also to the myth of Peter's extraordinary self-birth recounted by Rusi in his 'Finnish Legend'. This connects Iakko to the 'Western' Peter, which furthers the conflict between his native and adopted origins.

182). Iakko observes unseen what he assumes to be El'sa's wedding to Iusso, leaves a purse of money for her, and declares: 'The last thread is broken... my land is foreign to me [*zemlia moia – mne chuzhaia*]. Farewell, Suomi[21] – farewell for ever! And greetings to Russia, my real fatherland[22] [*moia otchizna*]!' (176 / 183). It is important that Iakko no longer calls Finland his 'homeland' (*rodina*) – 'place of birth' – but simply 'my land' (*zemlia moia*). Russia, on the other hand, takes on full identity as Iakko's 'fatherland': *otchizna* comes from the same root as 'father' (*otets*). In breaking his connection to El'sa, and the possibility of an incestuous union with her, Iakko represses the crisis of his unknown birth origins in Finland. As Part II of *The Salamander* will reveal, rather than clearing up the mystery, his switch of national allegiance anticipates a still greater crisis of engendering.

V

Part II of *The Salamander*, 'El'sa', begins with two epigraphs. The second is taken from the *Autobiography of Benvenuto Cellini*:

> We were sitting in front of the fire; suddenly father hit me so hard that I cried. 'Don't cry', said father, 'you've done nothing wrong'; at that moment the Salamander appeared in the fire; 'I hit you so you don't forget it and so you'll pass this event on to your children'. (p. 177)

As happens frequently in Odoevskii's incorporation of other texts into his own, the quotation serves a dual purpose. Explicitly, of course, the excerpt introduces the concept of the Salamander, the 'spirit of the element of fire'.[23] Implicitly, however, the quotation signals the question of generations that haunts the first part of the novella. A child is violently instructed to pass the memory of being violently instructed down to his descendants. The irony captures the central theme of the entire novella – the problematic nature of a national identity based on the law of the father.

---

[21] Finnish word for 'Finland'.
[22] I have modified Cornwell's translation, changing his 'motherland' to 'fatherland', to emphasise my point.
[23] In Russian, '*dukh stikhii ognia*'; see Sakharov's note to *Salamandra* in *Sochineniia v dvukh tomax*, vol. 2, p. 352.

That theme is foregrounded in the opening image of 'El'sa' – a house which is reputed to be haunted by spirits of the dead. In his introduction to *The Oxford Book of Gothic Tales*, Chris Baldick writes:

> Gothic fiction is characteristically obsessed with old buildings as sites of human decay. The Gothic castle or house is not just an old and sinister building; it is a house of degeneration, even of decomposition, its living space darkening and contracting into the dying-space of the mortuary and tomb.[24]

It is fitting that Baldick uses the term '*de*generation', since the house in *The Salamander* is the place of cross-generational connection. The narrator's uncle speaks of the house in question as 'the house of the father' (*ottsovskii dom*: 179 / 186):[25]

> Yes indeed! I've known that house for forty years. In my day it used to belong to Prince A., with whom I was friendly in my youth. In those days the nobility lived more like boyars: at every step in the house you could see that its owner had a father, a grandad and a great grandad and their ancestors [*otets, ded, praded i predki*], which is not a thing you notice in the rented apartments of today, in which our top historical names languish so tediously and lavish their wealth... (179 / 185)

For the uncle, the house is a metonymy of the family's patrilineage. If so, however, the moans and shrieks from the 'strange room' betray a crisis within that paternal line which the house most represents, as the uncle points up when he excuses the lack of patrilineal evidence in the 'new generation' ('*novoe pokolenie*'). As he says to his nephew: 'you are cleansing your fathers' sins' (*vy ochishchaete grekhi ottsovskie*: 179 / 185).[26]

---

[24] Baldick, 'Introduction', p. xx.

[25] I alter Cornwell's translation here, originally 'the house of his fathers' (p. 179).

[26] Although space considerations here prohibit lengthy comment, it should be noted that the uncle (a double of Faust from *Russian Nights* [*Russkie nochi*] and Odoevskii himself) serves in this story as the cultural translator between the 'folk' and the 'rational'. After the nephew has given a complex, 'rational' explanation for the moaning sounds in the house, the uncle then explains to the merchant (who believes in the house's 'brownies' [*domovymi*]) that his nephew will 'get rid of the goblins' (*vyvedet domovykh*: 179-81 / 186-8).

The Gothic house typically embodies a memory of the past that resists the revisions of time. In *The Salamander* it is the nephew-narrator who reflects upon the nature of memory:

> When we entered the old boyar dwelling, I sadly examined the princely coats of arms which were generously dispersed over the walls; the rows of family portraits whose origins [*nachalo*] were lost back in the legendary periods of our history ... and my heart shrunk at the thought that coarse mechanical work was to take the place of lofty moral acts. ... Calico and printed cloth! Are you worth this? Under your mills will vanish the memory of our ancestors' ancient virtue [*pamiat' o drevnem dobre nashikh predkov*]; our history will vanish! [*ischezaet istoriia!*] (180 / 186-7)

Although the house's memory causes problems for its new owner from the *nouveaux riches*, the narrator recognises that the imminent loss of that memory constitutes a kind of crisis as well. Without memory we no longer recognise our fathers, and therefore our origins. This crisis is recognised both on the familial level – the coat of arms and portraits of one family's ancestral fathers are hung in the house – and on a national level: the fathers were boyars with responsibility to Russian society, a moral code partly destroyed by Peter I's service reforms, and the beneficiaries were the class represented by Iakko. When the nephew tries to refute the importance of the past, his uncle argues with him, affirming the house as a storehold of historical memory: 'You may laugh, Mister Philosopher, but it's quite certain that there are places to which the whole past is as though attached, on which are traced in secret letters for people who are centuries removed from us their thoughts, their will...' (p. 183).[27] The rest of Part II of *The Salamander* is devoted to exploring this past in an attempt to understand the crisis of its origins as represented in its present ghosts.

Recounted by the nephew, the uncle's narrative commences in 1726, where Iakko is introduced by his Russian identity, 'Ivan Ivanovich'. The death of his Russian father-figure, Peter I, has put Iakko in terrible straits: orphaned again as he was at the beginning of Part I, he is living

---

[27] The nephew's lament for the loss of memory is in fact also identified with Iakko in Part I. Trying to win Iakko's affections, El'sa poses Iusso as his competitor; when Iakko asks, 'Who's Iusso?', El'sa responds, 'Don't you know Iusso, Iukhano's son? You've forgotten all your own people, the *Veineleisi* have knocked your memory out of you' (*Ty vsekh svoikh pozabyl, Iakko, veineleisi sovsem otbili u tebia pamiat*: 163 / 171).

in Moscow,[28] married to Mar'ia Egorovna, now a nag and a drunk, and enslaved to a miserly old count as an alchemical assistant. 'Spurned and scorned' as a 'poor Finn', Iakko naturally looks to the only Finnish family left him – El'sa, his 'little sister' (*sestritsa*), on whose 'white breast' (*belaia grud'*) he wishes to sleep and listen to his 'native songs' (*rodimye pesni*: 189 / 196). As before, Odoevskii uses epithets containing the Russian root *rod-* to emphasise that what is 'native' is that which is connected to us through birth. Iakko's fatherless position is parodied by his selfish wife, who complains of her own misfortune:

> Oh, what a poor, miserable orphan I am! [*Akh, ia bednaia, goremychnaia sirota!*] I have neither mother nor father, neither family nor tribe, there's no one to stand up for me; God treated me to married life with an accursed Finn, a sorcerer, a heretic... (190 / 197)

Longing for El'sa, Iakko eventually conjures her in the alchemist's furnace, where she appears as the spirit of fire, the Salamander. This reunion of Iakko with El'sa in both her spiritual and earthly forms restates the crisis of their relationship. El'sa repeatedly refers to Iakko as 'brother' (*brat*) and 'old chap' (*bratets*, a diminutive of *brat*), and Iakko continues to call her by 'sister' (*sestra*) or 'little sister' (*sestritsa*). Their sexual passion, however, remains in conflict with their familial relationship, however metaphorical. The omnipresent fire motif represents not only the sexual desire inherent in Iakko's and El'sa's relationship, but also once again the danger of possible incest in any such consummation. The *dvoemirie* (or double-worldness) of El'sa's form, between that of the simple Finnish peasant girl and the powerful sorceress in the flames, is really a mirror reflection of the *dvoemirie* of her relationship with Iakko. This relation reaches a crisis, which Iakko subconsciously represents in his bizarre dream-like visions[29] in the athanor's fire. As the old count sleeps, Iakko observes skeletons, dead bodies, vulturous birds, and 'then he saw El'sa in the form of a

---

[28] In the mythology depicting the relationship between Moscow and St. Petersburg, Moscow is typically seen as the female and folk, and St. Petersburg--as the male and modernised. Therefore, after the death of Peter (metaphorical father of Iakko and the new capital) it makes sense that Iakko would relocate to the heart of the motherland, Moscow.

[29] See Victor Frankenstein's reflection of his own incestuous crisis in his 'wildest dreams' which come after the creation of his monster (*Frankenstein*, p. 35).

Salamander, with a crown on her head. The Salamander splashed voluptuously in the fiery sea and two flaming jets were issuing forcefully from her virginal breasts' (*iz ee devstvennykh persei*: 198 / 205). Earlier, Iakko had idealised El'sa's 'white breast' (a source of milk for infants); here the fire that comes out of these 'virginal breasts' indicates the danger in Iakko's sexual desire. El'sa as the Salamander realises the dual nature of Iakko's attraction to her – as family and as sexual object – when she metaphorises the search for the alchemist's stone, saying, 'From our breasts [*iz sobstvennykh nashikh grudei*] we must secrete the life-giving moisture which alone can awaken its dead power' (199 / 206). Here the Russian word is again *grud'*, identifying the mother's breast with El'sa's 'white breast', rather than with the Salamander's 'breasts' (*persi*).

With the help of El'sa, Iakko accomplishes his first alchemical triumph: to make an indigo-like dye, which he produces to great economic profit. With Mar'ia comfortably inebriated all day and El'sa running his business, Iakko can devote all his time and energy to searching for the true alchemist's stone: the magic elixir, the 'seed of metals' (*semia metallov*),[30] which, as the count assures Iakko, 'saves the body from rotting' and 'can endlessly prolong human existence' (191 / 198).[31] The use of such an elixir would halt the natural progression of generation and degeneration. Such a transgression of the laws of life and death again reflects the central transgressive nature of Iakko's sexual desire for El'sa. This crossing of boundaries between life and death is also revealed by the Salamander, who says, 'Iakko, Iakko! the embryo of life – is death...' (*zarodysh zhizni--smert'*: 202 / 209). This seemingly cryptic pronouncement bespeaks the contradictory nature of the incestuous sister-desire as well as the warning to Iakko that ends are located in origins.

During his year of working toward the completion of the elixir, Iakko grows closer to the human El'sa. One night she sneaks in to the laboratory, and he embraces her, saying:

---

[30] See the reference above to *The Kalevala*'s story about the origins of iron, which also informs Charles XII's birth myth.

[31] This life-prolonging elixir is jokingly foreshadowed by narrator of Part II when he begins his narrative with: 'There lived in Moscow an uncle cf mine, a man no longer at all young, but with a mind, a heart and an education - and in these three qualities, they say, there lies the secret of never growing old' (p. 177).

'You are my only consolation, you take the place of everything for me – both wife and family... [*i zhena, i semeistvo*]. Your father brought me up when I was a poor, helpless orphan. When again penury visited me, you took on your father's role [*ty mne stala vmesto ottsa*] ...' (203 / 210).

This passage serves to show how easily El'sa, shown to be a full heroine-transgressor in Part I, transgresses traditional relational boundaries: she is both family (of the same 'seed' as Iakko) and wife, and now both sister and father. This confusion of roles leads to the second part's climax. First, Iakko must be included in the transgression: earlier, El'sa as the Salamander had told him, 'It is enough just to desire' (*dovol'no tol'ko pozhelat'*: 196 / 203). The same night that Iakko professes his love for El'sa, and thus acknowledges her three-part role for him as sister, father, and lover, he also expresses the desire that he be married not to the despicable Mar'ia but to El'sa. Mar'ia then bursts into spontaneous flame in her bed and dies a painful but quick death, and El'sa begins to assume her role as the next wife. After creating the real alchemist's stone, with the ability to turn anything into gold, Iakko also desires to take the place of the count, in order to spend his new-found wealth freely and take a place in society. Once again, his wish is granted: the boundaries between personal identity are transgressed, and Iakko becomes the grey-haired old count.

The deaths of Mar'ia and the count thus give birth to a new life of wealth and prestige for Iakko. He moves to the count's estates, transports his gold, and assumes an active (and, surprisingly to all, youthful) role in society. Rumours circulate that the old count has the intention of marrying the sixteen-year-old Princess Vorotynskaia. Negotiating the marriage with the girl's mother, the count (Iakko) is described as '*plammenyi*', which is understood metaphorically as 'impassioned', but literally means 'fiery' or 'flaming' (210 / 217). The fire again signifies transgression: the threat of inappropriate sexual desire is repeated here (now the desire of an old man for a young girl), but the real issue this time, of course, is that Iakko has transgressed against the primary transgressor – El'sa. In a scene which evokes the wedding-night events of *Frankenstein*, El'sa comes to visit Iakko on his wedding day to the princess, asks him naively when they will be married, and, having received a condescending rebuff, murders him in a raging fire.

El'sa's act of violence cannot simply be construed as a lover's revenge; as in *Frankenstein*, the pre-consummation murder of Iakko, like that of Elizabeth, takes place at the intersection of multiple engendering crises in the texts. Iakko dies never having resolved the questions of his origin or of his sibling/lover relationship to El'sa, as Victor dies without being able to extinguish the destructive force to which he gave birth. This moment of crisis is reflected in the house's haunting. The narrator's uncle grasps the unresolved nature of the crisis when he asks the house's moaning 'poor wretches', 'When are you going to pay off your debt for this?' (p. 186). The recognition that engendering crises are in actuality debts that can never be repaid is the true Gothic revelation of *The Salamander*.

VI

As a closing note to this essay, I would like to comment briefly on the problems of engendering in Part II of *The Salamander*. The text bespeaks its own search for origins in its structure. Like *Frankenstein*, and unlike the relatively straightforward telling of Part I, 'El'sa' is an embedded narrative, typical of the Odoevskii of *Russian Nights* (*Russkie nochi*). The nephew is the exterior narrator, who presents the frame of the story: his exploration of a supposedly haunted house in Moscow. The nephew therein introduces his uncle as the interior narrator, who actually tells the story of Iakko and El'sa. This mixing of beginnings and endings not only intensifies the Gothic element in *The Salamander* of an oral tale of warning passed down through generations, but confuses the issue of where the origins of the tale – and the plot – lie. Thus the novella's structure reflects its content. Both Parts I and II refract the problem of configuring the act of narrative and cultural transmission in paternal terms. It is through this prism of the crises of origins and engendering, of fathers and sons, that *The Salamander* can be seen as achieving its greatest insights and it greatest unity.

ELENA GAN AND THE FEMALE GOTHIC IN RUSSIA

CAROLYN JURSA AYERS

When Ellen Moers devoted a chapter of her influential survey *Literary Women* to a category she called the 'Female Gothic', she used the term simply to refer to works by women writing in the Gothic mode.[1] Beginning with Ann Radcliffe, Moers charted a tradition carried on in the nineteenth century by Mary Shelley, Emily Brontë, and Christina Rossetti, and most notably in the twentieth century by Carson McCullers. She explained the female appropriation of the Gothic in terms of the way Gothic conventions seem to suit a particularly female conception of the self. Female Gothic writers share a compulsion to visualise the self and to represent literally anxieties about the boundary between self and other. As the assumption of an adult identity has traditionally been defined for women as sexual maturity, anxieties about female identity have centered on the representation of sex in terms of a mortal threat to the female self. The (traumatic) transition to adulthood, which for male characters often takes shape in a quest or adventure plot, gives birth in the Gothic imagination to visions of monsters and madness. Sexuality emerges in the Female Gothic either as a threat from the outside, or as woman's 'dark side', strongly associated with (self) fear and loathing.

Since Moers, the term 'Female Gothic' has come into wide use in Anglo-American criticism, acquiring along the way a broader range of meanings and associations than Moers had originally identified. The 'popular gothic', for example, refers to a certain kind of formula fiction which uses many of the standard Gothic devices (exotic locales, sexual threats, flight and pursuit of an innocent woman) to appeal to a largely female readership with escapist narratives. The term 'domestic gothic', on the other hand, is sometimes used to describe narratives which situate the heightened emotional pitch of the Gothic and its concern

---

[1] Ellen Moers, *Literary Women.* London, The Woman's Press, 1978 (first published Garden City, New York, Doubleday, 1976).

with sexual threat in a realistic context.[2] The tradition which Moers identified as originating in the eighteenth and nineteenth centuries has continued throughout the twentieth in the works of Sylvia Plath and Angela Carter, among others. Reworkings of the Female Gothic are still quite viable today, Margaret Atwood's novels being a notable example.

Discussions of the Gothic in Russia, however, have so far not seriously considered the possibility of a female version. The introduction of the Gothic into Russia followed closely the historical period in which the Gothic flourished in England and Germany, namely the late eighteenth and early nineteenth centuries. Ann Radcliffe's novels were for a time wildly popular in Russia; this vogue corresponded roughly with the Russian craze for Shakespeare. In his book *The Russian Gothic and its British Antecedents,* Mark S. Simpson makes a case that Russia proved to be a congenial home for the Gothic. The landscape provides a fitting background, both in the wild and gloomy regions of the mysterious north, and among the urban tenements of Moscow and St Petersburg, with their dark, winding and dilapidated staircases. This setting, along with a predilection for antirational thought, a tolerance of – if not a preference for – the emotional apprehension of reality, and a fear of the spread of revolution, all contributed to creating an atmosphere in which the Gothic could easily take root.[3] In general, the Gothic movement in Russia is associated with the names of Karamzin, Marlinskii, and, later, Dostoevskii. Of course, Gothic overtones have been noted as well in individual works by other writers: Pushkin's *The Queen of Spades*, Lermontov's *Demon*, Turgenev's *Bezhin Meadow*, and so on.

Among several 'other writers' whose work Simpson mentions in the context of the Gothic movement, we find the name of only one woman: Elena Gan (1814-42). Simpson goes no further than this brief mention, noting in passing 'a strong and continuing Gothic undercurrent' in Gan's stories of 'passionate, articulate young women', who find themselves under onslaught from 'boredom, emotional and physical

---

[2] The 'domestic gothic' is identified by Joan Lidoff, 'Domestic Gothic: The Imagery of Anger in Christina Stead's *The Man Who Loved Children*', in Juliann E. Fleenor, editor, *The Female Gothic*, Montreal and London, Eden Press, 1983, pp. 109-22.
[3] Mark S. Simpson, *The Russian Gothic and its British Antecedents,* Columbus, Ohio, Slavica, 1986.

cruelty', and men in general.[4] It is certainly true that Gan was and is recognised for her representation of exceptional women.[5] Her heroines are nearly always intelligent, sensitive women who through some accident of fate have acquired a wide, morally grounded education. These women then face a difficult confrontation with the banalities of life in a society which neither shares their lofty attitudes nor appreciates their gifts. Often their unusual talent, perceived as a threat to other women, is interpreted by others as moral or sexual laxity, while in fact their characters are remarkably pure.

In terms of genre, Gan is usually associated with the society tale, which, in turn, is often considered as a precursor to the realist novel, and so might be expected to shun Gothic features.[6] Discussions of Gan's style, however, usually deal uneasily with her 'excess of the pathetic' and other breaches of aesthetic restraint.[7] Gan's obvious narrative devices and occasionally ecstatic tone have cost her the esteem of some readers.[8] Yet it is precisely these dubious characteristics that account at least in part for the 'strong Gothic undercurrent' in her writing. Moreover, the Gothic in Gan's work may function as more than a source for stock devices. Given that female

---

[4] Ibid., p. 50.

[5] See Joe Andrew, *Narrative and Desire in Russian Literature, 1822-49: The Feminine and the Masculine*, New York, St Martin's Press, 1993, p. 85ff.; and Hugh A. Aplin, 'M.S. Zhukova and E.A. Gan. Women Writers and Female Protagonists, 1837-1843', unpublished Ph.D. dissertation, University of East Anglia, 1988.

[6] Interestingly enough, before the relatively recent acknowledgement and reconsideration of the society tale and its place in the Russian literary tradition (see, for instance, Neil Cornwell, editor, *The Society Tale in Russian Literature*, Amsterdam and Atlanta, GA, Rodopi, 1998), this genre too was generally dismissed as a non-essential sidetrack to Russian prose, in terms strikingly similar to those now used to dismiss Gothic elements in various Russian narratives: imitative of Western European trends, reliant on stock clichés, providing material for great writers to work with but not worthy of attention in its own right, etc. In the light of this, one might hope for similarly promising results from a reconsideration of the role of the Gothic in Russian literature. Elena Gan's work, coincidentally, figures in both traditions.

[7] In the introduction to the anthology *Dacha na petergofskoi doroge,* V. Uchenova notes regretfully that Gan's work is 'not free ... from an excess of the pathetic, a drawing out of certain episodes, and romantic phraseological clichés': *Dacha na petergofskoi doroge: Proza russkikh pisatel'nits pervoi poloviny XIX veka.* Moscow, 1986, p. 10.

[8] For example, see Hilde Hoogenboom, 'The Society Tale as Pastiche: Mariia Zhukova's Heroines Move to the Country', in *The Society Tale in Russian Literature*, op. cit., pp. 85-97 (92, note 11).

sexuality seems to be a real problem in Gan's fiction,[9] her Gothic
inclinations are worth investigating, particularly in the light of some of
the tendencies that have been linked to the female appropriation of the
Gothic.

Of all Gan's tales, *Society's Judgement* (*Sud sveta*)[10] is most
conspicuous in its Gothic trappings. While this novella, even more than
Gan's other works, displays all the conventional formulas of the society
tale (and has generally been read as one), it contains a Gothic episode
at its heart. This episode is related in a letter that the hero, Dmitrii
Egorovich Vlodinskii, leaves for his niece to read after he dies. In this
letter, he discloses the secret which has compelled him to live as a
recluse for almost twenty years. For most of his youth Vlodinskii had
led the usual profligate, unthinking, and unfeeling life of a Russian
officer. However, on one occasion he falls so ill that he is unable to
travel with his military unit. When the unit is transferred, Vlodinskii is
taken to recover in the country house of a German baron in the
neighbourhood. This country house turns out to be a dilapidated castle,
set in surroundings recognisably Gothic:

> The estate of Baron Gorch, situated in a gorge between the mountains, was
> surrounded on all sides by forest and dense parkland; day and night the wind
> howled in the bare trees, mist constantly blanketed the surroundings; in short,
> everything was desolate and wild. The Baron's house itself, which dated back to
> feudal times, lay half in ruins. (p. 64)

Vlodinskii goes on to describe the room 'in which the malicious doctor
had condemned me to spend a prolonged confinement' (ibid.). This
room features Gothic architectural details and furnishings, including the
all-important window out onto the surrounding landscape. Particularly
disturbing to Vlodinskii are several portraits, 'which, more than once,

---

[9] Catriona Kelly also notes 'often strong overtones of sexual revulsion' in Gan: see her
A History of Russian Women's Writing, 1820-1992, Oxford Clarendon Press, 1994, p.
114.
[10] 'Society's Judgement,' in *Russian Women's Shorter Fiction: An Anthology 1835-
1860*, translated by Joe Andrew, Oxford, Clarendon Press, 1996, pp. 50-121;'Sud
sveta', in *Russkaia svetskaia povest' pervoi poloviny XIX veka*, pp. 207-70. Moscow,
1990 (first published in *Biblioteka dlia chteniia*, 1840). Page references incorporated in
the text refer to the English translation.

during my attacks of nervous irritability, had infuriated me by their imposing, haughty bearing (particularly of the women)' (p. 65).

Here Vlodinskii endows not just the setting, but his whole experience with Gothic overtones, and, immediately introduces representations of women as an integral problem. According to his own account, he begins to behave accordingly. Confined to his room, cut off from most social contact, he hones his sensibilities: 'I caught the slightest rustle, listened ardently to every creak of a door...' (p. 65). Most of his time is spent gazing out of the Gothic window, 'and if it happened that an early bird, circling and soaring in the air, was carried down to the lower heavens, I followed it with sad eyes, envying the freedom of this inhabitant of the air' (ibid.). Interestingly enough, Vlodinskii's description of his confinement recalls not the traditional male perspective, but the experience of the typical Gothic *heroine*.[11] This supports Joe Andrew's contention that Vlodinskii's emotional transformation during this period of his life 'takes the specific form of his demasculinisation or feminisation'; Andrew notes as well the 'traditional feminine iconography' (feverish trembling and other extreme physical manifestations of emotion) applied to Vlodinskii throughout his first encounters with Zenaida, the heroine.[12]

Zenaida herself is introduced into the narrative as the object of Vlodinskii's Gothic gaze:

> Then, looking mindlessly at the garden path which began beneath my window to be lost among the distant, thick group of trees, I saw a human figure. Such a phenomenon was so unusual around the castle that I gave it all my attention. The figure was approaching rather quickly; I was already able to distinguish the dark colour of its dress; a few moments later, I could clearly see a woman, wrapped in a cloak, and wearing a veil which had been carelessly thrown over her head. (p. 66)

Unable to make out Zenaida's face in the twilight, Vlodinskii imposes on her an image of his own invention. This in itself is in keeping with the Gothic preference for imagination as a way of apprehending reality; like the conventional Gothic hero, Vlodinskii ascribes the 'strange

---

[11] There is, however, ample precedent for male confinement and sensibility: Vivaldi, the hero of Radcliffe's *The Italian,* is certainly endowed with a Gothic temperament which is tested when he undergoes confinement in the vaults of the Inquisition.

[12] Andrew, *Narrative and Desire*, p. 119.

impression' made by the appearance of a woman in the garden to the 'morbid irritability' of his nerves (ibid.). Indeed, Vlodinskii is conjuring not just a face for Zenaida, but the entire Gothic framework for his experience, as he himself realises:

> The next morning I woke up with thoughts of the strolling beauty: this was how I imagined her; and I must admit that, had an ugly old woman been hidden beneath the dark cloak and veil, I would have considered myself truly miserable, if only for a time. (p. 66)

Vlodinskii continues for several days to indulge in his Gothic fantasy, watching anxiously for Zenaida's nightly appearance in the garden. She seems to him to appear and vanish into the evening mist 'like a spectre', and he is especially taken with her shawl and veil, which sometimes hide, sometimes reveal glimpses of her face. Even when he finally has occasion to examine her face and features at length (the day is warm and she uncovers her head), he manages to superimpose a Gothic filter of perception over the decidedly non-Gothic reality that he also recognises perfectly well: 'I saw a young woman with a pleasing, but ordinary appearance, with a face which would pass unnoticed in a crowd' (p. 68). Still he continues, through an act of sheer will, to impose on Zenaida the image that has grown in his own imagination:

> In my thoughts and with my eyes I followed her and each time she reached the end of the avenue, my stranger returned towards me, and I discovered new charms in her [...] I could not tear myself away from the window: I stood like a prisoner chained to the bars of his cell by the sight of the magnificent sun, which he has not seen for many months, I stood and did not take my eyes off her. After an hour had passed I was ready to call her a beauty: my imagination created in her a beauty which was invisible to the indifferent.... (pp. 68-9)

Vlodinskii's fantasy soon bumps up against mundane reality, when the next morning his servant identifies his mysterious woman as 'our Frau Generalin'. This 'cold, heavy phrase' and the details of her life story 'tore away the flowers of mystery with which my imagination had garlanded my strange lady' (p. 70). Yet, despite even this double disillusionment, Vlodinskii continues to react to Zenaida according to a conventional Gothic pattern. When he is eventually introduced to her, he is overcome to the extent that he becomes inarticulate. When she plays the piano and sings for him, he is overwhelmed with emotion and rushes from the room.

As Vlodinskii and Zenaida draw close to each other, Vlodinskii finds that some of his expectations fall naturally by the wayside, and he grows to love her as he now sees her: 'Soon the Frau Generalin and all my fantastic visions were erased from my memory: I recognized her as a woman...' (p. 72). Nevertheless, she retains some of her mysterious aura. 'In our lengthy conversations Zenaida rarely mentioned her husband and never spoke of herself: I knew nothing of her childhood, her family, her marriage, of her fate, but I guessed that she was not happy' (ibid.).

While Zenaida herself sheds some of her 'Gothic veils', Vlodinskii continues to experience this time together in a rather Gothic tonality. He relaxes his dependence on reason and gives way to pure emotion. He is carried away; his love for Zenaida takes place in what Cynthia Griffin Wolff describes as 'a never-never land, existing beyond the reach of spatial or temporal constraints':[13] 'Day followed day; I no longer counted them. In the presence of Zenaida time seemed miraculously to fuse for me into a single, complete, lofty pleasure. I did not divide the day into hours, I did not think, nor live; I merely felt emotions...' (ibid.) The relationship, however, remains absolutely chaste, as Vlodinskii suppresses all sexual passion in favour of a more 'lofty' love.

As if these conventional formulas were not enough to place Vlodinskii's experience in a Gothic framework, he draws specific associations between his current feelings and certain sensations he had experienced in his youth when visiting Switzerland, home to the sublime mountain landscapes that figure quite often in traditional Gothic narratives (p. 75). Clearly, this is a conscious allusion to the literary genre on which Vlodinskii is modeling his narrative. The reader, consequently, awaits the next twist to the plot with some foreboding.

Soon enough, the 'real world' of society does intrude on the private world of Zenaida and Vlodinskii, and the plot proceeds according to conventional society-tale formulas. Zenaida's husband returns; the two

---

[13] Cynthia Griffin Wolff, 'The Radcliffean Gothic Model: A Form for Feminine Sexuality', in Fleenor, *The Female Gothic*, pp. 207-23 (211).

are forced to part, but a year or two later fate brings them together again. This time Zenaida's appearance is preceded not by a mystery, but by trivial rumour. Vlodinskii hears from his female relatives numerous malicious judgements about Zenaida's eccentric behaviour and immoral habits. The seed of doubt is sown in Vlodinskii's heart; when he catches a glimpse of Zenaida with another man, he leaps to society's conclusions, challenges his rival to a duel, and kills him. As it turns out, Vlodinskii has been mistaken about the presence of a rival, and the man he has killed is Zenaida's brother. Vlodinskii himself falls desperately ill, but recovers, only to find that he has indirectly sent to the grave both Zenaida's father (who dies of shock, grief, and shame) and Zenaida herself (who withers away out of despair). At this point Vlodinskii decides to become a recluse himself, condemning himself to live out the rest of his life in miserable self-recrimination, isolated from the world which had corrupted his judgement, treasuring only his final letter of forgiveness from Zenaida. The final portion of *Society's Judgement* consists of this letter, in which Zenaida explains to Vlodinskii (and the reader) how her peculiar situation has come about. In contrast to Vlodinskii, Zenaida does not resort in her account to Gothic narrative tropes; on the contrary, she provides a sober realistic appraisal of her life in an unkind society. While she recognises that her fate has been unlucky, she represents herself at all times as capable of making her own reasonable decisions. Significantly, her voice is given the final word in Gan's narrative.

In his reading of *Society's Judgement*,[14] Joe Andrew takes the Gothic episode to be possibly parodic; he notes its set conventionality, and he also points to a devaluing of the Gothic mentality at the plot level. Because Vlodinskii's expectations are deflated, Andrew considers that the exotic atmosphere of the German castle serves only to endow his spiritual 'rebirth' with a magical, fairy-tale essence. Yet this seems insufficient justification for the appearance of this and other Gothic elements in the work. The Gothic, besides consisting of a number of conventional literary devices, is indicative of a particular emotional or psychological outlook. Through its very conventional tropes, its architectural enclosures that may be either prisons or refuges, its secret letters and documents of identity, and its emotional excesses, the Gothic conveys an anxiety about the nature of the self. People are not

---

[14] Andrew, *Narrative and Desire*, pp. 117-31 (especially 122).

necessarily who they seem to be; there are secrets that lie underneath day-to-day existence. The boundaries of the self are fluid, the integrity of the self is questioned. Vlodinskii recognises these troubling implications himself as he describes the course of his love, and perhaps this awareness accounts for his choice of the Gothic mode in which to present his story:

> For Zenaida, I had forgotten friends, family, obligations, I had forgotten my very self, I saw and remembered only her; everywhere and always her alone, but, like a child who, when it has scratched its face, frowns, runs past the mirror, so as not to see its wounds and the blood, I also feared to look into my soul, I avoided all reflections, all stock-taking with myself. (p. 76)

Vlodinskii's narrative, then, raises the question of personal identity and selfhood – both his and, ultimately, Zenaida's. The Gothic tonality serves to express an anxiety about the position of the self in the world. The uncertainties Vlodinskii acknowledges in himself, questions of whether his personal identity is linked to family, to social obligations, or to his individual temperament and experience, will play themselves out, with tragic consequences, in Zenaida's life story.

Thus far I have discussed only those Gothic features that Vlodinskii himself attaches to his time with Zenaida in the castle. But the Gothic overtones in *Society's Judgement* extend well beyond this episode. Not only do the other characters seem to fall in with Vlodinskii's interpretation of the situation (the Baron calls him 'my dear captive' more than once) but there are Gothic details in the novella which do not depend on Vlodinskii's narration at all. For example, the family situations of both Vlodinskii and Zenaida conform to Gothic conventions in that they have lost their mothers at a young age. Zenaida grows up virtually unsupervised, until she is brought under the care of relatives who do not have her best interests at heart. Her marriage is likewise more the result of an extortion than of a courtship; she is sacrificed to the General for the sake of her brother's career.

There is even a hint of incest in the tale. Not only Vlodinskii but many of Zenaida's casual social acquaintances confuse her brother with the man they suspect of being her lover. This ambiguity is perhaps foreshadowed by the narrator's reference to Vlodinskii's own 'strange reputation' in later life:

> Many romantic incidents were ascribed to him, people talked of some terrible
> events, of a crime. Some told stories of how, in national uprisings he had fallen
> in love by mistake with a princess; sensitive maidens of the country concerned
> still played a melancholy waltz, which, it was alleged, he had once composed in
> a fit of amorous insanity. Others saw him as a replica of the fugitive of
> Bornholm, and were only concerned that his sister was much older than he....
> (p. 58)[15]

Granted, there is a good deal of parody in this passage, directed against
the same provincial society that refuses to accept women writers.
Nevertheless, it is significant that the narrator of *Society's Judgement*
supports Vlodinskii in situating the story in a Gothic framework. It is
she, in fact, who introduces Vlodinskii himself as a sort of mystery
character with a dark, secret sorrow:

> She [Vlodinskii's niece, the narrator's childhood friend] did not know what
> storm had reduced his life to ashes ... whether the tears of which she only saw
> the traces in the mornings were shed by him to heal his wounds or to wash
> away the bloody stains of an indelible sin ... (p. 58)

His niece's decision to give up society and come and care for him in his
isolation is compared by the narrator to 'taking the veil'. Yet, 'she was
deprived of the best, the highest consolation – of healing the soul of the
mourner – because she did not know, nor could even guess the cause of
the eternal grief which gnawed at him like a worm in the grave...'
(ibid.). All of this is completely external to Vlodinskii's own narrative;
it takes place eighteen years later, in a different country, and is related
by a different character (the narrator), whose experiences and
temperament are closer to Zenaida's than to Vlodinskii's. Yet the
references are too pointed to be accidental; Gan clearly makes these
associations intentionally.

   If there is one convincing argument for recognising as significant
the pervasive presence of the Gothic in *Society's Judgement*, it relates
to the overt theme of the work. In this novella Gan is very concerned
with the representation of female sexuality, which Wolff identifies as

---

[15] The reference is to Karamzin's Gothic story *The Island of Bornholm* (*Ostrov
Borngol'm*), which concerns an incestuous love between brother and sister; see Derek
Offord's essay in the present volume.

'the underlying problem of Gothic fiction.'[16] The plot of *Society's Judgement* turns precisely on the question of Zenaida's sexual behaviour and reputation. Not only society, but Vlodinskii as well, seem obsessed with the idea that all traces of a sexual life must be disassociated from her (curiously, her husband seems to be the only person not particularly concerned about this). Thus Vlodinskii scrupulously avoids acknowledging his (or Zenaida's) physical desire and consciously maintains their relations on a spiritual plane, 'devoid of any depraved thought'. On some level he has 'a premonition that my passion's awakening would be terrible' (p. 76) This attitude goes far beyond the concern for a woman's reputation generally treated in society tales. The night Zenaida's husband visits the castle, Vlodinskii is driven nearly to distraction by the sight of casual physical contact between them, and by the thought that the General may [!] have paid a conjugal visit to his wife.

Zenaida is naturally the one, however, who suffers most from the sexual dilemma into which she is cast. Vlodinskii, on the one hand, sees her as the pure, virtuous ideal of femininity (again, an image he himself has imposed on her), and cannot accept her in any other context. When he is forced by the arrival of her husband to consider his own physical attraction to her, his attitude and behaviour toward her change: 'My former respectful love for her was now intermingled with tempestuous thought of earthly pleasure...' (p. 77). Vlodinskii's passion then takes the destructive form of jealousy; he is especially unwilling to hear 'this angel in a woman's body' discussed in the context of 'offensive' gossip. Eventually, it is the apparent possibility that Zenaida has not lived up to Vlodinskii's image of her, rather than the fact that he is barred from seeing her, that drives Vlodinskii to his ill-fated duel:

> Had she been as pure and holy as the image I carried in my soul, then no envy, no malice would have dared to raise its poisonous sting against it....No, the charm had disappeared!.. The dreams, the love, everything was gone!.. (p. 96)

If Vlodinskii can only recognize Zenaida as pure and virtuous, society, on the other hand, sees in her only the threat of the sexual predator. Vlodinskii's aunt explains how her behaviour is viewed by most of her acquaintances:

---

[16] Wolff, 'The Radcliffean Gothic Model', p. 217.

> If you really are a pure woman, virtuous, spotless, then you should love, my dear girl, only your husband and have relations with him alone, for you have no business at all with these young admirers of incomprehensible feminine virtue. [...] Don't inflame their imaginations with your spiritual charms because they can't have your bodily charms: that too is coquetry, and even more dangerous, more immoral than the usual kind [...] This type of coquetry is the surest means of crushing a man for the rest of his life, of rendering him incapable of any lawful pleasure, of cultivating in him a revulsion for accessible sources of real, practical happiness. (pp. 87-8)

In this view of the world, women are exclusively sexual beings and dangerous temptresses of men. If their sexuality is not expressed blatantly, the only possible alternative is that it must be teasingly disguised.

Gan seems to recognise sexuality as a problem especially for talented women. While any deviation from 'normal' feminine behaviour is regarded with suspicion, women who write are imagined, in fact, as monsters. *Society's Judgement* contains in its opening pages Gan's most famous passage on how the woman writer is visualised in the eyes of provincial society:

> ... she is not merely a woman, but a woman writer, which is a special kind of creature, a capricious whim of nature or, more properly: a degenerate of the female gender. After all, there are people who are born with a bird's head and the feet of a goat, —why then can't it be that her soul, created in the image and likeness of a chameleon, will pretend to be such and such, will make a copy of herself and, what's more, will turn into a different form. (p. 54)

Confronted with the woman writer, people 'fantasize about the satanic smile on her lips, the satirical powers of observation in her eyes, the treacherous spying...' (p. 55) Writing, then, is interpreted as a moral and even physical transgression, an aggressive act against 'the natural order of things'. From this, it is not so far a leap to the idea of writing as a sexual act, an association noted more explicitly in Gan's other works.[17]

What is interesting about Gan's representation, however, is that, in addition to reversing expectations by ascribing the Gothic interpretation

---

[17] See Andrew, *Narrative and Desire*, p. 136; and Kelly, *A History*, p. 115.

of experience to Vlodinskii rather than to Zenaida, she reverses the traditional Female Gothic sexual dichotomy. According to the pattern developed by generations of women writers in England, the heroine's social self is conventionally passive and innocent, while a second, sexually threatening self lurks somewhere underneath 'normal' life. But in *Society's Judgement*, the female self that is visible to society is already depraved and sexual. This is the female identity which society takes for granted, while the lurking woman – the one of which Vlodinskii gets only a fleeting glimpse – is the pure one. Rather than unacknowledged sexual desire threatening to dislodge a socially constructed image of virtuous femininity, the desire for virtuous femininity, which seems to be linked directly to exceptional creativity, is threatened by the socially constructed image of woman as a sexual predator. And rejecting female sexuality ultimately causes as much anxiety as recognising it, because it is bound in a duality with the image Gan's heroines cherish of themselves as pure. The words of Vlodinskii's aunt, while they may be misdirected, are not entirely misconceived.

There may be a bit of self-loathing, and certainly some 'anxiety of authorship' here on Gan's part as well. She is ironic about the world's judgment, but at the same time she creates no female characters that I know of who are not trapped by this dual image of femininity. In order to reject for her exceptional heroine society's vision of femininity as centered on sexuality, Gan rejects sexuality entirely. Yet in identifying her narrative voice so closely with the sensibility of the injured Zenaida, she draws attention to her discomfort with the image of herself as a woman writer. Just as Zenaida's lofty vision of humanity does not survive in the hard, cruel world, Gan's image of inspired creativity is also under threat, and the narrator, at least, feels this acutely. Thus in uncovering Vlodinskii's story, she (the narrator) reveals some of her own secrets as well.

While *Society's Judgement* offers Gan's most extensive appropriation of the Gothic, Simpson is right to suggest that a Gothic tonality runs through most of her writing. The fact that this tonality manifests itself differently in different works only supports the contention that Gan's use of the Gothic represents not just a casual borrowing of devices, but more of a natural affinity. In *The Ideal* (*Ideal*, 1837), this affinity surfaces mainly in the sensibility of the heroine Olga, who experiences

her arranged marriage, the military transfers of her husband, and her
near-seduction by a celebrity poet, as something like a Gothic plot in
which she is continually threatened by males with demonic
tendencies.[18] Olga's eventual safe haven is found in a setting
reminiscent of the Gothic convent, a small chapel situated among the
mock ruins in the gardens of Tsarskoe Selo. When the attendant leads
her 'through the thick bushes' and opens the door to the tower, Olga is
overcome with 'a feeling of reverence'. She is flooded with memories
of her childhood, including an image of 'the ancient church on the high
crag', on which she used to gaze. Light pours through the Gothic
window to the chapel and, in a decidedly Gothic moment, Olga
achieves a kind of sublime reconciliation with her fate.[19]

In a later work as well, *Recollections of Zheleznozavodsk*
(*Vospominaniia o Zheleznozavodske*, 1841), Gan draws on some of the
more sensational Gothic features, chief among which is a sequence of
abduction, flight and pursuit across an exotic landscape. Clearly she felt
in command of these devices, and, more importantly, recognised in
them the possibility to represent and explore her imaginings of the
female self.

Granting, then, that the Gothic lens provides new possibilities for
enhancing our interpretation and appreciation of Gan's work, we should
still ask whether her adoption of the Female Gothic is a single case.
Can she in any way be thought of as part of an ongoing tradition? After
all, it is in terms of a continuing, evolving appropriation that the Female
Gothic is defined. The search for a Female Gothic tradition in Russia is
made problematic, first and foremost, by a persistent downplaying of a
separate female tradition in literature at all. Andrew, notwithstanding
his own admirable efforts to draw attention to Russian women writers,
recognises this, and characterises the development of the female
tradition in Russian letters as 'decidedly spasmodic, with as many
discontinuities as continuities'.[20]

---

[18] 'The Ideal', in *Russian Women's Shorter Fiction*, pp. 1-49; 'Ideal', in *Russkaia
romanticheskaia povest'*, Moscow, 1992, pp. 215-54 (first published in *Biblioteka dlia
chteniia*, 1837). Andrew (*Narrative and Desire*, p. 92) calls attention to 'the
sacred/demonic lexicon which saturates the text'.
[19] 'The Ideal', pp. 45-7.
[20] Andrew, *Russian Women's Shorter Fiction*, p. vii.

Despite this apparent lack of a continuous female tradition in Russian literature, there are, we might say, several individual examples which could conceivably be brought under the Female Gothic umbrella. Nadezhda Durova, roughly a contemporary of Gan and most famous for her military memoirs,[21] herself acknowledged that she had read and been inspired by Ann Radcliffe.[22] Some of her fiction displays unmistakable Gothic elements; graveyard settings and secrets of identity feature prominently.[23] In a manner very different from Gan's, Durova problematised female sexuality in her life as well as her writing, and thus it is not at all surprising that she should have had recourse to Gothic modes of representation. Yet Durova is somehow always classified as outside any literary tradition, with the possible exception of autobiography.[24]

More remotely, Mariia Zhukova, another contemporary, employs the occasional Gothic trope in several of her stories. Associating Zhukova with the Gothic is again not likely to be a popular interpretive strategy, as she is also the woman writer perhaps most likely to be accepted as one of the pioneers of Russian realism. The 'madwoman in the garden', who turns out to be Zoia, in her tale *The Dacha on the Peterhof Road* (*Dacha na Petergofskoi doroge*, 1845), may indeed represent 'a character from another genre', used self-consciously by the narrator in order to demonstrate the inappropriateness of 'Romantic' behaviour and sensibility.[25] On the other hand, it seems not too much of a stretch to see Zoia as Mary's dark double-figure in the tale, the embodiment of her irrational desire (the fact that they both desire the same man supports this reading). There is no reason, indeed, why she cannot serve

---

[21] Durova's remarkable memoir of her participation in the Napoleonic campaigns (she was able to join the cavalry dressed as a man) is recorded in *The Cavalry Maiden. Journals of a Russian Officer in the Napoleonic Wars*, translated with introduction and notes by Mary Fleming Zirin, Bloomington, Indiana University Press, 1988; originally published as *Kavalerist-devitsa*, St Petersburg, 1836, and *Zapiski Aleksandrova (Durovoi)*, Moscow, 1839.

[22] See chapter 13 of *The Cavalry Maiden.*

[23] See, for example, the story *Pavil'on*, in N.A. Durova, *Izbrannoe*, Moscow, 1984, pp. 233-406.

[24] Durova is included in an upcoming survey of Russian autobiographies: see Ulrich Schmid, *Ichentwürfe: Die russische Autobiographie zwischen Avvakum und Gercen* (forthcoming: pp. 89-104). However, Kelly calls Durova's 'interest in Radcliffean intensity ... an individual quirk' (*A History*, p. 56).

[25] Andrew's interpretation: see *Narrative and Desire*, p. 183.

both functions at once. It is true that Zhukova's plot provides none of the suspense characteristic of the Gothic; we already know Zoia's dismal fate from the beginning of the story. Yet even if she does appear in the text primarily as an icon from romantic fiction, it is noteworthy that she is there at all. Despite her rationalist 'society' mentality, Mary can not be rid of Zoia, who throughout the story intrudes at precisely the inappropriate moments which should be Mary's social triumphs.

In the twentieth century, there is no longer a question of women writers appropriating outdated romantic strategies 'by mistake', or in order to demonstrate by contrast a preference for realism. Yet the issue of how to represent female self-consciousness and the female self persists. Even quite recently, however, Russian women writers themselves seem reluctant to identify with a specifically female tradition. Helena Goscilo, observering contemporary attitudes toward women writers and women in general in Russia, notes and laments the persistent association of the label 'women's prose' with purely derogatory features, such as superficiality, a philistine outlook, and empty decoration.[26] All of this makes a positive appropriation of the Female Gothic unlikely. Again, Gothic tendencies are remarked in individual writers: for example, Nina Sadur's evocation of the 'lurking other', a threat of evil lurking under the 'thin veil of everyday life'.[27] Few claims are made, however, for a continuous tradition.

Moreover, according to Goscilo, much new women's prose displays no qualms about representing the female self directly as body; thus the 'dark' threatening side of sexual desire is not represented metaphorically, as in the Gothic, but literally.[28] And yet, sexuality is still rendered problematic as regards the integrity of the female self. Kelly comments that, '[a]s in the nineteenth century, so in the late twentieth, celibacy is frequently presented as a guarantee of independence, and the incompatibility of physical and intellectual matters asserted'.[29] So long as women writers continue to see

---

[26] Helena Goscilo, *Dehexing Sex: Russian Womanhood During and After Glasnost*, Ann Arbor, University of Michigan Press, 1996, p. 16.

[27] See 'Nina Sadur', in Marina Ledkovsky, Charlotte Rosenthal, and Mary Zirin, editors, *Dictionary of Russian Women Writers*, Westport, CT and London, Greenwood Press, 1994, p. 555.

[28] Goscilo, 'Inscribing the Female Body in Women's Fiction: Stigmata and Stimulation,' in *Dehexing Sex*, pp. 87-116.

[29] Kelly, *A History*, pp. 361-2.

themselves in terms of this 'split identity', in which sexuality is understood as a threat to the female self, the tropes of the Female Gothic lurk in the shadows of the literary pantheon, less perhaps as signs of an unwanted intruder than as a familiar 'other' mode of self-representation.

SUPERNATURAL DOUBLES:
VII AND *THE NOSE*

PRISCILLA MEYER

Vse proiskhodit naoborot.
Everything happens in reverse.
N.V. Gogol, *Nevsky Prospect* (1835)

Gogol's hilarious tale about how Major Kovalev's nose detaches itself from his face and zips around St Petersburg so astonishes critics that Saul Morson has called it a 'parable of explanation'.[1] Morson thinks that only the Nose, who says 'I understand absolutely nothing', interprets the story correctly, and concludes: 'The adventures of the nose are neither a freak of nature nor a supernatural occurrence nor a delusion: they are not *explicable in any way*. They exceed (but invite) explanation in terms of any system, even an alternative logic'.[2] I would like to propose an alternative logic that has yet to be explored: a reading of Gogol's Petersburg tale through the lens of one of his Ukrainian tales written at the same time.

Vii and *The Nose* (*Nos*) were written between 1833 and 1834, a time of transition in Gogol's work. The tales double each other structurally, in their motifs, and in their deepest thematic concerns.[3] Before doing a close analysis, it is helpful to examine the larger system governing Gogol's transposition of the supernatural *Vii* into the mundane *The Nose*.

---

[1] Once again I am grateful to Susanne Fusso for reading my manuscript with her usual insight, expertise and skill and making many valuable suggestions.
See Gary Saul Morson, 'Gogol's Parables of Explanation: Nonsense and Prosaics', *Essays on Gogol: Logos and the Russian Word*, edited by Susanne Fusso and Priscilla Meyer, Evanston, Illinois, Northwestern University Press, 1992, pp. 200-39 (227): hereafter *Essays on Gogol*.
[2] Ibid., p. 233.
[3] The motifs of *A May Night* and *The Overcoat*, written at the earliest and the latest periods of Gogol's career, follow the same pattern as those in *Vii* and *The Nose*: See P. Meyer, 'False Pretenders and the Heavenly City: "A May Night" and "The Overcoat"', in *Essays on Gogol*, pp. 63-74.

1. The Ukraine versus Petersburg

Gogol's Ukrainian tales teem with devils and supernatural terrors, while his Petersburg stories take place against such an everyday background that they were taken as social satire by contemporaries.[4] The abyss between the two sets of tales was bridged by Iurii Mann, when he showed how elements of Ukrainian diabolism appear in masked form in the Petersburg tales: unexplained traces of the supernatural are carried by, for example, the interference of animals, or involuntary motion (dancing, winking, grimacing).[5] The relationship between the two sets of stories may be even more systematic: Gogol seems to construct the Ukrainian and Petersburg worlds as complements to one another. Markers of what is transcendent in the rural setting become emblems of the mundane when moved to the urban milieu.

Gogol presents a world clearly divided between two realms that scholars have defined variously: as magical/everyday,[6] phenomenal/noumenal,[7] or sacred/profane.[8] But as John Kopper points out, Gogol's understanding of German romantic philosophy was part of a general Russian oversimplification of it. The Russian understanding was built on Schelling's version of Plato's opposition between real and

---

[4] And by later critics. G.A. Gukovskii, discussing *Old World Landowners*, characterises Petersburg as a world of evil - the government centre full of *chinovniki*, artificiality and false passions (see his *Realizm Gogolia*, Moscow-Leningrad, 1959, p. 92). If the word 'evil' is replaced with 'mundane', or 'parody of the transcendent', his definition can be extended to all the Petersburg stories, and beyond the realm of social satire.

[5] Iurii Mann, 'Evoliutsiia gogolevskoi fantastiki', in *K istorii russkogo romantizma*, edited by Iurii Mann *et al.*, Moscow, 1973, pp. 219-58; and idem, *Poetika Gogolia*, Moscow, 1978 (especially pp. 62-132).

[6] Michel Gorlin, *N.V. Gogol und E. T.A. Hoffmann*, Leipzig, 1933, pp. 46-7; and Iurii Lotman, 'Problema khudozhestvennogo prostranstva v proze Gogolia', *Trudy po russkoi i slavianskoi filologii*, 11, Tartu, 1968, pp. 5-50.

[7] John Kopper, 'The Place of the Thing-in-itself in Gogol's Aesthetics and the Journey out of Dikanka,' in *Essays on Gogol*, pp. 40-62. Kopper gives a useful survey of the discussion of Gogol's *dvoemirie* in Soviet criticism. Susanne Fusso discusses the *dvoemirie* of *Dead Souls* in relation to that of Zhukovskii in her *Designing Dead Souls*, Stanford, Stanford University Press, 1993, pp. 68-93 (especially pp. 68-73).

[8] Madhu Malik, '*Vertep* and the Sacred/Profane Dichotomy in Gogol's Dikan'ka Stories,' *Slavic and East European Journal*, 34, 3, 1990, pp. 332-47.

ideal; this opposition underlies all Russian romanticism,[9] and may be used to subsume the other terms.

One of the difficulties of understanding Gogol's work stems from the seemingly contradictory ways the ideal realm is implied. When writing clearly within the German romantic tradition of Hoffmann and Tieck, Gogol uses the usual images of the artist and muse within a secular, realist framework, as in *Nevsky Prospect* (*Nevskii Prospekt*). In the Ukrainian tales he uses both Christian imagery and pagan folklore, drawing simultaneously on worldviews that for Gogol are not contradictory but mutually illuminating.[10] Gogol's peculiar synthesis of high German and popular Ukrainian *dvoemirie* (two-world system) is analogous to the sacred/profane (Christian) opposition in the Ukrainian *vertep* (puppet theatre) that so informs Gogol's stories:[11] the Herod plays were staged in two-level puppet theatres with the divine story placed physically above the secular.[12] The Petersburg stories are bewildering in part because all of these systems are used simultaneously, as in a multiply-printed lithograph, with occasional bleeding edges.

---

[9] Cf. Michel Gorlin, 'Hoffmann en Russie', in M. Gorlin and R. Bloch-Gorlina, *Etudes littéraires et historiques*, Paris, Institut d'études slaves, 1957, pp. 189-205; and Jesse Zeldin, *Gogol's Quest for Beauty: An Exploration into his Works*, Lawrence, Regents Press of Kansas, 1978.

[10] I disagree with Mikhail Weiskopf's implication that the pagan is absolutely negative for Gogol (see his 'Nos v Kazanskom sobore: o genezise religioznoi temy u Gogolia', *Wiener Slawistischer Almanach*, Band 19, 1987, p. 40). It is only in the Petersburg setting that the pagan is demoted to mere magic. As suggested by Sergei Bocharov's analysis of Gogol's use of the mirror ('Zagadka "Nosa" i taina litsa', in *Gogol', istoriia i sovremennost'*, Moscow, 1985, pp. 124-61 [p. 146]), each motif may have a meaning corresponding to each term of the opposition real/ideal: used to observe one's exterior, the mirror abets the trivial (cf. Kovalev's use of it); used to look into one's soul, it is positively valued, with Biblical overtones: cf. *Selected Passages*: N.V. Gogol, *Polnoe sobranie sochinenii*, 14 vols, Moscow-Leningrad, 1937-52, vol. 12, p. 348 (hereafter *PSS*).

[11] See Malik, op. cit. For a detailed account of the *vertep*, complete with plot summaries, see V.N. Perets, *Kukol'nyi teatr na Rusi*, St Petersburg, 1898. For one example, see also Catriona Kelly, *Petrushka: the Russian Carnival Puppet Theatre*, Cambridge, Cambridge University Press, 1990.

[12] The same system was used by the medieval pageant wagons in England. See 'The World's Classics' edition of *The York Mystery Plays: A Selection*, edited by Richard Beadle and Pamela M. King, Oxford, Oxford University Press, 1995 (Introduction, pp. ix-xxx; especially p. xix).

In some of his more complex stories, Gogol blends Ukrainian folk mythology, puppet theatre and fairy tales with Christian texts, rituals and images, and dresses them in romantic stylistics. In the Petersburg tales, however, he appears to abandon the Ukrainian material altogether, adopting a blend of the conventions of German romanticism with the newly developing Russian Natural School. His use of low physical realist detail, that the Russian Naturalists learned from the French physiological sketches,[13] masks the divine, the supernatural and the comic elements that Gogol transposed from the Ukrainian tradition.[14]

In *Nevsky Prospect* the opposition between the high romantic and the low comic is used as the structuring device. Gogol contrasts the romantic tale of the artist driven to madness by the loss of his ideal with its comic travesty; the German idealist aesthetic philosophy of Piskarev's tale has its mundane counterpart in Pirogov's burlesque encounter with the drunken German craftsmen Hoffmann and Schiller, whose names hint at the lost ideal. Here, where the romantic sacred and profane are placed side by side in parallel anecdotes, it is easier to see the 'negative sign of a positive essence...or...of its presence in an...extremely travestied...form', as Mann says in another context.[15] It is the method of realist art to imply the ideal through its travesty in the real, to imply the poet in Hoffmann, the 'rather good bootmaker' and

---

[13] See V.V. Vinogradov, 'Shkola sentimental'nogo realizma', in his *Evoliutsiia russkogo naturalizma*, Leningrad, 1929, pp. 293-390 (translated in *Dostoevsky and Gogol: Texts and Criticism*, edited by Stephen Rudy and Priscilla Meyer, Ann Arbor, Ardis, 1979). Vinogradov's formulation ('The dream of a synthesis of natural forms with the principles of religious-civic sentimentalism tormented and consumed Gogol': English version, p. 171) omits the Ukrainian material.

[14] V.V. Gippius (in his *Gogol'*, Leningrad, 1924; reprinted Providence, Brown University Press, 1966) has discussed these components in a general way; Victor Erlich (in his *Gogol*, New Haven and London, Yale University Press, 1969, pp. 62-9) weights the German romantic influence more heavily. Mann's use of E.T.A. Hoffmann's tales as a background against which to read Gogol's is illuminating: the dreamer-idealist Anselmus of *The Golden Pot* is contrasted to Akakii Akakievich (*Poetika Gogolia*, p. 386). Plato's contribution to German romantic aesthetics is discussed by John Kopper, op. cit.; Gogol's specific use of Platonic images is discussed by Mikhail Weiskopf ('The Bird Troika and the Chariot of the Soul: Plato and Gogol', in *Essays on Gogol*, pp. 126-42). The interplay of these disparate components has yet to be analysed, to my knowledge, in the study of a single work.

[15] Iurii Mann, '*I uzhas okoval vsekh*: Gogol's Poetics of Petrification', in *Essays on Gogol*, pp. 75-88 (84).

Schiller, 'the tinsmith'; as Harry Levin said, every realist is a failed idealist.

The Ukrainian tales are explicit about the missing ideal, while the Petersburg stories only imply it. The two cultural worlds are presented as opposites: while the Ukrainian characters are constantly terrified by the eruption of devils and witches into their everyday reality, Petersburgers are immune to amazement: everyone readily accepts Kovalev's vagrant nose, seeing nothing in it that might hint at the presence of supernatural forces. Together, *Vii* and *The Nose* can be viewed as Gogol's paired *vertep* presentation of the world, with the Ukraine on the upper level and Petersburg below, a Ukrainian and a Petersburg variation on the problematic nature of divine and earthly beauty and how they are masked in the everyday.

For Gogol, following the Platonic tradition, beauty is a means to absolute truth, a source of all that is good, capable of transfiguring man. But the world abounds with false images of beauty that are diabolic deceptions.[16] Divine intention is disguised: Gogol's characters are ruined by their inability to discern it, while the reader is made to work to unveil transcendent truth lurking in the everyday. This is why vision, both physical and spiritual, is the focus of Gogol's system of motifs.[17]

---

[16] See Zeldin, op. cit., pp. 1-9.

[17] Many scholars have addressed the theme of vision in Gogol. Leon Stilman, 'The "All-Seeing Eye" in Gogol', in *Gogol from the Twentieth Century*, edited by Robert Maguire, Princeton, Princeton University Press, 1974, pp. 376-89, relates Gogol's use of vision to 'the all-seeing eye of God' (300). F.C. Driessen, *Gogol as Short Story Writer*, The Hague, Mouton, 1965, surveys Gogol's use of the demonic gaze (pp. 152-3), discussing Gogol's own fear of being seen in terms of sexual guilt (p. 163). Donald Fanger, *The Creation of Nikolai Gogol*, Cambridge, Mass., Harvard University Press, 1979, pp. 252-5, rejects the psychological approach in his survey of the motif, relating Gogol's own fear of the 'annihilating gaze' to the fixing of his identity as a writer. The present reading is closer to those of Weiskopf and Bocharov. Weiskopf ('Nos v Kazanskom sobore', p. 39) relates Gogol's use of vision and related objects (glasses, mirrors) to the words of the apostle Paul: '*Vidim ibo nyne iakozhe zertsalom v gadanii, togda zhe poznaiu, iakozhe i poznan bykh*' (I Corinthians 13:12). Bocharov (op. cit., pp. 152-4) discusses eyeglasses and nearsightedness as part of the theme of spiritual fragmentation in *The Nose*.

2. Pagan and Christian beauty in *Vii*

In *Vii*, Gogol presents divine beauty as seen on earth in two ways: in nature, which is represented in pagan terms, and in religious worship, represented by the Russian Orthodox Church.

When Khoma Brut is being ridden by the witch, he sees a water spirit (*rusalka*). She is the divine counterpart to the witch. While in Russian folklore the *rusalka* is part of the 'unclean spirits' (*nechist'*) and has no soul, in *Vii* the imagery surrounding her suggests that the water spirit evokes man's thirst for immortal beauty. This thirst is represented sensually, but as the *rusalka* is an unattainable object of desire in this life, the desire is to be read metaphorically.[18] The description emphasises clarity of vision and relates it to penetration of the soul through ringing sound:

> Khoma...felt some langorous, unpleasant and at the same time sweet feeling assailing his heart. He bent his head and saw that the grass that had almost been under his feet seemed to be growing far below, and that above it there was water transparent as a mountain spring, and the grass seemed to be at the bottom of some bright sea, transparent to its very depths; at least he saw clearly how he was reflected in it together with the old woman sitting on his back. He saw that instead of the moon some kind of sun was shining there. He heard the bluebells [*kolokol'chiki*], inclining their little heads, ringing [*zveneli*]. He saw a rusalka swim out from behind the reeds, flash her back and leg, plump, springy, all shining and trembling. She turned to him – and her face, with bright eyes, gleaming, piercing, with a song penetrating the soul, was approaching him, was already at the surface, and trembling with shining laughter, was moving away; and now she turned on her back, and her cloudlike breasts, matte white like unglazed china, gleamed in the sun at the edges of their white, soft and supple roundness. Little bubbles of water like beads bedewed them. She was all quivering and laughing in the water ...
>
> Was he seeing this or not? Was he awake or dreaming?...Was it wind or music ringing, ringing [*zvenit, zvenit*], and winding, and approaching, and piercing the soul with some unbearable trill ... (II, 186-7 / 2, 140-1)[19]

---

[18] In A. Afanas'ev's definition, 'Slavic ... *rusalki* are from head to waist young maidens of marvelous, seductive beauty, and below have a fish tail' (*Drevo zhizni*, Moscow, 1982, p. 213). Some *rusalki* have legs, although here the singular (*noga*) is ambiguous. Her function in *Vii* matches Afanas'ev's description: 'they sing enchanting songs and lure incautious youths', but Khoma is too busy struggling with the demonic forces of the witch/beauty to respond to the call from the other world.

[19] Citations are from Gogol', *PSS*, indicated in the text by volume (in Roman numerals) and page number, followed by the same (volume number in Arabic numerals) for the English translation, taken from the *The Complete Tales of Nikolai Gogol*, edited by

The *rusalka* shimmers under the reflecting surface that divides the temporal world from the eternal. In the reflection the two worlds are inverted: the moon shines above the water while the sun seems to shine beneath the surface, suggesting another world below. Such disorienting reversals are the problem Khoma is meant to solve: the old woman turns out to be a beauty; the beauty turns out to be a witch. The church is a holy place but filled with demons; the witch's corpse is alive but the church is dead. The description of the *rusalka* describes Khoma's dilemma: he is caught between earthly (the witch/beauty on his back) and otherworldly sensuality; the first leads to his death, while the soul-piercing song of the *rusalka* accompanied by the ringing of the bluebells from below summon him to eternal life. Here, as throughout the tale, Khoma has difficulty distinguishing between the confused categories[20] – only when he is flying over a forest does Khoma think 'Ehe, this is a witch' (II, 186 / 2, 140). Beauty and sensuality are ambiguous: they may signify divine beauty or mask the diabolic. The *rusalka* is a pagan icon of an ideal form of feminine beauty (breasts like clouds). The other women Khoma encounters – the witch/beauty (the *pannochka*), the young widow Khoma sins with after beating the *pannochka*, and the coquette in the *sotnik*'s (Ukrainian officer's) kitchen – are to be measured against her.

The connection becomes explicit through the motif of the ringing of little bells. By punning on bluebells (*kolokol'chiki*), Gogol connects the *rusalka*, the *pannochka* and the church. Shortly after Khoma sees the bluebells at the bottom of the *rusalka*'s lake, he beats the witch; her transformation into the beautiful *pannochka* is marked by the sound of *kolokol'chiki*: the wild howls of the witch 'at first were angry and menacing, then grew fainter, sweeter and clearer, then rang [*zveneli*] gently like silver bells [*kolokol'chiki*] that went straight to his soul' (II, 187 / 2, 142). The two beauties appeal to Khoma's soul, the first a pagan spirit, the second a bewitched woman. The parallel between the two descriptions is reinforced by Khoma's doubt: as he had wondered about the *rusalka*, he asks himself, 'Was he seeing this or not?', and

---

Leonard J. Kent, Chicago, University of Chicago Press, 1985, 2 vols. I have made some alterations in the translation.

[20] Driessen's psychological analysis of Khoma's and Gogol's Oedipus complex is based on collapsing these oppositions, removing the essential ambiguity of the artistic text.

'Was it really the old woman?': Khoma doubts the reality of both events; he must discriminate between divine and diabolic beauty.

Vii opens with the ringing of the 'rather ringing [*zvonkii*] seminary church bell [*kolokol*]' (II, 177 / 2, 132) and closes with church bells – Khoma's friend Khaliava becomes the bellringer (*zvonar'*) of the highest belltower (*kolokol'nia*) (II, 218 / 2, 168). Thus the tale of the godless seminarian Khoma is framed by the potential saving powers of Christian faith, and his test is to identify forms of female beauty, with the eternal, mythical, natural ideal of the *rusalka* at one extreme and the deceptive shape-changer on the other.

After beating the *pannochka*, Khoma 'got to his feet and looked into her eyes: the sunrise glowed, and the golden cupolas of the Kiev churches gleamed in the distance' (II, 187 / 2, 142). The churches could save him from her had he faith but, like his fellow seminarians, he is preoccupied with fleshly appetites – food, sensuality, tobacco. That Khoma's Christianity is too much a travesty to protect him is indicated by his comic double, the bellringer Bogoslov (theologian) Khaliava.

3. Doubling through Signs of Soullessness: *Vii* and *The Nose*

Khoma and Kovalev are doubles, and each has his own comic double, who plays an important role at the end of the tale. The ending of *Vii*, involving the seemingly irrelevant Bogoslov Khaliava, actually contains the moral of the tale, emphasising Khoma's spiritual emptiness. That the two seminarians are doubles is hinted at by their mirrored initials – Kh. B. and B. Kh. – as well as by a tobacco motif: on the first page, the 'philosophers' such as Khoma are said to have tobacco roots (*koreshki*) in their pockets (II, 177 / 2, 133), and on the last page Khaliava, now himself become a philosopher, is said to smell of these tobacco roots (*tabachnymi koreshkami*) (II, 218 / 2, 168). As will be seen, tobacco is part of Khoma's downfall.

The comic double of Major Kovalev (pronounced 'Kovalióv') is Ivan Iakovlevich. Their names too are phonemically similar (KOVaLioV / iaKOVLeVich) and, like Khoma and Khaliava, both are noted tobacco users. After Kovalev tells him his hands stink and he denies it, Ivan Iakovlevich takes a pinch of snuff before lathering him (III, 51 / 2, 218). Kovalev becomes enraged at the newspaper man for offering him snuff when he has no nose: 'May the devil take your tobacco!' (III, 63 / 2, 229) and resumes aggressively taking snuff when his nose returns – 'deliberately taking out his snuff box, he stuffed ... for an extremely long time his nose at both entries' (III, 74 / 2, 238).

Both Khaliava and Ivan Iakovlevich are linked to fish. Khaliava steals a carp which Khoma in turn pulls out (*vytashchil*) of his pocket; and Ivan Iakovlevich uses fish as his excuse for looking under the bridge where he hopes to dispose of the evidence of his guilt. In both tales, the comic doubles are corrupt. Khaliava smokes and drinks excessively; Ivan Iakovlevich, like every decent Russian workman, 'was a terrible drunk' (III, 51 / 2, 218). Khaliava carries off (*utashchil*) a boot sole; the policeman who returns Kovalev's nose accuses Ivan Iakovlevich of having 'filched [*stashchil*] a strip of buttons from a shop' (III, 66-7 / 2, 232).

Khoma and Kovalev are womanisers. After Khoma escapes from the witch/beauty, he takes up with 'a young widow in a yellow bonnet who was selling ribbons, shot and wheels', after which he is seen in a tavern 'smoking a pipe as his habit was' (II, 188 / 2, 142). Kovalev would tell 'a woman on the street selling shirt fronts' or 'some pretty little baggage' to go round to his house (III, 53 / 2, 220). Further sign of the heroes' soullessness, bearing in mind Mann's tracing of the motif of demonic motion,[21] is their dancing: Khoma 'when he was drinking, always engaged musicians and danced the *trepak*' (II, 181 / 2, 136). At the peak of his fear, before the third night he is to read over the corpse of the *pannochka*, Khoma gets drunk and dances such a prolonged *trepak* that the servants (*dvornia*) watching him spit and walk off (II, 215 / 2, 166). Kovalev, overjoyed by the return of his nose to his face, 'almost danced the *trepak* barefoot about his room, but the entrance of Ivan stopped him' (III, 73 / 2, 237). Khoma dances from terror at his impending trial in church; Kovalev dances from relief at the conclusion of his ordeal. Khoma fails the test of faith and pays with his life, while with restored nose Kovalev happily continues his soulless existence.[22]

The comic doubles provide the anticlimaxes of the tales of the heroes' terrifying adventures. After Khoma perishes from demon-induced terror, Khaliava 'spent a whole hour plunged in thought' (II, 218 / 2, 168). His friend's terrifying death means nothing to him, for he has been made 'bellringer of the very highest belfry', which only

---

[21] Mann, *Poetika Gogolia*, pp. 123-5.
[22] Bocharov briefly compares Khoma's and Kovalev's 'ordeals' in 'Zagadka nosa'.

increases his dandyism and tendency to reek of 'spirits and coarse tobacco'. The tale's climax, his carrying off the sole of an old boot by force of habit, is an inverse moral apotheosis.

In *Vii* young Khoma dies tragically and nothing changes – Khaliava's bad habits only get worse. The seminarians' lack of spiritual dedication has caused Khoma's death, but Khaliava continues in his spiritually slovenly ways. But in *The Nose*, after Kovalev's 'tragedy' has been happily resolved, Ivan Iakovlevich is a changed man: 'There it is, sure enough. What can it mean? He went on pondering, and for a long while he gazed at the nose. At last, lightly, with a cautiousness which may well be imagined, he raised two fingers to take it by the tip' (III, 74 / 2, 238). When Kovalev admonishes him, he is 'flustered and confused as he had never been before', and learns to shave Kovalev without holding on to his nose. Thus while Khoma's death goes unredeemed by his double, Kovalev's mock tragedy leads to his double's mock reformation. In *The Nose* everything takes place within the comic secular plane; in *Vii* only the last page does. In both cases, the comic low detail heightens all the characters' lack of spirituality.

Mirrors reveal the heroes' spiritual crisis.[23] Khoma had seen himself reflected in the lake when he saw the *rusalka*; he sees himself in a mirror after the second night in church has turned his hair grey. He is shown his grey hair by a 'coquette' who works in the *sotnik*'s kitchen, where she keeps a triangular fragment of a mirror, 'fly-spattered ... in front of which were stuck forget-me-nots, periwinkles and even a garland of marigolds, indicating its purpose for the toilette of the finery-loving coquette' (II, 211 / 2, 162).

The *rusalka*'s clear, bright lake is contrasted to the dirty fragment belonging to the flirtatious kitchen maid, and marigolds (*nagidki*), instead of bluebells, adorn the mundane temptress, a 'not-yet middle-aged babenka in a tightly-tied apron that showed her round, firm waist' (II, 212 / 2, 162). The marigolds link her to the *pannochka*: the *sotnik* calls his daughter 'my field marigold' (*polevaia nagidochka*) (II, 198 / 2, 151). The ribbon she wears also links her to the ribbon-selling young widow Khoma sinned with in Kiev. Through these associations with the three temptresses of the tale, the mirror, which reflects the real

---

[23] Weiskopf and Bocharov find the mirror to be a measure of spirituality in Gogol (Weiskopf, 'Nos v Kazanskom sobore', pp. 39-40; Bocharov, op. cit., pp. 145-6: see note 10 above).

effects on Khoma of his supernatural experience, suggests the possible consequences of sensuality.

Major Kovalev looks at himself in a mirror seven times during the tale. The mirror reveals the loss of his nose, the absence of which keeps him from his lady-killing, in particular in the Kazan cathedral, where he sees a woman whose dress 'very nicely described her slender waist' (III, 56 / 2, 223) as the coquette's apron had displayed her firm waist. The mirror also shows the nose's return, which allows Kovalev to say to himself: 'Take that, you women, you hens! [*vot, mol, vam, bab'e, kurinyi narod*!] And I won't marry the daughter anyway' (III, 74 / 2, 238). He resumes his promiscuous ways with new gusto: 'And after this [he] could be seen...pursuing absolutely all the pretty ladies'.

Mirrors in *Vii* reveal the extremes of divine and mundane, providing an eternal view of sensual sins. In *The Nose* the divine becomes merely a parody of the supernatural (the nose's adventures) and the sensual predominates. Petersburg daily life is even more terrifying than Ukrainian devils, because it is entirely devoid of meaning.

The heroes comment on the meaninglessness of events, but not to the point. The refrain of death/disappearance (*propadat'*) 'for nothing' reinforces the implied parallel between Khoma's soul and Kovalev's nose: The wandering seminarians looking for shelter ask the witch, 'How is it possible that Christian souls would perish for nothing at all [*propali ni za chto, ni pro chto*]?' (II, 184 / 2, 138); and after Khoma's death Khaliava says: 'He perished for nothing [*propal ni za chto*]' (II, 218 / 2, 168). Kovalev laments, 'If at least it had been cut off at war or in a duel, or I had somehow been the cause; but it disappeared for no reason at all [*propal ni za chto, ni pro chto*], for nothing, not for a penny!!...'(III, 64 / 2, 230). The equation of Christian souls with Kovalev's nose is strengthened in Kovalev's scene with the doctor. The doctor offers to buy the nose, to which Kovalev screams: 'No, no! I won't sell it for anything! [*ni za chto ne prodam*]...better let it be lost! [*propadet*]' (III, 69 / 2, 234). The doctor, with his pitch-black [*smolistye*] sidewhiskers, is a parodic devil trying to buy Kovalev's soul. His diabolic aspect is confirmed by association with the *pannochka*'s curses, which 'gurgled hoarsely, like the bubbling of boiling pitch [*smoly*]' (II, 210 / 2, 161). The echo of the Ukrainian supernatural setting of these words resounds eerily in Petersburg.

4. Structure and Spirituality

As *Vii* begins and ends with church bells, *The Nose* begins and ends with an evocation of Christian faith: March 25th (Old Style) is April 7th (New Style), Annunciation Day on the Orthodox Church calendar. What could have been a conversion tale, beginning without faith but gaining faith through catharsis, turns out instead to be an identity: Kovalev with nose restored is no more different from the Kovalev who has not experienced nose loss than March 25th is from April 7th, and the miracle of immaculate conception and divine birth goes unremarked (though hinted at by Ivan Iakovlevich's reformed behaviour). The faithless Khoma, however, undergoes the great change of moving from this world to the next.

Ivan Iakovlevich lives on Voznesenskii Prospect (Ascension Avenue), but the resurrection of the spirit is less miraculous to him than the reappearance of Kovalev's nose on his face. Ascension Day, which takes place forty days after Easter, is also known as Holy Thursday. Khoma confesses to the *sotnik* that he once sinned 'with the baker woman on Holy Thursday itself' (II, 197 / 2, 150). In *Vii* these church holidays have meaning for the characters. Unlike any of the characters in *The Nose*, Khoma is aware that he is a sinner, although he uses this knowledge only to try to save his life when trying to get the *sotnik* to release him from the third night of reading over the *pannochka*: 'I myself am the devil knows what [*sam ia chort znaet chto*]. I have no appearance at all [*Nikakogo vidu s menia net*]' (II, 197 / 2, 150).

Ivan Iakovlevich is also involved with a 'baker woman' – his wife. She throws him the roll (*odin khleb*) (III, 49) in which he finds the nose, and calls him a drunkard and a trollop (*potaskushka*). In *The Nose* it is more difficult to identify the characters' sins: Kovalev knows that Ivan Iakovlevich shaved him a whole day before the nose disappeared and must therefore be innocent, but the policeman who returns Kovalev's nose says: 'It's strange that the main participant in this affair is the scoundrel barber on Ascension Street ... I have long suspected him of drunkenness and thievery, and just three days ago he filched a set of buttons from a certain shop' (III, 66-7 / 2, 232). In Petersburg the sins are more diffuse and ambiguous than in Gogol's Ukrainian world. As to spiritual self-knowledge, when Kovalev says 'without a nose a man is the devil knows what' (*bez nosa chelovek – chert znaet chto*: III,

64 / 2, 230), he is speaking only of his 'libellous appearance' (*ekoi paskvil'nyi vid*!: III, 65 / 2, 230). The two phrases are almost the same ones Khoma uses to describe his sinful soul to the *sotnik*.

God and the devil are definite presences in *Vii*, but appear only as epithets in *The Nose*. Demons whose visible presence has scared Khoma to death remain caught in the church apertures defiling the *sotnik*'s church. Kovalev has no fear of God or the devil. He invokes the devil nine times in twenty-six pages, but uses God's name only on four occasions, twice in tandem with the devil's.[24] He projects his own lack of godliness onto his nose – 'for this person nothing was sacred' (III, 58 / 2, 224). Only when trying to convince the newspaper man that he has no nose does Kovalev suggest respect for the Lord: 'I swear to you, as God is holy!' (III, 62 / 2, 228). However weak his faith, Khoma knows the effects of the Lord's word on evil spirits and successfully uses it to keep them at bay for the first two nights in church. Thus multiple references to Christian faith, starting with the parallel openings of the two tales and appearing in *The Nose* disguised as everyday street names, reveal a clear opposition between the spiritual universes of Khoma and Kovalev.

Natalie Moyle has shown the folktale structure of *Vii*.[25] The three seminarians – Tiberii, Khoma and Khaliava – parody the traditional three brothers of the Russian fairy tale; the middle brother is the hero who fails in his task, instead of the traditionally successful youngest brother. There are many more uses of the fairy tale threes: the old woman in the barn comes at Khoma three times with outstretched arms, just as the *pannochka* does on the three successive nights he reads over her corpse; and several utterances come in threes, for instance: '*vot podnimetsia...Chto, esli podnimetsia... esli podnimetsia?*' (II, 207); '*nemnogo strashno... ne strashno... sovsem ne strashno*' (II, 210).

The Nose parodies the supernatural tale rather than the fairy tale, and so condenses and disguises the leisurely threes. Kovalev goes to three places in his quest for his nose: to the police commissioner, to the

---

[24] Kovalev uses the word '*chert*' on III, 54, 55, 60, 63, 64, 69, 71, 73 74; '*bog*' or '*bozhe*' on III, 52, 54, 62, 64. Ivan Iakovlevich uses '*chert*' once (III, 50); the narrator uses '*bog*' twice (III, 58, 60); and the servant, advertising for his mistress's dog, says '*ei-bogu*' (III, 59).

[25] Natalie K. Moyle, 'Folktale Patterns in Gogol's *Vii*', *Russian Literature*, 7, 1979, pp. 665-88.

newspaper office and to the police inspector. When these civic agencies fail, Kovalev returns home and deals with three possible helpers: the policeman who returns the nose, the doctor who fails to affix it, and Madame Podtochina who might undo the spell, if one were cast. Phrases and words are also repeated three times, such as '*Chert poberi*' (II, 57, 73, 74) and '*paskvil''* (II, 61, 65, 69).

In keeping with the shift from a Ukrainian farm world to urban St Petersburg, Gogol reduces the number of characters in *The Nose*, while replacing the witch/beauty of *Vii* with two women: the mother and daughter Podtochina. Kovalev suspects the mother of having cast a spell on him, either herself or by hiring witches (*koldovok-bab*: III, 65). Like the witch, Podtochina is after Kovalev. But while the witch wants to seize Khoma's soul, Podtochina only wants to marry Kovalev to her daughter. Kovalev resists. Khoma also resists: first the witch's apparently sexual advances, then the sensual allure of the beauty she becomes, and finally her clutches as a demonically possessed corpse. Khoma becomes convinced that he is dealing with unclean powers, a conclusion validated by the *sotnik*'s men who tell tales of the *pannochka*'s vampirism, while Kovalev readily dismisses his own accusation of Podtochina's supernatural powers.

5. The Church
The opposition between the two tales is clearest in the paralleled church scenes. Khoma's belief in transcendent powers is displayed when he reads the prayers for the dead in the *sotnik*'s church. Kovalev's absence of faith is displayed in the Kazan cathedral, whither he pursues his nose.

As the place where the earthly and the divine conjoin, the church is the proper setting for Khoma's and Kovalev's encounters with their respective nemeses. For Khoma these are the leader of these powers, the Vii, and the *pannochka*, a mortal beauty possessed by unclean powers. For Kovalev, these are his nose, possibly possessed by unclean powers controlled by Madame Podtochina, and the beauties whom his noselessness prevents him from courting, represented in church by one particularly ethereal example.

The 'rustle/noise [*shum*] of a multitude of wings' (II, 210 / 2, 161) of the spirits that finally terrify Khoma to death is replaced in *The Nose* by the 'pleasant rustle/noise [*shum*] of a woman's dress' in the Kazan cathedral. Parallel to Madame Podtochina and her daughter, the beauty/witch of *Vii* is represented in the Kazan cathedral by a beauty and her 'middle-aged' mother. Kovalev's beauty is a 'light little lady', whose innocence is the opposite of the sensual, demonic beauty of the *pannochka*:

> There approached...a slender little lady, in a white dress, very nicely describing her slender waist, in a little straw hat light as a pastry ... he saw under her hat a round little chin of a bright whiteness and part of her cheek, illuminated with the color of the first spring rose.
> ... like a little spring flower, [she] bowed slightly and brought her white little hand with semi-transparent fingers to her forehead.
> (III, 56-7 / 2, 223)

The description emphasizes purity. The *pannochka* is also described in terms of her facial features, but they are described sensually:

> Never, it seemed, could features have been formed in such striking yet harmonious beauty. .. the lovely forehead ... ; the even brows ... rose proudly above the closed eyes; the eyelashes that fell like arrows on the cheeks glowed with the warmth of secret desires; the lips were rubies ... (II, 199 / 2, 151)

In these features, Khoma sees 'something terrifyingly penetrating. He felt that his soul began to ache in some sick way' (II, 199 / 2, 151), while Kovalev is merely 'reduced to despair' (III, 57 / 2, 223) by his inability to pursue a new flirtation.

Khoma sees a tear coming out from under the beauty's lashes, 'and when it stopped on her cheek, he clearly made out that it was a drop of blood' (II, 207 / 2, 158). Kovalev's beauty's cheek is rose-coloured and Kovalev's own eyes fill with tears of vexation (III, 57 / 2, 223). Khoma is appropriately terrified by his powerlessness against the bewitched *pannochka*; Kovalev 'leaps away as if burned' from his mundane beauty (dressed in pseudo-ideal white) because he remembers his noselessness.

Both encounters involve beauty, the diabolical and motifs of vision. Vision unites the motif system of Gogol's earliest Ukrainian tales, as well as of his last Petersburg stories[26] and links *Vii* and *The Nose*. The motifs of eyes, eyelids, eyebrows, eye-glasses, mirrors, reflections, transparency/opacity, tobacco and looking/not looking are related

---

[26] See note 17 above.

through vision to the problem of beauty central to both tales. Gogol associates tobacco with the diabolical because it obscures vision, whether through sneezing, a haze of smoke, or the distraction of snuff-taking.[27] Motifs of facial features – eyes, eyelids, eyebrows, the nose, nostrils – and verbs of looking link the two church scenes.

Khoma, locked in the church, is alone with the terrifying *pannochka*. He longs for tobacco: 'It's a shame that in God's temple you can't smoke a pipe!' (II, 206 / 2, 157) and again later trying to allay his fear: 'Oh for a sniff of snuff: Ekh, good tobacco! Wonderful tobacco! Fine tobacco!' (II, 207 / 2, 158). Tobacco plays a role in Kovalev's encounter with his beauty too: 'Behind [her] stopped and opened his snuffbox a tall footman with big sidewhiskers and a whole dozen collars' (III, 56 / 2, 223). In both scenes the tobacco is a sign of the hero's inattention to his soul. Sergei Bocharov draws a parallel between the failures of Khoma and Kovalev to look into their souls, to '*smotret' zrachkami v dushu*'.[28] While Khoma wants to smoke to avoid looking at the beauty, the footman's snuffbox merely mortifies Kovalev by underscoring his lack of a nose, that prevents him from approaching his beauty. As Kovalev says, his nose is 'almost the same thing as' Kovalev himself, a mock representation of his soul. He feels its lack acutely in his encounter with the beauty in this church scene.

For Khoma, looking at the beauty is terrifying. On his first night in church Khoma tries not to look at the *pannochka*, but is unable to hold out, while she, on the other hand, looks at him fixedly, at first with closed eyes and then with unseeing eyes. The second night too is described in terms of who looks at whom: Khoma decides 'not to raise his eyes from the book', but after an hour 'he took his horn out of his pocket and, before bringing the tobacco to his nose, timidly turned his eyes to the coffin', to find the corpse standing on the protective line he

---

[27] Several anti-spiritual motifs have been identified in Gogol's work. In addition to those mentioned by Mann, Weiskopf ('Nos v Kazanskom sobore', pp. 25-46) identifies coffee and eye-glasses. Tobacco plays this same role of distractor from a (mock) spiritual quest in *A May Night* and *The Overcoat*.

[28] Bocharov (op. cit.) discusses the interrelationship among 'the material, the bodily, the spiritual, and the human personality', and briefly compares Brut's ordeal to Kovalev's as the ordeal of isolated man, of man cut off from his inner self, a part removed from the whole, just as the nose is an alienated part of the face. Weiskopf discusses the origins of these images in the writings of Skovoroda ('Nos v Kazanskom sobore', p. 26).

has drawn, fixing him with her dead eyes (II, 208 / 2, 159). Khoma, 'looking out of one eye', sees that the corpse cannot see him. On the third night Khoma 'has not the spirit to look' at the claws and wings of the unclean spirits surrounding him, but sees the two eyes of a hairy monster that has 'slightly raised eyebrows'. 'Everything looked at him but could not see him'. When the Vii is brought in, it demands that its floor-length eyelids be raised. '"Don't look!" some inner voice whispered to the philosopher. He couldn't hold out, and looked ... and right away his spirit flew out of him from terror' (II, 217 / 2, 167).

In church both heroes come face to face with the object of their horror: Khoma is in constant terror during his three nights in the church with a living corpse. Kovalev experiences *uzhas* when he first recognises his nose on the street: 'everything whirled before his eyes; he felt that he could barely stand; ... he trembled as if in a fever ... he almost went out of his mind' (III, 55 / 2, 221); and later, when he is unable to stick it back on his face. The *pannochka* was a living creature, has died, and is terrifyingly reanimated after death; the nose, apparently an inanimate thing when cut off from its living source, is also terrifyingly reanimated in the form of a superior government official. But Kovalev's *uzhas* is directed at the threat to his social status and love life, not at the supernatural transformation.

In *The Nose* the church scenes of *Vii* are condensed, and the mundane again replaces the supernatural. While Khoma is forced into the church, tries not to look at the beauty or at the Vii with the extraordinary eyelids, and prays fervently in self-defence, Kovalev hurries into the Kazan cathedral, 'searches for the Nose with his eyes in all the corners', and is 'so upset that he could not pray' (III, 55 / 2, 222). Unlike the beauty and the Vii, the Nose 'hid his face completely in his large standing collar', and after Kovalev approaches him, 'looked at the Major, and slightly knit his eyebrows' (III, 56 / 2, 222), echoing the 'slightly raised eyebrows' of one of Khoma's monsters. The long-lidded Vii is an emanation from another world, the head of the gnomes, so powerful that exposure to him claims Khoma's very life. But the supernatural power that animates Kovalev's own nose does not terrify him as much as the necessity of suspending his deceitful habits.

6. The supernatural

The witch's transformation into the beauty causes Khoma to ponder 'about such an incomprehensible occurrence' (*o takom neponiatnom proizshestvii*: II, 188 / 2, 142) all the way to Kiev, where he spends an evening with a young widow and stops thinking about 'his extraordinary occurrence' (*o svoem neobyknovennom proizshestvii*: II, 188 / 2, 142); Kovalev 'doesn't even know how to think about such a strange occurrence' (*o takom strannom proizshestvii*: III, 55 / 2, 221) as the transformation of his nose into a government official.

Khoma and Kovalev both have occasion to wonder whether they are dreaming. Khoma, when he sees the *rusalka*, thinks: 'Was he seeing this or not? Was he dreaming or awake?' (II, 187 / 2, 141). After his first night in church, 'the whole night event seemed to him to have taken place in a dream' (II, 208 / 2, 160). Kovalev wonders when he discovers the absence of his nose: 'Wasn't he asleep?' (III, 53 / 2, 219). After his three visits to officials, Kovalev returns home and, trying to explain the event with the usual devices of supernatural tales – sleep or drunkenness – hopes that 'this was probably being dreamed or simply day-dreamed'; he pinches himself, which convinces him 'that he was acting and living in a wakened state' (III, 65 / 2, 230). Throughout the stories, Khoma recognises the appearance of spirits that can steal his soul from his body, while Kovalev has no way to understand the mock-miraculous incarnation of his nose-spirit in the body of a civil councillor.

Secondary characters echo the problem of spiritual vision suggested by the heroes' difficulty in interpreting events. The Cossack Dorosh at the *sotnik's* tells a tale about how the bewitched *pannochka* once took the form of a dog: A woman opens the door to the dog and 'sees that this was not a dog, but the *pannochka*' (II, 204 / 2, 156). The policeman who returns Kovalev's nose reports: 'the strange thing was that I myself took him first for a gentleman. But fortunately I had my glasses with me, and I saw at once that this was a nose' (III, 66 / 2, 231). Again, Gogol inverts: the dog is a woman, the man is a nose – the movement is in the direction of the inanimate.[29] The first tale is a

---

[29] But parallel to Dorosh's tale, a dog turns out to be a man in the newspaper clerk's account of the lost poodle 'who turned out to be a cashier of some institution' (III, 61-2 / 2, 227).

horrifying tale of vampirism – the dog-*pannochka* drinks a child's blood. The second tale appears to be merely an absurd parody of a supernatural transformation, but if you think about it, there is something in it: can a person be so reduced that he is equivalent to a body part whose importance is mostly appearance? It seems only 'a strange thing' to the policeman, whose glasses cope with the material but not the spiritual universe. Kovalev's nose is the opposite of the Vii's eyelids: raising the eyelids opens the gulf into another world, while the nose is associated only with this one.[30]

The deepest terror in both tales is clothed in the comic everyday, and comes at the end in a separate section. The final sentence of *Vii* shows Khaliava carrying off 'the old sole of a boot' (II, 218 / 2, 168). The boot sole is as lowly a mundane object as can be imagined. Spirid, comparing the old houndsman to the new one in *Vii*, uses the Russian expression 'he's not worthy of being his boot resoling' (*v podmetki emu ne goditsia*: II, 202). Boots appear in Gogol's work as an emblem of concern with the trivial: In *Dead Souls* (*Mertvye dushi*) boots are the obsession (*zador*) of the officer in the hotel room; in *The Overcoat* (*Shinel'*) Bashmachkin's *bashmak* is even lower than the footwear of his relatives, who 'went around in boots, which they merely resoled about three times a year' (III, 142 / 2, 305); Hoffmann, the bootmaker of *Nevsky Prospect*, is defined as the opposite of the German master of supernatural literature – he is '*not* the writer Hoffmann' (III, 37 / 1, 230). Boot soles, then, are an even lesser object of concern, and used ones must be at the bottom of the hierarchy of material objects. They appear in *The Nose* as well. At the end of a long list of newspaper advertisements for dubious goods and services is 'a summons to those wishing to buy old boot soles, with the invitation to appear at the bidding from 8 to 3 in the morning' (III, 60 / 2, 226). Khaliava picks up one random boot sole, but in Petersburg people are placing advertisements for, selling and purchasing these used boot soles almost around the clock.

Although he has the honour of being a conspicuous servant of God as the bellringer of the tallest belfry, Khaliava has no spiritual fervour. Presumably his love of drinking contributes to the fact that he is 'almost always to be seen with a damaged nose, as the wooden

---

[30] As emphasised by Bocharov and Weiskopf. This reading can readily accommodate the nose-as-phallus interpretation.

staircase to the belfry had been extremely carelessly made' (II, 218 / 2, 168). Khaliava's damaged nose suggests that he neglects his duty to God, as did the carpenter who built the staircase, making a descent out of what should be an ascent. Spiritual negligence is everywhere, even in church.

Khoma dies for his spiritual poverty, but Kovalev gets his nose back and becomes an even greater lady-killer and impostor, buying a ribbon of some order that he is not entitled to wear. All of Petersburg is as indifferent to the condition of Kovalev's nose as was his servant Ivan. Only the narrator reacts. He is outraged, but neither because he sees Kovalev's spiritual poverty go unpunished nor because he sympathises with Kovalev. The narrator plays the role played by Khaliava: he extends the story's moral to include all of Russia. By raging against the 'indecency' of the events described (but by whom, then?), at the story's being 'of no use to the fatherland', he personifies the spiritually blind reader, transposing the 'you're laughing at yourselves' of *The Government Inspector* to address the whole audience, all of Russia.

In *Vii* Gogol depicted the absence of spirituality in a folkloric Ukraine. In that setting, an urbane audience would see the supernatural events as mere literary convention. Transposing his horror tale into the language of Petersburgers, Gogol rendered it apparently purely secular and realist, rather than religious and supernatural. To literate contemporaries, *The Nose* looked like a parody of the tales of E. T. A. Hoffmann, so popular at the time in Russia. And there are many points of contact with *A New Year's Eve Adventure* (1816), a story in which the hero loses his reflection through the agency of the diabolic Dr Dapertutto.[31] The doctor figure in *The Nose* can be taken as a comic version of Hoffmann's Devil, one blended with elements taken from the *vertep* version of *Petrushka*.[32] Had Gogol limited his sources for *The*

---

[31] See E.T.A. Hoffmann, *The Best Tales of Hoffmann*, edited by E.F. Bleiler, New York, Dover, 1967, pp. 104-29. Points of contact include a tobacco box polished like a mirror that offends the reflectionless man (110); the rustling sound that heralds the approach of Giuletta, the devil's sensual bait (117); the accusing shrieks of the wife angered by the supernatural loss (124); and the hero's terror at his reflection's independent actions which achieve the hero's desires (127).

[32] In *Petrushka* a gypsy sells Petrushka a horse who throws him; Petrushka summons a doctor who pokes him with his finger, etc. In another scene, Petrushka inspects his bride as if she were a horse. Kovalev's doctor treats him similarly, causing him to throw

Nose to Hoffmann's tales and the Ukrainian comic elements, even including the Christian thematics, the tale might have remained merely a comic parody of the supernatural tale with its customary social satirical elements. But by his deep incorporation of the terrifying pagan forces contained in *Vii*,[33] Gogol gave his apparently whimsical *Nose* its profound uncanniness, the feature that is so hard to locate in the Petersburg stories.

Iurii Mann says that the evil forces in the Ukrainian tales become invisible in the Petersburg tales. They may be invisible to the characters who are characterised by their clouded vision, and in a city where all becomes clouded with fog during events that can only be supernatural, but the reader is able to glimpse the unrealised transcendent world that is intimated by its travesty in the real one.[34] The spiritually annihilating gaze of the Vii becomes the socially humiliating look of – a nose. Exorcism of the Vii by prayer is replaced by a quest for the nose through the (corrupt) civil agencies of Petersburg – the newspapers, the officials, the police. Having glimpsed the supernatural forces that Gogol has recostumed in Petersburg dress, it becomes impossible to read *The Nose* as merely a social satire, a parody of the supernatural genre, a sexual fantasy, or absolute nonsense.

---

his head back 'like a horse whose teeth are being inspected' (III, 68 / 2, 233). See V.N. Perets, op. cit., pp. 82-4.

[33] Studies by Soviet scholars explore the connections of Gogol's Ukrainian lore to Indo-European mythologies; notably, Viacheslav Ivanov has connected the characterisation of the Vii to a mass of folklore ('Ob odnoi paralleli k gogolevskomu Viiu', in *Trudy po znakovym sistemam*, 5, vyp. 284, Tartu, 1971, pp. 133-42; idem, 'Kategorii "vidimogo" i "nevidimogo" v tekste: eshche raz o vostochnoslavianskikh fol'lklornykh paralleliakh k gogolevskomu Viiu', in *The Structure of Texts and the Semiotics of Culture*, edited by Jan van der Eng and Mojmir Grygar, The Hague, Mouton, 1973, pp. 151-76) from Ukrainian and Russian, as well as Indo-European mythologies. He suggests a connection to children's games of Baba Iaga, interpreted as games about death in which the blindfolded grandmother or grandfather tries to catch someone.

[34] But cf. G.A. Gukovskii, op. cit.: 'V Peterburgskikh povestiakh fantasticheskoe - eto vovse ne sily ada, raia, i t. p., ne mifologicheskie sushchestva, i k problemam morali, dukha, religii ono ne imeet maleishego otnosheniia...' (p. 271).

THE GOTHIC IN DOSTOEVSKII AND GOGOL: THE BRITISH CONNECTION

IGNAT AVSEY

And everywhere there is a connection, everywhere there is
illustration: no single event, no single literature, is adequately
comprehended except in relation to other events, to other
literatures.

Matthew Arnold, *On the Modern Element in Literature.*

There is no new thing under the sun.

Ecclesiastes [1:9]

Any discussion of the Gothic element in literature must inevitably include Horace Walpole. In *The Castle of Otranto: A Gothic Story*, he not only established a new trend in the nascent English and indeed European art of novel writing, but also applied the name, or rather classification, 'Gothic', to define it. The term had, of course, been in use a long time, though not in literature; it was commonly employed in calligraphy and printing and, most widely, in architecture, typified by upwardly vaunting and tapering shapes. Russians have another name for it as applied to architecture – *strel'chatyi stil'*,[1] (i.e. ogival). However, even in architecture, for many centuries what we know as Gothic was not so termed; it was simply the prevailing form of building. As soon as the name was applied, the Gothic style was born: style only, an associative reference, rather than actual cultural heritage, for the savage Goths themselves never constructed a single Gothic cathedral.[2] In literature – from the Bible, to Shakespeare to Charles

---

[1] *Entsiklopedicheskii slovar'*, St Petersburg, Brockhaus-Efron, 1890-1907 (see the entry under *Goticheskoe zodchestvo*).
[2] C. Baldick, editor, 'Introduction', *The Oxford Book of Gothic Tales*, Oxford, Oxford University Press, 1992, p. xii.

Perrault – there are numerous allusions to Gothic themes, though the genre was not yet recognised as such. Trees existed, but the concept of 'forest' did not. The first associative references to the Gothic in poetry belong to Thomas Wharton (*Observations on the Faerie Queene of Spenser*, 1754) and Richard Hurd (*Letters on Chivalry and Romance*, 1762). Walpole's genius, however, lay in going a step further, and staking out a category of his own by boldly applying the name to the novel. As soon as the name was applied, the trend was set, a trend which persisted and burgeoned throughout the succeeding centuries. The first direct product, after Walpole, of the newly-extended literary scene was Clara Reeve's *The Champion of Virtue* (1777), alternatively entitled *The Old English Baron*, followed by Sophia Lee's *The Recess: A Tale from other Times* (1783-85), introducing a sub-category – the historical Gothic – and, perhaps the most famous of all exponents of the genre, Ann Radcliffe: to be outshone perhaps only by Mary Shelley with her *Frankenstein* (1818).

The epoch-making mainstream of English literature that followed also absorbed the Gothic appeal and influence in various ways. Meanwhile, 'over the three decades between 1790 and 1820 ... the English novel and the Gothic novel were one and the same species', writes Fredrick Frank.[3] From Jane Austen's parody *Northanger Abbey* (1818), via Charlotte Brontë's *Jane Eyre* (1847) and Emily Brontë's *Wuthering Heights* (1847), to Edgar Allan Poe and Robert Louis Stevenson, and later to H.P. Lovecraft, Wyndham Lewis and Mervyn Peake – and indeed right up to the present day (Ursula Le Guin, David Gemmel, Stephen King, to name but a few): all drew inspiration from the Gothic and all ultimately owe a debt to Walpole.

There is some debate over the origins of the specifics of the plot of *The Castle of Otranto*. Alice M. Killen[4] mentions the Rev. Thomas Leland's *Longsword, Count of Salisbury* (1762), which she suggests foreshadowed in considerable detail the Gothic trend. Clara F. McIntyre[5] goes back even further, to the early seventeenth century, in establishing the inspirational source; she cites, amongst others,

[3] S.F. Frank, *A Guide to the Gothic*, Metuchen, NJ, and London, Scarecrow Press, 1984, p. ix.
[4] A.M. Killen, *Le Roman 'terrifiant' ou roman 'noir' de Walpole à Anne Radcliffe et son influence sur la littérature française jusqu'en 1840*, Paris, Champion, 1915, p 5.
[5] Quoted by P. Lewis, in *Notes and Queries*, 25, 1978, pp. 52-4.

Tourneur's *The Atheist's Tragedy* (1611) and Shakespeare's *Hamlet, Macbeth* and *Romeo and Juliet*. The themes and preoccupations which Walpole distilled into the Gothic novel – the supernatural, the mysterious, the macabre, the fantastic – had thus already been explored a century and a half earlier. But the honour of initiating a major new literary scion belongs to Walpole.

Thanks to Walpole, the Gothic novel proper is recognised as a peculiarly English phenomenon, albeit that the roughly contemporaneous German hyper-romantic *Sturm und Drang* movement afforded a variant outlet for kindred sentiment. But *Sturm und Drang* was *nach vorne gerichtet*, self-assertive to the point of being combative, emotionally progressive – not bedevilled by the treacherous psychological undertow of the English Gothic, in which traditional values are inverted and accepted standards disarranged, the observer being left at best ethically disorientated, at worst misled. Be it at Elsinore or Otranto, there is scarcely a hard and fast moral code that cannot be up-ended. The discursive Hamlet, holding forth on man in general but patently referring to himself ('how noble in reason, how infinite in faculties... in apprehension how like a god... the paragon of animals'), presents a lofty positive façade, but subjacently is well able to operate outside traditional moral codes and behave as a harsh, disturbingly uncompromising and, incidentally, overtly misogynistic force. By contrast, and in illustration of the complex interrelationship of good and evil depicted within the Gothic mode, the 'mildewed ear' Claudius, 'that incestuous, that adulterate beast', can articulate redeeming, heartfelt words of succour ('How do you, pretty lady?') to comfort and reassure with disarming economy of words the very victim of Hamlet's unnecessary cruelty and heartlessness. Tom Stoppard, re-writing Shakespeare with remarkable aplomb, has succeeded in dredging up bewilderingly unexpected qualities, even in such abject knaves as Rosenkrantz and Guildenstern.

The moral strands in *The Castle of Otranto* may, if anything, be even more intertwined. Matilda, mortally wounded, harshly rebukes the priest Jerome for denouncing her father Manfred, who has just stabbed her. The victim pronounces the exposer of the crime more culpable than its perpetrator. Such filial devotion to her murderous parent, which she reaffirms with her dying breath ('I can, I do [forgive], and may heaven confirm it'), recalls with graphic symbolism Christ's resolute death on the cross – the supreme and extreme, the absolute sacrifice. And it is precisely this absolutism being emulated by Matilda that has exposed Christ to the charge of introducing the cult of suffering, of martyrdom. But he was God, and therefore may be 'forgiven'. For man to go so far, is in fact to go too far. There is some danger in what the Gothic heroine Matilda does, namely of protesting too much, of going morally 'over the top', *za chertu* (in the Dostoevskian sense). However, that is in the nature of the Gothic: to favour extreme psychological solutions.

The Castle of Otranto, being a seminal novel, helped to establish a paradigm, a set of characteristic features for the Gothic novel. It was a frail child, conceived with some misgiving, its author-father – we read in the two prefaces – appearing initially to have little faith in his offspring, expecting it to be stillborn or, worse still, if it did survive precariously, prepared to disown and abandon it to its fate. This he did. But the foundling, as is not uncommon, immediately captured the popular imagination and, touchingly, the father himself, on seeing the success of his progeny, came forward to 'own it without a blush'.[6] Walpole clearly took parental delight in the tender charms of his newly-born offspring. Casting aside all false modesty after the unprecedented success of the first edition, he went on to predict its future destiny, prophetically anticipating much more glory for it in the future, in the hands of 'men of brighter talents'[7] – the successive generations of literary giants to whom he freely and magnanimously offered his shoulders to stand on that they might see farther. The first and most famous of these was Sir Walter Scott who, with the acquisitive eye of an artist, immediately perceived it to be grist to his mill.[8] His encomia of the novel flew in the face of all the received opinion at that time, perhaps even in violation of a sound critical judgment, very likely coloured by a practising writer's quest for ideas and inspiration to feed his own creative needs. The second and equally acquisitive literary giant was Dostoevskii. If Scott pursued the historico-romantic route, Dostoevskii focused on the internal mental labyrinths of his heroes, and developed what might be called the psychological Gothic, which had

---

[6] H. Walpole, *The Castle of Otranto*, 'Preface to the Second Edition', in *Three Gothic Novels*, edited by Peter Fairclough, Harmondsworth, Penguin, 1968, p. 43.

[7] Ibid., p. 44.

[8] See W.S. Lewis, 'Introduction', *The Castle of Otranto*, Oxford, Oxford University Press, 1969, p viii. (quoting from Walter Scott, introduction to *The Castle of Otranto*, Edinburgh, 1811).

already been explored by Matthew G. Lewis (1775-1818) and Charles R. Maturin (1782-1824). It is a mark of Walpole's genius that he clearly foresaw the eventuality of others developing and embellishing his original idea. Thus his novel paradoxically assumes a greater significance, because of its shortcomings rather than because of its merits, in that creative minds had chosen to look beyond its deficiencies and had assessed it according to their own lights and attitudes. As one commentator puts it:

> He may... be regarded as a wholehearted rebel, who led the forlorn hope in a cause which, years after, had its day of triumph. It is that which makes *The Castle of Otranto* a marked book—even more marked perhaps for its ultimate bearing on foreign literature than on our own.[9]

* * *

Dostoevskii would almost certainly have first come across *The Castle of Otranto* in a French translation (as far as it has been possible to ascertain, the first Russian translation of *The Castle of Otranto* did not appear until the 1960s).[10] Dostoevskii's own avowed respect for and indebtedness to Western European, more particularly English, literature could help to explain how readily he might have gravitated towards such a significant and famous work as *The Castle of Otranto*. Talking of the English readership, he wrote:

> Their poets are for us as close, at least for the more enlightened amongst us, as they are to the people in the West. I maintain and repeat that any European poet, thinker, philanthropist besides his own native land is always received and understood more readily in Russia than anywhere else in the world.[11]

And in 1861 he had said: 'English literature is without doubt incomparably more familiar in Russia than in France and perhaps in Germany'.[12] By way of a corrective, the editor of his *Full Collected*

---

[9] C.E. Vaughan, 'Sterne and the Novel of his Times', *The Cambridge History of English Literature*, edited by Sir A.W. Ward and A.R. Waller, Cambridge at the University Press, 1952, vol. 10, p. 61.

[10] Kh. Uolpol, *Zamok Otranto*, Leningrad, 1967.

[11] F.M. Dostoevskii, *Polnoe sobranie sochinenii v tridtsati tomakh*, Leningrad, 1972-90, vol. 23, p. 31: hereafter 'Dostoevskii, *PSS*' (unless acknowledged, all translations from Russian sources are my own: IA).

[12] Ibid., vol. 19, p. 17.

Works observed that Dostoevskii had, of course, said this in the heat of
'polemical ardour'.[13] This instance of polemical ardour on
Dostoevskii's part is, however, very revealing in what it says about the
man himself. Like Hamlet, purporting to speak for the whole of
mankind but thinking only of himself, Dostoevskii with similarly
disarming modesty speaks for the whole of Russia.

In the clear line of succession from Walpole via Ann Radcliffe to
Byron, who 'in his self-dramatization ... [as] a worldly romantic ...
[borrowed] from the picture of Schedoni'[14] (Radcliffe's villainous hero
of *The Italian*), it would be most surprising if Dostoevskii had not,
together with Scott, drawn vitality and inspiration deep from the Gothic
taproot. We read in Dostoevskii's *Diary of a Writer* that: 'a great deal of
what we borrowed from Europe, and transplanted to our soil, was not
just slavishly imitated ... but was assimilated by our organism to
become part of our very flesh and blood'[15] (the active-voice Russian
construction is even stronger '... *privili k nashemu organismu, v nashu
plot' i krov'*). To appreciate what Dostoevskii really meant: for 'we',
read 'I'; and for 'our' read 'my'. But Dostoevskii had. of course, the
advantage of being a writer who could – and did – create his own
virtual world, his own virtual Russia.

As if to drive the point home about the popularity of English
literature, in the fictional world of the trial scene in *The Karamazov
Brothers* (*Brat'ia Karamazovy*), the defence counsel Fetiukovich,
addressing the jury drawn from the good and true inhabitants of the
town of Skotoprigonevsk, deep in Russia's heartland, refers to *The
Mysteries of Udolpho* as if it were common domestic reading. It would
certainly be 'polemical ardour' to presuppose such extensive reading in
a German or a French provincial town – or, come to that, even in an
English one by the 1860s – let alone a Russian town, unless of course it
was a figment of Dostoevskii's own virtual reality, steeped as he was in
English, especially Gothic, literature. Overlaying all this is the hilarious
realisation that the very name 'Skotoprigonevsk' (say, 'Cattletown') is
itself the ultimate in zany, slapstick, knockabout semantic spoofery.

'*We* all emerged from beneath *The Overcoat*' [my emphasis: IA] is

---

[13] Ibid., vol. 23, pp. 364-5 (note to p. 31).
[14] W.L. Renwick, *English Literature 1789-1815*, Oxford, Oxford University Press,
1963, p 89.
[15] Dostoevskii, *PSS*, vol. 23. p. 31.

yet another instance of Dostoevskii's hyper-egotism (in this famous, though possibly apocryphal, statement). Who but Dostoevskii alone ever emerged from beneath Gogol's *Overcoat* (*Shinel'*)? Yet, true to form, it is 'we', 'we all' in fact. Even the word 'emerged' has to be taken with a pinch of salt. If the truth be told, having been 'born' under *The Overcoat* – one only has to think of *Poor Folk* (*Bednye liudi*, 1846) – he did not emerge from beneath it at any time, but stayed enveloped in its folds to his dying day: 'the apparel oft proclaims the man'.

But Gogol apart, the influence that Walpole had on Dostoevskii, though much more restricted, is nonetheless significant: not only because the work in question is *The Karamazov Brothers*, but because not a few of its themes and central characters are traceable to *The Castle of Otranto*. Both novels begin with an authorial preface (two in Walpole's case), touching upon the crucially important question of the status and persona of the author in relation to the reading public. In the preface to *A Hero of our Time*, Lermontov, preceding Dostoevskii by some forty years, confronts the self-same issue, and would appear to have been influenced by Walpole in equal measure. 'An Introduction commonly signals there's someone or something important to follow', writes Valentine Cunningham.[16] Both *The Castle of Otranto* and *The Karamazov Brothers* are novels whose authors were convinced of the importance of their mission, and signalled in their respective introductions that something important *was* to follow. The former sought 'to blend two kinds of romance, the ancient and the modern'; the latter to write the definitive, the unifying novel of his time, the Russian *Divine Comedy*,[17] again in emulation of Gogol. It is interesting that, although the artistically lesser *The Castle of Otranto* succeeded in its mission, the undoubtedly creatively superior *The Karamazov Brothers*, following in the footsteps of *Dead Souls* (*Mertvye dushi*) failed, not least because the project in its entirety envisaged an even grander sequel, which of course did not materialise.

As to the status of the author, Walpole (as already mentioned), had initially attempted to disown his authorship, claiming merely the role of translator who, by a stroke of good luck (serendipity!), 'had found [the

---

[16] V. Cunningham, 'Allow me to introduce...', *Compass: The Oxford World's Classics Magazine*, no. 1, March 1998, p. 6.
[17] Walpole, 'Preface to the Second Edition', *Three Gothic Novels*, op. cit., p. 43; Dostoevskii, *PSS* (editor's notes to *The Karamazov Brothers*), vol. 15, p. 400.

work] in the library of an ancient Catholic family in the north of England'.[18] We know that, by the time of the second edition, the pretence was dropped and Walpole admitted his authorship. One could argue that the initial attempt to conceal his identity was part and parcel of a grand hoax, and even the very idea of the novel a mere self-indulgence on the part of a rich and eccentric member of the English aristocracy. But this would leave more questions unanswered than resolved. A more intellectually honest explanation would be that he was indeed doubtful whether 'he was entirely [..]equal to the task he had undertaken', and was prepared, in modern parlance, to be 'economical with the truth' – paradoxically, perhaps, due to a naïve uncertainty of whether he would be able to exploit the translator/narrator figure as a literary device. Gogol and Dostoevskii had no such difficulty. In their case, the narrator is a familiar and accepted figure, acquiring, in the hands of Gogol, and later in even fuller measure in Dostoevskii's hands, the added sophistication of being semi-competent,[19] to ever greater dramatic effect and verisimilitude. As Allan Lloyd Smith puts it:

> The Gothic writer, working to produce incredulity, mystery, and suspense, sets off one account of events against another, usually subsumed within a moralised but generally incompetent master-narrative whose function is to *fail* [author's italics] to explain and thereby allow access to subdued and repressed realms of knowledge and experience.[20]

The preface to *The Karamazov Brothers*, entitled 'From the Author', is permeated by the notion of failure: failure to convince and to persuade, resulting in the fear of the ultimate failure of failing to entertain. The author is challenging and provocative, as only a person can be who speaks from a position of weakness: 'Of course, nobody is under any obligation; anyone is free to close the book after two pages... never to open it again'.[21] There is anxiety, bordering on desperation, in

---

[18] Walpole, 'Preface to the First Edition', *Three Gothic Novels*, p. 39.
[19] R. Peace, 'Introduction' to Nikolai Gogol, *Village Evenings near Dikanka and Mirgorod*, translated by Christopher English, Oxford, Oxford University Press, 1994, p. viii.
[20] Allan Lloyd Smith, 'Postmodernism/Gothicism', in *Modern Gothic*, edited by Victor Sage and Allan Lloyd Smith, Manchester, Manchester University Press, 1996, p. 12.
[21] Fyodor Dostoevsky, *The Karamazov Brothers*, translated by Ignat Avsey, Oxford,

this; but, oddly enough, strength too – because, in retrospect, we know the novel did get written, and the public does continue to read it. The enigmatic thumbnail blueprint sketch that is the preface, which is then gloriously enlarged into the Gothic pile that is the novel proper, is in itself an expression of the very essence of the Gothic state of insecurity, rooted as it is in identifiable personal and historical anxieties.

The novel's structural complexity, its labyrinthine arguments, its thematic dead ends, and its multiplicity of characters in a kaleidoscope of perspectives, are bewildering and destabilising. The rather dispassionate narrator, a throw-back to the vague, shadowy, indeterminate kind we find in Gogol's *Dead Souls*, but more prepared to posit questions and raise issues for which he readily and beguilingly declares his inability to find solutions, is not one to inspire confidence. Unlike Sergei in *The Village of Stepanchikovo* (*Selo Stepanchikovo i ego obitateli*) and Vania in *The Insulted and the Injured* (*Unizhennye i oskorblennye*), who were timid and ineffectual enough, the anonymous narrator in *The Karamazov Brothers* is non-participatory, avoiding all direct contact with the protagonists and unable to resolve issues which have outstripped his powers of analysis. Not for him Sergei's heroically combative posturing to challenge and reform, or Vania's desperate attempts to assert himself and establish his credibility as a romantic lover. The narrator in *The Karamazov Brothers* adopts a passive role and merges into the background. Like the author himself, he prefers not to agonise over the spectres conjured up by the run-away characters. He is reluctant to pursue, his creative palette in hand, the monstrous Russian muzhik beating his wretched horse; the general unleashing his pack of borzoi hounds; the sadistic Turk taking the life of an infant for, as Losskii has noted, 'these are not the people into the most sacred recesses of whose souls Dostoevskii chooses to take us; the deepest motivations of their actions remain unexplained to us'.[22]

Evil is as difficult to process creatively as pure goodness, though Dostoevskii, like Shakespeare, has been rather more successful with the former than the latter: Foma Fomich Opiskin and Iago come to mind. Totally distinct though these archetypal characters may be in terms of cultural and historical settings, there is yet an underlying likeness

Oxford University Press, 1994, p. 6.
[22] N. Losskii, 'O prirode sataninskoi (po Dostoevskomu)', in *O Dostoevskom*, edited by V. Borisov and A. Roginskii, Moscow, 1990, p. 296.

between them – cruelty for cruelty's sake: a characteristic which is to be found in all times, in all cultures and in all guises! Cunning and shrewd, they both demonstrate an irrepressible, irrational urge to inflict pain and suffering; in this they are of the same ilk as the barbaric muzhik, the dehumanised general, the sadistic Turk. The deliberative psychological inquisitor that is Opiskin, the relentless insentient annihilator that is Iago: neither can have apologists. They are to be excluded from the pantheon of Gothic positive heroes, as surely as must be the mindless Dracula. The prerequisite for the Gothic hero must be a passionate nature with a sound rational mind, tragically torn between good and evil. Such a categorisation is both possible and necessary, precisely because both types have been depicted in literature and must be clearly differentiated. Claudius can be regarded as conforming to the truly Gothic: seen through Hamlet's jaundiced eyes, he has no redeeming features. But Hamlet has had his own way for too long; Belinskii set the record straight, overstating his case, perhaps, in going on to claim that the King was a very good man; nevertheless, one could certainly agree that: 'the King... is not a villain, merely a weak man, and even if he is a villain it is due to weakness of character, rather than the ferocity of an imperious nature'.[23]

Via Manfred in *The Castle of Otranto*, Fedor Pavlovich Karamazov is in direct line of succession from Claudius. For too long he has been misrepresented by Mitia, right down to the crucially important matter of his unprepossessing physical appearance. As in the case of Hamlet, Mitia had his own axe to grind and can hardly be considered an impartial commentator. Grushen'ka herself is silent on this matter, as are all the other personages, so that it is Mitia's view that prevails. And practically everything that Mitia says and does turns out in the end to be a red herring, in order to keep the reader on a false scent in the 'who-dunnit' guessing game. According to L.P. Karsavin: 'Fedor Pavlovich is gross, but he is sensitive to beauty; he is perverse, but he yearns for purity and sanctity'.[24]

To Fedor Pavlovich must go the title of the ideal Gothic type. Paying a little more heed to Grushen'ka's silence, which is so significant in the context, one could arrive at a visual construct, perhaps not at all

---

[23] V.G. Belinskii, *Sobranie sochinenii v deviati tomakh*, Moscow, 1977, vol. 2, p. 48.
[24] L.P. Karsavin, 'Fedor Pavlovich Karamazov kak idealog liubvi', in *O Dostoevskom*, op. cit., p. 265.

displeasing to the eyes of a passionate, sensual woman. It is only within the non-visual bounds of the novel that one is liable to fail to recognise the true state of affairs. On stage or film, Fedor Pavlovich has to cut a much more presentable romantic figure, or the supposition that he could be a serious rival to his son becomes simply untenable. Any serious dramatist or director must bear this in mind. The more romantically attractive Fedor Pavlovich is, the more threatening he is to Mitia, and the more powerful the conflict between them for their ultimate prize, Grushen'ka. Mitia's capacity for self-delusion is legendary, his father's physical grossness being largely a figment of his imagination. After all, he himself makes no attempt to raise the subject of his father's ugliness with Grushen'ka, in order to settle the matter once and for all. The weight of evidence therefore is in favour of Fedor Pavlovich being at least as attractive to Grushen'ka as Claudius is to Gertrude, making Mitia's silence on the subject that much more understandable, and his patricidal intention that much more plausible.

Before considering Manfred in *The Castle of Otranto,* who in fact bears a closer relation to Fedor Pavlovich than does Claudius, let us look at one or two further parallels. Grigorii is as much of a 'rash intruding fool' as Polonius, and very nearly meets the same sorry fate. The case of Smerdiakov, however, is altogether more intriguing and deserves especial consideration. He too, no less than Fedor Pavlovich, is a gigantic Gothic presence, originally descended from the 'waterfly' Osrick of Elsinore, who, via John Smauker, 'the powdered-headed footman in gorgeous livery' of *The Pickwick Papers*, mutated into Vidopliasov in *The Village of Stepanchikovo.*

Vidopliasov, the man with the multiple aliases (from Orleandrov to Essbouquetov), burdened with an acute identity crisis, is the first of the effete lackey figures, and the one who comes oddly and sadly a cropper on the altar of learning. He pays dearly for the thirst for knowledge that his mentor Foma Fomich Opiskin has inspired in him and, significantly, winds up in a madhouse, where he meets his end. '*Gore ot uma* (woe from wit) and some danger in hero worship too', one could comment and close the book with a wistful smile, lulled into a sense of euphoria at the author's beguiling promise of another story, amid the prevailing mood of optimism and good cheer with which the novel ends. But something is not quite right; that the innocuous Vidopliasov, with his hypersensitive awareness of his own self, should wind up in a

madhouse strikes a sinister and disturbing note. Nothing really prepares
the reader for such an eventuality. Significantly, he is the last character
to be mentioned, and *The Village of Stepanchikovo* ends with the
narrator promising to enquire after him: a brilliant device – to close the
book on one story, while holding out the promise of another. But the
sequel was a long time in coming, over twenty years in fact. When we
meet Smerdiakov in *The Karamazov Brothers*, it is as though
Vidopliasov has been resurrected, his mind reconstituted (but not
quite!) after his incarceration in the madhouse. And what a name to be
lumbered with – Smerdiakov! (from the verb *smerdet'*, to stink).
Especially when we remember how sensitive his prototype Vidopliasov
was on this very point. It is, however, Smerdiakov's hero-worshipping
syndrome, predicated on the thirst for learning inherited from
Vidopliasov, that causes all hell to break loose.

Smerdiakov (and the parallel, as far as it goes, between Smerdiakov
and Vidopliasov was noted by Konstantin Mochulskii[25]) is a sad and
doomed figure. By the time of *The Karamazov Brothers,* the beguiling
comic element that typified the earlier lackey figures has been
completely discarded. There is not a shred of humour left in
Smerdiakov. In honest Grigorii's eyes, he is less than human, the
'spawn of bathhouse slime', a congenital un-Christian, a Godless
revisionist, perversely and maliciously questioning the very foundations
of Orthodox religious beliefs.[26] His early childhood propensity for
sacrilegious rituals involving animals, complete with liturgical censer
and white chasubel,[27] is Gothic at its most deadly serious, even such as
to please Montague Summers – notorious for his disapproval of
anything frivolous in Gothic.[28]

By a totally independent route, Dostoevskii had arrived at his own
version of a Frankenstein monster. Physical deformity, a key factor in
Mary Shelley's work, is pretty much irrelevant here. For all we know,
Lizaveta Smerdiaschaia's offspring might have been quite presentable,
and indeed he very likely was (there is nothing like a touch of romantic
dash to enliven the Gothic! 'Smerdyakov with a guitar'[29] says it all).

[25] K. Mochul'skii, *Gogol', Solov'ev, Dostoevskii*, Moscow, 1995, p. 306.
[26] Dostoevskii, *The Karamazov Brothers*, op. cit., p. 157.
[27] Ibid., p. 156.
[28] See M. Summers, 'Introduction', *The Supernatural Omnibus*, London, Blacken
Books, 1994, p. 27.
[29] Dostoevskii, *The Karamazov Brothers*, p. 279.

Though his sexual orientation is always far from clear, he could easily turn on the romantic charm to devastating effect to melt Mar'ia Kondrat'evna's heart, if only to prove that he too is a Karamazov, infected by the virus of sexuality. He is a Frankensteinian freak whose mind, rather than body, is a composite monstrosity, a rag-bag of disowned thoughts. Humanity, as represented by Fedor Pavlovich's hostile household, has rejected him. The pathetically insignificant servant woman Mar'ia Kondrat'evna is the exception that proves the rule – a tiny refuge of sympathy in a disordered and irrational world. After pandering to the basest and the most repressed of his mentor's wishes, after committing the heinous crime of patricide, Smerdiakov suffers the fate of all over-zealous, fawning hero-worshippers who are ruthlessly cast aside and disowned after serving their purpose. One is reminded here of King Henry II's knight-barons after the murder of Thomas à Becket in the cathedral. Even the non-participatory narrator-author (Lev Karsavin distinguishes between 'author' and Fedor Mikhailovich Dostoevskii himself),[30] we feel, rejects Smerdiakov in a way that the author of *Frankenstein* never rejected her grief-stricken creature. And that is the unkindest cut of all. In Smerdiakov, therefore, a still deeper level of despair and spiritual desolation has been plumbed, beyond which lies only self-annihilation.

If Smerdiakov's sexuality is doubtful, Fedor Pavlovich's is not. Together with Claudius, and more especially Manfred, he is one of a trio of inordinately passionate men in their maturity, who have skeletons in their cupboards and are resolutely unrepentant. Each has an adverse agency operating to destroy his peace of mind and bring about his downfall. Claudius, the murderer, and usurper of Elsinore, is plagued by Hamlet; Manfred, the usurper of Otranto, with the blood of his daughter on his hands, is harassed by supernatural portents, largely the imaginings of his guilt-ridden subconscious; Fedor Pavlovich, who has putatively misappropriated inherited wealth, has his *enfant-terrible* Mitia to contend with. Of the three, only Manfred escapes death, to seek salvation in a monastic setting.

The seminal status of *The Castle of Otranto* makes it a point of reference, if not a yardstick, for the Gothic genre. Fedor Pavlovich's obsession with Grushen'ka bears a close psychological parallel with Manfred's deluded belief in his ability to gain the favours of Isabella. In

---

[30] Karsavin op. cit., p. 264.

both cases there is the barrier, and challenge, of the generation gap. Fedor Pavlovich's lust is unrequited, and he does not engage in any visual or epistolary, let alone carnal, intercourse with the object of his desire. He nurtures an idealised construct of Grushen'ka, with which he indulges his fancy and is able to bolster his male ego. Her actual physical presence would disturb and unsettle him. The very measures he adopts to convey his loyalty and attachment, such as placing the money in an envelope and addressing it to Grushen'ka, and especially the addition of the endearing pet-name as an afterthought, while they may apparently give the impression of being ploys to lure her into his 'parlour', are really a subconsciously devised attempt to feed his own self-delusion and impart an air of normality and purposefulness to the proceedings. Writing her name on the envelope, while it does not totally exclude his expectation of Grushen'ka's arrival, does strongly suggest that it was added for his own benefit, as a deliberate act of make-believe. Furthermore, the relationship is demonstrably unilateral. We are given next to no background details of how he became acquainted with Grushen'ka, nor of the history of his infatuation with her. There is a symbolically significant void here. Living alone in his large, bleak, Gothic house, with distant memories of his former wives and the violent harrowing conflicts as reminders of his unfitness to sustain a normal conjugal relationship, he builds up a comforting, idealised concept of a woman to suit his personal predicament. It is entirely rootless and incorporeal. Fixated on one woman, it embraces all womanhood: *Das Ewig-Weibliche,/ Zieht uns hinan!* (though not as Goethe meant it!).

A Faust manqué, Fedor Pavlovich, without the benfit of the pimp Mephistopheles to assist him in his sexual aspirations, is tormented by the most exalted yearning conceivable, the yearning for the unattainable. This yearning is manifested even in his philosophical inquisitiveness. It is he who poses the most significant, and ultimately unanswerable, questions. His tongue-in-cheek ontological enquiries, in the full knowledge that no empirically demonstrable answer is possible, is a kind of dialectical cat-and-mouse game with his interlocutors. From the vantage point of his parental authority, he adopts a mocking, patronising tone with his sons, probing and testing the strength of their convictions, above all their faith in themselves, goading them into arguing, and enjoying flaunting his own ignorance in front of them. He feels he can get the better of them; he is a clown, a jester whose mission is to challenge by provoking mirth, and to mock. In this he is a faithful disciple of Manfred, who taught him the art of incisive tongue-in-cheek banter. But where the aristocratic Manfred had been subtle and refined, as when expressing his exasperation to the three knights, 'since mirth is not your mood, let us be sad', Fedor Pavlovich in true muzhik fashion would be as likely to tell a crude indecent anecdote when in a tight corner. One of his most remarkable characteristics is his ability to generate excitement; his knack of always being centre stage, a true clown in a circus ring, a born showman. With the showman's unerring instinct, he can feel the pulse of his audience and detect any potential source of danger. But up against Smerdiakov he is powerless.

In the Greek myth, Oedipus's father Laius had the benefit of the oracle to warn him. Fedor Pavlovich has no premonition of the danger emanating from his murderer. The intense horror of Smerdiakov's role is that he is able to commit the atrocity under the cloak of innocence, without arousing any suspicion in his intended victim. Above all, his intent to kill is motiveless, and therefore undetectable by his victim's instincts of self-preservation. The real locus of the demonically murderous intent resides in Ivan and, true to his percipient nature, Fedor Pavlovich perceives it unerringly. He is aware of the danger and is in mortal dread of Ivan, whose demonism – frightening as it is to him – is irresistibly alluring to the congenital proselyte, Smerdiakov. This intricate causal interrelationship within the Karamazov household cannot be explained simply in terms of the classical Greek myth, in which, significantly, Oedipus has no intention of killing his father,[31] but is best regarded from a Gothic perspective, with the demonic element to the fore. By linking the Oedipal and the hero-worshipping syndromes, Dostoevskii has, in his convoluted Gothic world, provided a more complex pathogenesis of man's destructive genius than was ever dreamt of – even in thy philosophy, Sigmund!

* * *

Ivan's alter ego, the shabby devil with the amenable countenance who visits and torments him in his nightmare, is as far removed from the traditional cloven-footed, long-tailed variety that plagues Father

---

[31] J. Lempriere, *A Classical Dictionary*, London, T. Cadell, 1824 (see entry under *Oedipus*, pp. 512-13).

Therapon, as is Gogol's early village devil, with 'the goat's beard beneath his chin',[32] from Pavel Ivanovich Chichikov of *Dead Souls*; and yet Dmitrii Merezhkovskii saw the connection and recognised the Satanic, the Antichrist,[33] in the urbane gentleman arriving in the town of N- in his smart, well-sprung carriage. This is the new, the modern Gogolian devil, whose greatest strength resides in 'his ability to appear that which he is not'; he is the eternal parasite, the great pretender, the Ape of God (*der Affe Gottes*).[34] It could well have been Chichikov sitting across from Ivan Fedorovich Karamazov, on whom he might have called (and not for the first time!) to see if he couldn't finally settle that little matter of buying his, Ivan's, soul. Merezhkovskii insists on the ominous symbolism of Gogol's personages: 'The two principal heroes created by Gogol – Khlestakov and Chichikov – are but two thoroughly modern faces in a crowd of Russians, two images of a diptych depicting eternal and universal evil'.[35]

Edmund Wilson too, in Merezhkovskii's wake, points to the presence of the demonic and, by implication, the Gothic element in Chichikov, and indeed suggests that the landowners themselves amongst whom he had come are also of the devil.[36] At this point, one is tempted to extend the comaprison to R.S. Surtees's Mr Soapey Sponge, to see what *the devil* that red-coated pseudo-gentleman is up to in the English countryside. If there is merit in cross-cultural fertilisation, it is when new and stable creative forms evolve without stifling or displacing the indigenous cultural icons in their own environment. The Gothic came to Russia from abroad, specifically England, and provided a stimulating creative environment, particularly for the culturally receptive Dostoevskii. But what of Gogol?

Mark Simpson is of the opinion that Gogol's Gothicism has few English antecedents, though he admits that the question must ultimately

---

[32] Gogol, *Village Evenings near Dikanka and Mirgorod*, op. cit., p. 98.

[33] D.S. Merezhkovskii, *Gogol i chert*, Moscow, 1906, p. 65 (translated as 'Gogol and the Devil', in *Gogol from the Twentieth Century: Eleven Essays*, edited by Robert A. Maguire, Princeton, Princeton University Press, 1974, pp. 55-102).

[34] Ibid., p. 4. *Handwörterbuch des Deutschen Aberglaubens*, Berlin and Leipzig, 1927 (see entry under *Affe*).

[35] Merezhkovskii, op. cit., p. 5.

[36] E. Wilson, 'The Demon in the Overgrown Garden', in N. Gogol, *Dead Souls: The Reavey Translation, Backgrounds and Sources, Essays in Criticism*, edited by George Gibian, New York, Norton, 1985, p. 544.

remain open.[37] Direct Gothic antecedents? – perhaps not, although it is impossible to ignore Scott, '[without whom] there would be no Gogol,'[38] according to an assertion of Belinskii's that Anna Elistratova (in her by and large excellent study *Nikolai Gogol and the West European Novel*), does not attempt to challenge; in fact she points to *Dead Souls* as being specifically influenced by Scott.[39] However, the fact that her discussion of Scott's romanticism omits any mention of Horace Walpole must be regarded as a serious lacuna, for it is through Scott that Gogol is indisputably linked to the very heart of Gothicism. With Mr Soapey Sponge fresh in mind, an attempt may be made to establish a connection.

Janko Lavrin would have us believe that, 'although not the first to introduce the humble "little man" into Russian fiction, Gogol was largely responsible for his literary canonization'.[40] Lavrin does not enlighten us as to who was 'the first', though intellectually 'canonization' is a far greater feat, than 'introduction'. However, more of *The Overcoat* later. Let us at this stage consider Surtees's Soapey Sponge alongside Chichikov and Khlestakov. Although the serialised edition of *Mr Jorrocks' Jaunts and Jollities* appeared as early as 1831-34 (second edition, 1838), one could safely say that neither Dostoevskii nor Gogol were guilty of imitating the 'jolly, free-and-easy, fox-hunting grocer'. Incidentally, it may be surprising that Gogol does not boast a 'free-standing' – and apparently quintessentially Gogolian – character such as Mr Jorrocks in his *oeuvre,* though one can still feel that sooner or later he would surely have come up with his own Russian version. It fell to Dostoevskii to supply the missing link, in the person of Mr Bakhcheev (of *The Village of Stepanchikovo*), using the prototypes of Sir Toby Belch and Falstaff.

Mr Sponge's Sporting Tour did not see the light of day until 1853, but neither is it likely that Surtees had any inkling of *The Government Inspector* (*Revizor*, 1836) or of *Dead Souls* (1842). It is therefore safe to assume that the picaresque troika of Khlestakov, Chichikov and

---

[37] Mark S. Simpson, *The Russian Gothic Novel and its British Antecedents*, Columbus, Ohio, Slavica, 1986, p. 97.
[38] Quoted by A.A. Elistratova, *Gogol' i problemy zapadnoevropeiskogo romana*, Moscow, 1972, p. 55 (republished in English as Anna Yelistratova, *Nikolai Gogol and the West European Novel*, translated by Christopher English, Moscow, Raduga, 1984).
[39] Ibid., p. 58.
[40] J. Lavrin, *Nikolai Gogol'*, London, Sylvan Press, 1951, p. 77.

Soapey Sponge were independently conceived and evolved separately.
What then are the features that identify them as birds of a feather? All
three are confidence tricksters *par excellence*. Khlestakov is a born liar;
Chichikov a wheeler-dealer; and Soapey Sponge a professional hanger-
on, an opportunist and more than a bit of a rogue. As to whether they
can be classed as picaresque: the answer is an unqualified 'yes' in the
case of Soapey Sponge, only marginally less so in the case of
Chichikov,[41] and pretty much unqualified in the case of Khlestakov.
They are all likeable enough, and therein perhaps lies their chief threat
to the ethical welfare of the community at large: it is the sugar that
masks the poison in the pill. In Soapey Sponge one can still detect
remnants of the swashbuckling rogue and adventurer *à la* Barry
Lyndon, but he is much more likely to find himself 'and his horse
floundering about in the black porridge-like mess'[42] of a bog, than
galloping 'round the ring, saluting his Highness the Duke... and
performing the most wonderful exercises with my bay'.[43] This is a
decisive leap away from Thackeray and into Gogolian territory, where
the only vestige of Chichikov the knight-errant are his wet
accoutrements (Chichikov's visit to Korobochka after being caught in a
downpour).

It is in the person of this 'de-frocked' knight of the wet
accoutrements that Merezhkovskii recognised the modern devil of the
day: stripped of all romanticism, he is condemned to wander the earth,
performing the sacred capitalist rites of acqusitiveness – *Dead Souls*,
chapter 11 ('any old souls!'), with echoes of St Paul: 'Covetousness is
the root of all evil'[44] – demonstrating the irresistible lure of security
and contentment to those with feet of clay. Security and contentment,
mediocrity, the middle way: all are encapsulated in the near-mythical
Russian word *poshlost'* (or, as Nabokov would have it, *'poshlust'*), and
is borne by Chichikov like a hallmark. Elistratova is at pains to discuss

---

[41] T.E. Little, *'Dead Souls'*, in *Knaves and Swindlers: Essays on the Picaresque Novel
in Europe*, edited by Christine J. Whitbourn, published for University of Hull, by
Oxford University Press, 1974, p. 138.
[42] R.S. Surtees, *Mr Sponge's Sporting Tour*, Ware, Hertfordshire, Wordsworth
Classics, 1995, p. 134.
[43] W.M. Thackeray, *The Memoirs of Barry Lyndon, Esq.*, Oxford, Oxford University
Press, 1984, p. 148.
[44] 'The First Epistle of St Paul unto Timothy', Chapter 6, William Tyndale, *Tyndale's
New Testament*, New Haven, Yale University Press, 1995, p. 313.

the word *poshlost'*, not only with reference to Gogol, but to Western European literature as well, including *Don Quixote*.[45] (The 'middle-way', bourgeois comfort, globalisation – *poshlost'* rules, OK!) Merezhkovskii quotes Smerdiakov's words to Ivan Karamazov, '...and above all you like a comfortable life... that more than anything, sir'. He continues:

> And even in the awesome visage of the Grand Inquisitor one can detect not only the features of Fedor Pavlovich Karamazov, but of Pavel Ivanovich Chichikov too. The kingdom of Antichrist, which the Grand Inquisitor juxtaposes with the kingdom of Christ – those 'thousands of millions of happy children', that gratified satiety, that 'relaxed sense of well-being' of the whole of mankind in their comfortable 'aluminium palaces', in their Tower of Babel of social democracy, is but the kingdom of Chichikov, the universal and eternal Chichikov *sub specie aeterni*, for his kingdom is indeed 'the kingdom of this world': in Chichikov – as Gogol puts it – was '*all that one needs for this world*'.[46]

Gogol and the Devil is a truly pioneering work, containing vintage Merezhkovskii. The inimitable Vladislav Khodasevich, poet and critic, writing in 1934, called it 'the most profound and significant pronouncement on Gogol made hitherto'.[47]

V.V. Zen'kovskii is correct in maintaining that Herzen's and Leont'ev's analysis of *meshchanstvo* (another problem word: roughly equivalent to 'bourgeoisie'; or, figuratively, 'the attitudes of the bourgeoisie') paved the way to a deeper understanding of *poshlost'*;[48] but he is less than fair in dismissing Merezhkovskii's contribution as 'witty but unconvincing' (especially as his own arguments are no more convincing and certainly less witty). For a matching assessment, of Khodasevich's view of Merezhkovskii as a literary critic, one may turn to Aleksandr Blok.[49] In any event, one can agree with Louis Allen's editorial comments on Zen'kovskii and Vasilii Gippius, that, 'in place

---

[45] See Elistratova, op. cit., pp. 64-70.

[46] Merezhkovskii, op. cit., p 42.

[47] V. Khodasevich, 'Pamiati Gogolia', in his *Sobranie sochinenii v chetyrekh tomakh*, Moscow, 1996, vol. 2, p. 293.

[48] V. Zen'kovskii, *N.V. Gogol'* [with V. Gippius, *Gogol'*], St Petersburg, 1994, p. 243.

[49] See the reviews and articles on Merezhkovskii (1903-17), in A. Blok, *Sobraniie sochinenii*, 8 vols., Moscow-Leningrad, 1960-63, vol. 5, pp. 360-6, 635-6, 657; vol. 6, pp. 393-5.

of Gogol the realist and chronicler, Gogol the denouncer of Nicholas's Russia, [they] have given us Gogol the romantic, the writer of the fantastic, the mystic, the visionary'.[50] However, Merezhkovskii had already done that a few years earlier.

The other Ape of God – the father of all lies, of the facile and the insubstantial, the modern man of the moment, Ivan Aleksandrovich Khlestakov, the second member of Gogol's Gothic diptych – differs from Chichikov and his English counterpart, Mr Soapey Sponge, in that he is essentially less of a travelling man (at least, in the sense that the other two are). A born optimist, an opportunistic imposter and the classical example of the mistaken-identity-man: arguably, he has no equal in world literature or theatre – although there is over-compensation from the countless variants in the world of cinema, where the mistaken identity motif is a stock-in-trade. Ostensibly, Gogol has orchestrated the role for laughs but, as with all great comedy, every guffaw is but a hair's breadth from the serious or the ominous. On this point, one would have to take radical issue with Vasilii Gippius, who asserts that 'on the whole, Gogol does not *mix* [my italics: IA] the comic and serious with the demonological theme.'[51] For conclusive refutation of Gippius's assertion, the reader may be referred to Ershov's eerie, haunting and, it must be added, intensely funny film version of *Vii.*

Even *The Castle of Otranto* could be played for laughs and Walpole, perhaps unwittingly, provided excellent opportunities for this. In fact, comedy might be the only mode in which to present it to a modern and visually sophisticated audience, given that its original Gothic paraphernalia is well past its view-by date. For an instance of comedy in *The Castle of Otranto*, one need only consider the scene between the exasperated Manfred (clenching and unclenching his fists, foaming at the mouth) and his vassal servants Jaquez and Diego (potentially a Bobchinskii and Dobchinskii pair):

> '…have you found the princess?'
> 'We thought we had, my lord,' said the fellow, looking terrified; 'but—'
> 'But what?' cried the prince; 'has she escaped?'

---

[50] V. Gippius, *Gogol'*. V. Zen'kovskii, *N.V. Gogol'*, op. cit., publisher's blurb (back cover).
[51] Ibid., p. 31.

'Jaquez and I, my lord—'

'Yes, I and Diego,' interrupted the second, who came up in still greater consternation.

'Speak one of you at a time,' said Manfred; 'I ask you, where is the princess?'

'We do not know,' said they both together; 'but we are frightened out of our wits.'

'So I think, blockheads,' said Manfred.[52]

This exemplifies the thin dividing line between high drama and comedy. So, too, Mr Soapey Sponge (along with Khlestakov, surely one of the great comic characters of literature) transcends the narrow world in which he is made to operate, and his timeless humour ensures that he will be taken seriously long after the Walpolean – not to mention the Orwellian – types are confined to the literary-historical archives. Not only did Surtees write of 'an England for all time',[53] but, like Gogol, he wrote of a human condition for all time.

Brief consideration must now be given to one additional character of Gogol's – Pliushkin. This is prompted principally by V.N. Toporov's immensely interesting and original treatment of him in his recent study of myth and ritual.[54] Bearing in mind Merezhkovskii's famous dictum, that Dostoevskii is to be seen as the seer of the spirit and Tolstoi as seer of the flesh, Gogol (on the basis of Toporov's analysis) should be regarded as the seer of the inanimate object; this view would have been approved by Andrei Belyi, who noted Gogol's anthropomorphism of the object – namely, the overcoat, in the eponymous story.[55] Man's complex relationship to the inanimate is developed further on the pages of *Dead Souls*, with Pliushkin depicted as high priest of the cult of the inert object. Whereas Chichikov is motivated by personal acquisitiveness, Pliushkin, on the other hand, is motivated by destructive acquisitiveness. According to Toporov:

> Pliushkin is a saint of miserliness because, through love for things as such – in all their pettiness and insignificance – he makes enormous sacrifices and loses

[52] Walpole, in *Three Gothic Novels*, p. 67.

[53] Molly Keane, quoted in Surtees, *Mr Sponge's Sporting Tour* (introduction and back cover).

[54] V.N. Toporov, 'Veshch' v antropotsentricheskoi perspektive (apologiia Pliushkina)', in his *Mif, Ritual, Simvol, Obraz - Issledovaniia v oblasti mifologicheskogo*, Moscow, 1995, pp. 7-111.

[55] A. Belyi, *Masterstvo Gogolia*, Moscow, 1934, p. 19.

real wealth. Mills, spinning-houses, textile workshps – all go to rack and ruin, because the rubbish underfoot – an old shoe sole, an iron nail, a piece of broken earthenware- is valued above money and gold.[56]

As with Khlestakov, who was lying for lying's sake, so Pliushkin hoards for hoarding's sake. Art for art's sake: it is the act, rather than the fact of hoarding – the creative delight, the spotting and picking up of the object – that appeals to Pliushkin:

> ... he wandered about the streets of his village every day looking under the bridges, under the planks thrown over puddles, and everything he came across, an old sole, a bit of a peasant woman's rag, an iron nail, a piece of broken earthenware, he carried them all to his room and put them on the heap which Chichikov had noticed in the corner.[57]

Toporov, in vaguely identifying the unique, ritualistic nature of Pliushkin's miserliness, rather spoils his accomplishment by lamenting that 'Gogol could not, or did not want to, look into the soul of his character to see what motivated him'.[58]

Gogol's achievement, surely, lay in defining a type whose symbolic parameters and contours may be adjusted according to the lights and scope of our own imagination. Pliushkin is one of the most frightening figures in literary creation. Is it not, therefore, better that he remain masked by the greasy dressing-gown in which he appears before Chichikov? Any attempt to find out what makes him tick would involve unfastening that terrible dressing-gown – to reveal, perhaps, a hideous outline of the bare skeleton beneath, as in an H.P. Lovecraft-type horror story.[59] Or perhaps, for that matter, nothing at all: just dust and must, the inevitable and prophetic concomitants in centuries to come of Adam Smith's disastrous economic doctrine of acquisition. Gogol, with the intuitive eye of the artist, saw ('divined': *ugadal* – Pushkin's term) all

---

[56] Toporov, op. cit., p. 89.

[57] Nikolai Gogol, *Dead Souls*, translated by David Magarshack, Harmondsworth, Penguin, 1961, p. 126.

[58] Toporov, p. 89.

[59] See H.P. Lovecraft, *At the Mountains of Madness and other Tales of Terror*, New York, Ballantine 1982. The cover illustration depicts a woman undoing her cape to reveal that her body is a skeleton; this illustration does not refer to any story in the book, nor to any other work by Lovecraft known to me, and is in all likelihood a case of the editor's, and the illustrator's, artistic licence.

too clearly the consequences of unfettered economic free-for-all. Gogol
the novelist encapsulated in literary terms the biblical 'ashes to ashes'
verity, and from his pen came the first entropic character in world
literature. This truly dead soul (the embodiment and graphic illustration
of the law of entropy,[60] according to which the physical world is
destined to end in the form of the rubbish heap that Chichikov, the
Antichrist and the buyer of dead souls, comes across on the floor of the
miser's residence) is a truly frightening and cautionary figure. Let us
therefore hurry away from this Dantesque scene of melancholy and
hopelessness and, for light relief, momentarily contemplate the more
up-beat aspects of Gogolian Gothic.

*A Night in May, or the Drowned Maiden (Maiskaia noch', ili
Utoplennitsa)* may be an appropriate story to quote, the more so since it
re-establishes the correlation between architecture and literature which
the Gothic concept invites. Gogol is here at his most optimistically
buoyant in his use of the upwardly surging, escalating –indeed,
vaunting – images and metaphors:

> 'Look, look over there!' she continued... raising her eyes upward to the infinite
> vault of the warm blue Ukrainian sky.... 'See those teeny stars twinkling over
> there?.. Just imagine if people had wings, like birds, and we could fly up there,
> high up in the sky... it fills you with dread! There isn't a single oak tree tall
> enough to reach the stars. But they say there is one, somewhere, in some
> faraway land, whose topmost branches rustle in heaven, and God walks down
> them to earth on the night before Easter Sunday.'
> 'No, Hanna: God has a ladder that reaches from heaven right down to earth.'[61]

Yet, there is no such joyous sentiment or lyrical optimism in *A Terrible
Vengeance (Strashnaia mest')*. The atmosphere is tense and doomladen,
one in which the forces of evil are continually gaining the upper hand.
Even love and compassion appear to have lost their redemptive power.
The Landlady (Khoziaika, 1847) was Dostoevskii's rather too faithful
imitation of *A Terrible Vengeance*, complete with the retention of the
same name for the heroine (Katerina) and the stylised, folkloric and
mystically-charged language with which he was patently ill at ease.
Fortunately, Dostoevskii never again returned to that style of
composition.

---

[60] On this subject, see J. Rifkin, *Entropy: A New World View*, London, Paladin, 1985.

[61] Gogol, *Village Evenings near Dikanka and Mirgorod*, p 53.

* * *

We conclude with a brief word on Gogol's epoch-making *The Overcoat*, to which reference has already been made. The significance of Akakii Akakievich, the 'nobody', the unimportant down-trodden individual, desperately fighting for survival, cannot be overestimated. In creating a man whose strength is his weakness, Gogol ensured that he remains invincible. Dostoevskii tried hard to match Gogol's feat but, in the end, came nowhere near it: every one of his 'weak' personages is undermined by powerful, and ultimately destructive, reserves of strength. Nevertheless, in success as in failure, both Gogol and Dostoevskii made their own significant contributions to the Gothic genre by idiosyncratically blending fantasy and realism in their works. Essentially, such an artistic policy may be said to represent a continuation of what Horace Walpole had attempted a century or more earlier, except that, in his case, the blend between 'the ancient and the modern' had charted a new course in literary genre.

THE ECHOING HEART:
FANTASIAS OF THE FEMALE
IN DOSTOEVSKII AND TURGENEV

LEON BURNETT

> He feeds upon her face by day and night
> ...
> Not as she is, but as she fills his dream.
> (Christina Rossetti, 'In an Artist's Studio')

Let us start by quoting a passage from the first page of *The Brothers Karamazov* (*Brat'ia Karamazovy*). It reads, in Constance Garnett's unrevised translation:[1]

> I knew a young lady of the last 'romantic' generation who after some years of an *enigmatic passion* for a gentleman, whom she might quite easily have married at any moment, invented insuperable obstacles to their union, and ended by throwing herself one stormy night into a rather deep and rapid river from a high bank, almost a precipice, and so perished, entirely to satisfy her own *caprice*, and to be like Shakespeare's Ophelia. Indeed, if this precipice, a chosen and favourite spot of hers, had been less *picturesque*, if there had been a *prosaic* flat bank in its place, most likely the *suicide* would never have taken place. This is a fact, and probably there have been not a few similar instances in the last two or three generations. [italics mine: LB]

---

[1] For the Russian text, see F.M. Dostoevskii, *Polnoe sobranie sochinenii v tridtsati tomakh*, Leningrad, 1972-90, vol. 14, p. 8. English translations of *The Brothers Karamazov* consulted for the preparation of this paper are those published by: Constance Garnett (London, Heinemann, 1912); David Magarshack (Harmondsworth, Penguin, 1958); Ralph E. Matlaw (New York, Norton, 1976: a revised version of Garnett, see note 2); Richard Pevear and Larissa Volokhonsky (London, Quartet, 1990; re-issued London, Vintage 1992); David McDuff (Harmondsworth, Penguin, 1993); and Ignat Avsey (Oxford, Oxford University Press, 1994). Two further translations - by Andrew R. MacAndrew (Toronto, Bantam, 1970) and Julius Katzer (Moscow, Progress, 1980) - were not available to me. All versions after Garnett follow her in translating the Russian title as *The Brothers Karamazov*, with the exception of Katzer and Avsey (*The Karamazov Brothers*).

Whether one is inquiring into the nature of the 'Romantic', the 'Gothic', the 'fantastic' or any combination of these three, this passage should hold some interest for the reader. It is also interesting from the point of view of literary translation, for the translator is, after all, not a neutral intermediary but a mediator in the text.[2] What I have in mind here, particularly, is Garnett's rendition of the Russian phrase *'posle neskol'kikh let zagadochnoi liubvi'* as 'after some years of an *enigmatic passion'*. A literalist might well object that *liubov'* should be translated as 'love', reserving the word 'passion' for *strast'*. Garnett's choice, however, may be defended on the grounds that the qualification of *liubov'* – as *zagadochnaia* – functions to modify the concept of love. In other words, her translation offers an example of dynamic, as opposed to static, equivalence. Love is one thing, an enigmatic or mad love (*amour fou*) is another.[3]

I intend to use this anecdote as a template for examining the function of the erotic as an active component in the reading of mid-nineteenth-century Russian fiction. I am interested, in particular, in what is signalled in the expression translated by Garnett as 'enigmatic

---

[2] For a full discussion, see Rachel May, *The Translator in the Text: On Reading Russian Literature in English* (Evanston, Illinois: Northwestern University Press, 1994). On Constance Garnett's mediation in the Dostoevskian text, see Ralph E. Matlaw, 'Afterword: On Translating *The Brothers Karamazov*', in Fyodor Dostoevsky, *The Brothers Karamazov*; translated by Constance Garnett, revised and edited by Ralph E. Matlaw, New York, Norton, 1976, pp. 736-44; and A.N. Nikoliukin, 'Dostoevskii in Constance Garnett's Translation', in *Dostoevskii and Britain*; edited by W.J. Leatherbarrow, Oxford, Berg, 1995, pp. 207-27 (this essay, here translated by Leatherbarrow, had been originally published in *Russkaia literatura*, no. 2, 1985). When Matlaw 'revised' the Garnett translation for the Norton Critical Edition of *The Brothers Karamazov*, he re-introduced the qualification made by the Dostoevskian narrator at the end of the last sentence in the extract: 'This is a fact, and probably there have been not a few similar instances in the last two or three generations *in our Russian life*'. Garnett, we may presume, omitted this phrase because she felt it redundant, since the central motive for her monumental effort in translating Dostoevskii and other nineteenth-century Russian novelists was to bring to her English readers the strangeness of a whole world of Russian fiction, hitherto unexplored. With the exception of Magarshack, all the later English translations that I have consulted include this important qualification. We are, in effect, dealing here with the *Russian* Gothic and this has a significance for any interpretation of the material.
[3] J.H. Matthews defines *amour fou* as passion 'undisciplined by reason, expressive of irrational impulses and therefore assertive of freedom': see his *Toward the Poetics of Surrealism*, Syracuse, New York, Syracuse University Press, 1976, p. 169.

passion', and by a later translator as 'mysterious love'.[4] What I want to argue is that these two alternative translations may be taken as indicative of the distance between Dostoevskii's and Turgenev's presentations of Eros. That is to say, what Dostoevskii might regard as an enigmatic passion is, for Turgenev, a mysterious love.

My interest here lies not so much in exploring eroticism *in* the text as in positing what might be called an erotics *of* the text or, more specifically, an erotics of the tale (*rasskaz*). The distinction I make between an enigma and a mystery is intended to suggest a contrast between the erotic questioning in Turgenev's *Faust* and that which is presented in, for example, Dostoevskii's *A Meek Girl* (or 'A Gentle Creature': *Krotkaia*), a tale which also takes Goethe's *Faust* as a point of reference. Both *Faust* and *A Meek Girl* serve as instances of the late Gothic in nineteenth-century Russian fiction, so 'late' indeed that they are more frequently defined as belonging to a 'fantastic' sub-genre of realism that one may qualify either as 'mysterious' or as 'enigmatic'.[5]

I have italicised certain key words in the passage quoted above. Dostoevskii's narrator tells us how the mood (*caprice*) and setting (the *picturesque*), as constituents of the erotic (the *enigmatic passion*), help decide the outcome (*suicide*). Had the location been less 'romantic' (i.e. had it been what Dostoevskii calls *prosaic*), the ending would 'most likely' (*mozhet byt'*) have been different, and, in all probability, the 'enigmatic passion' would have lacked the necessary grounding, or interest, to become a story worth the telling. Caprice and the picturesque, or an inherent predisposition in the character and a 'chosen and favourite' (*namechennyi i izliublennyi*) location, combine to induce a state of mind that drives the individual to act in an extraordinary manner, outside the normal orbit of human conduct. This state of mind may be defined as a form of *possession*. The romantic young lady is led to behave like a person possessed. Possession, of course, has long been recognised as state of mind associated with the Dostoevskian character, a recognition reinforced by Constance Garnett's choice of title – *The Possessed* (1914) – for her translation of the novel *Besy* (1871).[6]

---

[4] Namely, McDuff. Pevear-Volokhonsky use the literal (static) 'enigmatic love'.

[5] I have explored the contrast between 'mystery' and 'enigma' as narrative orientations in a paper entitled 'The Vanishing Point: Dostoevskii and the "New Word"', given to the Neo-Formalist Circle (Oxford, September 1998: publication forthcoming).

[6] Garnett was following the example of Derély, the French translator, whose *Les Possedés* appeared in 1886; and Putze, whose German version, *Die Besessenen*, was

Although it is possible to identify two different types of possession –
the erotic and the religious – it is often difficult to distinguish between
them, since they frequently make use of the same vocabulary.[7]

The fact that an element of choice is involved in the young lady's
amour fou makes her passion for self-destruction enigmatic (rather than
mysterious). There is, however, another aspect to the enigma that
should be noted. The young lady wanted 'to be like Shakespeare's
Ophelia'. What does it mean to be like Ophelia (*pokhodit' na Ofeliiu*),
and how complete is the identification? Must her 'gentleman', as a
consequence, be like Hamlet? Must she have a garrulous, interfering
father who ends up murdered by her lover? Is it, perhaps, a secret wish
to espouse Danish nationality? Or, as is 'most likely', does it mean
simply that she wishes to die a 'romantic' death, like her Shakespearean
predecessor? One is tempted to ask, recalling the play's most famous
soliloquy, whether, in fact, she desires 'to be' or 'not to be' (that is to
say, to die), like Ophelia. If so, the wish to be like Ophelia is a wish not
to be. This paradox expresses the enigmatic 'fantasia', which led her to
choose a watery death.

The word that I shall use to define the wish to be like another
character is *projection*. She projects herself as Ophelia or, to be more
circumspect, the narrator tells the reader that she projects herself as
Ophelia. It is important to entertain such circumspection in reading
fiction, and in particular first-person narratives, for what the reader is
given is not the lyrical sensation, '[f]elt in the blood, and felt along the
heart' (to quote Wordsworth's memorable image for unmediated,
romantic passion), but a narrated 'echo' of that truth.[8] The fantasia of

---

published in Dresden in 1888. When Magarshack's Penguin edition appeared in 1953,
the title was translated as *The Devils*, but the alternative - and established - title, *The
Possessed*, was printed after it in parentheses. Pevear-Volokhonsky provided a third
English option in 1994 (London, Vintage) by entitling the new translation *Demons*.

[7] For an authoritative account of spirit possession, see I.M. Lewis, *Ecstatic Religion:
An Anthropological Study of Spirit Possession and Shamanism*, Harmondsworth,
Penguin, 1971. Georges Bataille identifies three types of eroticism - physical,
emotional and religious: see his *Eroticism*; translated by Mary Dalwood, London,
Marion Boyars, 1987, pp. 15-16.

[8] William Wordsworth, 'Lines Written a Few Miles above Tintern Abbey, on
Revisiting the Banks of the Wye during a Tour, 13 July 1798', line 29. The contrast
between the narrative and the lyrical is well illustrated in the example of the heroine of
Hardy's *Tess of the D'Urbervilles*. In the novel, the reader follows the narrative account
of Tess's fatalistic path, but in Hardy's poem, 'Tess's Lament', the erotic impulse is

the female, then, has a twofold perspective. It is simultaneously the lyrical fantasia that takes possession of her (or the fantasia that she lives) and the narrative fantasia projected upon her by the male storyteller in his attempt to understand her 'otherness'.

There is a further point to be noticed in the projection of Dostoevskii's *devitsa*. She wants to be like *Shakespeare*'s Ophelia. *Literary* desire has a particular significance in the configuration of the Gothic-fantastic, understood as an offshoot of the Romantic. In projecting herself as Ophelia, she allows Shakespeare's *story* to take possession of her and thus, in a sense, to nullify her.[9] If this projective tendency is characteristic of 'the last two or three generations' in the cultural life of Russia in the middle of the nineteenth century, as Dostoevskii's narrator informs us, one might wish to add that Hamlet is one of the three most potent and enduring male figures drawn from outside the nation's literary heritage to exercise an analogous, albeit not always so fatal, influence on the masculine psyche in this period.[10]

* * *

The present inquiry, however, is into the female fantasia. Dostoevskii's narrator introduces the anecdotal account of the suicide at the beginning of *The Brothers Karamazov* in order for it to serve as an illustrative alternative to the choice made by Adelaida Ivanovna Miiusov, who married Fyodor [Fedor] Karamazov, the father of the ill-fated family. Adelaida Ivanovna chose the course of action rejected by

---

shown clearly to be one of willed self-destruction. The lament, as she expresses it in the poem, could serve as epitaph for Dostoevskii's 'romantic' maiden: 'I'd have my life unbe.' In this connection, Bataille's link between the *dissolute life* and *dissolution* is noteworthy: 'The passive, female side is essentially the one that is dissolved as a separate entity. But for the male partner the dissolution of the passive partner means one thing only: it is paving the way for a fusion where both are mingled, attaining at length the same degree of dissolution' (*Eroticism*, p. 17).

[9] Cf. 'Possession can only occur if at the same time there is a "depossession" of the self' (Lewis, *Ecstatic Religion*, p. 46).

[10] The other two are Don Quixote (whom Turgenev, in a celebrated essay, identified as a complementary, or antithetical, type to Hamlet) and Faust. Robert A. Johnson, *Transformation: Understanding the Three Levels of Masculine Consciousness*, New York, HarperCollins, 1991, draws upon these three literary figures to define his three levels of masculine consciousness. According to him, Don Quixote is two-dimensional, Hamlet three-dimensional and Faust four-dimensional.

the romantic young lady. She married her suitor. The narrator proceeds
to inform the reader of Constance Garnett's version that:

> Adelaida Ivanovna Miiusov's action was [...], no doubt, an echo of other
> people's ideas, and was due to the irritation caused by lack of mental freedom.
> She wanted, perhaps, to show her feminine independence, to override class
> distinctions and the despotism of her family. And a pliable imagination
> persuaded her, we must suppose ...

Here we have it, an indisputable case of *amour fou*: unreasonable
behaviour coupled with an assertion of independence, which may be
put down to 'a pliable imagination'. This is, of course, a curious and,
perhaps, modern (*sovremennyi*) kind of independence, for – like the
suicide's – it is 'an echo of other people's ideas'. Now, while Garnett's
'enigmatic passion' (for *zagadochnaia liubov'*) was found acceptable
on the grounds of dynamic equivalence, on this occasion it is difficult
to defend her rendition of *ogoloskom chuzhikh veianii*. Her translation,
as Matlaw claims (in his 'Afterword'), 'vitiates' the Russian original: it
conceals more than it reveals. The phrase 'echo of other people's ideas'
misses what post-Bakhtinian translators find easier to spot, namely the
dialogical resonances in the Russian word, *chuzhoi*. The Pevear-
Volokhonsky edition, which is generally the most literal and source-
oriented of the translations, comes the closest to capturing the nuance
in the original with 'an echo of foreign influences'.[11]

Nina Perlina has written perceptively on the function of quotation in
The Brothers Karamazov.[12] In the Russian original of the passage
quoted above, we find a particularly subtle (and fully motivated) use of
quotation to which the translator needs to be attuned. Dostoevskii
follows the remark *about* 'an echo of foreign influence' *with* an echo of
an alien voice by means of a subtextual reference to a poem written by

---

[11] Matlaw revises Garnett with 'an echo of *foreign* ideas' (italics added). The other
translators have 'a reflection of other people's ideas' (Magarshack); 'a response to
foreign influences' (Avsey); and 'an echo of trends and ideas acquired elsewhere'
(McDuff) - a cumbersome circumlocution which merits a 'sic!'.
[12] Nina Perlina, *Varieties of Poetic Utterance: Quotation in The Brothers Karamazov*,
Lanham, MD, University Press of America, 1985. She does not refer, however, to the
particular Lermontovian quotation that I discuss.

Lermontov,[13] thereby offering a notable instance of what Bakhtin has called 'double-voiced discourse'.[14] Garnett misses this allusion entirely and translates awkwardly: 'and was due to the irritation caused by lack of mental freedom'. With the exception of the Pevear-Volokhonsky translation, other translators fare little better.[15]

As one may readily observe, there is considerable variation in the translations, but what is just as striking in this case is the uniformity in the decisions of the translators as how to render the Russian noun in the expression that Garnett transcribes as 'a pliant imagination', even if there is no agreement among them as to the preceding epithet.[16] Yet, the equivalent word for 'imagination' in the original is not, as one might be led to expect from the consistency of the translations, *voobrazhenie*: but *fantaziia*.[17]

---

[13] 'Ne ver' sebe' ('Trust Not Thyself', 1839). The injunction is addressed to the 'young dreamer'. The fourth line of this poem reads: '*il' plennoi mysli razdrazhen'e*'; it is also quoted by Dostoevskii in *A Meek Girl*.

[14] See, for a schematic representation of the forms of 'internal dialogization', Mikhail Bakhtin, *Problems of Dostoevsky's Poetics*; edited and translated by Caryl Emerson, Manchester, Manchester University Press, 1984, p. 199; and compare Perlina's claim that, in *The Brothers Karamazov*, 'quotation organizes the whole architectonics of the novel' (*Varieties of Poetic Utterance*, p. 39).

[15] The Pevear-Volokhonsky version translates the Lermontovian phrase as 'the chafings of a mind imprisoned' and adds a footnote to explain the provenance of the expression. While Matlaw's revision had 'remedied' the deficiency in Garnett by substituting 'foreign' for 'other people's', and had also added a footnote (placed ambiguously in the text) to indicate the Lermontovian source, he nevertheless manages to outdo Garnett in his prosaic rendition of the poetic allusion by adding a redundant 'also': 'and was *also* due to the irritation caused by lack of mental freedom' (italics added). In the other translations, Magarshack makes a stab at alliteration, coming up with 'and the impulse of a mind cribbed and confined'; McDuff has 'and also the "fretting of a captive mind"', a quasi-Lermontovian locution placed, contrary to Dostoevskii, in quotation marks (note the recurrence of the redundant 'also'); Ignat Avsey, who systematically reduces the roughness of Dostoevskii's stylistic idiosyncrasies in the interests of English readability, offers 'and an act of defiance of an enslaved soul'.

[16] Matlaw leaves Garnett unaltered (although he tinkers with the word order in the sentence); Magarshack has 'an *accommodating* imagination'; Pevear-Volokhonsky 'an *obliging* imagination'; McDuff 'her *complaisant* imagination'; and Avsey 'her *fertile* imagination'.

[17] Dostoevskii's phrase is '*usluzhlivaia fantaziia*'. The 'fantasia' of the female in this reference may be compared with the 'fantasia' of Europe in *The Idiot*. The last words uttered by any of the characters in *The Idiot* belong to Mrs Epanchin. In her translation, Constance Garnett retains the allusion to 'fantasy' (Dostoevskii's *fantaziia*): 'And all

* * *

The genre most frequently employed by both Dostoevskii and Turgenev as a vehicle for the fantasia is the *rasskaz*. The *rasskaz* (short story, or tale) that I shall focus on in this paper is one that Turgenev wrote relatively early in his literary career, and which he entitled simply *Faust* (1856).[18] It is the first of several tales that the author wrote which draw upon the repertoire of the 'Gothic' while, at the same time, anticipating a trend towards the 'fantastic', in the period of literary history better known for its production of works of realism.[19] Turgenev chose Goethe's drama as the source and the site of the erotic tale with which he began what was to prove a sustained exploration of the fantasia of the female. Unlike Dostoevskii, who availed himself of a dialogic approach in approaching the 'dark' forces of 'enigmatic passion' that lurk beneath the social exterior, Turgenev preferred a more restrained dialectic of presentation for which, when it came to the power of 'mysterious love', the trappings of the Gothic tale provided a suitably ambivalent texture.

Turgenev's *rasskaz* bears all the hallmarks of an erotic fantasia: caprice, the picturesque, a literary projection that amounts to the 'echoing' of a named 'foreign' text, a reminder of the 'safe', prosaic alternative, and, finally, death. We find all these elements in this *Faust*

---

this, all this life abroad, and this Europe of yours is all a fantasy, and all of us abroad are only a fantasy'. Magarshack substitutes 'delusion' for Garnett's 'fantasy'.

[18] The translation quoted in this article ('Faust: A Story in Nine Letters') is by Constance Garnett, and included in *A Lear of the Steppes etc*, volume 12 of *The Novels of Ivan Turgenev*, London, Heinemann, 1920 (first published 1898), pp. 151-223. Page references given here in the text are to this edition. For the Russian text, see I.S. Turgenev, 'Faust: Rasskaz v deviati pis'makh', *Polnoe sobranie sochinenii i pisem*, 28 vols., Moscow-Leningrad, 1960-68, vol. 7 (*Sochineniia*), pp. 7-50. Alternative, or more recent, English versions may be found in the Turgenev selections: *The Mysterious Tales*, translated by Robert Dessaix, Canberra, Australian National University, 1979; and *Stories and Poems in Prose*, translated by Olga Shartse *et al.*, Moscow, Progress, 1982.

[19] The incorporation of the 'fantastic' within the realist genre is associated less with Turgenev than with Dostoevskii, however, and it is for the latter's compositions that the description 'fantastic realism' is usually employed, taking the lead from the subtitle that Dostoevskii himself appended to *A Meek Girl* (1876), written toward the end of his career. I see these two first-person narratives (*Faust* and *A Meek Girl*) as standing at the beginning and the end of a single period of *transitional realism* in Russian literature, a period which coincides approximately with the third-quarter of the nineteenth century.

– but *à la* Turgenev, and not at all in the Dostoevskian manner. Thus, an act of caprice (in Dostoevskii a psychologically motivated form of unpredictable behaviour) is transformed into a mystery (which, even though it is just as unpredictable, is aesthetically determined by forces that lie outside the control of the individual).[20] Similarly, the pathological, but undefined, desire 'to be like Shakespeare's Ophelia' is replaced by a desire stimulated by carefully orchestrated readings from Goethe's *Faust*. The fact that the volume read is not a translation, but in the original German, borrowed from the narrator's own library, is a typically Turgenevan touch, as is the series of vignette descriptions: an evening storm, a boat ride on the lake, an impressionistic sketch of light on leaves, a lover's vigil in the dark. There is even the 'chosen and favourite spot' where the fateful book is read: a Chinese summer-house. This outdoor location is the setting for the erotic encounter described in the last letter. Its counterpart is the favourite interior space (*liubimoe mesto*), beneath the 'gloomy portrait' of Madame El'tsov, which is mentioned in the third letter. Priimkov, the heroine's husband, represents the prosaic alternative to the temptations offered by exposure to a Faustian world.

The heroine of Turgenev's *Faust* is Vera Nikolaevna, daughter of Colonel and Madame El'tsov, and grand-daughter on her mother's side of Ladanov and his wife, a peasant woman, whom he had seduced, from Albano in Italy. The family history, replete with passionate intrigues and premature deaths, is used to hint at a latent eroticism within Vera, the 'angel of peace' (*mirnyi angel*). All that we learn about Vera's enigmatic passion/mysterious love, however, are second-hand traces, revealed in her reported words and actions, or else through the surmises and speculations of the male narrator.

The story, told in an episodic manner with an accelerating narrative pace, takes the form of a sequence of nine letters written by Pavel Aleksandrovich B- to his friend Semion Nikolaevich V-. The span of the action is from July to September 1850, the time of the narrator's return to his old estate in M- village after an absence of nine years. This is also the period in which all the letters are written, with the sole exception of the last letter, penned in 1853, which contains the

---

[20] On 'caprice' in Dostoevskii see my 'Dostoevsky, Poe and the Discovery of Fantastic Realism', in *F.M Dostoevsky (1821-1881): A Centenary Collection*, edited by Leon Burnett, Colchester, University of Essex, 1981, pp. 58-86 (64-7).

denouement. Through the nine letters, the reader learns of Pavel Aleksandrovich's encounter with his neighbour, Priimkov, who, it turns out, has married Vera Nikolaevna, the woman whom the narrator had met and fallen in love with some twelve years before. The epistolary device allows the reader to follow the narrative development of the plot through a series of diary-like commentaries, written from the perspective of the male protagonist. At various points in the narration, the writer's limited perspective is emphasised. In the seventh letter, for example, he acknowledges: 'Now I understand what I wrote to you in my first letter; I understand now what was the experience I had missed' (p. 204). What the letters record is a growing attachment between Pavel Aleksandrovich and Vera Nikolaevna until, in the last (delayed) letter, an account of their mutual declaration of love – and its aftermath – is given. Typical of the concatenated effect produced by means of this epistolary device is the dramatisation of a series of shifts in the writer's sensibility,[21] until, climactically, in Letter Nine, he confesses ingenuously: 'This is how I learnt that Vera loved me. First of all I must tell you (and you will believe me) that up to that day I had absolutely no suspicion' (p. 209). One is given the impression that what is being set down – except in the last letter – is an immediate response to events as they are happening, an account, moreover, which can only be reported to the most intimate and confidential of friends.

The temporality of the tale combines chronological progression, marked objectively by the exact date at the head of each letter, with a gradual unfolding of events as recorded by a subjective, that is to say, a circumscribed, interpretation of their significance. The most explicitly Gothic note is sounded in the narrator's response to a striking portrait of Vera's mother, hanging in the drawing-room, over a sofa:

---

[21] Some indication of the shifts may be given by the following excerpts. In Letter One, Pavel Aleksandrovich announces: 'A sort of inward calm has come upon me since I have been settled here ... one is too lazy for thought, but not too lazy for musing; two different things, as you know well' (p. 156); in Letter Three (ten days later), he reports a change of mood: 'I am very glad of such neighbours, glad of this opportunity of seeing something of an intelligent, simple, bright creature. And as to what comes of it ..., you shall hear in due time' (p. 177); and in Letter Seven (on August 22), when events have moved on apace, he exclaims: 'I can't hide my feelings any longer! ... How wretched I am! How I love her! You can imagine with what a thrill of bitterness I write that fatal word' (p. 203).

It caught my eye directly I went into the room. It seemed as though she were gazing sternly and earnestly at me. ... I could not help continually glancing at the gloomy portrait of Madame Eltsov. Vera Nikolaevna was sitting just under it; it is her favourite place. (p.172).

The all-too-animated portrait of the dead person is, of course, a well-known prop in the repertoire of the Gothic, which Turgenev is loath to relinquish. Later in *Faust*, after the narrator has dared to challenge the wish expressed by the 'strange woman' that her daughter should not read any works of the imagination, he stands in front of the portrait thinking triumphantly: 'I have read your daughter a forbidden book!' (p.185). The consequence of these defiant words is reported to his correspondent:

All at once I fancied – you have most likely noticed that eyes *en face* always seem fixed straight on any one looking at a picture – but this time I positively fancied the old lady moved them with a reproachful look on me. (pp. 185-6)

The Pushkinian subtext, from *The Queen of Spades* (*Pikovaia dama*), prepares us for the fact that the Faustian man will be defeated – for a second time – in his encounter with the dark forces represented by the 'old woman'. If a supernatural agency is implicit in the Gothic trappings of the 'gloomy portrait', then the scientific explanation is supplied by a series of pointed references to heredity. In the sixth letter, for example, he speculates that Vera may have inherited the sensuality of her Italian grandmother, a legacy of the 'luxuriance' (*roskosh'*) and 'power' (*sila*) that is displayed in another portrait, the miniature contained inside a gold medallion which Vera owns:

But what a face the Italian woman had, voluptuous, open like a full-blown rose, with prominent, large, liquid eyes, and complacently smiling red lips! Her delicate sensual nostrils seemed dilating and quivering after recent kisses. ... The artist (a master) had put a vine in her hair, which was black as pitch with bright grey highlights; this Bacchic ornament was in marvellous keeping with the expression of her face. ... And what is most wonderful of all, as I looked at the portrait, I recalled that in Vera too, in spite of the utter dissimilarity of the features, there is at times a gleam of something like that smile, that look. . . . Yes, I tell you again; neither she herself nor any one else in the world knows as yet all that is latent in her. . . .' (pp. 202-3)

In both instances, projection (what the narrator sees in the likenesses) and possession (the power that he supposes the dead to exercise over the living) are played off against each other. The latent erotic impulse noted in Vera is inherited from an ancestor whose actions resemble those of Adelaida Miiusov, in that she rebelled against 'the despotism of her blood and family'. Indirectly, the formation of Vera's character is construed as 'an echo of foreign influences, the chafings of a mind imprisoned', as she is put under similar pressures by the complicit act of reading a 'forbidden book'. Yet the 'Bacchic' projections so erotically imagined exist only in the mind of the narrator.

I have said that, in *Faust*, caprice is transformed into mystery, but this distinction should not obscure the fact that one of the defining features of capriciousness, namely the suddenness of the unexpected change in behaviour or mood, remains a central element in Turgenev's story. The consequences of *suddenness*, so often implemented to powerful effect in Dostoevskii, are exploited by Turgenev in *Faust*. The suddenness of Vera's caprice – her abandonment of familial duty for the sake of an erotic love – is in part what lends the tale its Gothic quality. When the narrator returns to his home village, what he first notices everywhere and in everyone (including himself) is change, except, that is, in Vera:

> When she came to meet me, I almost cried out in amazement; it was simply a little girl of seventeen! Only her eyes are not a little girl's; but then her eyes were never a child's, even in her young days, – they were too clear. But the same composure, the same serenity, the same voice, not one line on her brow, as though she had been laid in the snow all these years. And she's twenty-eight now, and has had three children... It's incomprehensible! [*neponiatno*] (p.171)

The fact that she is unchanged 'in face or in figure' – her *neizmennost'*, as he calls it – makes a negative impression upon him. 'A woman of eight-and-twenty, a wife and a mother, ought not to be like a little girl [*pokhodit' na devochku*]' (pp. 171-2), he reflects. Significantly, there is another, and more particular, aspect to her Ophelia- or Gretchen-like innocence and naïvety: 'Imagine my amazement; Vera Nikolaevna has never read a single novel, a single poem – in fact, not a single invented work as she expresses it!' (p. 172).

'Not one line on her brow' and not one line of poetry in her head: Vera Nikolaevna, at this stage in the narrative, presents the narrator with a blank surface, like the snow that he mentions, a surface upon which a literary image may be projected. The serenity of her unchanging, and untroubled, appearance is reinforced by the name she bears. (*Vera*, in Russian, signifies faith, belief, trust: compare the English *veracity*). Faith, which takes the love of others on trust, stands in opposition to fantasia, that 'pliable' faculty, as Garnett translates it. Vera first places her trust in her mother's love (*verila ei slepo*) and then in the narrator's, because from childhood she has never known deceit: 'she is accustomed to truth, it is the breath of her being' (Letter Five). Turgenev distinguishes carefully between this emotional dependence and an independence of mind: 'She takes nothing on trust [*na veru*]; there's no overawing her with authority' (p. 191). Psychologically, this independence is a necessary precondition for her moral *volte face*. Marital fidelity depends upon such trust. When Vera contemplates an illicit liaison, she ceases, in a sense, to be Vera.

Faust is a story of how belief is destroyed by too fiery an imagination: too fiery because it is the product of erotic longings. The end of the story is prefigured in the simile of the young woman, who had been laid in the snow. For years her spiritual development has been arrested – frozen – under the dominion of her dead mother. In life, her mother had impressed the narrator as 'a very strange woman, a woman of character, of strong will and concentration' (p. 165). We are told that she had her *idées fixes*, one of which was being 'mortally afraid' [Garnett's translation of *kak ognia boialas'*] 'of anything that might work upon the imagination' (p. 166). In death, however, she herself becomes a haunting presence – to the narrator, when the eyes in her 'gloomy portrait' seem to move 'with a reproachful look', and to Vera, when she returns to this world as an apparition to thwart the erotic rendez-vous. As a result of what the narrator calls 'this incomprehensible [*neponiatnoe*] intervention of the dead in the affairs of the living' (p. 220), Vera dies. Her death is left medically 'undefined', but symbolically the cause is clear.[22] The fire of passion has dissolved the Ice Maiden.

---

[22] From an anthropological perspective, Vera's situation is akin to what Lewis terms *central*, as opposed to peripheral, *possession:* 'Whereas those cults we call peripheral involved spirits which were sublimely indifferent to the moral conduct of mankind, now we are concerned with mystical powers which are regarded as sternly moralistic.

In the last of the nine letters, as he awaits the meeting with Vera that is destined never to take place, the narrator recalls Madame El'tsov's words to her daughter: 'She had said to her once, "You are like ice; until you melt as strong as stone, but directly you melt there's nothing of you left [*a rastaesh', i sleda ot tebia ne ostanetsia*]"' (p. 215). No trace (*sled*), that is to say, except an echo. The ice metaphor itself is an 'echo' of Madame El'tsov's words, which, as the narrator confides 'Vera had repeated to me'. At the end of the tale, the echo comes from Vera's heart, not her mind. In the fifth letter, at a mid-point in the *rasskaz*, the narrator recalls the young girls, who 'would sometimes repeat one's own words to one, as they well knew how, and one would be in ecstasies over the echo, and possibly be quite impressed by it, till one realised what it meant' (p. 191). Vera's one talent, her peculiar ability, twice mentioned in the final letter, is keeping silent until the last minute. Turgenev underlines the association between Vera and the personified Echo of Greek mythology in the same letter. Waiting in the dark for the meeting destined not to take place, the narrator informs his correspondent, 'I called Vera, in a whisper, called a second time, a third. ... No voice called back' (p. 216). But later that night, after his return home, he wakes up to hear 'a voice of entreaty' calling him: 'A distinct moan broke into the room and, as it were, hovered about me. Chilled with terror, I drank in its last dying echoes [*vnimal ia ego poslednim, zamiravshim perelivam*]' (p. 218).

In the sixth letter, a remarkable passage precedes, indeed precipitates, the reference to the medallion portrait of Vera's grandmother. The narrator reports a 'strange conversation', triggered by the topic of 'apparitions' (*privideniia*). As Pavel Aleksandrovich writes to his friend, 'We began talking of imagination, of the power of imagination' (p. 199). The narrator relates to Vera and her husband his favourite fantasia, which is to imagine a Venetian interlude with the woman he loves.[23] Vera's response to this scenario is cool.

... Their task is to uphold and sustain public morality.' (*Ecstatic Religion*, p. 34). Lewis subdivides 'central possession religions' into two types: those involving ancestor spirits and those involving autonomous deities. Vera's possession clearly falls within the former category.

[23] It is to be noted that, in Turgenev, the *fantasia* of the female and the *fantasia* of Europe frequently coincide. In *Faust*, the Italian motif extends from Albano to Venice.

> She listened to my nonsense, and said that she too often dreamed, but that her
> day-dreams [*mechtaniia*] were of a different sort: she fancied herself
> [*voobrazhaet sebia*] in the deserts of Africa, with some explorer, or seeking the
> traces of Franklin in the frozen Arctic Ocean. She vividly imagined all the
> hardships she had to endure, all the difficulties she had to contend with ...
>   'You have read a lot of travels,' observed her husband. (p.200)

The triteness of Priimkov's response sets the latent yearning of his wife
in its domestic context. Yet it is not only the sheer imperviousness, the
lack of imagination, in Priimkov (that qualified him in the judgement of
Vera's mother as the ideal partner for her daughter), which makes
Vera's fantasia so significant. The contrastive imaginations of the male
and female in the two juxtaposed fantasias, one the product of an
imagination pampered by culture and the other elemental in its
starkness, present what, superficially, may seem to be merely a clash
between pleasure and purpose.[24] Yet Vera's day-dream 'in the deserts
of Africa', or 'seeking the traces of Franklin in the frozen Arctic Ocean
[*otyskivaet sledy Franklina na Ledovitom okeane*]', is also revelatory of
the dichotomy within her. The two alternatives correspond to the two
traits that Vera has inherited: the fiery impulsiveness of her
grandmother and the life-denying *idées fixes* of her mother – the heat of
passion and the cold of denial.[25]

The Arctic imagery takes up, and extends, the earlier simile in
which Vera was described as being 'of the same composure, the same
serenity, the same voice, not one line on her brow, *as though she had
been laid in the snow all these years* [*tochno ona vse eti gody
prolezhala gde-nibud' v snegu*]', and anticipates the reference to the
melting ice at the end.[26] Vera projects herself (at least, according to the

---

[24] This opposition has already been established in the story in a conversation, reported
in Letter Two, between Pavel Aleksandrovich and Madame El'tsov.

[25] Frank Seeley takes a more patronising view: '... her very daydreams were of
arduous achievement amid the perilous wastes of the Sahara or the Arctic - typical
adolescent daydreams - in stark contrast to her friend's banal fantasies of happiness in
the guise of honeymooning in Venice': see his *Turgenev: A Reading of his Fiction*,
Cambridge Cambridge University Press, 1991, p. 151.

[26] In Russian the link is more evident, since the Arctic Ocean (*Ledovityi okean*) is
literally the ocean of ice (*led*). Garnett's translation compensates for the different
association in English by translating it as the 'frozen Arctic ocean'. The deliberate
placing of these three allusions to snow or ice in the third, sixth and ninth letters,

narrator's account) as engaged in 'seeking the traces of Franklin'. This reference to Franklin is at the heart of a symbolic constellation. It functions on several different levels. First of all, the frozen aspect of the northern ice reinforces the sense of arrested development that is central to this *rasskaz*. The second point to be made about Arctic wastes and African deserts is that to the mid-nineteenth-century European mind they represent 'regions unknown to man'[27] (just as dabbling in alchemy did in an earlier, Faustian epoch).[28] The third significance of the Franklin reference appertains to the fact that he is an historical figure and not – like Ophelia – a literary creation. One effect of this is to modulate the fantasia of the Gothic by an explicit reference to a contemporary event that would have been of considerable interest to the early readers of Turgenev's *Faust* – and, indeed, one that continues to exercise a fascination at the end of the twentieth century.[29]

In *Faust* there are two ways of responding to the Unknown, just as there are two ways of looking at literary compositions. They may be seen either ingenuously as 'invented works' (*vydumannye sochineniia*), clever products of the human mind, as Vera sees them; or superstitiously as black magic, verbal catalysts capable of releasing 'those secret forces on which life rests and which, rarely, but so

---

through their exploitation of the magical significance of the number three, may be read as the aesthetic signature of the author.

[27] The phrase 'regions unknown to man' occurs in a passage in Hardy's *The Return of the Native* which refers to Franklin: 'Glacial catastrophes, snow-storm episodes, glittering auroral efects, Polaris in the zenith, Franklin underfoot, - the category of his commonplaces was wonderful'. Quoted from Gillian Beer, 'Can the Native Return?', The Hilda Hulme Lecture, 1988 (University of London, 1989), p. 16 (I am indebted to Peter Hulme for drawing my attention to this lecture).

[28] In Letter Two, we are told that Ladanov, Vera's grandfather, on his return to Russia, 'never left his house, nor even his study; he devoted himself to chemistry, anatomy, and magical arts; tried to discover means to prolong human life, fancied he could hold intercourse with spirits, and call up the dead' (p. 164).

[29] Numerous books and pamphlets on the 'search for Franklin' were published in the early 1850s and have continued to appear sporadically until the discoveries of the 1980s and 1990s, detailed on various Internet sites. See 'The Franklin Trail' Home Page (URL http://www. franklintrail.com), which provided a 'daily log' of the 'archeological survey of evidence and artifacts relating to the final days of the Franklin expedition' in April 1998; and the Home Page on 'Sir John Franklin: His Life and Afterlife' (URL http://home.navisoft.com/ekkhs/frank1.htm). See also the books by David C. Woodman: *Unravelling the Franklin Mystery: Inuit Testimony* (1989) and *Strangers Among Us* (1995), both published by McGill-Queen's University Press, Montreal.

suddenly [*izredka, no vnezapno*], break out' (pp. 166-7), in the narrator's own words. Similarly, the Unknown may be regarded either as a construct of the mind – what I have called a projection – or as an autonomous realm with the coercive power of possession.[30] The former view prevails at the start of the story, but the latter view gradually insinuates itself until, in the final letter, the narrator submits and renounces worldly pleasures as an illusion:

> Renunciation, continual renunciation – that is [life's] secret meaning, its solution [*razgadka*]. Not the fulfilment of cherished dreams and aspirations [*ispolnenie liubimykh myslei i mechtanii*], however lofty they may be – the fulfilment of duty, that is what must be the care of man.[31]

Perhaps the most interesting point from a Gothic-fantastic perspective – and one that brings me back to where I began – has to do with the problem of possession. Vera dies because she falls prey to a fatal possession. Projection presupposes the agency of an egoistic impulse (an imprinting of a Faustian text upon an untrammelled soul), but possession implies the suspension of the ego (when the latent psyche is most susceptible to the forces of the Unknown, 'the secret play of fate, which we in our blindness call blind chance': p. 221).[32] Turgenev leaves us in doubt – in a state of hesitation – as to how we should interpret the forces of the Unknown. Did Vera's mother really

---

[30] One of the early books speculating on Franklin's fate which appeared before Turgenev had composed his *Faust*, and authored by the unlikely sounding Alfred Cridge, was entitled: *Epitome of spirit-intercourse: a condensed view of spiritualism, in its scriptural, historical, actual and scientific aspects; its relations to Christianity, insanity, psychometry and social reform; manifestations in Nova Scotia; important communications from the spirits of Sir John Franklin and Rev. Wm. Wishart, St. John, N.B., with evidences of identity and directions for developing mediums* (published Boston, B. Marsh, 1854).

[31] This statement (p. 222) constitutes the Faustian moral of the tale, flagged by its palindromic epigraph from Part One of Goethe's play: *Entbehren sollst du, sollst entbehren.*

[32] There is a moment (in Letter Seven, p. 204) when - for the narrator - the forces of Eros and Narcissus appear to be held in balance. The narrator recognises what it means to love a woman [*ia tol'ko teper' uznal, chto znachit poliubit' zhenshchinu*], but, with his next words, acknowledges that all love is egoism [*Liubov' vse-taki egoizm*]. At the end of the letter, he exclaims: 'Give me time; I will come to myself, and possess my soul again [*ovladeiu svoeiu dushoiu*]'. This is, eventually, what happens, but it is not presented as a triumphant recovery.

exercise a custodial watch from beyond the grave, or was it a self-destructive passion in her blood, inherited from her grandmother, which consumed Vera? In either case, it could be said that her mother played a decisive role in the transmission. It is the reader's inability to decide conclusively *on the evidence presented* which perspective is correct, the rational or the supernatural, that, as one influential definition of 'the fantastic' has it, qualifies Turgenev's *Faust* (like Pushkin's *The Queen of Spades*) as a classic example of the genre.[33]

* * *

Post-scriptum: Franklin's Tale
As I noted in my discussion of *Faust*, Vera projects herself as engaged in 'seeking the traces of Franklin'. Sir John Franklin was the master of an expedition, comprising the ominously named *Erebus* and *Terror*, which set out in 1845, 'packed to the gunwales with pickled potatoes, pemmican, and a relatively new invention – canned meat, Goldner's Patent',[34] to find the North West Passage. Franklin died on 11 June 1847, but news of his death did not reach Europe until 1854, when Dr John Rae, a surveyor for the Hudson's Bay Company, published information on the expedition's fate. One aspect of Rae's report on the last days of the expedition aroused a great public outcry, and transformed the nature of the *cause célèbre*, namely his remark that 'from the mutilated state of many of the corpses, it is evident that our wretched countrymen had been driven to the last resource – cannibalism – as a means of prolonging existence'.[35] Charles Dickens, among others, expressed outrage at the very idea that a man could be a Victorian Englishman and a cannibal at the same time.[36]

Half a century later, when one of the greatest of all the tales of 'regions unknown to man' was told, Charlie Marlow started his account

---

[33] See Tzvetan Todorov, *The Fantastic: a structural approach to a literary genre*; translated by Richard Howard, Ithaca, New York, Cornell University Press, 1980 (see also Claire Whitehead's Todorovian analysis of *The Queen of Spades* in the present volume). In the words of an anthropologist: 'For those who believe in them, mystical powers are realities both of thought and experience' (Lewis, *Ecstatic Religion*), p. 28.
[34] Taken from the Home Page 'Sir John Franklin: His Life and Afterlife'.
[35]　　　Quoted　　here　　from　　'The　　Franklin　　Trail'　　Home　　Page　　(URL http://www.franklintrail.com/ cannibalism.htm).
[36] Charles Dickens, 'The Lost Arctic Voyagers', *Household Words*, December 2 and 9, 1854. See also Beer 'Can the Native Return?', p. 17.

of a momentous journey (when there were still 'many blank spaces on the earth') by recalling 'Sir John Franklin', one of 'the great knights-errant of the sea':

> The tidal current runs to and fro in its unceasing service, crowded with memories of men and ships it had borne to the rest of home or to the battles of the sea. It had known and served all the men of whom the nation is proud, from Sir Francis Drake to Sir John Franklin, knights all, titled and untitled – the great knights-errant of the sea. It had borne all the ships whose names are like jewels flashing in the night of time, from the *Golden Hind* returning with her round flanks full of treasure, to be visited by the Queen's Highness and thus pass out of the gigantic tale, to the *Erebus* and *Terror*, bound on other conquests – and that never returned. [37]

Turgenev's heroine, then, was not the only fictional figure to have been attracted to the British explorer, but the allusion in *Faust* to Franklin is, as far as I know, the earliest reference that occurs in imaginative literature. It is a topical allusion, and the dating of events – fictional and historical – is, I believe, significant. The introduction of topical 'facts' into imaginative fiction has always been a popular device. As Dostoevskii recognised, the newspaper had an advantage over the novel in that it enjoyed the 'privilege of reality'.[38] 'Real life', as Dostoevskii was to write in discussing the two cases of suicide that provided the material source for *A Meek Girl*, will 'present you with something … that you never even suspected and that goes far beyond anything your own observation and imagination were able to create!'.[39]

Turgenev wrote his story in 1856. By this date, he and his first readers would have known from newspaper reports about Franklin's death and the revelations concerning the human diet. Yet he chose to set his story in 1850 (with the final letter written in 1853), thus precluding the possibility of any of his characters being aware of what had happened to the ill-fated expedition. Turgenev's fictional fantasia of 'seeking the traces of Franklin in the frozen Arctic Ocean',

---

[37] From the opening of *Heart of Darkness* (first published in *Blackwood's Magazine*, February-April, 1899): see Joseph Conrad, *The Complete Short Fiction*, vol. 3; edited by Samuel Hynes, London, William Pickering, 1993, p. 2.

[38] See Burnett, 'Dostoevsky, Poe and the Discovery of Fantastic Realism', p. 79.

[39] See the article 'Two Suicides' (October 1876), in Fyodor Dostoyevsky, *A Writer's Diary: Volume I, 1873-1876*; translated by Kenneth Lantz, London, Quartet, 1994, pp. 650-3.

remarkable for its being attributed to the heroine rather than the hero, is carefully situated in historical time. What the report of cannibalism could have told Vera, had she known of it, would have amounted to a warning as to what may happen *in extremis*, a warning that is vouchsafed to Marlow, for example, before his physical and psychological journey into the heart of darkness.

A short exchange occurs between Marlow and the doctor who examines him for his suitability to undertake the expedition:

> 'I always ask leave, in the interests of science, to measure the crania of those going out there,' he said. 'And when they come back, too?' I asked. 'Oh, I never see them,' he remarked; 'and, moreover, the changes take place inside, you know.'[40]

Too rapid a change brings derangement and horror, yet too slow a change can also have its surprises. I turn, in conclusion, from fiction to fact. In 1985, Owen Beattie led an expedition to seek 'the traces of Franklin'. To quote the report from the Home Page on 'Sir John Franklin: His Life and Afterlife':

> Owen Beattie opened the graves from Franklin's first winter camp, and found inside three remarkably well-preserved bodies [as a result of the permafrost], looking not much different from the way they did when first buried. One, John Torrington, his eyes open, looks almost as if he could yet be alive – a deceptive look for a man who had spent 139 years in a simple black wooden coffin.

This modern discovery, of course, is something that Turgenev could not have known, but what history's uncanny account sets before us is a Gothic symmetry in the reversal of conventional gender roles. The fictional Vera casts herself as a would-be intrepid explorer, while the explorer John Torrington usurps the fictional role of the Sleeping Beauty (give or take 39 years). There is more to the 1985 discovery than this, though. Beattie, we are also told in the same report:

> ... measured lead levels in the soft tissue and hair from these bodies, as well as from bones recovered from King William Island, and found that at least some

---

[40] Conrad, op. cit., p. 10. Compare Vera's artless remark, soon after her reunion with the narrator: 'Every one tells me that I am very little changed externally, though indeed I have remained just the same inwardly too' (Letter Three, p. 175).

of the Franklin crew-members were suffering from lead-poisoning brought about by their canned foods. Yet whether this ailment, or scurvy, or starvation was the ultimate killer, one fact remains: not a single survivor ever returned.

What this admits, and what may, perhaps, be too grim an irony for our bourgeois sensibilities to digest, is the possibility that eating people kept some of Franklin's crew alive, whereas the consumption of tinned meat killed them!

Yet, to revert from ironic conjecture to the central mystery in Turgenev's Gothic tale, we may note, in conclusion, how retrospective re-collection and a sense of immediacy have worked together within *Faust* to construct a reading of the deceased Other that prepares the narrator for his return from the romantic *fantasia* and the echoing heart to the practicalities of a resigned living in the world of the real that awaits him. This is a characteristic resolution for Turgenev's heroes. As regards the verisimilitude of a 'psychological sequence' charting the enigma of passion, for that we must turn to Dostoevskii.

UNKNOWN FORCE:
GOTHIC REALISM IN CHEKHOV'S
THE BLACK MONK

ANN KOMAROMI

> ... he kept glancing at the door as if afraid of being taken
> over again by that unknown force, which in a mere two
> years had caused such destruction in his life and the life of
> those near to him.[1]
>
> A.P. Chekhov, *The Black Monk* (1894)

The authoritative historian of Russian literature D.S. Mirsky claimed that, out of Anton Pavlovich Chekhov's *oeuvre*, *The Black Monk* (*Chernyi monakh*) was 'the only story that is quite certainly a failure'.[2] Why should this story receive such particular, if dubious, distinction? Perhaps the prominence of romantic ideology and the supernatural in the story seemed awkward and incomprehensible, coming from a writer like Chekhov, who is famed elsewhere for his sober objectivity. The strange appearance of a legendary vision, the romantic linkage of madness and greatness, and the Gothic degeneration of family and estate in this story all appear rather out of place among Chekhov's other works. Furthermore, Chekhov uses these elements in an unorthodox, unexpected fashion, which makes interpretation of this story yet more difficult.[3] Confusion surrounding Chekhov's works is nothing new,

---

[1] From the ninth and final section of Chekhov's *The Black Monk*, p. 312 (all quotes are taken from the Goslitizdat edition of Anton Chekhov, *Sobranie sochinenii v dvenadtsati tomakh*, vol. 7, Moscow, 1956, and identified by page numbers in the text; translations are my own).

[2] Chekhov apparently wrote *The Black Monk* in 1893, and it appeared for the first time in the journal *Artist*, 1894, no. 1. In his discussion of Chekhov's works, Mirsky identified *The Black Monk*, in passing, as the only foray Chekhov made outside the bounds of rigorous realism and, presumably for this reason, a failure: D.S. Mirsky, *A History of Russian Literature,* New York, Knopf, 1949, p. 364.

[3] Chekhov did not associate himself with any particular school or movement. As he wrote to Peshcheev on October 4, 1888: 'I'm not a liberal, or a conservative or a gradualist, or a monk, or an indifferentist. I should like to be a free artist and that's all

however. He was for his contemporaries, and remains for commentators today, one of the most 'difficult' of Russian writers. Vittorio Strada pointed out that this difficulty is due to the slippery nature of Chekhov's works: '... under a maximum of apparent transparency lies hidden a core resistant to all critical formulations'.[4] Chekhov is a 'hard nut to crack'. Without claiming to have produced a definitive reading of *The Black Monk*, I propose to give an overview of Chekhov's use of romantic, fantastic and Gothic elements in the story. Chekhov employs light irony to deflate the romantic ideology behind these elements. He also confines them largely to Kovrin's sick perspective, which is characterised as part of a relatively objective portrait of illness and psychological pathology. However, a Gothic sense of mystery and fear pervades the entire piece and remains at the end. Typically for Chekhov, the 'solution' to the story – i.e. how the author judges the situation, and how the tragedy could have been avoided – is not clear. Kovrin and the Pesotskiis are all engulfed by a nearly fantastic destruction, without knowing how or why. Alongside the story's realism, something of the spirit of mystery and terror essential to the Gothic aesthetic remains.

The Romantic Idealisation of Madness

The eerie apparition of the black monk realises the link between madness and greatness for Kovrin. He appears in order to satisfy Kovrin's longing for a grand purpose. The monk tells Kovrin: 'Yes. You are one of those few who are justly called God's chosen', and that Kovrin and the other chosen 'will lead humankind to the reign of eternal truth a few thousand years earlier than it would be achieved otherwise'. The monk further explains: 'You are the incarnation of the divine blessing which rests on the people' (pp. 297-8). The appearance of the black monk to Kovrin and the message he imparts hearken back to a tradition of romantic idealisation of madness. E.T.A. Hoffmann fantastically dramatised the idea of 'voluntary madness' in *The Golden Pot*, of 1813. Prince Vladimir Odoevskii developed this same theme for

...': quoted by Gordon Mc Vay, in *Reference Guide to Russian Literature*, edited by Neil Cornwell, London, Fitzroy Dearborn, 1998, p. 216.

[4] Vittorio Strada, 'Anton Tchekhov', in *Histoire de la littérature russe: L'Age d'argent*, edited by Efim Etkind *et al.*, Paris, Fayard, 1987, p. 52.

his story *The Sylph* (*Sil'fida*), which was written in 1836.[5] In these works, the heroes desire escape from the baseness of this world into madness, for in this other reality select individuals can find a path to true greatness and fulfilment of desires. In Hoffmann's story, the student Anselmus finds that, in lieu of the worldly fortune of which he had dreamed, his 'childlike, poetic character' suits him to life in the realm of 'poesy'. In that world, Anselmus acquires special knowledge and becomes the husband of a beautiful princess.[6] In Odoevskii's story, too, the 'new, secret world' to which the hero Mikhail Platonovich abandons himself seems to him to be a path to significant discoveries and extraordinary greatness.[7] These other realms represent for the mad heroes a higher plane of existence, where knowledge of a purer truth is possible. They also provide escape from the 'baseness' (*nizost'*) and 'immorality' (*beznravstvennost'*) of everyday people and life.[8]

Echoes of these romantic themes appear in Chekhov's story, and they work strongly on Kovrin's imagination prior to the monk's visitations. Sitting on the balcony one evening at the Pesotskiis' estate, Kovrin concentrates on the romantic serenade being played and sung by Tania and other guests indoors. In the song a girl hears secret sounds so strange and beautiful that she confesses them to be a 'sacred harmony' (*garmoniia sviashchennaia*), which, incomprehensible to most 'dead' mortals, flies away to the heavens.[9] This serenade motivates Kovrin to

---

[5] R.G Nazirov associated Chekhov's *The Black Monk* with this tradition of 'flight into madness', noting that the basic romantic plot of madness, introduced by Odoevskii into the Russian literary tradition, was adapted, too, by Lermontov in his story *Shtoss* and by Turgenev in *Phantoms* (*Prizraki*): Nazirov, 'Chekhov protiv romanticheskoi traditsii', in *Russkaia literatura 1870-1890 godov*, sb. 8, Sverdlovsk, 1975, pp. 96-111.

[6] See E. T. A. Hoffmann, 'The Golden Flower Pot', in *The Best Tales of Hoffmann*, edited by E.F. Bleiler, New York, Dover, 1967, pp. 1-70 (elsewhere *Der goldne Topf* is usually translated as 'The Golden Pot').

[7] V.F. Odoevskii, *Deviat' povestei*, New York, Izd. imeni Chekhova, 1954.

[8] Odoevskii's Mikhail Platonovich rails against the baseness and immorality of urban intellectuals and ignorant provincials alike (see Odoevskii, pp.160-1). Hoffmann's narrator laments the 'paltriness of everyday life', which sickens him with 'tormenting dissatisfaction' (Hoffmann, p. 66).

[9] These 'secret sounds' may suggest the tinkling of crystal bells which accompanies the appearance of the fantastic snakes to Anselmus. Even more, they suggest the echoes of holy music discussed in another of Hoffmann's stories, 'Automata' (ibid., p. 97). They also may recall heavenly sounds of the angel's song which possess a young person's soul in Lermontov's 'Angel' (1831). On the ringing of bluebells in Gogol's tale *Vii*, see Priscilla Meyer's essay in the present volume.

tell Tania about the legend of the black monk, which has been on his mind since morning. Shortly thereafter, the black monk appears to Kovrin for the first time.

The exhilarating prospect of being one of God's chosen, able to lead humankind toward the realm of 'eternal truth', contrasts sharply with the unpleasant, mundane reality of Kovrin's life. Kovrin acknowledges explicitly the nature of this reality after his 'cure'. He realises that, in order to achieve a most modest amount of academic success before the age of forty, he was required to work day and night for fifteen years, to suffer serious psychological illness, to survive an unsuccessful marriage, and to commit all manner of stupidities and injustices. For all this, he was given the privilege of a professorship in which he could 'expound ordinary and, moreover, others' thoughts in a flat, boring, heavy tone' (p. 313). This reality seems not only mundane, but absolutely futile. Notably, Chekhov placed this confession of the world's unpleasantness *after* the hero's experience of madness and cure. Rather than proceeding from the hero's state of mind, as he slips toward escape into madness (as in the other works), this confession gives the impression of a more sober evaluation of objective, and inescapable, reality. Thus, the contrast between frustrating reality and the manic grandeur of Kovrin's delusion strikes the reader with great psychological force. In the end, Kovrin manages to escape reality only as he is seized by his fatal tubercular fit.

Does Chekhov endorse to any degree romantic ideology in this story?[10] Given the allusions to a tradition of romantically idealised madness, we should consider whether we are meant to understand that Kovrin's madness signifies extraordinary potential of some kind. Kovrin himself certainly subscribes to the romantic view that it does. He rails bitterly at the less imaginative Pesotskiis for ridding him of his tremendous potential through treatment:

---

[10] Several critics believed that Chekhov sympathised with Kovrin's romantic idealism. While acknowledging that *The Black Monk* may be unique among Chekhov's works, V.I. Kuleshov argued that Kovrin represented Chekhov's own longing for ideals and sense of distaste at low reality, which had been aggravated by his recent visit to Sakhalin: see Kuleshov, 'Realizm Chekhova v sootnoshenii s naturalizmom i simvolizmom v russkoi literature kontsa XIX i nachala XX veka', in *Chekhovskie chteniia v Ialte*, Moscow, 1973, p. 34.

How fortunate were Buddha and Mohammed or Shakespeare, that good relatives and doctors did not cure them of their ecstasy and inspiration! ... If Mohammed had taken potassium bromide for his nerves, worked only two hours a day, and drunk milk, then as little would have remained after this remarkable person as after his dog. (p. 308)

Kovrin implies that, without his cure, he could have been as significant as any of these great figures. Indeed, the black monk expressed the corollary to this view earlier, when he discussed Kovrin's illness with him: 'My friend, only ordinary people, people of the herd are healthy and normal' (p. 299).[11] The idea of a 'fixation of genius' (*genial'naia oderzhimost'*) or a 'divine sickness' (*bozhestvennaia bolezn'*) was widespread in decadent circles contemporary to Chekhov. Chekhov became intimately acquainted with decadent ideas during his travels through Europe with A.S. Suvorin in 1891, just two years before writing *The Black Monk*. D.S. Merezhkovskii and Z.N. Gippius numbered among their acquaintances in Paris, and they discussed together the aesthetics and philosopy of decadence to its roots.[12]

However, it is only with some difficulty that we can suppose that Chekhov meant to endorse a romantic idealisation of madness. Chekhov explicitly stated his intention to portray a clinical condition of illness. In letters to M.O. Men'shikov (of January 15, 1894) and A.S. Suvorin (of December 18, 1893) Chekhov described his story as 'medical', depicting 'a young man suffering from a mania of greatness' (*maniia velichiia*). Sukhikh suggested that Chekhov based his portrayal of Kovrin's illness on the description of the 'mania of greatness' that appeared in S.S. Korsakov's book on psychiatry (*Kurs psikhiatrii*),

---

[11] In another variation on this theme, Mikhail Gromov noted that many critics felt that, according to Chekhov, it is not Kovrin who is sick, but the world around him. This identification of the age, not the apparently mad hero, as sick strongly informed Odoevskii's *The Sylph*. One epigraph to this story characterises the 19th century thus: '!?!?'. According to several commentators, the world reveals itself to be sick when 'greatness departs from life and remains only in the dreams of maniacs, when ecstasy becomes the domain of the psychologically unwell' (quoted by Gromov, in his *Kniga o Chekhove*, Moscow, 1989, p. 276; also by Kuleshov op. cit., p. 30, who attributes it to G. Bialyi, in *Trudy iubileinoi nauchnoi sesii Leningradskogo universiteta*, Leningrad, 1946, p. 301). A. Gornfel'd had previously subscribed to this same view: see his analysis of *The Black Monk* in *Krasnaia nov'*, 1939, 8, p. 399.

[12] See Gromov, p. 299.

which was published in 1893, and was in Chekhov's library.[13] As a doctor, Chekhov devoted himself to health: 'My holy of holies is the human body ...'.[14] Nazirov asserted that Chekhov, throughout his work, praised health and advocated a 'Pushkinian' harmony, very different from the 'sacred harmony' of romantic and neo-romantic ideology: 'Chekhov praised corporal and spiritual health in his entire body of works and fought for the re-establishment of Pushkinian harmony ... he *had to* come out against the aestheticisation of madness' [italics in original].[15] Chekhov would not positively valorise that which he saw as illness.

In addition, Chekhov deflates the romantic ideals discussed by Kovrin and the monk with irony. The discussion of these ideals proceeds with ironic carelessness ill-suited to the loftiness of the subject:

> 'And what is the goal of eternal life?' asked Kovrin.
> 'Like the goal of any life – pleasure [*naslazhdenie*]. True pleasure in cognition [*poznanie*]; and eternal life will present countless and inexhaustible bases of cognition ...'
> 'If you only knew how nice it is to listen to you!' said Kovrin, rubbing his hands in glee.
> 'So happy'. (p. 298)

The reduction of the long expositions in Hoffmann's and Odoevskii's stories – on a harmonious synthesis, higher existence, and a pure truth – to, simply, pleasure and vague 'cognition' – trivializes these ideals. Furthermore, Kovrin's ecstatic response to the monk's banal words seems quite absurd, and the monk's dry response resembles a social pleasantry, out of place in a serious, elevated discussion.

The Fantastic

Chekhov appears rather to polemicise with the romantic idealisation of madness and to poke a certain amount of fun at romantic ideals. Nevertheless, fantastic and Gothic elements pervade the entire work. The fantastic genre proceeds from the romantic tradition. The French writer Charles Nodier, for one, understood the fantastic as the human

---

[13] I. Sukhikh, 'Zagadochnyi "Chernyi monakh"', *Voprosy literatury*, 6, 1983, p. 112.
[14] From Chekhov's letter to Pleshcheev, of October 4, 1888.
[15] Nazirov, op. cit., p. 104.

spirit's recourse against 'the repulsive realities of the real world'.[16] Commentators later observed that: 'It seems that for Nodier the fantastic was less an intrusion of the unreal into the real than a means of perceiving the real to the point of perishing from it'.[17] The fantastic can be a window into a possible higher reality.

The appearance of a legendary vision 'in reality' certainly seems eerie, but does the appearance of the black monk to Kovrin qualify as a fantastic device? According to Tzvetan Todorov, the fantastic operates in a gap, characterised by hesitation, that exists between the 'marvellous' and the merely 'strange'. The fantastic tale obliges its reader to believe the world of the characters to be similar to the reader's own and to hesitate between a supernatural and a rational explanation of the fantastic event.[18] A reader not yet overwhelmed by the consistent realism of Chekhov's other works may respond to the black monk's first appearance with the hesitation characterising the fantastic. However, even during this first visit, the narrator hints at a rational explanation of the monk's appearance. After the first sighting of the monk, Kovrin does not try to explain to himself the 'strange phenomenon', but is 'satisfied with the mere fact that he managed to see so closely and clearly not only the black dress, but even the face and the eyes of the monk ...' (p. 290). The narrator implies that the reader, unlike Kovrin, should try to explain the vision rationally. Other clues in the opening sections, including Kovrin's agitated nerves and his unhealthy lifestyle, rationally suggest Kovrin's decline into clinical mental illness.

Chekhov turned the device of the fantastic on its head in Kovrin's second meeting with the black monk. Kovrin expresses puzzlement over the monk's ability to sit and talk with him, as this does not correspond to the legend from which he supposedly proceeds. The monk responds calmly: 'It doesn't matter ... Legend, mirage, myself – it's all a product of your stimulated imagination'. To Kovrin's question, 'So, that means you don't exist?' the monk engages in a bit of sophistry: 'Think what you want ... I exist in your imagination, and your

---

[16] This comment appeared in an article in the *Revue de Paris*, entitled 'Du fantastique en littérature'; cited in *Précis de la littérature française du XIX-e siècle*, edited by Madeleine Ambrière, Paris, Presses Universitaires de France, 1990, p. 163.

[17] Ibid., p. 233.

[18] Tzvetan Todorov, *Introduction à la littérature fantastique*, Paris, Editions du Seuil, 1970, p. 37. See Claire Whitehead's essay in the present volume for a detailed application of Todorov's theory to Pushkin's *The Queen of Spades*.

imagination is a part of nature, so that means that I exist in nature' (p. 297). The black monk does not even try to maintain his objective existence. Kovrin then asks the black monk directly: 'You are a spectre, a hallucination. That means that I am psychologically sick, abnormal?' The black monk, unconcerned with concealing the fact, responds: 'Suppose that is so. What's the harm in it? You are sick, because you have over-worked yourself and are exhausted ...' (p. 298). Chekhov played with the conventions of the fantastic, which was, in a certain sense, already a defunct genre,[19] by dramatising the meta-literary question. The scene neutralises the reader's hesitation: the black monk is no more than a product of Kovrin's sick mind, and even Kovrin himself knows this. Mental illness provides a rational explanation of the monk's appearance, and it is thus neither fantastic nor marvellous, but strange.

Kovrin's mental illness has a basis in several objective circumstances made obvious by Chekhov to the reader. Overwork and exhaustion have strained Kovrin's nerves. The first sentence of the story introduces his condition: 'Andrei Vasil'ich Kovrin, *magister*, had become exhausted and his nerves were irritated' (p. 282). It is for this reason that he decides to take a rest in the country. But in the country he maintains the same fatiguing lifestyle. He works too much, drinks, smokes, and sleeps so little, that all are 'amazed' (p. 287). His immoderate chatter and avid attention to music when it is played suggest that these habits have contributed to a nervous condition. But these factors alone do not account completely for Kovrin's psychological state. Chekhov depicts other dynamics shaping Kovrin's condition.

A Gothic View, A Realistic View
In several senses, *The Black Monk* recalls the Gothic tradition, which is closely allied to the fantastic, although Chekhov does not construct a

---

[19] Strictly speaking, *The Black Monk*, published in 1894, does fall outside the chronological boundaries of the fantastic, at least as suggested by Todorov, in whose view: '... the fantastic had a relatively short life. It appeared in a systematic manner round the end of the eighteenth century with Cazotte; one century later one finds in the stories of Maupassant the last aesthetically satisfying examples of the genre' (Todorov, pp. 174-5).

typical Gothic story.[20] Paul Davies describes the Gothic thus: 'The attributes of Gothic fiction are numerous, but the primary characteristic, present in all variations, is concern for the workings of the mind manifest though the supernatural ...'.[21] The black monk constitutes a pseudo-supernatural manifestation of Kovrin's mental condition. According to Davies, the supernatural is normally associated with the villain, who represents the decay of the old order, while the young hero or heroine, symbolising the new order, struggles against the allure of and potential entrapment by the past: 'The plots are frequently convoluted but pivot on the need to understand the self as a unique entity as well as part of a family and of society, hence the emphasis on inheritance, lost wills, usurpation, family lines and incest ...'.[22]

Chekhov's story exhibits some of these Gothic traits, although we cannot simply identify Egor Pesotskii as a villain, and the 'supernatural' phenomenon is not directly associated with him. However, Egor Pesotskii, Kovrin's father figure, morbidly fears the destruction of his work, represented by the garden, and he fears the loss of his daughter.[23] Egor appeals to the young Kovrin, his former ward,

---

[20] The Gothic genre, like the fantastic, enjoyed its heyday before Chekhov's time. As Paul Davies explains: '... Gothicism is now applied to a particular literary form first codified by Walpole in his *The Castle of Otranto*, 1764'. Clearly, however, Gothic traits persisted in works written shortly before, and indeed contemporary to, *The Black Monk*: for example, R.L. Stevenson's *The Strange Case of Dr Jekyll and Mr Hyde* (1886), and Bram Stoker's *Dracula* (1897). See Paul Davies, 'Gothicism', in *Encyclopedia of Romanticism, Culture in Britain, 1780s-1830s*, edited by Laura Dabundo, New York, Garland, 1992, pp. 239, 242.

[21] The supernatural here need not be taken as a strictly 'marvellous' phenomenon. Like Walpole's *The Castle of Otranto*, Ann Radcliffe's *The Mysteries of Udolpho* is also considered prototypical for the genre (Davies, p. 241). These works fall on either side of fantastic, with the supernatural in Walpole's work being 'genuine' (or 'marvelous'), while Radcliffe's supernatural elements find rational explanation, consigning them to the realm of the merely 'strange' (or 'uncanny').

[22] Davies, p. 240.

[23] Neil Cornwell, in his examination of links between Stevenson's *Will o' the Mill* and *The Black Monk*, identified 'Gothic' as 'engaging with the fall of a house (literally or dynastically or both), and the consequent disposal of an inheritance - often in close association with the flourishing and decay of a garden or landscape - frequently accompanied or aided by supernatural or quasi-supernatural agencies ...'; see his 'Two Visionary Storytellers of 1894: R.L. Stevenson and Anton Chekhov', in *Beauty and the Beast: Christina Rossetti, Walter Pater, R.L. Stevenson and their Contemporaries*, edited by Peter Liebregts and Wim Tigges, Amsterdam and Atlanta, GA, 1996, pp. 171-

to save them, and consequently entangles Kovrin in his family with tragic consequences. Kovrin's problematic relationship to Tania carries subtle overtones of incest, due to their sibling-like relationship (there are hints, too, that there might have been a relationship between Egor and Kovrin's deceased mother). Tania and Kovrin's perceptions of a powerful but mysterious destructive force corresponds to the Gothic as well. Edmund Burke, writing in 1757, at the time of the emergence of a Gothic aesthetic, associated the beautiful with the agreeable and the sublime with violent emotions, such as terror or stupefaction. The sublime proceeded originally from natural spectacles that evoke a sense of colossal power, mystery and fear.[24] In the spirit of this Gothic aesthetic, Kovrin and Tania both sense an overwhelming destructive force in their lives that they cannot understand. Against the background of this atmosphere and these circumstances, Kovrin's desperate struggle to establish his own reputation in the world and his place in the Pesotskii family is, to a certain degree, a Gothic plot. In portraying this struggle, Chekhov mixed Gothic elements into a realistic depiction of the complex psychological dynamics surrounding Kovrin's mental illness.

Chekhov's realistic description of the psychological conditions of Kovrin's situation includes several aspects. The characters' attitude toward work is one. Kovrin begins to ruin his health with work, and this sphere of activity reveals much about the nature of Kovrin's struggle for his own identity. Quite remarkably, Chekhov never explicates the content of Kovrin's diligence. Kovrin responds to Egor's inquires about his work by telling him that he reads psychiatry, but generally studies philosophy (p. 286). No elaboration appears here or elsewhere in the story. Nevertheless, the opening of part two of the story tells us:

---

85 (176). According to this definition, *The Black Monk* possesses significant Gothic elements.

[24] Gita May has noted: 'The end of the eighteenth century saw the emergence of an aesthetic of the sublime, of the picturesque, of the "gothic," and the fantastic ... it was Edmund Burke who, in *A Philosophical Enquiry into the Origin of Our Ideas of the Sublime and Beautiful* (1757), ... made the sublime an aesthetic value superior to that of the beautiful ...': see 'Du beau au sublime', in Denis Hollier, editor, *De la littérature française*, Paris, Bordas, 1993, p. 432.

> In the country he continued to lead the same nervous and agitated life that he
> had led in the city. He read much and wrote, studied Italian, and, when he was
> out walking he thought with pleasure that he would soon sit down to work
> again. (p. 287)

What Kovrin read and wrote we do not know, and we do not hear of
particular progression or successes in his work. The style of Kovrin's
work matters more than its content for the purposes of Chekhov's story:
Kovrin maintains a hectic pace which he finds exciting, but which
progressively aggravates his nervous condition. With no evidence from
the work itself to justify Kovrin's manic activity, we must look for other
motivations.

In fact, Kovrin seems to be attempting to fulfil the excessively high
expectations the Pesotskiis have of him. During Kovrin's first
conversation with Tania after his arrival, she refers to clearly long-held
beliefs about Kovrin. She reminds him:

> You already know that my father adores you. Sometimes it seems to me that he
> loves you more than me. He is proud of you. You are educated, you have made
> a brilliant career for yourself, and he is sure that you are what you are because
> of what he reared you to be. (p. 285)

Tania's articulation of their high opinion of Kovrin suggests a familial
type of obligation that Kovrin has to her father and hints at some
sibling rivalry she might feel toward him. Egor later brags about Kovrin
to one of his gardeners. As a child his good qualities had been obvious:
most especially he had always surprised them with his mind. Egor
irritably insists: 'It is to no purpose that he is a *magister*! No purpose!
But just see, Ivan Karlych, what he will be in ten years!' (p. 303). Tania
referred to Kovrin as a great man (*velichina*) already, but Egor expects
much greater things of him. The force of the Pesotskiis' beliefs about,
and expectations of, Kovrin pervade their relationship and shape
Kovrin's behaviour.

Unfortunately, it appears unlikely that Kovrin will ever be able to
satisfy people as nervous and demanding as Egor and his daughter.
Reading Egor's articles on gardening, the themes of which seem
innocuous enough, Kovrin wonders at 'such an agitated, uneven tone;
such nervous, almost sick passion!' (p. 293). He reflects, too, on Tania,
who exhibits much of this same nervous passion. He recalls how her

eyes are 'wide-open, dark, intelligent, always looking somewhere and searching for something ...', concluding that she must be 'nervous in the highest degree' (p. 294). Egor himelf has toiled ceaselessly over his tremendous garden. His constant and excessive ranting and raving over his garden suggest that he cannot be at rest himself, nor can he be satisfied with others' work. Kovrin observes on the first day after his arrival what appears to be typical behaviour on Egor's part. Egor responds to a small incident with enormous anger and distress:

> 'Who is it that tied a horse to the apple tree?' his desperate, soul-rending cry was heard. 'What scoundrel, what slime dared to tie a horse to the tree? My God, my God! Thoroughly spoiled, thoroughly befouled, thoroughly besmirched, thoroughly ruined! The garden is lost! The garden is dead! My God!' (p. 286)

Neither he nor Kovrin comment on the outburst, as though it is unremarkable or discussion would be pointless. Elsewhere Egor confesses that his garden is 'wonderful, exemplary', not just a garden, even, but a 'whole institution, possessing great governmental importance'. It already constitutes a 'step into a new era of Russian agriculture and Russian industry'. But Egor, unsatisfied with this accomplishment, asks, 'to what purpose? What is the goal?' (p. 291). The garden, a living creation, requires attentive maintenance and care. Egor fears the decline that constantly threatens it. Nervous and irritable, accustomed to ceaseless battle, Egor appears unlikely ever to be satisfied with any accomplishment that he or those around him may achieve. Kovrin emulates Egor's constant work, which offers no hope of final satisfaction or rest.

Irritability manifests itself as well in Egor's and Tania's relationship with each other. The narrator informs the reader straightforwardly at the beginning of part four: 'Egor Semenych and Tania often quarrelled and said unpleasant things to one another' (p. 295). Kovrin smooths over the consequences of one typical quarrel. Egor has attacked Tania for making a suggestion regarding the labour in the garden. Tania expresses to Kovrin her confusion over the deeply hurtful nature of Egor's attack, which seemed to her most unmerited. However, her own response seems out of proportion to the situation. She locks herself in her room and cries all day, in turn inflicting distress on Egor. Kovrin marvels at the force of Tania's grief:

> He felt sorry for her so much the more, that the cause of her grief was not
> serious, but she suffered deeply. What trifles were sufficient to make a creature
> unhappy for a whole day, and even for a whole life! (p. 296)

Kovrin glimpses at this point the mysterious force, which the reader
may identify realistically as emotional instability, that threatens them
all with destruction. At the same time, he realises that Tania and her
father are the only family he has and he feels an unhealthy attraction to
her:

> And he felt that the nerves of this crying, trembling girl respond, like iron to a
> magnet, to his own half-sick, frayed nerves. He could never love a healthy,
> strong, red-cheeked woman, but he liked this pale, weak, unhappy Tania. (p.
> 296)

The Gothic suggestion of incest and the unhealthy attraction of one ill
person to another correspond to the Gothic sense of wonder Kovrin
feels contemplating the powerfully destructive force that seems to have
possession of the Pesotskiis.

Kovrin struggles to find a place in this dysfunctional family. The
Pesotskiis treat Kovrin as their own, yet not their own. They expect his
success, yet subtly reproach him for it. Kovrin has trouble defining his
place with them, and his sexual relationship with Tania lies at the crux
of this problem. During their first conversation, Kovrin notices with
some pleasure that the child Tania has already matured into a woman.
In response to his remark on the passage of time, Tania sighs and asks
him seriously:

> 'Tell me, Andriusha ... have you grown apart from us? But what am I asking?
> You are a man, you live your own interesting life, you are a great person
> [*velichina*]. ... Estrangement [*otchuzhdenie*] is so natural! But despite that,
> Andriusha, I want you to consider us your own. We have a right to that'. (pp.
> 284-5)

Tania implies that Kovrin, as a 'great man', could not be expected to
regard the provincial Pesotskiis as fondly as he had formerly. She
somewhat argumentatively asserts that they have a right to expect him
to consider them his family, although Kovrin has said nothing to

indicate that he does not. Tania implies that Kovrin needs to show that he accepts them as his family: marrying Tania would be one way to do that. The subsequent development of Kovrin's attraction to Tania follows a suggestion by Egor that he would be pleased to see a relationship between the two of them:

> 'I will speak plainly: you are the only person to whom I would not be afraid to give my daughter. You are an intelligent person with a heart, and you would not allow my beloved work to die. And the main reason – I love you, like a son ... and I am proud of you. If you and Tania worked out somehow a romance – well, what of that? I would be very happy and even fortunate. I say this plainly, without affectation, as an honest man.'
>
> Kovrin began to laugh. Egor Semenych opened the door to go out and stopped on the threshhold.
>
> 'If you and Tania had a son, then I would make a gardener out of him', he said, having thought a moment. 'However, these are empty dreams ... Good night. (p. 293)

Egor wants to preserve his garden and family and would like to count on Kovrin. However, he regards these as 'empty dreams'. Presumably he, like Tania, regards Kovrin as someone apart from them now, who would not deign to join himself to this provincial family. However, he gives Kovrin no chance to respond to the suggestion or his last statement. Kovrin's inappropriate laughter indicates tension on his part. Perhaps he understands Egor's suggestion as another tremendous expectation of him. In order to assume a place in this family (and he has no other), he should do what Egor suggests, even if Tania had seemed to him merely a kid sister before. There is a larger problem, however: binding himself to this family means subjecting himself to their temperaments.

The storms of their personalities begin to engulf Kovrin as soon as he makes a step towards joining their family. Kovrin proposes to Tania, but the Pesotskiis respond with distress to what should be a welcome event. Tania reacts to Kovrin's marriage proposal with visible, physical distress, even while she accepts him. Kovrin, for his part, finds Gothic-like pleasure in her tormented mien. Having just come from a conversation with the monk, it seems Kovrin has abandoned himself to this obviously destructive course, just as he abandoned himself to his delusion. Although Egor had professed a strong desire for such a union, the news of their betrothal agitates him in the extreme. In turn, Egor's obvious, though unarticulated, distress subsequently upsets Tania and provokes another day-long fit of crying (pp. 300-01). For the wedding, however, Egor insists on a loud, long celebration. The resulting spectacle is unpleasant and gratuitous. The narrator comments that, 'due to the bad hired music, the screech of toasts and the servants' bustle, due to the noise and the crush of people no one appreciated the taste of either the expensive wines or the amazing *hors d'oeuvres* ordered from Moscow' (p. 303). The scene encapsulates the Pesotskiis' unpleasant tendency to over-dramatise events, to insist on great noise and spectacle to the exclusion of genuine appreciation or enjoyment of life. Furthermore, the wedding scene seems to symbolise the chaos and decay to which they willingly submit. Kovrin, himself quite ill, is expected to save this family, but the forces of destruction it carries within itself are strong.[25]

Kovrin does not seem strong enough to assert himself either independently of, or within, the Pesotskiis' family. He can neither satisfy their expectations of him, nor provide a foil for their own destructive tendencies. The black monk, however, allows Kovrin temporarily to think that he can. The monk's assurances of Kovrin's greatness soothe his anxieties over his own identity. And this alternate reality becomes Kovrin's 'truth', enabling him for a time to be what the Pesotskiis want him to be. After the monk first outlines Kovrin's divine calling, Kovrin, armed with the self-assurance given him by the monk's words, finds Tania in the park and moves easily from ecstatic exclamation of his own happiness to impassioned proclamations of his love for her. Tania reproaches Kovrin for ignoring her and her father for the past two days, assigning to it the usual explanation: 'We are insignificant people and you are a great man'; Kovrin meets this self-

---

[25] As opposed to the 'Kovrinists' (see note 10 above), the 'Pesotskiist' critics believed that the author's sympathies sided with the Pesotskiis. V.B. Kataev employed the terms *'Kovrinisty'* and *'Pesotskiisty'* in reference to critics of this story in his book *Proza Chekhova: Problemy interpretatsii*, Moscow, 1979, p. 193. Nazirov, for example, felt that the Pesotskiis, with feet planted firmly in the soil of their garden, were a healthy contrast to the ill Kovrin's ecstatic romanticism. In his view, Kovrin alone, by repudiating his 'moral responsibility' to 'life and work' (*zhizn' i trud*) caused the ruination of the garden and family: see Nazirov, p. 110. In my view, although the romantic Kovrin and the more prosaic Pesotskiis are opposed by their natures, they all suffer nervous conditions and all three contribute to their mutual destruction.

abasing hostility directly and brushes it aside, saying, 'No, we will speak seriously' (p. 300). Likewise, the emotional storm subsequent to the announcement of Kovrin's and Tania's engagement does not disturb Kovrin. While Egor rants and raves, 'Kovrin worked with his former determination and did not notice the commotion' (p. 303). The monk's appearance to Kovrin, at dinner with the Pesotskiis, inspires him to speak particularly eloquently and charmingly, as the Pesotskiis' smiles attest. Although Kovrin questions the reality of the black monk, he concludes that it does not matter. The black monk, as a creation of Kovrin's own mind, tells him what he wants and needs to hear, like a self-justifying double. While he appears to Kovrin, he provides him with assurance of his own identity and allows him to assume a satisfactory place in the Pesotskiis' family.

The loss of Kovrin's delusion illustrates the importance it had for stabilizing both Kovrin and the Pesotskiis. After his cure everything deteriorates quickly. Without his vision, Kovrin becomes just as irascible and unhappy as the Pesotskiis. Tania reproaches Kovrin for the change in his behaviour: 'You, an intelligent, unusual person, irritated by trifles, involving yourself in squabbles ... Such petty things bother you ...' (p. 309). Tania cannot manage the emotional instability to which they are all subject. She 'wanted to understand and could not, and for her the only clear thing was that their relationships were becoming worse and worse with every day ...' (p. 308). Egor particularly irritates Kovrin and he cannot treat Egor other than with scorn and hatred. Tania pleads with Kovrin to stop this behaviour and asks for an explanation. Kovrin refuses to explain why he treats Egor so badly. Tania cries out: 'I cannot, I cannot understand! ... Something incomprehensible and terrible is happening in our house' (p. 309). In Gothic fashion, she senses a tremendous destructive force which she cannot comprehend and against which she is powerless. This perception transforms her. Kovrin later remembers that Tania became, by the end of their marriage, a grotesque creature. She was, finally, like the living dead, the only remaining living feature being her 'big, fixedly staring intelligent eyes' (p. 311). Kovrin himself, no longer able to work, not believing in himself and beginning to hate the Pesotskiis, leaves them. After his departure the Pesotskiis endure a truly Gothic fall. Two years later, Tania informs Kovrin by letter that her father is dead and the garden is being ruined in the hands of others. Kovrin already feels guilt over his treatment of the Pesotskiis. Although Chekhov does not explicitly state this, we can assume that the shock of Tania's news, combined with the hatred and guilt she heaps on Kovrin, provokes his fatal attack.

Chekhov provides concrete physical – and sophisticated psychological – motivations for Kovrin's mental illness. He realistically motivates the collapse of the Pesotskiis, as well. In this respect the story seems realistic. On the other hand, a number of features suggest a Gothic atmosphere. Kovrin's struggle for self and position in a family whose estate and members are threatened with decline; Kovrin's nearly-incestuous relationship to Tania and his unhealthy attraction to her; the black monk's visitations; and the perception of a mysterious destructive force – all contribute to a Gothic atmosphere in the story that is difficult to ignore. The romantic, Gothic, and fantastic elements do not undermine the realism of *The Black Monk*, but they do colour the story significantly.

The End

If we look carefully at the romantic, fantastic and Gothic elements of *The Black Monk*, we could argue that they are confined to Kovrin's sick perspective. After his cure, he sees reality much more prosaically (one might say depressively), although he still believes for a time that his madness held real potential. Part eight and the beginning of part nine, following Kovrin's cure, do not depart from prosaic realism. Tania's letter destroys Kovrin's equilibrium, however, and fantastic elements begin to infect the narrative in part nine, increasing to a romantic crescendo at the end. Seeing Tania's handwriting on the envelope reminds Kovrin of the grotesque, zombie-like appearance Tania acquired by the chaotic end of their relationship. Kovrin reads her horrible letter and 'he was overcome by an anxiety similar to fear'; although he hears his companion's breathing, and voices and laughter from the floor below, it seems to him, fantastically, that there is not another living soul in the hotel. At this point, he apprehends and fears the 'unknown force' that brought such destruction to their lives (p. 312). He recognises in the violin and voices from below the same romantic serenade he heard before his visions began, about a girl in a garden who heard the 'sacred harmony'. The serenade deeply affects him: 'Kovrin's breath caught and his heart ached with sadness, and a wonderful, sweet happiness, which he had long forgotten, trembled in his chest' (p. 313). It triggers his romantic delusions, and the black monk appears once again. That these delusions are inextricably connected to the Pesotskiis, we guess from Kovrin's inability to call his companion: he can repeat only Tania's name. Overcome by romantic emotion he invokes, too, 'the big garden with its luxurious flowers, sprinkled with dew', as well as 'his youth, bravery, happiness', and 'life, which was so wonderful'. In conjunction with this romantic vision, the pool of blood beside Kovrin and his rapid decline to death render the scene Gothic, and the story ends on this note.

The Unknown Force

Although Chekhov deflates romantic, fantastic, and Gothic notions in *The Black Monk*, something of the spirit of Gothic romanticism remains at the story's end. The reader can explain the monk's appearance, and the reader finds little reason to take the monk's romantic ideology seriously. Madness did not make Kovrin a genius; rather, he was mentally ill, due to a number of identifiable physical and psychological factors. Nevertheless, something in the vicious destruction which claims the characters inspires awe. The emotional volatility and abusive nature of their relationship to one another produces terrible consequences on an alarming scale. Neither Kovrin's philosophy nor the Pesotskiis' pragmatic prosaicism could provide an antidote to the situation. Chekhov, the unbiased observer, offers no solution, no positive instruction and no moral. Critics who looked for positive aims, ideals and solutions in Chekhov's work were always disappointed. As his fame grew in the late 1880s, Chekhov came under attack by journalists and critics for this lack. As Gordon McVay has put it:

> In response to such attacks, between 1888 and 1890, Chekhov gradually formulated his own concept of the dispassionate, objective, non-judgmental author. ... He emphasized that the writer's task was to pose a question correctly, but not to offer solutions.[26]

Chekhov does not offer a solution. But perhaps he is not completely dispassionate in this story. He does convey a sense of wonder at the self- and mutual destruction of which people are capable. Tania and

---

[26] McVay, op. cit., p. 215.

Kovrin both express this wonder, and the reader, left with no idea how the tragedy could have been avoided, feels it too. The paradox of loving someone, yet being unable to restrain from abusing them, and the complex, difficult task of attempting to find one's own place within the world and within one's family challenge rational comprehension. The story's realism does not dispel the impression of Kovrin's final, pathetic happiness in his romantic delusions. Nor does it dispel the Gothic horror of the very real death and destruction surrounding him. In the end, the reader, too, marvels at that 'unknown force' that destroyed their lives.

NOTES ON CONTRIBUTORS

Ignat Avsey is a former Senior Lecturer at the University of Westminster. He is the translator of Dostoevskii's *The Karamazov Brothers* (Oxford World's Classics, 1994) and *The Village of Stepanchikovo* (Penguin, 1995). He is completing a translation of Merezhkovskii's drama *Paul I* and is preparing a monograph on the early works of Dostoevskii (with special reference to *The Village of Stepanchikovo*).

Carolyn Jursa Ayers is a Postdoctoral Fellow in Comparative Literature at the University of Groningen, The Netherlands. She has written articles on the Russian society tale and various aspects of representation in narrative. She is co-editor of *Appropriated Narratives: Autobiographical Strategies for Writing the Self from the Colonial Era to the Present Day* (Sheffield Academic Press, 1999), and is currently working on a study of the representation of education and learning in nineteenth-century Russian prose.

Leon Burnett is Reader and Head of the Department of Literature, University of Essex. He edits the journal *New Comparison* and has published articles on Russian poetry, on nineteenth-century Russian prose, and on translation and comparative literary studies. He is the editor of *F.M. Dostoevsky (1821-1881): A Centenary Collection* (University of Essex, 1981); and of *Poetry, Narrative, Translation* (University of Essex, 1997. He is currently researching a book to be entitled *Faces of the Sphinx: Literary Encounters between Russia and the West*.

Roger Cockrell is Senior Lecturer and head of Russian, University of Exeter. He has edited (with D.J. Richards) two collections of essays on nineteenth-century Russian literature and his edition of Odoevskii's *Kosmorama* was published by Bristol Classical Press in 1998. He has also written widely on Aleksandr Fadeev.

Neil Cornwell is Professor of Russian and Comparative Literature, University of Bristol. He is the editor of *Reference Guide to Russian Literature* (Fitzroy Dearborn, 1998) and of *The Society Tale in Russian*

Literature (Rodopi, 1998), the author of two books on V.F. Odoevskii, and translator of a selection of his stories into English. He has also published studies in other areas of nineteenth and twentieth-century Russian literature and on comparative themes. He is the Bristol Classical Press series editor for Russian Texts and Critical Studies in Russian Literature.

Ann Komaromi is a doctoral candidate at the University of Wisconsin - Madison (Department of Slavic Languages and Literatures). She is currently planning her doctoral dissertation on Venedikt Erofeev's *Moskva-Petushki* and is publishing an article on 'The Aporia of Temporal Existence in Sep-Szarzynski's Poetry' (*SEEJ*, forthcoming).

Priscilla Meyer is Professor of Russian Language and Literature at Wesleyan University (Middletown, Connecticut). She is author of *Find What the Sailor Has Hidden: Vladimir Nabokov's 'Pale Fire'* (1988) and co-editor of *Essays on Gogol: Logos and the Russian Word* (1992). Her articles on Gogol and Hoffmann (*The Nose* and *A New Year's Eve Adventure*), Karolina Pavlova and Louise Colet, Andrei Bitov's *Man in Landscape*, and Dostoevskii and Jules Janin (*Crime and Punishment* and *La Confession*) are forthcoming.

Derek Offord is Professor of Russian and Head of the Department of Russian Studies at the University of Bristol. He has published several books on Russian intellectual history, two on the Russian language, and a number of articles on nineteenth-century Russian literature. He is currently researching eighteenth-century social and political thought.

Richard Peace is Professor Emeritus of the University of Bristol, where he taught Russian from 1963 to 1994 (with an interlude from 1975 to 1984 as professor at Hull University). He has published widely on nineteenth-century Russian literature, including books on Dostoevskii, Gogol, Chekhov and Goncharov.

Michael Pursglove was Senior Lecturer in Russian at the University of Exeter and currently teaches at the University of Bath. He specialises mainly in nineteenth-century literature and has published a monograph on, plus a book-length translation of, Grigorovich, as well as articles on

Pushkin, Gogol and Tolstoi. He has also edited four titles in the Bristol Classical Press Russian Texts series.

Cynthia C. Ramsey is a doctoral candidate at the University of Wisconsin-Madison (Department of Slavic Languages and Literatures). She is currently researching an article on Tsvetaeva's Pushkin texts and working on the short stories of David Albahari.

Alessandra Tosi is a post-doctoral researcher at the Department of Slavonic Studies, University of Cambridge, where she completed her doctoral dissertation on Russian prose in the age of Alexander I (1998). She is currently publishing articles in this area and preparing an expanded book-length investigation of this neglected topic.

Claire Whitehead is a research student at the University of Bristol, writing a doctoral dissertation on fantastic narratives in France and Russia in the nineteenth century. She currently occupies a position as lectrice at the Université Michel de Montaigne, Bordeaux III.

SELECT BIBLIOGRAPHY

1 *ANTHOLOGIES*

Russian Romantic Prose: An Anthology, edited by C. Proffer, Ann
    Arbor: Translation Press, 1979 (hereafter 'Proffer, 1979')
Russkaia romanticheskaia povest', Moscow, 1980
Russkaia romanticheskaia povest' (pervaia tret' XIX veka), Moscow,
    1983
The Ardis Anthology of Russian Romanticism, edited by C. Rydel, Ann
    Arbor: Ardis, 1984 ('Rydel, 1984')
Russian 19th-century Gothic Tales, compiled by Valentin Korovin,
    Moscow: Raduga Publishers, 1984 ('Korovin, 1984')
Sil'fida: Fantasticheskie povesti russkikh romantikov, Moscow, 1988
Russkaia i sovetskaia fantastika, Moscow, 1989
Russkaia romanticheskaia novella, Moscow, 1989
Russian Tales of the Fantastic, edited and translated by Marilyn Minto,
    London: Bristol Classical Press, 1994 ('Minto, 1994')
Russian Women's Shorter Fiction: An Anthology, 1835-1860, translated
    by J. Andrew, Oxford: Clarendon Press, 1996 ('Andrew, 1996')

2 *MAIN PRIMARY TEXTS*

Apukhtin, A.
Mezhdu zhizn'iu i smert'iu (1892); translated as 'Between Life and
    Death' (Minto, 1994)
Bestuzhev-Marlinskii, A
Zamok Eizen (1825)
Vecher na Kavkazskikh vodakh v 1824 godu (1830)
Latnik (1831)
Strashnoe gadan'e (1831); as 'The Terrible Fortune-Telling' (Korovin,
    1984)
Chekhov, A.
Chernyi monakh (1894); as 'The Black Monk' (various)

Dostoevskii, F.
Dvoinik (1846); as *The Double* (various)
Khoziaika (1847); as 'The Landlady' (various)
Brat'ia Karamazovy (1879-80); as *The Brothers Karamazov* / *The Karamazov Brothers* (various)
Gan, E.
Sud sveta (1840); as 'Society's Judgement' (Andrew, 1996)
Garshin, V.
Krasnyi tsvetok (1883); as 'The Red Flower' (in V. Garshin, *From the Reminiscences of Private Ivanov and Other Stories*, Angel Classics, 1988)
Gnedich, N.
Don-Korrado de Gerrera, ili Dukh mshcheniia i varvarstva Gishpantsev (1803)
Gogol, N.
Strashnaia mest' (1832); as 'A Terrible Vengeance' (in *Village Evenings...*)
Vii (1835); as 'Viy' (in *Village Evenings...*)
Portret (1835-42); as 'The Portrait' (in *Plays & Petersburg Tales)*
Nos (1836); as 'The Nose' (in *Plays & Petersburg Tales*)
Village Evenings Near Dikanka and Mirgorod (OUP, 1994)
Plays and Petersburg Tales (OUP, 1995)
Karamzin, N.
Ostrov Borngol'm (1794); as 'The Island Bornholm' (in *Selected Prose*)
Selected Prose of N.M. Karamzin (Northwestern UP, 1969)
Lermontov, M.
Vadim (1832-4); as *Vadim* (Ardis, 1984)
Shtoss (1841); as 'Shtoss' (Rydel, 1984; and Minto, 1994); as 'Stuss' (Korovin, 1984)
Leskov, N.
Belyi orel (1880); as 'The White Eagle' (Minto, 1994)
Odoevskii, V.
Sil'fida (1837); as 'The Sylph' (in *The Salamander* ...: see below)
Prividenie (1838); as 'The Ghost' (in Minto, 1994)
Kosmorama (1839); as 'The Cosmorama' (in *The Salamander*)
Salamandra (1841-4); as *The Salamander*
Zhivoi mertvets (1844); as 'The Live Corpse' (in *The Salamander*)
Russkie nochi (1844); as *Russian Nights* (Northwestern UP, 1997)

The Salamander and Other Gothic Tales (BCP; Northwestern UP, 1992)

Pogorel'skii, A.
Dvoinik, ili moi vechera v Malorossii (1828); as *The Double, or My Evenings in Little Russia* (Ardis, 1988)

Polevoi, N.
Blazhenstvo bezumiia (1833)

Pushkin, A.
Pikovaia dama (1833); as 'The Queen of Spades' (various)
Complete Prose Fiction (Stanford UP, 1983)

Pushkin, A. and Titov, V.
Uedinennyi domik na Vasil'evskom (1828); as 'The Lonely Cottage on Vasilev Island' (in *Complete Prose Fiction)*

Somov, O.
Kievskie ved'my (1833); as 'The Witches of Kiev' (Korovin, 1984)

Tolstoi, A.
La famille du vourdalak (*c* 1840)
Upyr'(1841); as 'Vampire' (in Korovin, 1984)

Turgenev, I.
Faust (1856); as 'Faust' (in *Mysterious Tales*, etc.)
Prizraki (1864); as 'Visions'; 'Phantoms'; 'Ghosts' (various)
Stuk... stuk... stuk! (1871); as 'Knock, Knock, Knock' (*Mysterious Tales*, etc.)
Pesn' torzhestvuiushchei liubvi (1881); as 'The Song of Triumphant Love' (in Minto, 1994; *Mysterious Tales*)
Klara Milich (1882); as 'Klara [Clara] Milich' (*Mysterious Tales* etc.)
The Mysterious Tales (Australian NU, 1979)

Zagoskin, M.
Vecher na Khopre (1834); includes *Nezhdannye gosti*: as 'Unexpected Guests' (Korovin, 1984)

Zhukovskii, V.
Donika (1831)
Lenora (1831)
Sud v podzemel'e (1834)

3 SECONDARY LITERATURE: GENERAL STUDIES ON GOTHIC-FANTASTIC

Botting, Fred, *Gothic*, London: Routledge, 1996

Clute, John, and John Grant (editors), *The Encyclopedia of Fantasy*, London: Orbit, 1997

Cornwell, Neil, *The Literary Fantastic: from Gothic to Postmodernism*, New York and London: Harvester Wheatsheaf, 1990

Kilgour, Maggie, *The Rise of the Gothic Novel*, London: Routledge, 1995

Howard, Jacqueline, *Reading Gothic Fiction: A Bakhtinian Approach*, Oxford: Clarendon Press, 1994

Jackson, Rosemary, *Fantasy: The Literature of Subversion*, London: Methuen, 1981

Lloyd Smith, Allan, and Victor Sage (editors), *Gothick Origins and Innovations*, Amsterdam and Atlanta, GA: Rodopi, 1994

Miles, Robert, *Gothic Writing 1750-1820: A Genealogy*, London: Routledge, 1993

Mulvey-Roberts, Marie (editor), *A Handbook to Gothic Literature*, Basingstoke and London: Macmillan, 1998

Punter, David, *The Literature of Terror: A History of Gothic Fictions from 1765 to the present day*, second edition, 2 vols, London: Longman, 1996

Punter, David (editor), *Companion to the Gothic*, Oxford: Blackwell (in press)

Sage, Victor (editor), *The Gothick Novel: A Casebook*, Basingstoke and London: Macmillan, 1990

Siebers, Tobin, *The Romantic Fantastic*, Ithaca and London: Cornell University Press, 1984

Tinkler-Villani, Valeria, and Peter Davidson (editors), *Exhibited by Candlelight: Sources and Developments in the Gothic Tradition*, Amsterdam and Atlanta, GA: Rodopi, 1995

Todorov, Tzvetan, *The Fantastic: A Structural Approach to a Literary Genre*, translated by Richard Howard, Cleveland and London: The Press of Case Western Reserve University, 1973; Ithaca, New York: Cornell University Press, 1975 (first published Paris, 1970)

Williams, Anne, *Art of Darkness: A Poetics of Gothic*, Chicago and London: University of Chicago Press, 1995.

Ziolkowski, Theodore, *Disenchanted Images: A Literary Iconology*, Princeton: Princeton University Press, 1977

4. SECONDARY LITERATURE: GENERAL STUDIES WITH RELEVANCE TO RUSSIAN GOTHIC-FANTASTIC

Botnikova, A.B., *E.T.A. Gofman i russkaia literatura (pervaia polovina XIX veka). K probleme russko-nemetskikh literaturnykh sviazei*, Voronezh, 1977

Brown, William Edward, *A History of Russian Literature of the Romantic Period*, 4 vols, Ann Arbor: Ardis, 1986

Cornwell, Neil (editor), *Reference Guide to Russian Literature*, London and Chicago: Fitzroy Dearborn, 1998

Grossman, Joan Delaney, *Edgar Allan Poe in Russia: A Study in Legend and Literary Influence*, Würzburg: jal-Verlag, 1973

Ingham, Norman, *E.T.A. Hoffmann in Russia, 1822-1845*, Würzburg: jal-Verlag, 1974

Izmailov, N.V., 'Fantasticheskaia povest'', in *Russkaia povest' XIX veka: Istoriia i problematika zhanra*, edited by B.S. Meilakh, Leningrad, 1973, pp. 134-69

Kelly, Catriona, *A History of Russian Women's Writing, 1820-1992*, Oxford, Clarendon Press, 1994

Kostka, Edmund, *Schiller in Russian Literature*, Philadelphia: University of Pennsylvania Press, 1965

Leighton, Lauren G., *The Esoteric Tradition in Russian Romantic Literature*, University Park, Pennsylvania: The Pennsylvania State University Press, 1994

Levin, Yu.D., 'English Poetry and Russian Sentimentalism', in his *The Perception of English Literature in Russia: Investigations and Materials*, translated by Catherine Phillips, Nottingham: Astra Press, 1994, pp. 127-95

Mandelker, Amy, and Roberta Reader (editors), *The Supernatural in Slavic and Baltic Literature: Essays in Honor of Victor Terras*, Columbus, Ohio: Slavica, 1988

Mersereau, John, Jr, *Russian Romantic Fiction*, Ann Arbor: Ardis, 1983

Moser, C. (editor), *The Russian Short Story: A Critical History*, Boston: Twayne, 1986

Moser, C. (editor), *The Cambridge History of Russian Literature*, Cambridge: Cambridge University Press., 1992

O'Toole, L.M., *Structure, Style and Interpretation in the Russian Short Story*, New Haven: Yale University Press, 1982

Passage, Charles E., *The Russian Hoffmannists*, The Hague: Mouton, 1963

Reid, Robert (editor), *Problems of Russian Romanticism*, Aldershot: Gower, 1986

Rydel, Christine (editor), *Russian Literature in the Age of Pushkin and Gogol: Prose* (*Dictionary of Literary Biography*, vol. 198), Detroit: Gale Research, 1999

Rosenthal, Bernice Glatzer (editor), *The Occult in Russian and Soviet Culture*, Ithaca and London: Cornell University Press, 1997

Simpson, Mark S., *The Russian Gothic Novel and its British Antecedents*, Columbus, Ohio: Slavica, 1986

Tosi, Alessandra, 'The Forgotten Years: Russian prose in the Age of Alexander I, 1801-1825', unpublished PhD dissertation, University of Cambridge, 1998

Vatsuro, V.E., 'Roman Klary Riv v russkom perevode', in *Rossiia i Zapad*, edited by M.P. Alekseev, Leningrad, 1973

Vatsuro, V.E., 'Iz istorii "Goticheskogo Romana" v Rossii (A.A. Bestuzhev-Marlinskii)', *Russian Literature*, 38, 1995, pp. 207-26

Vatsuro, V.E., 'A. Radklif, ee pervye russkie chitateli i perevodchiki', *Novoe literaturnoe obozrenie*, 22, 1996, pp. 202-25

INDEX

Andrew, Joe 175, 178, 184
Apukhtin, A. 19
Austen, Jane 11, 212
  Northanger Abbey, 11, 212
Avsey, Ignat 18, **211-34**, 241
Ayers, Carolyn Jursa 15, **171-
  87**

Bakhtin, M. 9, 17, 241
Baldick, Chris 164
Balzac, Honoré de 11, 20
  Melmoth reconcilié 20
  Séraphita 20
Baratynskii, E. 3
Batiushkov, K. 85
Beckford, William 40, 67
  Vathek 40
Belinskii, V. 14, 96, 100, 127,
  129, 130, 220, 227
Belyi, A. 19, 231
Bestuzhev-Marlinskii, A. 14,
  63, 81, 172
  Castle Eisen 14
  Cuirassier, The 15
  *Evening at a Caucasian Spa,
  An* 15
  *Terrible Fortune-Telling,
  The* 15
  Traitor, The 14
Bocharov, S. 191, 204
Borel, Pétrus 10
Bosley, Keith 148, 151

Brambeus Baron [see
  Senkovskii]
Brontë, Charlotte 212
Brontë, Emily 171, 212
Brown, Charles Brockden 10
Bulgakov, M. 19, 33, 34
  Master and Margarita, The
  33, 34
Bürger, Gottfried 11, 13, 20,
  85, 87, 88, 89, 90, 92
  Lenore 11, 13, 20, 85, 87,
  88, 90, 92, 93, 94
Burke, Edmund 54, 266
Burnett, Leon 19, **235-55**
Byron, Lord 11, 20, 79, 87,
  152, 216

Camõens, Luis de 26, 27, 29,
  35
  Lusiads, The 25, 26, 35
Cazotte, Jacques 10, 11, 20,
  264
  Devil in Love, The 10, 20
Chekhov, A. 19, 34, 35, **257-
  75**
  Black Monk, The 19, **257-
  75**
  Ward No. 6 19
Chulkov, M. 28
Cockrell, Roger 17, **127-43**
Coleridge, Samuel T. 11, 83
  Christabel 83
Conrad, Joseph 253, 254

Cornwell, Neil **3-21**, 84, 92, 135, 146, 265
Cuthbertson, Catherine 13
  Romance of the Pyrenees, The 13

Dacre, Charlotte 10
  Zofloya 10
Dante 24, 29, 30
  Divine Comedy, The 24
Davies, Paul 265
Dickens, Charles 252
  Great Expectations 19
  Pickwick Papers, The 221
Doppelgänger 8
Dostoevskii, F. 3, 8, 12, 15, 17, 18, 19, 20, 32, 33, 34, 63, 81, 82, 103, 104, 124, 125, 129, 132, 172, **211-34, 235-55**
  Bobok 34
  Devils [Possessed], The 32, 237
  Double, The 18, 32, 129
  Karamazov Brothers, The 18, 33, 216, 217, 218, 219, 220, 222, 225, 235, 239, 240
  Landlady, The 15, 18, 233
  Meek Girl, A 237, 242, 253
  Village of Stepanchikovo, The 219, 221, 222, 227
Dumas, Alexandre (*père*) 11
Durova, N. 185
dvoemirie 8, 146, 166, 191

Eichendorff, J.F. von 20
Elistratova, A. 227, 228

fantastic, the 3, 6, 7, 10, 11, 14, 17, 18, **103-25**, 129, 130, 134, 135, 138, 143, 236, 258, 262, 273, 274
  'fantastic realism' 8
Franklin, Sir John 249, 250, 251, 252, 253, 254, 255
Freud, Sigmund 5, 31, 225
Friedrich, Caspar David 6
Fuentes, Carlos 19, 20
  Aura 19

Gan, E. 15, **171-87**
  Ideal, The 183, 184
  Recollections of Zheleznozavodsk 184
  Society's Judgement 15, **171-87**
Garnett, Constance 235, 236, 237, 240, 241, 242, 247
Garshin, V. 19
  Red Flower, The 19
Gautier, Théophile 11, 20
Gei, N.K. 121
Genette, Gérard 106, 107
Gippius, V. 229, 230
Gnedich, N. 13, **59-82**, 87
  Don Corrado 13, **59-82**
  Moritz 61, 62, 68, 77
Goethe, J.W. von 28, 60, 79, 128, 138, 139, 140, 242, 243
  Faust 128, 138, 139, 140, 224, 237, 242, 243
Gogol, N. 3, 12, 15, 16, 19, 20, 29, 30, 31, 32, 33, 81, 93, **189-209, 211-34**, 259
  Christmas Eve 30

Dead Souls 31, 32, 207, 217, 219, 226, 227, 228, 231, 232
Evenings in a Village near Dikanka 29
Government Inspector, The 208, 227
Nevsky prospect [Nevskii Prospect] 30, 32, 189, 191, 192, 207
Night in May [May Night], A 189, 233
Nose, The 16, **189-209**
Overcoat, The 30, 32, 189, 207, 216, 217, 227, 234
Portrait, The 16, 32
Terrible Vengeance [Revenge], The 15, 32, 233
Vii 16, 31, 93, **189-209**, 259
'graveyard' poetry 5, 13, 37, 60, 68, 76, 83, 84
Gray, Thomas 41, 84
Elegy in a Country Churchyard 84
Griboedov, A. 87
Grot, Ia. 148
Gumilev, N. 96

Hardy, Thomas 238, 250
Hawthorne, Nathaniel 19
Hoffmann, E.T.A. 4, 8, 10, 12, 15, 16, 17, 18, 20, 28, 81, 128, 191, 192, 207, 208, 209, 258, 259, 262
Devil's Elixirs, The 12, 18
Entail, The 12, 17
Gambler's Luck 18

Golden Pot, The 8, 192, 258
New Year's Eve Adventure, A 208
Homer 148
Iliad, The 13, 23, 32, 59, 148, 149
Odyssey, The 23, 148
Hugo, Victor 11, 15

Irving, Washington 10, 14, 20
Izmailov, N.V. 13, 14

Jakobson, Roman 105
James, Henry 10, 19
Aspern Papers, The 19
Janin, Jules 11

Kahn, Andrew 18
Karamzin, N. 13, 19, **37-58**, 62, 63, 66, 67, 69, 82, 92, 172, 180
Island of Bornholm, The 13, **37-58**, 62, 67, 180
Letters of a Russian Traveller 38, 48, 49, 50, 55, 58
Natal'ia, a Boyar's Daughter 47
Poor Liza 13, 37, 39, 47
Karlinsky, Simon 146, 155
Karsavin, L. 223
Katenin, P. 87, 100
Katz, Michael 85
Kelly, Catriona 174, 185, 186
Khodasevich, V. 229
Kleist, Heinrich von 11

Beggarwoman of Locarno,
   The 11
Foundling, The 11
Komaromi, Ann 19, **257-75**

La Fontaine, Jean de 138, 139
Lanser, Susan 106, 107, 109,
   113
Lee, Sophia 40, 212
   Recess, The 40, 212
Lermontov, M. 3, 15, 17, 84,
   100, 172, 217, 241, 259
   Demon 84, 100, 172
   Shtoss 15, 259
   Vadim 15
Leskov, N. 19, 34
Lewis, Matthew 9, 10, 13, 20,
   40, 65, 67, 68, 69, 75, 80,
   85, 215
   Monk, The 13, 40, 65, 69,
   75
Lönnrot, Elias 147, 148, 149
   Kalevala, The 147, 148,
   149, 150, 151, 155, 156,
   167
Lovecraft, H.P. 212, 232

Maikov, V. 12, 26, 27, 30, 31,
   35
   Elisei, or Bacchus Annoyed
   26, 35
Mann, Iurii 190, 192, 197, 209
Marlinskii [see Bestuzhev-
   Marlinskii]
Matlaw, Ralph E. 240, 241
Maturin, Charles Robert 11,
   20, 67, 215

Melmoth the Wanderer 11,
   20
Maupassant, Guy de 11, 264
McKenzie, Anna Maria 13
McVay, Gordon 274
Mel'nikov-Pecherskii, P. 34
   In the Forests 34
Melville, Herman 10
Merezhkovskii, D. 34, 226,
   228, 229, 230, 231, 261
Mérimée, Prosper 11, 20
Meshchevskii, A. 85, 100
Meyer, Priscilla 16, **189-209**
Milton, John 24, 25, 28, 29,
   33, 35, 60, 61, 68, 75, 79
   Paradise Lost 61
Mirsky, D.S. 257
Moers, Ellen 171

Narezhnyi, V. 29
Nerval, Gérard de 11, 12
   Aurélia 11
Nightwatches of Bonaventura,
   The 11
Nodier, Charles 11, 20, 262,
   263
Novalis 131

O'Brien, Fitz-James 17
Odoevskii, V. 3, 6, 14, 16, 17,
   20, 28, 81, **127-43**, **145-69**,
   258, 259, 261, 262
   Cosmorama, The 16, **127-
   43**
   Ghost, The 17
   'Improvisor, The' 17
   Living Corpse, The 3, 143

Russian Nights 16, 17, 20,
128, 164, 169
Salamander, The 16, **145-69**
Sylph, The 17, 259, 261
Offord, Derek 13, **37-58**
Ossian 39, 41, 61, 75, 149

Panaev, I.I. 129
Peace, Richard 13, **23-35**
Piranesi, G.B. 6, 17
Plato 139, 190, 192, 193
Poe, Edgar Allan 10, 12, 20,
212
William Wilson 20
Pogorel'skii, A. 3, 14, 29
Double, The 14
Polevoi, N. 15
Bliss of Madness, The 15
Potocki, Jan 9
*Manuscript Found in
Saragossa, The* 9
Praz, Mario 10, 74
Preromanticism 13, 14, 39, 40,
46, 55, 68, 76
Punter, David 135, 136
Pursglove, Michael 13, **83-101**
Pushkin, A. 3, 17, 18, 19, 20,
32, 33, 59, 81, 87, 96, 100,
103-25, 146, 172, 232, 245,
252
Queen of Spades, The 14,
17, 18, 19, 33, **103-25**,
172, 245, 252

Radcliffe, Ann 9, 10, 13, 14,
40, 41, 43, 44, 63, 64, 65,
66, 67, 9, 80, 83, 85, 93,

147, 171, 172, 175, 185,
212, 216, 265
*Castles of Athlin and
Dunbayne, The* 40
Italian, The 40, 93, 175,
216
Mysteries of Udolpho, The
40, 85, 216, 265
Romance of the Forest, The
40, 85
Sicilian Romance, A 40, 43,
44
Ramsey, Cynthia 17, **145-69**
Reeve, Clara 13, 40, 41, 62,
212
Old English Baron, The 13,
40, 62, 212
Roche, Regina Maria 40, 43
Children of the Abbey, The
40, 43
Clermont 40
Rosa, Salvator 6
Rosenthal, Bernice G. 8
Rossetti, Christina 171, 235
Rousseau, Jean-Jacques 37, 53

Sade, Marquis de 5, 10
Sakulin, P.N. 130, 138
Saint-Martin, Louis Claude de
20
Schelling, F.W.J. 8, 14, 20,
143, 190
Schiller, Friedrich 11, 12, 14,
20, 60, 61, 68, 69, 73, 76,
77, 79, 80, 82, 85
Don Carlos 69
Fiesko 61, 76
Ghost-Seer, The 11, 12, 20

Robbers, The 73, 77
Scott, Walter 10, 11, 14, 15, 85, 92, 94, 97, 98, 99, 100, 214, 216, 227
Marmion 97
Senkovskii, O. 3, 14
Sentimentalism 13, 39, 40, 46, 48, 58, 64, 66, 74, 79, 88
Shakespeare, William 14, 46, 47, 60, 61, 68, 79, 80, 82, 172, 211, 213, 219, 235, 238, 239, 243
Hamlet 138, 139, 213, 220, 223, 235, 238, 239
Shelley, Mary 10, 20, 152, 153, 171, 212
Frankenstein 10, 20, 151, 152, 154, 166, 168, 169, 212, 223
Shelley, Percy Bysshe 20, 152
Simpson, Mark S. 79, 172, 183, 226
Sologub, F. 34
Somov, O. 3, 29, 63
Southey, Robert 85, 93, 94, 95
Stevenson, R.L. 212, 265
Surtees, R.S. 226, 227, 231
Mr Sponge's Sporting Tour 227
Swedenborg, E. 115

Tennyson, Alfred 131
Terras, Victor 128
Thackeray, W.M. 228
Barry Lyndon 228
Thomson, James 39, 41
Tieck, L. 28, 81, 191

Todorov, Tzvetan 5, 6, 7, 8, 10, 13, 17, 84, 88, **103-25**, 134, 135, 252, 263
Tolstoi, A.K. 3, 19, 20
Vampire 3, 19
Family of the Voudalak 19
Tolstoi, L. 33, 35, 231
Anna Karenina 33
Toporov, V.N. 231, 232
Tosi, Alessandra 13, **59-82**
Turgenev, A.I. 86, 93
Turgenev, I. 18, 34, 172, **235-55**, 259
Clara [Klara] Milich 19, 34
Faust 19, 243, 245, 246, 247, 250, 252, 253, 255
Knock... Knock... 34
Phantoms [Ghosts] 19, 34, 259
Song of Triumphant Love, The 34

Varma, Devendra P. 66, 79
Vatsuro, V.E. 4, 13, 14, 40, 41, 48, 62, 82, 84, 94, 147
Vel'tman, A. 29, 30, 32, 81
Adventures, Drawn from the Sea of Life 32
Heart and Thought 30
Vigel, F. 86, 87
Voeikov, A. 86

Walker, George 13
Walpole, Horace 5, 6, 9, 10, 16, 45, 47, 67, 80, 151, 211, 212, 213, 214, 217, 227, 230, 234, 265

Castle of Otranto, The 5,
45, 67, 80, 151, 152, 211,
212, 213, 214, 215, 217,
220, 221, 223, 230, 265
Whitehead, Claire 17, **103-25**
Wilde, Oscar 9
Wilson, Edmund 226
Wordsworth, William 238

Young, Edward 41

Zagoskin, M. 3
Zhukova, M. 185
Zhukovskii, V. 11, 13, 60, 63,
66, 67, 82, **83-101**, 140
Donika 93, 94, 95, 96, 100
Lenora 13, 87, 88, 90, 92,
94, 96
Liudmila 13, 87, 88, 92, 96
Svetlana 13, 87, 88, 92
*Twelve Sleeping Maidens,
The* 96
Underground Judgement 92